International Studies on Social Security

Volume 5

Chief Series Editor
STEIN RINGEN

Series Editors
PETER BEZEMER
ALAN DUNCAN
PHILIP R. DE JONG
JUN-YOUNG KIM
PER-GUNNAR SVENSSON

Fighting Poverty: Caring for Children, Parents, the Elderly and Health

Edited by
STEIN RINGEN
PHILIP R. DE JONG

Routledge
Taylor & Francis Group

LONDON AND NEW YORK

First published 1999 by Ashgate Publishing

Reissued 2018 by Routledge
2 Park Square, Milton Park, Abingdon, Oxon OX14 4RN
711 Third Avenue, New York, NY 10017, USA

Routledge is an imprint of the Taylor & Francis Group, an informa business

Publisher's Note
The publisher has gone to great lengths to ensure the quality of this reprint but points out that some imperfections in the original copies may be apparent.

Disclaimer
The publisher has made every effort to trace copyright holders and welcomes correspondence from those they have been unable to contact.

ISBN 13: 978-1-138-31546-4 (hbk)
ISBN 13: 978-1-138-31552-5 (pbk)
ISBN 13: 978-0-429-45627-5 (ebk)

Contents

Preface

Jonathan R. Bradshaw and Han Emanuel

This volume is the fifth in a Series of International Studies on Issues in Social Security, and the fourth that contains an edited selection of papers presented at the annual International Research Seminars on "Issues in Social Security" held in Sigtuna, Sweden. This volume relates to the fifth seminar, held in June 1998.

The series is published in close cooperation with the Foundation for International Studies on Social Security (FISS) in Amsterdam which takes care of selecting, editing and formatting the texts to include.

Starting with this volume we have been fortunate to find Stein Ringen, professor of sociology at the University of Oxford, England, willing to accept appointment as Chief Editor of the series, succeeding Peter Flora of the University of Mannheim, Germany. Further members of the Editorial Board, appointed by the Board of Governors of FISS, are Peter Bezemer (social law, former Vice-President for Pensions of the Dutch Civil Service Pension Fund in Heerlen), Alan Duncan (economics department of the University of York, England, and Institute of Fiscal Studies, London), Philip R. de Jong (professor of the economics of social security, Erasmus University, Rotterdam, and partner in Aarts and De Jong social security research, The Hague, The Netherlands), Jun-Young Kim (professor of economics, Economics Department, Sung Gyun-Kwan University, Seoul), and Per-Gunnar Svensson (Director-General, International Hospital Federation, London).

The series can be seen as a platform for academic discussion between researchers and scholars of different disciplines and countries. Articles included should display studies and their results on different aspects of social security or welfare and/or their relationships with other aspects of society in a cross national setting or with at least cross national relevance. Though independent and academic many of these studies will naturally have and will spell out the relevance of the findings for practical issues in social policy formation. The articles are selected with an eye to their novelty and thoroughness. One of the series aims is to confront different academic approaches with each other and with public policy perspectives. Another is to give analytic reports of cross-nationally different approaches to the design and reform of welfare state programs. Articles included form an edited selection of papers presented at the conferences and seminars of FISS. Other articles, offered for publication, may be accepted in the future.

The present volume, edited by Stein Ringen and Philip R. de Jong, contains a selection of articles based on papers presented at the Fifth International Research Seminar on "Issues in Social Security", held by FISS on 13-16 June 1998 in Sigtuna, Sweden and organized in cooperation with the Swedish Federation of Social Security Offices (Försäkringskasseförbundet, FKF) in Stockholm, also acting as main financial sponsor, at the latter's conference and training centre "Sjudarhöjden".

Finally, we would like to thank Ton Koekkoek at Van Diest Word Processing in The Hague, The Netherlands, for providing excellent editorial assistance for this volume.

Jonathan R. Bradshaw, University of York, U.K., President of FISS
Han Emanuel, Secretary-General of FISS, Amsterdam, the Netherlands

Introduction and overview

Stein Ringen and Philip R. de Jong

This volume deals with different aspects of poverty and policies to reduce it. It has four parts. Part 1 deals with some general conceptual issues and cross country comparative data related to poverty. Part 2 contains various analytical and policy approaches to establish and/or alleviate child poverty and poverty among single parents. Part 3 deals with an important international debate on pension reform, the most important instrument to alleviate poverty among the elderly. Part 4, finally, deals with allocation and incentive issues in health care provision and disability insurance, and focuses on the design of sustainable programmes and policies.

In the opening chapter of part 1, *Robert H. Haveman and Andrew Bershadker* argue that poverty is not adequately measured by having an annual cash income stream at or below a norm income for a family of a particular size, as the United States and a number of other countries traditionally and officially do. Instead they look at some measure of being "self-reliant" indicated by a family's income generating capacity, net of child support and similar expenses which a family incurs when it fully exploits the earning capacities of its members. They then use the U.S. Current Population Surveys from 1975 to 1995 to obtain empirical estimates of this *net earnings capacity* and its development over time. By this measure the prevalence of poverty in the U.S. has increased, and shows a larger cyclical amplitude than the traditional cash income concept.

In the other chapter in this part *Lee Rainwater* presents data derived from the Luxemburg Income Study (of which he is a founder and co-director) on child poverty and poverty among the elders in 14 industrialised countries. Rainwater stresses social exclusion as the most worrying aspect of poverty and, hence, argues for a relative poverty concept.

Part 2 groups a number of articles on family matters. *Jonathan R. Bradshaw and Helen Barnes* and *Bernard M.S. van Praag and Erik J.S. Plug* deal with child poverty and welfare in families with children, the first from a sociological point of view and presenting cross national data; the second more analytical, within an economic framework. *Nadine Lefaucheur and Martin Rein* and *Katja Forssén and Mia Harkovita* treat poverty among lone parents. Both papers address sociological aspects of single parenthood, and the ways in which society tries to cope with it. Whilst the first takes a cultural-historical approach, the second compares data from eight countries in Western Europe and North America on single parents' labour force participation, and tests resulting hypotheses for Finland.

Part 3 contains an interesting debate which has been going on for the last two years between staff members of the World Bank (here represented by lead researcher *Estelle James*) and the I.L.O. (in the person of social security director *Colin Gillion*). The discussion is embedded in the confrontation of a neo-classical, dynamic, framework, in which incentives on individual savings behaviour explain the level of investment, and a more static, Keynesian approach in which investments appear as an exogenous variable determining aggregate savings. In a third article *Stefan Felder* uses te method of intergenerational accounting to analyse the effect of two alternative methods of financing the deficit occurring in the present Pay-As-You-Go Old Age insurance system in Switzerland as a result of demographic developments.

The final, fourth part of this volume opens with a study by *Barbara L. Wolfe and David Vanness* on inequality in access to and utilisation of health care and the possible role of the public sector. They address two questions: what is or should be meant by equity in the provision of health care, and how can it be achieved? They propose a range of alternative equity definitions, such as equality in health status, equality in access to health care, and equal unit cost of any medical care for everybody. They then explore how social insurance and other public regulations may help to achieve such equity goals. *Erik Schokkaert and Carine Van de Voorde* investigate risk adjustment, i.e. compensating insurers for differences in medical consumption between various groups, as a way to finance medical expenses in a manner which is both efficient and equitable. After a general introduction they compare recent reforms in that direction in

Belgium and Switzerland. They argue that the choice of risk-adjustment factors is not only a technical problem but also involves ethical and political considerations.

The article by *Leo J.M. Aarts and Philip R. de Jong* on "The cost of coercion: an empirical study of the willingness to pay for disability insurance" deals with issues of equity in Pay-As-You-Go (PAYG) financing of insurance against income loss due to permanent disablement. Starting from the Van Praag individual welfare function of income they calculate the individual extent of risk aversion and the maximum premium one is willing to pay for disability insurance above flat rate compulsory insurance. These individual maximums are, then, confronted with corresponding actuarially fair and PAYG premiums. The results allow analysing and assessing the pros and cons of different forms of risk equalisation.

The volume ends with an informative paper by *Ching Y. Choi* on reform issues in health care financing in Australia.

PART 1

POVERTY AND INCOME DISTRIBUTION

1.1 "Inability to be self-reliant" as an indicator of U.S. poverty

Robert H. Haveman and Andrew Bershadker

1. Introduction

Today, nearly all developed countries accept the social goal of reducing or eliminating "poverty" among their citizens. Across these nations, however, there is no commonly accepted measure of poverty, and hence no easy way to determine which countries have more or less poverty. Most nations, however, measure poverty by comparing some indicator of the access of families to current resources to a measure of the resource needs of the family. Money income often serves as the resource indicator, which is the case for the United States.[1]

In this paper, we present a new measure of poverty for the United States, one which rests on a family's *capacity for generating income*, rather than the *actual money income* of that family. Given the current political and social climate, which emphasizes the self-reliance of individuals and families, poverty measures that rest on the relationship of income realizations to needs appear to be of less interest to policy makers than in previous times, when income adequacy was a central concern. In contrast, our measure, *net earnings capacity (NEC) poverty*, rests on the concept of self-reliance and measures the size of the population *unable to be self-reliant*.

We first introduce the concept of "poverty" and its current measurement, and note some of the criticisms of this official measure. We next describe the conceptual basis for NEC poverty, with an overview of the mechanics of calculating the measure. We then describe trends in NEC poverty for the entire U.S. population and for demographic subgroups and compare these trends to trends in the official poverty measure. Next,

3

we examine the composition of the NEC poor population and compare the changes in this composition to trends in the composition of the officially poor population. We next ask what underlying trends in the U.S. economy could have accounted for the observed trends in NEC poverty and their differences from trends in official poverty. Finally, we offer some concluding remarks and policy implications.

2. The concept of poverty, and how we measure it

Like nations, poverty analysts and researchers also find it difficult to agree upon a single poverty measure. Researchers taking a sociological perspective often advocate a multidimensional poverty concept, one reflecting the many aspects of everyday life. Hence, they speak about people being deprived of social contacts (with friends and families), and refer to the degree of social isolation relative to some norm as indicating such "isolation" poverty. Similarly, people living in squalid housing are viewed as "housing poor", and people with health deficits as "health poor".

Economists tend to prefer a measure that somehow reflects economic well-being. However, even among economists, different view points exist regarding how best to measure such well-being. Some rely on the income of a family, and compare this to some minimum standard of income, or poverty line. Others look to the level of consumption as an indicator of the level of living. Still others rely on families' own assessment of their economic well-being, and move from this assessment to a judgement regarding who is poor.[2]

The United States was among the earliest countries to establish an official definition of poverty, which was done in the mid-1960s.[3] It was a unique definition, and rested on the views of economists by comparing the cash income of people to an assessment of their income needs. As a measure of "income poverty", it has been used to track the nation's "poverty rate" over time and to describe how the characteristics of the families and people who are "income poor" have changed through time.

The calculation of this measure, developed over thirty years ago, has remained largely unchanged over time. This official measure identifies poor families and the individuals living in them by comparing two numbers:

4

1) the level of *current, annual cash income* of the family unit in which people live, and
2) a figure that indicates the *income necessary for a family of a particular size and composition to meet a minimum level of consumption.*

This second number is the family's poverty line. If the income of the family fails to exceed its poverty line, the family is defined as "poor". The nation's poverty rate is the percentage of its citizens who live in poor families so defined (or families who live below their poverty line).[4]

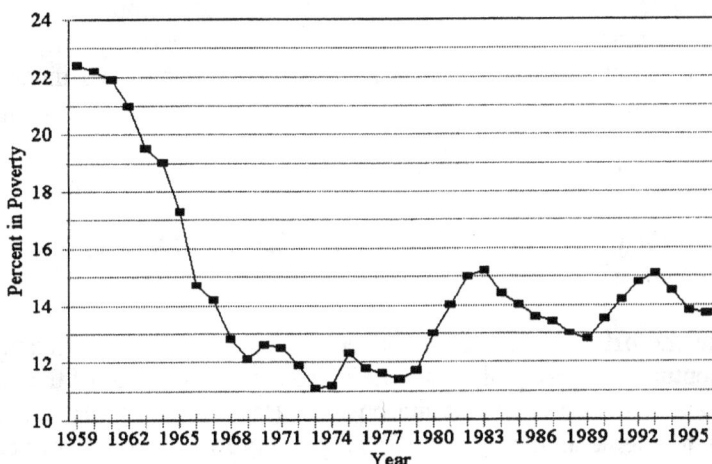

Figure 1.1.1   United States official poverty rate (all persons, 1959 to 1996)

Figure 1.1.1 shows the poverty rate for the U. S. from 1959 to the present. From 1959 to 1969, the poverty rate dropped sharply, in part due to the success of the federal government's "War on Poverty". After a slight rise due to a sluggish economy, the poverty rate reached its all-time low in 1973, when it stood at 11.1 percent. At that time roughly 23 million people were poor, 42 percent less than in 1959.

The rate oscillated between 11 and 12 percent from 1973 to 1979. After that, however, poverty increased steadily, reaching 15.2 percent in

1983. Over the next 10 years, the poverty rate fell, then rose. In the most recent period of job growth, the proportion and number of the poor have declined from a high in 1993 of 15.1 percent, or 39.3 million persons, to about 13.7 percent, or 36.5 million persons, in 1996.

While the nation has lived with this particular definition of poverty for a long time now, there are many reasons to be dissatisfied with it. Ruggles (1990) explores a wide variety of these concerns and discusses the strengths and weaknesses of alternative concepts for the measurement of poverty. Here we note that the official definition relies on a single year of cash income of a family, while for many families, annual income fluctuates substantially over time. Unemployment, layoffs, the decision to undertake mid-career training or to change jobs, health considerations, and especially income flows from self-employment may all cause the money income of a household to change substantially from one year to the next. Moreover, through its reliance on actual incomes, the official measure records as "poor", individuals whose low incomes reflect voluntary choices.

3. Does the official poverty indicator measure what people are interested in?

While the official measure of poverty is open to many criticisms, both conceptual and practical, it is widely used as an indicator of the nation is doing as a nation in combating poverty. Because many of the measurement problems afflicting the official poverty rate are relatively constant over time, analysts and policy makers feel confident in used this measure for assessing the trend of U.S. poverty, or direction in which the nation is moving in assuring a minimum level of living to our citizens.[5]

However, in recent years, many policy makers — reflecting the changing sentiments of some of citizens — have called into question the basic concept on which the official measure rests. While the official poverty measure tells us how we are doing in maintaining the incomes of cash-short families, so the discussion goes, the real problem of poverty is far more fundamental than just a lack of income. The real problem is that the nation has supplemented the low incomes of families through welfare and other transfers. This transferring of money has created a dysfunctional social class that is at the source of many of the nation's problems. In this view, it is likely that income support to cash poor families generates more poverty, as these people become dependent on government support.

To those who hold this view, the fundamental problem is this dependence of some people on welfare support from government. Having some people with low cash income is not the main problem, rather the problem is the reduction in self-reliance, as illustrated by a welfare dependent population.[6] This view is consistent with the trend in political rhetoric calling for a smaller economic and social policy role for government.

Evidence that being "self-reliant" or "economically independent" has taken on more weight in social policy is the provision in the 1996 U.S. welfare reform legislation for block grants to the states, titled Temporary Assistance for Needy Families (TANF). TANF eliminated the receipt of public transfer benefits by single-parent households as an entitlement, and imposed firm limits on the period that eligible families could receive support. The message to single parents, irrespective of their skills, training or home demands, was that they had to learn to "get by on their own". In short, independence was to come from income generated by their own work.

Similarly, advocates of the privatization of the Social Security retirement program envision that some portion of the contributions made on behalf of working-age individuals will be assigned directly to them, with the requirement that they manage these financial resources themselves (with constraints), and then make do in their retirement years on the accumulated assets in these private accounts. How they get by in their older years would reflect the choices and savings efforts they made during their working years. Proposals for medical savings accounts as a replacement for Medicare benefits, tighter eligibility criteria for disabled children's receipt of Supplemental Security Income benefits, the elimination of most legal immigrants from eligibility for public income support, the shift from defined benefit to defined contribution pension plans, and the emphasis on loans rather than grants to cover the rising costs of higher education are other manifestations of this emphasis on "self-reliance" as a substitute for public support.

In part because of the magnitude and the stridency of this view, the official measure of poverty appears to have become less relevant in policy discussions in recent years, and less attended to by policy makers. Indeed, to advocates of policy proposals emphasizing self-reliance, the official measure is but an indicator of failed social policy based on communitarian objectives. Increased public income support, it is noted, must more than offset any decrease in individual efforts if income poverty, as it is now measured, is to be reduced.

4. An alternative poverty concept and measure: do people have the capability to be "self-reliant?"

Given this judgement that people need to rely on their own energies and resources, it is interesting to ask the following reality-check-type questions:

-   What if there are people who do not have the capabilities to make it on their own in our sort of market society?
-   What collective responsibility does the nation have to them?

At one extreme, one could argue (as Charles Murray has) that the nation should simply go about its business, get the self-reliant message out, and let private charities provide whatever they wish to those families that are unable to be self-reliant. Government would get out of the business of trying to help the least able families, and presume that people would somehow make it on their own. This position is a harsh one, and perhaps more harsh than some advocates of the self-reliance position might be comfortable with.

Another option for those who sympathize with the self-reliance position would be to consider what policy options we have to counter this inability to be self-reliant, to ask what can be done to increase the ability of people who are not now economically independent to become so? For these advocates of self-reliance, then, the issue of poverty becomes recast; it does not vanish. The venue now becomes how best can public policy cope with a population unable to be self-reliant; what instruments are available, and which are the most cost-effective?

However, before alternative policy approaches to reducing 'dependence' and increasing self-reliance can be meaningfully discussed, there needs to be some way of determining if there are a group of people who are unable to be self-reliant. And, if there are citizens who cannot be economically independent on their own, how many of them are there? Have their numbers been rising or falling over time? And, what are their characteristics?

To enable us to discuss more meaningfully this issue of self-reliance, it is relevant to ask: "What sort of poverty measure might be relevant to those who place primary emphasis on self-reliance as a social objective?" Clearly, no measure of poverty consistent with this self-reliance concern now exists. If one were to design such a poverty measure, the objective would be to identify the size and composition of the population of citizens who cannot be self-reliant, to determine if this population has been growing or declining, and to identify the characteristics of this population.

Clearly, any such measure will have to rest on judgements, or norms, for there is no clear consensus on what it means to be "self-reliant", or "capable of being economically independent". Here we set forth one approach to this question, and draw out its policy implications. To capture this ability-to-be-self-reliant concept, we propose a measure that reflects a family's capability to achieve economic independence on its own, that is, to attain a minimum level of living only through the use of their own capabilities.

In order to develop an actual measure that would reflect this concept, we need to establish several norms, and to make several assumptions. First, we focus only on people who live in families that are headed by a working age person, someone aged 18-65. This makes sense, as the issue of self-reliance is directed to people who should — through their own work and efforts — be independent; few people would want to apply this criterion to the elderly.

Second, we need to find a way to identify the "capabilities" of people in such families, as any determination of the ability to be self-reliant requires some assessment of the resources that people can mobilize in order to "make it on their own". We do this by defining a concept we call "earnings capacity", which essentially asks how much adults, given their capabilities and characteristics, would be able to earn in the labor market if they were to work full time, full year. This work-level assumption is also a norm that we have adopted for the purpose of this study. Because full time, full year work is generally recognized as being "fully employed", this assumption, too, seems reasonable. Given these norms, then, we obtain a measure of adult capabilities or human capital for each adult in a representative sample of the population. As an indicator of capabilities or potential, this procedure carries no suggestion that everyone aged 18-65 *should* work full time, full year, or that anyone who does not engage in market work to that extent is not productive.[7]

9

We measure this earnings capacity value for each adult by using multivariate statistical techniques that, in effect, enable us to predict what each prime-aged adult would be able to earn if he or she worked full time, full year.[8] This imputation is based on observations of the actual earnings of full time, full year workers with various levels of "human capital" characteristics (like education, age, race and so on). In effect, the exercise here is to match each non-full time, full year working adult with a close-to-identical person who works full time, full year. We observe the full time, full year worker's earnings and take that observation as a prediction of how much the non-full time, full year adult in question could earn if he or she were working "at capacity".[9]

In making this prediction for each prime-aged adult, we implicitly adopt another norm, namely that people who do not work full time, full year are doing so voluntarily, and that they are not forced or constrained to not work at this level. However, such restrictions certainly do exist. We therefore adopt an adjustment procedure designed to reflect the constraints that some people face that keep them from working at this full-capacity level. Having an illness or a disabling condition are two such constraints. Moreover, people have characteristics that may hinder their job finding or job holding characteristics, hence constraining their ability to work at the full time, full year norm. While it is not possible to reflect these constraints with total accuracy, we develop a statistical procedure that utilizes information in our data base to make an educated estimate of the extent to which these constraints, in a steady state world, tend draw down the earnings capacity of people so constrained.[10]

Having estimated these adjusted earnings capacity values for each working-age adult, we reassemble these people back into their actual family units. By adding up the earnings capacities of all of the adults in the family, and adding to this the income that the family receives from their real property (e.g., income from rent, interest, dividends), we obtain the earnings capacity for the family itself. We call this value *gross earnings capacity*, or GEC.

We could use this value of GEC as an estimate of the capability of the family to generate earnings if they were to work at their full capacity, that is, how much income they could generate if they set all else aside and worked full time, full year. However, this would be a defective estimate of their ability to be self-reliant for at least one main reason. If all of the adults in families with children were to realize their full earnings capacity, they would necessarily incur substantial costs that are related to such a realization. The most important of these work-related costs are those necessary to provide adequate child care for their school age children. To reflect the costs of child care incurred were all adults in the family to work full time, full year, we subtract from each family's GEC, the amount required to purchase acceptable child care.[11] We call this value the family's *net earnings capacity*, NEC.[12]

In a final step, we compare the family's NEC to the official (family-size specific) poverty line for the family. This line, it will be recalled is interpreted as the amount of income that would enable a family of a specific size and composition to attain a socially acceptable level of living. If the NEC for a family is above this line, we classify the family as "self-reliant", or non-poor in NEC terms. Families who do not have the capacity to generate a net income stream (NEC) in excess of their poverty line are those we deem unable to be self-reliant.

As we emphasized above, many conventions, norms and assumptions have gone into this "self-reliant poverty" measure. To sum up the main ones:

- the *net earnings capacity* concept is an appropriate indicator of the "capability of a family to generate an income stream that could be used for meeting needs". It reflects the full capacity earnings capability of a family, and hence is a good index of the family's ability to generate income, and of the value of the stream of services that could be yielded by the family's human capital.
- The "norm" of full time, full year work is accepted as a social norm of the working time of people who are fully using their human capital. Values greater than, or less than, this amount could be used, but we accept this as a socially-determined full employment norm.
- The adjustments made for health, disability, and long-run unemployability reflect rough indicators of the adjustments that should be subtracted from a person's measured earnings capacity to obtain a more realistic estimate of the value of the potential services of his human capital.[13] We abstract from short-run constraints placed on a person's earnings capacity by the demand-side of the labor market. In particular, one could argue that earnings capacities *fall* during recessions. Our individual earnings capacities simply estimate what the individual *could* earn if he or she held a job paying a wage commensurate with his or her observed human capital characteristics.

11

The required costs of making full use of human capital (such as child care costs) should be subtracted from the gross value of the human capital (GEC) in arriving at an estimate of the ability of a family to attain a level of living that we call "self reliant". We take our estimates of the costs of adequate market provided care to be a reasonable estimate of these unavoidable work-related costs.

5. The level and trend of "inability-to-be-self-reliant" poverty

We use annual data from the March Current Population Survey (available from the U.S. Bureau of the Census) to estimate the rate of NEC poverty for families headed by a working-aged person in the United States from 1975 to 1995. The March Current Population Survey is an annual survey of over 50,000 American families, obtaining detailed information of the structure, income, and labor market activities and outcomes of the adults in the family. It is a stratified random sample, so that using the appropriate weighting factors (provided by the U. S. Bureau of the Census) yields a picture of the economic status and labor market activities of the entire American population.

We have also calculated the prevalence of U.S. poverty for families headed by working age individuals using the official definition and concepts of the U.S. Bureau of the Census. Our estimates of the overall prevalence of both NEC poverty and official poverty for the 1975 to 1995 period are shown in tables 1.1.1 and 1.1.2, respectively, and figure 1.1.2.[14]

While the official poverty rate over the period lies in the 10-14 percent range, the NEC poverty rate ranges from 6 to 11 percent. The primary factors that account for this difference in poverty rates between the two measures are:

1) the counting of transfer income (done in the official measure but not in the NEC measure);
2) the less than full time, full year work of many adults in the data (which affects the official poverty measure);
3) the adjustment for child care costs which offsets Gross Earnings Capacity in the NEC poverty measure.

12

Table 1.1.1 Percent of individuals in NEC poverty

	Average poverty rate		Growth rate [a]
	1975 to 1977	1993 to 1995	
All	5.79	10.54	3.38 %
Race of head			
Whites	3.55	6.5	3.41 %
Blacks	17.72	24.34	1.78 %
Hispanics	12.67	19.66	2.47 %
Other	4.52	9.57	4.26 %
Sex of head			
Males	2.84	5.77	4.02 %
Females	22.14	20.55	- 0.41 %
Education of head			
Less than high school	12.58	28.22	4.59 %
High school graduate	4.2	11.87	5.94 %
Some college	2.23	7.16	6.68 %
College graduate	0.47	1.22	5.46 %
Families with no children			
All	4.43	7.18	2.71 %
Couples	1.93	3.62	3.55 %
Single men	8.76	11.08	1.31 %
Single women	9.56	11.81	1.18 %
Families with children			
All	6.37	12.44	3.79 %
Couples	2.53	5.06	3.93 %
Single fathers	10.97	22.39	4.04 %
Single mothers	29.34	38.08	1.46 %
White	20.23	27.23	1.67 %
Black	39.08	46.72	1.00 %
Hispanic	40.86	48.1	0.91 %
Other	32.63	36.26	0.59 %
Single mothers on welfare	44.98	58.73	1.49 %
Single mothers not on welfare	17.72	26.16	2.19 %

a. The growth rate is calculated using the average 1975 to 1977, and 1993 to 1995 poverty rates, and assumes 18 years of growth.

Table 1.1.2 Percent of individuals in official poverty

	Average poverty rate		Growth rate [a]
	1975 to 1977	1993 to 1995	
All	10.19	13.72	1.67 %
Race of head			
Whites	6.67	8.28	1.21 %
Blacks	27.94	29.45	0.29 %
Hispanics	21.88	27.74	1.33 %
Other	13.64	16.66	1.12 %
Sex of head			
Males	5.94	7.89	1.59 %
Females	33.74	26.05	- 1.43 %
Education of head			
Less than high school	20.13	35.61	3.22 %
High school graduate	7.66	14.82	3.73 %
Some college	5.63	9.39	2.88 %
College graduate	2.29	3.09	1.67 %
Families with no children			
All	7.05	9.17	1.47 %
Couples	2.7	3.12	0.80 %
Single men	12.94	15.17	0.89 %
Single women	17.32	17.66	0.11 %
Families with children			
All	11.55	16.31	1.94 %
Couples	6.37	8.38	1.54 %
Single fathers	11	19.42	3.21 %
Single mothers	43.15	45.16	0.25 %
White	31.35	32.58	0.21 %
Black	56.71	55.22	- 0.15 %
Hispanic	55.03	57.37	0.23 %
Other	40.89	40.03	- 0.12 %
Single mothers on welfare	68.88	77.19	0.63 %
Single mothers not on welfare	24.05	26.59	0.56 %

a.   The growth rate is calculated using the average 1975 to 1977, and 1993 to 1995 poverty rates, and assumes 18 years of growth.

Figure 1.1.2 also shows the greater cyclical sensitivity of the official poverty rate than of the NEC poverty rate. While the official poverty rate rose nearly 40 percent during the recession of the early-1980s, the NEC poverty rate rose less than one-half of this amount. Given that the NEC measure reflects longer-term (or permanent) earnings potential as opposed to the shorter-term actual income amount reflected in the official measure, the closer tie between current labor market conditions and the official poverty rate is expected.

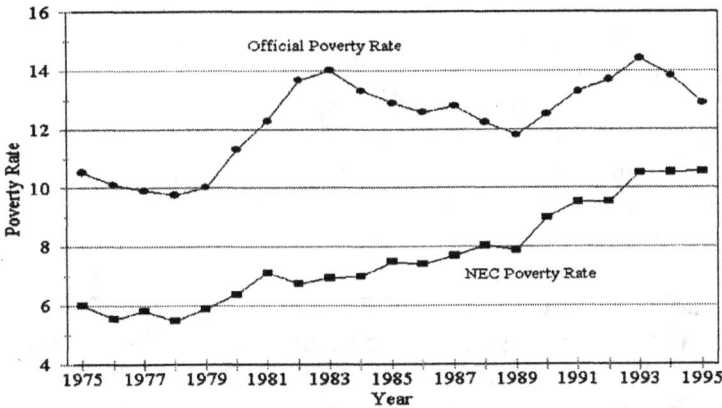

Figure 1.1.2   NEC and official poverty rate (all persons, 1959 to 1996)

As table 1.1.1 indicates, NEC poverty has grown at a substantially faster rate than has official poverty. Over the 1975-1995 period, the prevalence of official poverty grew by about one-third, reflecting an average annual growth rate of 1.7 percent. By contrast, the NEC poverty rate at the end of the period is nearly 185 percent of its initial level, reflecting a growth rate of 3.4 percent over the period, twice the rate of growth of the official poverty measure.

In our calculations, then, both the official poverty rate and especially the *net earnings capacity* poverty rate have risen from 1975 to 1995.[15] This growth in both the current income and self-reliant indicators of economic inadequacy is troubling when one considers what an affluent society the U. S. has become. Indeed, inflation-adjusted disposable income per capita in the U.S. has increased from $13,400 to $18,900 (1992 dollars) over the 1975-1995 period, an increase of over 40 percent.

This growth in the poverty rates that we have reported runs run counter to the findings of some other studies, where the trend in aggregate poverty has been negative, rather than positive. Perhaps the most prominent of these is Slesnick (1993), who bases his poverty measure on the level of consumption expenditures as an indicator of well-being. Like our study, he compares his indicator of economic position to a set of poverty thresholds. However, while we have accepted the official family-size specific needs standard as a norm, Slesnick computes an alternative set of poverty thresholds. These thresholds, however, have been strongly questioned.[16]

A second study that finds a downward trend in the poverty rate is that by Jencks and Mayer (1996), who calculate a poverty rate for children using an alternative price index (reflecting smaller price level increases than the official index) and a definition of family income that includes both the income of nonrelatives in the living unit and the value of public in-kind benefits.[17]

The rapid increase in the NEC poverty rate over the 1975 to 1995 period and the slower increase in the official poverty rate contrast starkly with the decreases in the poverty rate indicated in the Slesnick and Jencks-Mayer studies. The primary reason for these different patterns is clear. While the NEC poverty rate reflects the *potential* of a family to generate income, the other indicators seek to reveal income or consumption *realizations*. The rise in the NEC poverty rate indicates a decline in the potential of families to generate income. The decline in the Slesnick and Jencks-Mayer "consumption" poverty rate indicates a rise in consumption. Taken together, the two rates suggest that the *potential* earnings of some families is declining while at the same time the *realization* of that declining potential is rising.

The fall or slower rise in realized income or consumption poverty rates relative to the more rapid increase in the NEC poverty rate suggests an upward trend in the extent to which families with the lowest productive capabilities are in fact using these capabilities.

6. Trends in NEC and official poverty rates among some groups

The overall poverty trends that are described in figure 1.1.2 hide a variety of differential patterns of poverty growth among relevant subgroups of the U.S. population.

For example, the growth in NEC poverty among the population subgroups shown in table 1.1.1 ranged from -0.4 percent per year (for those living in families headed by a female) to over 6.6 percent per year (for those with some college). The family types with the highest growth rates are those which have experienced the largest *relative* losses in the capacity to escape poverty through their own work and earnings over the past two decades. The following summary lists the primary subgroups in table 1.1.1 with NEC poverty growth rates in excess of the national average (3.4 percent per year):[18]

Table 1.1.3 Subgroups with NEC poverty growth in excess of the national average

	Average Annual	
	Growth	NEC Poverty Rate in 1995
Whites	+ 3.4 percent	6.5 percent
Male heads of household	+ 4.0 percent	5.7 percent
Less than high school degree	+ 4.6 percent	28.2 percent
High school graduate	+ 5.9 percent	11.9 percent
Married couples without children	+ 3.6 percent	3.6 percent
Married couples with children	+ 3.9 percent	5.1 percent

From these comparisons, it is clear that the population subgroups experiencing the most rapid growth in NEC poverty include those in white, male-headed, and married-couple families; such families are not generally thought of as economically vulnerable. Nevertheless, even though these groups had large relative increases in NEC poverty, by 1995 the poverty rates for most of these groups were still low; the median among the groups listed is 6.5 percent relative to the overall 10.6 percent national rate.[19]

The most surprising story in table 1.1.1 concerns the groups that have experienced the lowest growth in NEC poverty over the period. The trends for these groups are well below the overall 3.4 growth rate in NEC poverty, and in several cases the trend is negative. These slow NEC poverty growth groups tend to be those with the highest overall levels of both NEC and official poverty. The following lists the primary subgroups in the table with the smallest trends in the NEC poverty index from 1975 to 1995:

Table 1.1.4 Subgroups with the smallest trends in the NEC poverty index

	Average Annual	
	NEC Poverty Rate in 1995	Growth
Blacks	+1.8 percent	24.3 percent
Hispanics	+2.5 percent	19.7 percent
Female family heads	-0.4 percent	20.6 percent
Black single mother families	+1.0 percent	46.7 percent
Hispanic single mother families	+0.9 percent	48.1 percent

Clearly, a large percentage of individuals in black and Hispanic families and in mother-only families are unable to be self-reliant. Among these groups, the NEC poverty rate in 1995 ranged from 19.7 percent to over 48 percent, compared to an overall NEC poverty rate of 10.5 percent.[20] However, these same least well off and most vulnerable groups in the nation have experienced either decreases or below average growth in NEC poverty. Among these groups, the rate of growth ranged from -0.4 percent per year to 2.5 percent per year, compared to the overall NEC poverty growth rate of 3.4 percent per year.

7. The composition of the NEC poor population

Evidence on levels and trends in poverty rates has implications for the characteristics of the groups in society who are included in the group designated as "poor". What are the characteristics of the NEC poor, and how has this composition changed over time? How do these patterns compare with patterns for those designated as poor by the official measure?

18

Table 1.1.5 Composition of individuals in NEC poverty, by characteristic of family head

	Average Poverty Rate [a]				Growth Rate [b]
	1975 - 1977		1993 - 1995		
Race of Head					
Whites	49.57	(0.94)	43.7	(1.02)	-0.70%
Blacks	36.87	(1.12)	30.4	(1.08)	-1.07%
Hispanics	12.34	(1.02)	22.06	(0.92)	3.28%
Other	1.21	(0.58)	3.84	(0.75)	6.61%
Sex of Head					
Males	41.5	(0.84)	37.07	(0.95)	-0.63%
Females	58.5	(1.15)	62.93	(1.03)	0.41%
Education of Head					
Less Than High School	66.47	(1.1)	41.85	(1.03)	-2.54%
High School Graduate	26.31	(0.97)	37.32	(1.04)	1.96%
Some College	5.75	(0.7)	17.95	(0.99)	6.53%
College Graduate	1.47	(0.36)	2.87	(0.51)	3.78%
Families with no Children	23.12	(1.11)	24.7	(1)	0.37%
Percent Comprised by					
Couples	28.51	(1.14)	27.47	(1.48)	-0.21%
Single Men	31.63	(1.07)	35.5	(0.93)	0.64%
Single Women	39.86	(0.88)	37.03	(0.85)	-0.41%
Families with Children	76.88	(0.97)	75.3	(0.99)	-0.12%
Percent Comprised by					
Couples	33.55	(0.72)	30.9	(0.79)	-0.46%
Single Fathers	2.33	(1.82)	6.39	(1.5)	5.75%
Single Mothers	64.11	(1.23)	62.71	(1.1)	-0.12%
Characteristic of Single Mother:					
White	35.89	(0.95)	31.47	(0.99)	-0.73%
Black	50.25	(1.01)	44.6	(1)	-0.66%
Hispanic	12.52	(1.09)	20.88	(0.99)	2.88%
Other	1.35	(1.19)	3.05	(1.08)	4.64%
On Welfare	65.37	(0.96)	56.45	(0.9)	-0.81%
Not on Welfare	34.63	(1.08)	43.55	(1.17)	1.28%

a.   The growth rate is calculated using the average 1975 to 1977, and 1993 to 1995 composition rates, and assumes 18 years of growth.

b.   The ratios of NEC poverty share to official poverty share are in parentheses.

Consider first the racial composition of poverty. In the mid-1970s, individuals living in minority headed families comprised more than one-half of the NEC poor group, and their share of the NEC poverty population grew over time; by the end of the period, minorities accounted for more than 56 percent of the self-reliant poor. Among the minority groups, the share accounted for by Blacks fell, while that of Hispanics grew rapidly. By 1995, people living in Hispanic families accounted for over 22 percent of the NEC poor population.

The officially poor population has a similar racial structure to the NEC poor population, as shown by the ratios of NEC poor population shares to officially poor population shares. In the mid-1990s, a slightly greater share of the NEC poor population lives in families headed by a Black, and a slightly smaller share of that population lives in families headed by a Hispanic. This is true despite the shift in the composition of the NEC poor population away from Black headed families towards Hispanic headed families; clearly that shift was more pronounced in the officially poor population.

In the mid-1970s, the NEC poor population was more heavily "female headed" than was the officially poor population. About 58 percent of those with the lowest earnings capacity relative to needs lived in "female headed" families at the beginning of the period, about 15 percent more than the percentage living in officially poor families. By the mid-1990s, almost 63 percent of the NEC poor lived in female headed families. Over the intervening years, the NEC poor and officially poor populations converged in terms of gender shares.

The share of the NEC poverty population with less than a high school degree was very high at the beginning of the period — about two-thirds of the total. However, as the number of working-age family heads without a high school degree decreased over time, their share fell to about 42 percent. Similarly, as education levels in the U.S. rose, the composition of the NEC poor population shifted towards families headed by more educated individuals. By the end of the period, almost 18 percent of the NEC poor population lived in families headed by individuals with some schooling beyond the high school level. Generally, however,

20

it remained true that the concentration of low education families in NEC poverty exceeded that in official poverty. In the mid-1990s, the share of NEC poor individuals living in families headed by a college graduate was still only half that group's share of the officially poor population.

Among NEC poor families with children, those living in a family headed by a single mother account for about 60-65 percent of the poor population. While this high proportion declined slightly for the capability poverty measure, it drifted upward for the official poverty measure. Despite this convergence, the share of NEC poor individuals comprised by single mother families was 10 percent higher than the corresponding share of the officially poor population in the mid-1990s.

Among NEC poor single mothers, the composition of the population shifted from families headed by a White or Black single mothers to families headed by Hispanic or Other single mothers. At the beginning of the period, individuals living in NEC poor families headed by a Black single mother comprised about half that population subgroup. Over time, this percentage decreased to about 44 percent. Correspondingly, the share of this subgroup living with Hispanic single mothers rose from 12.5 percent to 21 percent of the population.

Consistent with the group-specific poverty trends noted in section 5, the share of the NEC poor population comprised of individuals living in families headed by the most economically vulnerable individuals — high school dropouts, minorities, and single mothers — decreased over time.[21] Despite this decline, however, the NEC poverty measure is still more heavily comprised by these groups than is the official measure. The concentration of these groups in the capability poor population exceeds that in the official poor population.

8. What has accounted for these patterns?

In our discussion of the NEC poverty and official poverty measures, we have encountered several trends with interesting implications. The underlying economic, demographic, and cultural factors that have accounted for these patterns are numerous. Moreover, they interact in complex and difficult-to-understand ways.

An example of the puzzles that our analysis has uncovered concerns the different poverty growth patterns among the vulnerable and not-so-vulnerable groups in society. For example, in spite of the rapid growth of

21

NEC poverty overall, groups commonly thought of as being the most vulnerable — minorities, female-headed families, or families headed by a person with low schooling — recorded below-average increases in NEC (and to some extent, official) poverty, and increases that are less than those recorded for less vulnerable groups — whites, married-couple families, and those with relatively high levels of schooling.

What factors could have contributed to, or explained, some of these patterns? The catalogue of factors is very large. Indeed, any change that affects: a) the structure of work opportunities available in the economy (the demand side of the labor market), b) people's choices in response to these opportunities (the supply side of the labor market), or c) the demographic structure of the population will likely have some effect on the prevalence and the trend of both official poverty and poverty defined as the inability to be self-reliant. While it is impossible to assign responsibility for the observed changes in either of these poverty measures to individual factors, it is possible to identify the most important of the underlying changes, and to indicate the likely effect of them on these patterns.

In the following paragraphs, we summarize the effects of a number of economic and demographic changes over the 1975-95 period[22] on a few of the major changes in overall and subgroup poverty rates for both the official and NEC definitions.

Decreasing female poverty, increasing male poverty

As we have seen, although both the official and NEC poverty rates for those living in female-headed families exceed those of members of male headed families, the male poverty rate has risen while the female poverty rate has fallen.[23] The primary factors that are likely to have accounted for pattern include:

- the *decline in the real value of income transfers* (tends to increase relative female official poverty, but has no effect on NEC poverty);
- increased labor force participation of women (tends to decrease relative female official poverty, but has no effect on NEC poverty);
- increase in wage rates of females with low skills; decrease in low-skilled male wage rates (decreases both official and NEC female poverty, and increases male poverty under both definitions);

22

- increase in male joblessness (increases male official poverty rates, but has no effect on NEC poverty).[24]

We would speculate that the "gender twist" in both official but especially NEC poverty rates that we have documented is primarily the result of the relative erosion in both the quantity of labor supplied by low-skilled males (relative to females) and the absolute decrease in low-skilled male wage rates over this period.

Rising white, relative to black and hispanic, poverty

The low relative growth in the official and NEC poverty rates among blacks and Hispanics appears to be primarily attributable to the rather steady *increase in the absolute and relative wage rates of minority workers*, compared to white workers. Joblessness among low-skilled workers has also increased somewhat more for whites than minority groups, and this has contributed to the "racial twist" in the official poverty trend.

Rapid increases in poverty in families with headed by a low education worker

For both poverty measures (but especially the NEC measure), large absolute increases in poverty rates are recorded for families headed by high school dropouts and high school graduates. The *absolute fall in wage rates earned by those with little education and few skills* appears to account for the large increase in poverty rates for the groups with low schooling.[25] Because this eroding low-skill wage rate decreases actual earnings less than earnings capacity,[26] the negative impact of this erosion will be larger for the NEC poverty rate for those with low education than for the official poverty rate.[27]

Increasing overall poverty rates, especially NEC poverty

The main story that this analysis has revealed is the large increase in poverty defined as the inability to be self-reliant, relative to official income poverty — which itself has tended to rise over time. While several of the factors that we have already mentioned contribute to this disparate growth pattern, we speculate that the substantial *increase in wage inequality "within" age-race-schooling groups* over the period is

23

primarily responsible for this development. This rise in wage inequality serves to increase both the official and the NEC poverty rates, as it pulls those at the bottom of the wage distribution further away from the constant (in real terms) poverty line. Because the relative deterioration of wages at the bottom of the distribution weights all of the potential work hours of the low-wage population in the estimation of NEC poverty, but only the hours actually worked in the estimation of official poverty, the impact of this growth in wage inequality will be greater for NEC than official poverty. We attribute the large absolute and relative increase in the overall NEC poverty rate to this factor, together with the *absolute decreases in wage rates of males and less-educated workers*.

9. Conclusion and policy implications

To summarize, a new way to measure the population of the poor in the United States might be to look at which families lack the abilities necessary to earn, through their own efforts, an income sufficient to meet an official, minimally acceptable level of living. Such a measure may be of more interest to policy makers who emphasize self-reliance (and by extension, a smaller role for government) than is the current measure. We have shown that the level of poverty in the U.S., as measured by this alternative indicator, has increased substantially over the past two decades. There is a growing population of Americans who would remain below official poverty thresholds, even if they were to fully use their capabilities, their human capital.

We must stress that this measure is not intended to replace the current official measure of poverty, but rather to augment it. Certainly, the official measure identifies an important segment of the population, namely those families that lack sufficient *money income* to meet a minimum living standard. As such, it is well-suited to identifying those families in need of short-term cash or in-kind assistance. Our measure, in contrast, is better suited to identifying those families in need of *longer term* skill-enhancing assistance. Like a measure of "health poverty", which would identify those individuals with the lowest health levels, or a measure of "housing poverty", which would identify those individuals with insufficient housing, our earnings capacity measure identifies those individuals with insufficient skills, abilities, etc., to generate minimally acceptable earnings levels. As such, it views the poor population along a long term, human capital dimension.

The rapid growth in this type of poverty is discouraging for a society that prides itself on having an environment in which individuals are able to prosper and thrive by working hard, and playing by the rules. The message that it is necessary for workers and families to rely on their own resources in order to get by appears to have come at a time that underlying changes in basic demographic and economic trends have made it more difficult for those with few skills and little human capital to make it on their own.

In particular, we noted in section 7 the substantial increase in NEC poverty among our least educated individuals, and argued that the decline in wage rates for this group was primarily responsible for the NEC poverty trend. The decline in wage rates has been heavily researched in recent years.[28]

Explanations for it include changes in technology, which increased the demand for highly skilled and educated workers, and the decline in the influence of unions, whose members are often non among those with the highest skills.

This decline in capabilities highlights the dilemma faced by those who advocate the self-reliance objective. If income support measures are ruled out as eroding work effort, encouraging dependence, and fostering the growth of income poverty, what policy measures are available to reduce the prevalence of those who are unable to be self-reliant? Essentially, there are only two general policy strategies available:

- increasing the level of education, training, skills, and other income generating characteristics of those at the bottom of the human capital distribution, and
- increasing the "return" that individuals with low earnings capacity receive on the use of their human capital.

The first approach suggests targeting programs designed to improve schools and to provide education and training services on those with few skills and little human capital, and to increase the resources devoted to such targeted measures. Some programs, similar to Head Start, could be designed to increase the value of early education. Other programs, such as direct financial aid for post-secondary school, could stimulate later human capital investments. Similarly, job training programs designed to teach the skills needed in our "high technology" based economy could promote further human capital investments. A complete evaluation of these and other programs, is beyond the scope of this brief, however these are the types of programs that will be needed if self-reliance is our nation's main policy goal. How best to design and implement such programs, and to ensure that they are cost-effective, becomes a question of high importance.

The second approach is the more controversial, as it directly calls into question the productivity returns reflected in market-determined wages. Policy measures capable of reducing NEC poverty through increasing the returns to market work of those with little human capital often carry with them their own distortions and inefficiencies. Such measures include raising the national minimum wage, providing subsidized wage rates with those at the bottom of the wage distribution, or directly subsidizing the earnings of those whose work is insufficient to move their families above the nation's poverty line.[29] The nation's current Earned Income Tax Credit is an example of the last of these policies. All of these measures have both advantages and disadvantages; there is no "free lunch" here either. Again, the question is how best to design and implement such programs, and to ensure that they are cost-effective.

Some may argue that we have examined the trends in earnings capacity, but have ignored many of the choice-aspects of human capital accumulation and family formation. For example, should a individual with a terminal high school degree be considered "human capital poor" when that individual could have obtained a postsecondary degree? We would argue that while there are choice-aspects to postsecondary enrollment decisions, those choices may be made with less-than-good information, or under financing arrangements that constrain access for those from poor families. The individual choosing to attend college in 1979 made his or her decision at a time of declining "college earnings premiums", and may have believed that a college education was simply not worth the investment. Should that individual be held responsible for subsequent changes in labor market conditions? Do individuals who cannot afford postsecondary school or do not possess the ability to successfully pursue a postsecondary education *decide* not to attend? Or are these individuals constrained from augmenting their human capital stocks? Similarly, some may argue that NEC poverty among single mothers arises from decisions about family formation and fertility. We would respond that while there are choice-aspects to these decisions,

26

quite often single motherhood arises from abandonment, divorce, and the decisions made by fathers. Should these single mother families not be considered NEC poor because their expectations of family formation proved incorrect?

However, regardless of whether human capital accumulation, family formation, fertility and similar characteristics are choices or not, the fact remains that certain families and individuals lack the ability to be self-reliant, lack the ability to earn their way above minimum income thresholds. If self-reliance and economic independence are to be the standards by which we gauge our success as a nation, and if income maintenance is to be abandoned as a policy instrument, we cannot avoid answering the question of how best to provide the nation's lowest human capital families with the skills, capabilities, or returns on their efforts required for them to be self-reliant. In the face of underlying demographic and economic trends that appear to generate increases in the level of NEC poverty, finding an answer to this question assumes increased urgency.

Notes

1. Researchers have been able to compare poverty levels by assembling similar data sets from various countries, and then undertaking analyses based on a variety of poverty indicators. See Gottschalk and Smeeding (1997).

2. This approach has been called the "Leiden School" approach to poverty measurement, as most of the researchers who have pursued this question spent some time at Leiden University (the Netherlands). Bernard van Praag is the central figure in this area; the important papers are Hagenaars (1986); Hagenaars, van Praag, and van Weeren (1982). The approach of van Praag and his colleagues involves construction of an indicator of well-being that is comparable across people, based on income levels that individuals subjectively state to be "excellent", "good", etc.

3. See Fisher (1992).

4. An excellent study of the origins of the official poverty measure and of the analytical and empirical bases for it is Ruggles (1990).

5. Efforts are currently underway to revise the official measure to correct some of the problems mentioned above. A National Academy of Sciences panel was convened to study the official measure and to propose changes in it. Citro and Michael (1995) present the results of the panel's study, and discuss the revision of the measure proposed. This proposal is designed to secure a measure that better reflects the consumption "means" of a family relative to its needs than does the current official measure.

6. One of the earliest of the proponents of this view was Charles Murray (1984). His influential book, *Losing Ground* started a steady stream of writings, speeches and political candidacies that advocated the view that government policy — especially welfare and other income support measures — was really the problem, and not having a population of cash-short people. This, and related writings, followed this same track by suggesting that the nation lost the "War on Poverty", and that the government should get out of the business of assisting the destitute. Rather, social policy should emphasize individual self-reliance or, should private charities wish to help, voluntary contributions of time and money to the nation's most income poor.

7. To emphasize the fact that we are only interested in an indicator of people's capabilities, we could have called this measure "labor market potential", indicating that we are simply after a signal regarding just how much earnings potential people have. The indicator we have in mind is not substantively different from identifying the "health poor" as those who health status lies below some minimum norm.

8. This discussion is based on a larger, technical paper that describes in detail the procedures we use to estimate this "self-reliance" based poverty measure, and the norms on which it is based. See Haveman and Bershadker (1998).

9. In this procedure, each individual with the same set of characteristics is assigned the same earnings capacity, thus neglecting the role of unobserved human capital, and labor demand characteristics, and "luck" in the process by which earnings are determined. As a result, the distribution of earnings capacity that we would obtain would be artificially compressed. To adjust for this, we adopt a procedure that restores the effect of these unobserved factors. Technically, we apply a random shock reflecting the unexplained variation in the regressions to the estimated value for each observation. While this procedure requires a number of assumptions regarding the distribution of the unobserved factors, it is a reasonable way to secure a distribution of earnings capacities that avoids this narrowing of the distribution. See Haveman and Bershadker (1998) for a more complete discussion of this procedure.

10. This adjustment factor relies on what people state when answering questions about why they are not working full time, full year. These adjustments are rough, but they do capture characteristics about the health and the employability of people that should be taken into account. Most likely, our adjustments understate NEC poverty. First, they probably capture only the most disabled. They also fail to capture the reduction in wage rates for disabled who still work but at reduced productivity. Similarly, they fail to capture the constraints on work that affect parents with a disabled child. Or, take the case of a person who is a serious alcoholic but does not report a disability. We probably attribute too high an earnings capacity value to that person by not making a big enough estimate of his or her adjustment factor. Again, see Haveman and Bershadker (1998).

11. Note that the reason for needing this adjustment relates to the norm that we stated above, namely being out of the labor force is a voluntary choice. Because many people are uncomfortable with this norm in the case parents with young children, we

28

also make adjustment in this case (hence, positing yet another norm). We begin with estimates of the weekly cost of child care for children aged 0 to 5 ($90 per week in 1996) and 6 to 11 ($50 per week in 1996) (see U.S. General Accounting Office, 1997). We then adjust these estimates for region of the country, SMSA status, and year (see Casper, 1995). We multiply the adjusted cost estimate by the number of children in the family aged 0 to 5 or 6 to 11 as appropriate, and convert to nominal dollars. For further details on this procedure, see Haveman and Bershadker (1998). As an alternative to this procedure, we could attribute an earnings capacity of zero to one parent, or *the* parent, in case of single parents, in families with young children, and ignore required child care costs. Quantitatively, this would make a difference in our calculations only to the extent that the *difference* between the estimated earnings capacity for the parent and the child care expense is large enough to move the family from a position below its poverty line to one above it. Furthermore, to the extent that the percentage of families so affected is constant over time, such an adjustment would affect only the level and not the trend in NEC poverty. Finally, note that we have built in a single child care adjustment, when there is in fact a high variance to child care expenses. It would have been possible to have obtained information on this variance and then made arbitrary assignments as seemed appropriate. Such a procedure would have little effect on our overall estimate of the level or trend of NEC poverty.

12. There are clearly other costs that must be incurred if a person is working full time, full year. These include transportation costs to and from work, work-related clothing purchases, and food purchased away from home. We neglect these required costs that are associated with work. We also neglect the non-wage compensation that is paid to some full time, full year workers, such as health insurance and pension contributions.

13. In fact, we make the unemployability adjustment for all individuals who report not working full time, full year, but do not make it for individuals who are never in the labor force. Applying this adjustment to these individuals is impossible in that they do not report the reasons why they are totally out of the labor force. Some would argue that we should make a similar adjustment for the "discouraged worker" effect. Because of the difficulty of identifying discouraged workers, we have not made such an adjustment. To this extent, our NEC poverty measure is biased downward to some small degree.

14. Note that the official series in Figure 1.1.2 differs slightly from Figure 1.1.1 since the population in Figure 1.1.2 is restricted to individuals in prime-aged households.

15. This conclusion is consistent with that of Triest (1998), who has revisited the methods and implications of various poverty measures.

16. See Johnson (1996), U. S. General Accounting Office (1996), and Triest (1998) for a discussion of Slesnick's poverty threshold calculations.

29

17. Jencks and Mayer also report a separate calculation using consumption expenditures rather than income, and substituting for the official poverty lines alternative measures (with alternative inflation adjustments) that they judge to be more appropriate. While the official children's poverty rate increases from 14.3 percent to 18.2 percent from 1972-73 to 1988-90, or by 3.9 percentage points, the consumption-based children's poverty rate calculated by Jencks and Mayer falls by 0.9 percentage points. They find this pattern to be consistent with that for their revised income poverty figures.

18. The two highest education groups have been excluded from this listing, even though their percentage rates of growth were above average. It is difficult to interpret the percentage increase calculation, given that the base level is a very low number. See below.

19. Because the absolute size of these relatively mainstream groups is large relative to the population, the 82 percent increase in the overall NEC poverty rate over the period is largely attributable to the deterioration in their relative earnings capabilities.

20. The official poverty rates of these groups at the end of the period ranged from 26 percent to 57 percent as compared to the overall official poverty rate of 13.7.

21. The share comprised by individuals living in families headed by a woman have increased, however. This is largely explained by the increase in the proportion of female headed family units in the population.

22. These changes have been documented in numerous research articles and are commonly described in news stories.

23. "Male poverty" here refers to families headed by single men, with and without children, and married couples, with and without children. "Female poverty" here refers to single women, with and without children.

24. See Juhn (1992).

25. The converse of this, of course, is the increased "schooling premium", which has received so much attention in recent years.

26. In the first case, the wage rate is multiplied by actual hours worked, which in the case of low-skilled workers is often rather low; in the second case, the wage rate is multiplied by full time, year round work.

27. The relative increase in wage rates for minorities, which also tend to have relatively low levels of schooling, works to offset this effect of eroding relative low-skill, low-education wages.

28. See Levy and Murnane (1992), Bound and Johnson (1992), Katz and Murphy (1992), and Juhn, Murphy and Pierce (1993), for analyses of the changing structure of wage rates over the 1970s and 1980s.

29. For a discussion of such wage and employment subsidies as an anti-poverty strategy, see Haveman (1988).

References

Bound, John and George Johnson. 1992. "Changes in the Structure of Wages in the 1980s: An Evaluation of Alternative Explanations." *American Economic Review.* 82(3): 371-392.

Casper, Lynne. 1995. "What Does It Cost to Mind our Preschoolers?" *Current Population Reports P70-52.* Census Bureau.

Citro, Constance F., and Robert T. Michael, eds. 1995. *Measuring Poverty: A New Approach.* Washington, D.C.: National Academy Press.

Fisher, Gordon M. 1992. "The Development and History of the Poverty Thresholds." *Social Security Bulletin.* 55(4, Winter), 3-14.

Gottschalk, Peter and Timothy Smeeding. 1997. "Cross-National Comparisons of Earnings and Income Inequality." *Journal of Economic Literature.* 35(2), 633-687.

Hagenaars, Aldi. 1986. *The Perception of Poverty.* Amsterdam: North-Holland.

Hagenaars, Aldi, B.M. S. van Praag, and J. van Weeren. 1982. "Poverty in Europe." *Review of Income and Wealth.* 28: 345-359.

Haveman, Robert. 1988. *Starting Even: An Equal Opportunity Program to Combat the Nation's New Poverty.* New York: Simon and Schuster.

Haveman, Robert, and Andrew Bershadker. 1998. "Poverty as 'Inability to be Self-Reliant':Trends in Earnings Capacity and Official Poverty, 1975 to 1995." Discussion Paper, Institute for Research on Poverty, University of Wisconsin-Madison.

Jencks, Christopher, and Susan E. Mayer. 1996. "Do Official Poverty Rates Provide Useful Information about Trends in Children's Economic Welfare?" Harris Graduate School of Public Policy, University of Chicago.

Johnson, David. 1996. "The Two-Parameter Equivalence Scale and Inequality between and within Households." Paper prepared for meeting of the International Association for Research in Income and Wealth.

Juhn, Chinhui. 1992. "Decline of Male Labor Market Participation: The Role of Declining Labor Market Opportunities." *Quarterly Journal of Economics.* 57(1): 79-122.

Juhn, Chinhui, Kevin Murphy, and Brooks Pierce. 1993. "Wage Inequality and the Rise in Returns to Skill." *Journal of Political Economy.* 101(3): 410-442.

Katz, Lawrence and Kevin Murphy. 1992. "Changes in Relative Wages, 1963-1987: Supply and Demand Factors." *Quarterly Journal of Economics.* 107(1): 35-78.

Levy, Frank and Richard Murnane. 1992. "U.S. Earnings Levels and Earnings Inequality: A Review of Recent Trends and Proposed Explanations." *Journal of Economic Literature.* 30(3): 1333-1381.

Murray, Charles. 1984. *Losing Ground: American Social Policy 1950-1980.* New York: Basic Books.

31

Ruggles, Patricia. 1990. *Drawing the Line: Alternative Poverty Measures and Their Implications for Public Policy.* Washington, D.C.: Urban Institute Press.

Slesnick, Daniel T. 1993. "Gaining Ground: Poverty in the Postwar United States." *Journal of Political Economy.* 101(1): 1-38.

Triest, Robert K. 1998. "Has Poverty Gotten Worse?" *Journal of Economic Perspectives.* 12(1): 97-114.

U.S. General Accounting Office. 1996. *Alternative Poverty Measures.* GAO/GGD-96-183R.

U.S. General Accounting Office. 1997. *Implications of Increased Work Participation for Child Care.* GAO/HEHS-97-75.

1.2 Poverty among children and elders in Europe and North America

Lee Rainwater

Members of modern societies use a wide range of goods and services to effect their sense of social identity and their participation in activities and social relations. As a part of common cultural understandings members assume the necessity for particular material underpinnings to their activities in carrying out the social roles which constitute participation in their communities.

Because these are highly stratified societies the level of economic resources available to individuals and families varies greatly. People have a lively sense of what different levels imply in terms of both with whom an individual is likely to participate, and the kind of activities in social participation which are feasible.

The definition of poverty adopted by the European Community in 1984 reflects a conception of poverty grounded in an understanding of the nature of social stratification in prosperous industrial societies:

The poor shall be taken to mean persons, families, and groups of persons whose resources (material, cultural, and social) are so limited as to exclude them from the minimum acceptable way of life in the member state in which they live.

While Americans steeped in the tradition of an absolutely defined official poverty line often have some difficulty accepting such a conception of poverty, it is fast becoming the conventional wisdom in comparative poverty research. But it is not at all clear how widely understood are the sociological conceptions that lead to such a definition. (If I had to guess I'd say that the EU's definition was invented, or at least godfathered by, Brian Abel-Smith as a suitable bureaucratic formulation of Peter Townsend's theoretical approach to poverty.)

Relative income and social exclusion

The advanced industrial societies of the world have insured for their members a high standard of living, a standard unimaginable a century ago. As modern democracies, they also guarantee their members much security from arbitrary actions by powerful institutions and freedom of personal expression which has existed in few countries. Yet in some of these societies significant minorities are still excluded from full enjoyment of these advantages, and no advanced industrial society has succeeded in eliminating social exclusion.

Two perspectives contend in characterizations of economic well-being, the contrast being most apparent in conceptions of poverty. One emphasizes economic status per se; that is, people's command over goods and services. Poverty is material deprivation. An economic measure of well-being determines an income sufficient to provide a particular level of consumption of goods and services. Implicitly, the output of consumption is a given level of utility or satisfaction. One does not try to measure utility or satisfaction directly since this may involve subjective elements which are not relevant to the public policy issues involved.

A sociological measure of socioeconomic well-being is concerned not with consumption but with social participation. It is the participation in social activities which confers utility. While such a view is mainly identified with sociological (and anthropological) traditions, a few economists (Duesenberry in the 1940s, Lancaster, and recently Sen) have focussed on consumption as intermediate, that is, as an input into social activities which in turn confer well-being .

In this social perspective the problem of low income in relatively affluent societies is not seen as a problem of low consumption *per se*. The focus is instead on the consequence of the inability to consume at more than an extremely modest level. Without a requisite level of goods and services, the consequence, it is argued, is that individuals cannot participate as full members of their society. In the United States these more sociological concerns dominated the initial elite interest in poverty which prepared the groundwork for the launching of the War on Poverty. Michael Harrington's *The Other America*, first published in 1962, is generally credited with putting poverty on the agenda of the Democratic administration of John F. Kennedy. Harrington combined his own experience as a writer about the American working class with much sociological research during the 1950s on the inner city, on juvenile delinquency, and on slums. For Harrington there was "a language of the poor, a psychology of the poor, a world view of the poor. To be impoverished is to be an internal alien, to grow up in a culture that is radically different from the one that dominates society ... [The poor] need an American Dickens to record the smell and texture and quality of their lives. The cycles and trends, the massive forces, must be seen as affecting persons who talk and think differently."

In short, a focus on the merits of an absolute versus a relative poverty definition obscures a more important underlying difference between an economic and a social definition of poverty. Poverty as social exclusion directs our attention not so much to the amount of goods and services individuals can consume, but to the necessity for particular levels of consumption in order to be a fully participating member of society. Thus understanding economic deprivation or low income or poverty must proceed from a socially grounded understanding of the interpenetration of material and social well-being in modern societies.

As a shorthand for all this, we often say that poverty is relative. It is one way we talk about economic inequality in society. Much evidence from historical and community studies suggests that the minimum income for social participation as defined by members of society changes in step with changes in the average standard of living of the society. If the average standard of living increases by 50 percent, the perceived minimum for mainstream social participation also increases by 50 percent.

If one were to try to adhere to an absolute poverty standard over a long period of time or across countries one would end up with poverty amounts that are ridiculous on their face. Economic growth has been too great to maintain that what made for poverty in 1900, or 1930, or 1950 still applies. Similarly, the differences in standard of living across countries are such that we would react with disbelief to imposing one absolute standard on all.

Given that a relative approach to defining poverty assumes that the social definitions that mark some people as poor and some not change in step with changing levels of affluence, establishing socially relevant definitions of economic well-being should proceed by asking the experts - that is, the members of society. Some efforts along this line have proceeded through the use of survey questionnaires. Research in the community studies tradition of sociology and anthropogy threw useful light on the same questions despite the lack of quantification. And, of course, we are all also experts on our societies in our own right.

From these various sources a rough consensus has developed that people with less than half of the median income are surely poor. The reasoning sketched above, however, makes one conclude that there can be no sharp dividing line between the poor and nonpoor. Instead we are talking about gradations of social exclusion as income declines from the middle downward. We should be thinking of bands of low income rather than poor and nonpoor - say extremely poor, poor, near poor and just getting along.

Operationalizing measures of poverty

When we move to the stage of working with data it is necessary to consider how to measure the distribution of *relative equivalent disposable income*. There are several choices that have to be made - choices based on empirical evidence as much as possible but also on constraints imposed by existing income surveys (in my case as embodied in the LIS database).

Income refers to annual money income plus a few near money public transfers - housing allowances, food stamps, educational vouchers, heating allowances.

Disposable income refers to income after direct taxes are paid.

Equivalent income refers to income adjusted for family size and age to take into account the differing "needs" of families of different composition.

Relative income refers to the fact that we judge incomes high, middling or low in relation to the incomes of other people in the nation.

The most ambiguous of the adjustments to total money income is that of equivalence - the operations by which we adjust a household's income by an equivalence scale.

The logic of the social definition of economic well-being implies that what one wishes to establish are possibilities for equivalent social participation. From the perspective of economics equivalence scales are designed to establish equivalent consumption. From a sociological perspective, however, need and equivalence are issues of resources required for social participation. What must be established is the relation between family characteristics (size, age) and opportunities for social participation, and thus for activities that are the means for experiencing a particular level of well-being.

Based on my Boston survey of the early 1970s, a more elaborate Boston survey by Dubnoff, the analysis of Gallup Poll data on "the income necessary for your family to get along" for the period 1979-1986, and reading the papers by Bernard Van Praag and his associates I have concluded that a conservative standard of equivalence holds that need increases no more that in proportion to the cube root of family size. Based on the analysis of the same Gallup surveys and a Eurobarometer survey that asked roughly the same question I have concluded that need also varies by age of head - increasing roughly 1 percent a year to the mid forties and then decreasing at the same rate into old age.

In the analysis which follows, therefore, equivalent income (EI) can be defined as:

$$EI = Y / (S^{.33} * .99^{|A-45|})$$

That is, equivalent income is defined as disposable income divided by the product of (a) the cube root of family size and (b) .99 compounded by the number of years difference between an individual's age and 45.

This paper examines in detail patterns of child and elder poverty in 14 rich nations in the 1990s. Most of these countries are in Western Europe: Belgium, Denmark, Finland, France, Germany, Italy, the Netherlands, Norway, Spain, Sweden and the United Kingdom. In addition I consider economic well-being in two Commonwealth nations - Australia and Canada - and the United States. The data from the Luxemburg Income Study (LIS) are used.

Child poverty rates

Figure 1.2.1 graphs the poverty rates of children in the 14 countries. The United States has an extremely high poverty rate of 23 percent. That is, 23 percent of all children live in families with equivalent incomes below one-half of the median equivalent income. These are incomes so low that the child and others in his family are not able to participate in the ongoing activities of their particular community in a sufficiently full manner to allow them to perceive themselves and be perceived by others as regular members of their society.

37

Italy and the UK has the next highest rates at 18 and 19 percent. The two Commonwealth nations also have rather high rates - at 13 and 14 percent. Spain has a rate almost as high - 12 percent of Spanish children are poor.

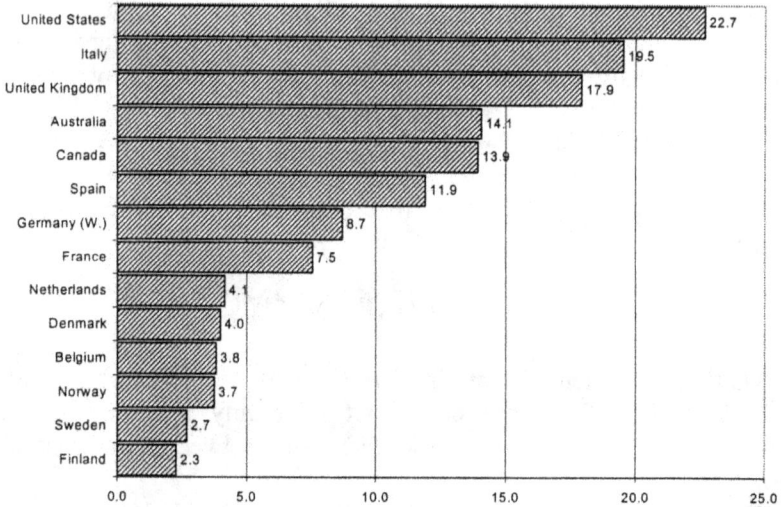

Figure 1.2.1   Child poverty rates

I'm puzzled as to how to deal with the great difference in incomes between the north and south of Italy. The social logic of a poverty line would suggest that we should have more local poverty lines. If that is the right choice it would make a lot of difference - the poverty rate for the South would be 21 percent, and that for the North quite a bit lower, grouping it with Australia and Canada at 14 percent. (Spain would also be a candidate for this treatment - in fact, if data were available we might wish to establish more local poverty lines in all countries.)

The rest of the countries have child poverty rates below 10 percent. Germany at 9 percent and France at 7 percent. The remaining countries have very low rates of below 5 percent. They constitute a northern continental European region of very low poverty - all of the Nordic countries and the Benelux countries.

Thus the poverty rate of American children is over 4 times as high as that of children in northern Europe. The child poverty rate of the United Kingdom is dramatically different from that of the northern part of the continent - over 3 times as high.

If one turns the question around and asks what the odds of escaping poverty in different countries are one see the contrast even more starkly. The odds of an American child escaping poverty are a little less than three-and-a-half to one, and of a British child about five to one. In contrast a child in the Northern European countries has odds of escaping poverty of almost 25 to one. Thus, these northern European children's chances of not being poor are well over 6 times greater than those of an American child and over 4 times greater than those of a British child.

If we broaden our focus to all of the countries for which LIS data exists we find no wider range in poverty rates but some interesting possibilities of comparison. We can add four Western European countries - two with data from the mid 1980s (Ireland and Switzerland) and two with more recently data - Austria and Luxembourg. Austria, Luxembourg and Switzerland fit neatly in the group of Northern continental countries with rates under 5 percent. Ireland on the other hand has a high poverty rate, right along side Spain, but not as high as that of the United Kingdom.

We have data from five Eastern European countries. Many people would not want to include these countries under the rubric of rich nations but we should keep in mind that their standards of living are not much lower than those of Western Europe some 40 years ago. By world standards they certainly are rich nations.

The most interesting observation to be made comparing these five Eastern European countries with each other is that the range in child poverty in these countries is great as it is in the countries of Western Europe. In fact the two countries with the very lowest rates of our twenty-five are the Czech Republic and Slovakia. Their child poverty rates are a bit lower than those of Sweden and Finland. Hungary appears in the middle of the range with about the same rate as France. Poland has a high poverty rate - about the same as Spain, Ireland, Canada and Australia. For Russia we find a very high poverty rate - a bit higher than in the United Kingdom although still not as high as in the United States.

Data are available for two other countries - Israel and the Republic of China (Taiwan). Both have higher rates than most European countries but lower than the two Commonwealth nations, the United Kingdom and the United States.

Broadening our scope from 14 to 25 countries tells us that within the range of economic development that these countries represent there is little relation between how rich a county is and how much child poverty it has. The West European countries with very low poverty rates have gross national products close to three times those of the Czech Republic and Slovakia and yet the poverty rates are not very different. Spain and Ireland have twice the real GDP as Poland but the three have very similar poverty rates. The United Kingdom, (southern) Italy and the United States versus Russia encompasses an enormous range in GDP yet these three have very high poverty rates.

Elder poverty

The question naturally arises as to whether there is something different about child poverty rates compared to rates for other persons. Since persons in the working ages are often parents we would not expect much difference in the poverty rates of working age adults and of children. There could be, and is, some difference because adults without children may have quite different rates from those with children. Large families may have poverty rates different from those of small families. Such difference will make for differences in the poverty rates of children versus the parental generation. However, in fact we find rather small differences in the rates of children and working age adults.

But, there is another large group which might fare very differently from children. The elderly seldom have minor children at home and derive their incomes in quite different ways from those in the working years.

Figure 1.2.2 plots the poverty rates for elders. Comparing the elder and child rates we find three countries with very high rates for both groups. In the United States elder poverty is almost 20 percent, not too different from the child rate of 23 percent. In the United Kingdom the elder rate is somewhat lower (15 percent) than the child rate of 18 percent. In Australia the child rate at 13 percent compares with a much higher elder rate of 25 percent.

In Canada it is the other way around - there is a much lower elder rate, about 8 percent, compared to a child rate of 14 percent. Italy has the same pattern - an elder rate of 13 percent compare to the child rate of 20 percent.

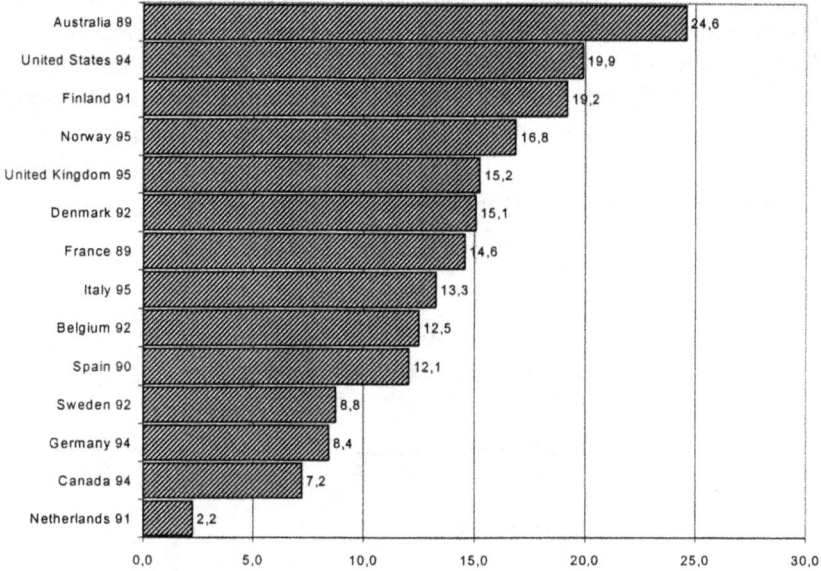

Figure 1.2.2   Elder poverty rate

There is no general pattern for the two rates be low or elevated together. (The correlation of child and elder rates is only .278). The group of countries with low child rates of under 10 percent vary all over the place in elder poverty. In general the elder rate is higher than the child rate, but how much higher varies.

If we wanted to understand elder poverty we would must move in rather different directions from where we need to go to understand child poverty. Note, for example, that although in the United States the child poverty rate is almost 10 times that of Finland, the elder poverty rate is barely higher. In Belgium, Denmark and Norway the elder rate is considerably higher than the child rate bringing these countries into the elder poverty range of Spain and the United Kingdom.

41

Child poverty in one and two parent families

In all of the countries we are comparing the great majority of children live in families headed by a couple who are married or living together as married. Ninety percent or more of children in Spain, Italy, Belgium, the Netherlands and France live in two parent families. In contrast in the United States only 72 percent of children live in two parent families and in the United Kingdom only 77 percent. The proportion in two parent families ranges between 82 and 89 percent in the remaining countries. Few children live with the father only so we will focus on children in two parent and in solo mother families.

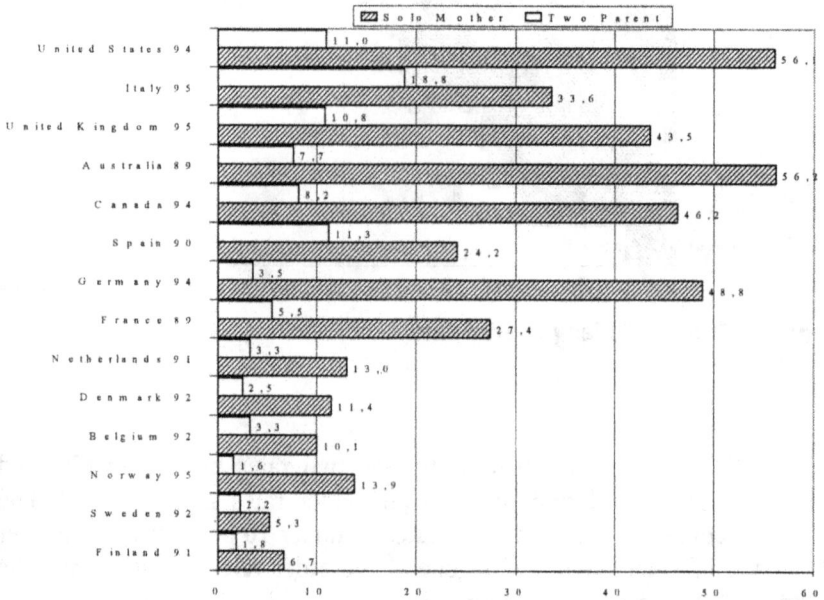

Figure 1.2.3   Child poverty by family type

Figure 1.2.3 shows that the proverty rates for children in solo mother families are extremely high in many countries compared to rates in two parent families. Almost or over half of the former are poor in Australia, the United States, Germany and Canada, and the United Kingdom is not far behind. In sharp contrast, in Sweden and Finland the solo mother rate is well under 10 percent. In fact the rate for children in solo mother families in those countries is lower than the rate for two parent families in six of the other countries. The rate is 10 percent or slightly more in an additional four countries - Belgium, Denmark, the Netherlands and Norway.

Elder poverty and family type

There is little similarity in the pattern of gender differences in elder and child poverty (Figure 1.2.4). For example, Finland's very low poverty rate for children in solo mother families is coupled with a very high rate of elder single woman's poverty compared to a very low rate for elder couples and a low rate for elder single men.

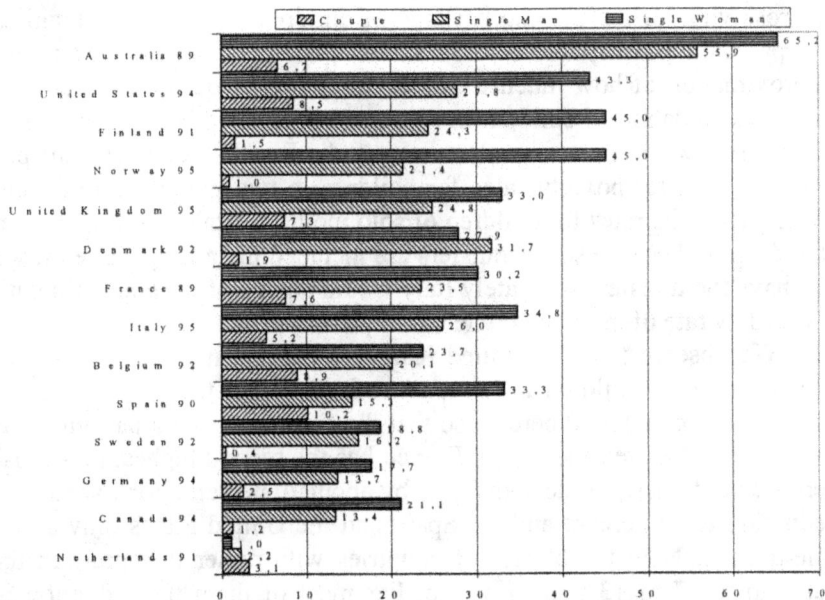

Figure 1.2.4   Elder poverty by family type

Norway also has a very high rate for single elder women and a moderately high rate for single elder men in contrast to low rates in child poverty. Both countries are more similar in this respect to the United States and Australia than to the other North European countries.

Elder couples in all counties have rather low poverty rates - less than 10 percent. (This is not a result of their being younger; these differences by family type are apparent at all elder age levels.)

With respect to child poverty we've noted that Canada and Australia are quite similar but they couldn't be more different in elder poverty. Canada is one of seven countries that come close to eradicating elder poverty among couples and has a lower rate of single elder poverty than all but a very few countries. Australia has very high rates of single elder poverty.

Earnings and transfers in the income package

A gross view of the income package of children's and elders' families compares the poverty rate before transfers and after. This allows a rough approximation of how much transfers move people out of poverty. Because the situation of children in solo mother and two parent families is so different we will examine them separately. Figure 1.2.5 shows the pre and post transfer poverty rates for children in two parent families and Figure 1.2.6 the rates for children of solo mothers. (Italy is omitted from this diagram because some transfers are included in earnings. Even if we did have the transfers separately Italy would be one of the countries with a very low rate of moving people out of poverty by transfers.)

We observe that the United Kingdom has the highest pre-transfer poverty rate for children in two parent families but that this rate is reduced by more than 50 percent so that the final rate is on a par with that of the United States and Spain. France has the second highest pre-transfer rate but transfers reduce that rate by about 70 percent. For Canada the reduction is 50 percent and for Spain and the United States only about one-quarter. Note the cluster of countries with rather low pre-transfer rates in the 7 to 13 percent range. For most of them the reduction is around 75 percent so that after transfers the poverty rates are 3 percent or lower. Overall, it is impressive that in 10 of the 13 countries the reduction in poverty is around 50 percent or greater.

44

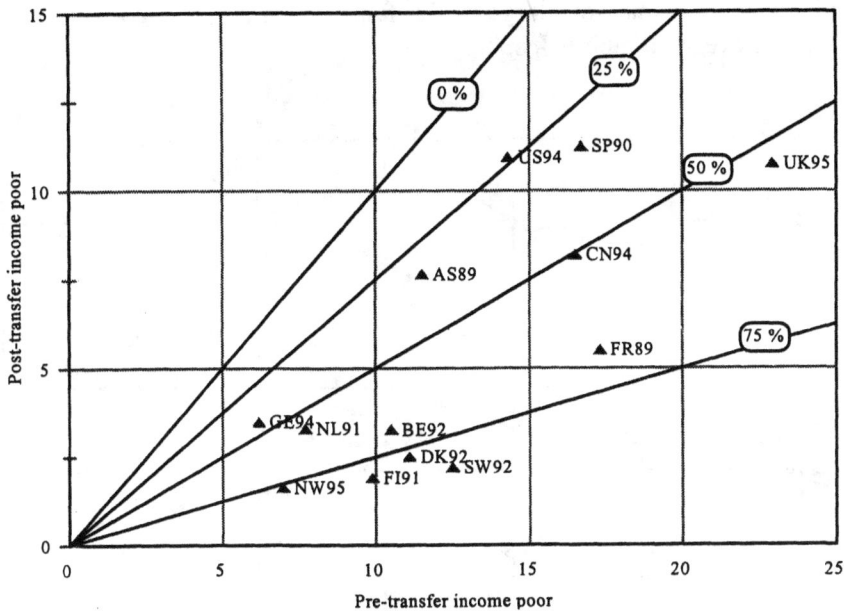

Figure 1.2.5   Earnings and transfers in two parent families

In the case of children in solo mother families the pre-transfer poverty rates vary upward from 40 percent in Finland to over 80 percent in the United Kingdom and the Netherlands. Note that the countries with very low solo mother rates of around 10 percent or less all also have reductions of three quarters or more. A majority of children from these families in the Netherlands, Norway and Sweden would be poor but not for transfers as would almost fifty percent of those in Denmark and Belgium. Yet after transfers their poverty rates are around 10 percent or less. Interestingly, despite a number of special programs for solo mother families French transfers move a smaller proportion of children in solo mother families out of poverty than in two parent families.

The social wage

Transfer programs in these countries represent a bewildering variety of principles and regulations. In general, for families with children no single transfer looms very large in the family income package. But, with income every little bit helps.

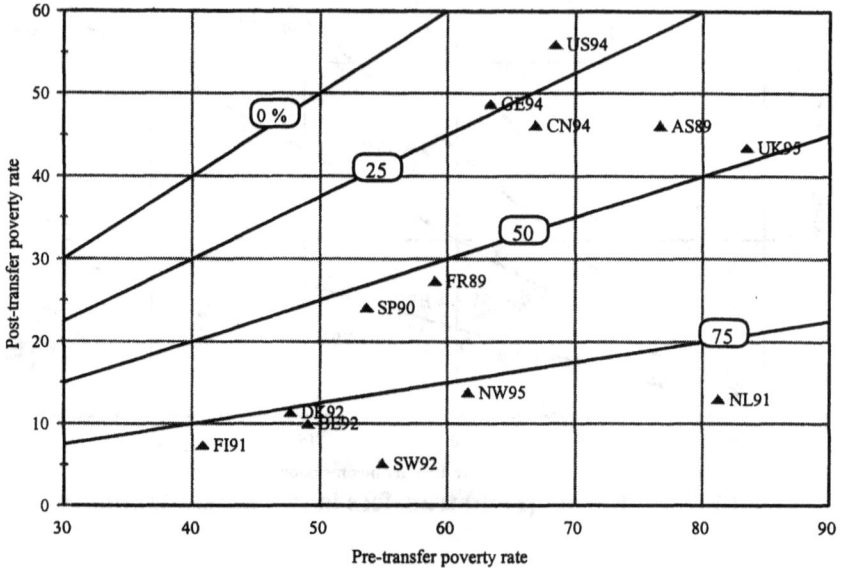

Figure 1.2.6   Earnings and transfers in solo mother families

We can identify two broad types of transfers and examine their impact on low income. First we consider programs that constitute a kind of social wage. These are programs that function mainly to supplement the income of families with earners - sickness payments, child allowances and child support payments, parental insurance, and unemployment insurance (on the assumption that most unemployed parents are not long term unemployed). Most children live in families with at least one person in the labor force. In the case of children in two parent families it is only in the United Kingdom, where only 86 percent of children live in families with earners, that the proportion falls below 94 percent.

Even for children with solo mothers we find that the proportion with an earner ranges upward from the high fifties (Australia, France, Germany) to 83 and 93 percent (Sweden and Finland) but with two outliers - the United Kingdom at 37 percent and the Netherlands at 33 percent.

These social wage transfers combined play a significant role in all countries, and a very central role in some. In eight countries they move 40 percent or more of pre-transfer poor in two parent families out of poverty:

- Australia 42%
- Belgium 69%
- Canada 44%
- Denmark 58%
- France 62%
- Finland 70%
- Norway 53%
- Sweden 73%

Spain, Netherlands and Germany are in the 20 to 30 percent range. The United Kingdom (17 percent) and the United States (which does not have a child allowance or social sickness insurance) at 14 percent bring up the rear.

For children in solo mother families the amounts needed to move them out of poverty are generally greater than in two parent families. But we do find that in four countries large proportions of children are moved from poverty by the social wage:

- Belgium 72%
- Denmark 53%
- Finland 45%
- Sweden 67%

France, Norway and Spain are in the 20 percent range. The United States, United Kingdom and (surprisingly) the Netherlands move fewer than 10 percent of solo mothers' poor children out of poverty with the social wage, and Australia and Canada move just a little over 10 percent.

Income tested programs

For many low income families income-tested programs provide a backup for the social wage. Such programs play the major role for children in two parent families only in the United Kingdom where the addition of income tested sources to the social wage moves 46 percent of children out of poverty. Such programs are also important in Denmark and Germany where they are required to move one-quarter of children out of poverty.

In solo mother families children are more often depended on income tested programs to escape poverty. In the United Kingdom and the Netherlands some sixty percent of pre-transfer poor children are moved from poverty by these programs. It Australia and France some forty percent are moved from poverty. And in Canada, Denmark, Finland, Germany and Sweden some twenty to twenty-five percent are lifted (but not very far) out of poverty.

Elder poverty and pensions

We don't need a diagram showing the effect of total transfers on elder poverty rates since almost all of their income comes from pensions. This is particularly the case for those elders who are in the lowest third of the overall distribution of income and therefore at greatest risk of being poor.

As might be expected elders are over-represented in families in the lowest third of the distribution. The over-representation ranges from slight in Italy, the Netherlands and the United States to close to two-thirds and more in Finland, Australia and Denmark (Figure 1.2.7). Note that there is no association with the elder poverty rates of these countries.

The average percent of total income represented by pension income for this low income group is 88 percent, and the range is from 80 percent in Australia to at least 95 percent in Belgium, Italy and the Netherlands. (We can't deal with the complexities of different kinds of pensions using the LIS data because the detail on pension programs is not consistent across countries - different countries combine their programs differently in the original income survey data.)

In 11 of the countries 98 percent or more of low income elders are in families that receive pensions - the low proportions are in Australia (88%), Spain (94%) and the United States (96%). On average earnings amount to less than 3 percent of total income, with the highest proportion being in Spain (7%) and the United States and Italy (5%).

Pensions alone are responsible for almost all of the reduction in elder poverty by transfers. The range in pre-transfer elder poverty is from 72 percent in the United States to 92 percent in Sweden. Eighty-five percent or more of the pre-transfer elder poor who are moved above

the poverty line are moved by pensions. Odds and ends of other resources play a minor role. But in a few countries income-tested assistance of one form or another (sometimes restricted to elders, other times
not) plays a significant role.

While in nine of our countries income-tested sources account for
less than 3 percent of the income of low income elders, these sources
play a somewhat stronger role in Spain and the United States accounting
for 5 percent of income, and are received by ten and 20 percent of elders
respectively.

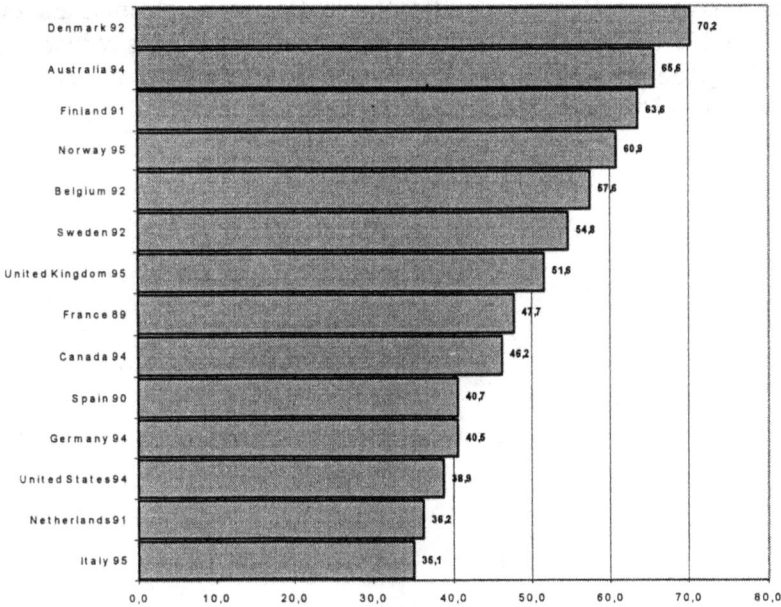

**Figure 1.2.7   Proportion of elders in lower 3rd of income
distribution**

In Denmark, Sweden and the United Kingdom income-tested
sources are much more important. Two-thirds of elders in Denmark
receive a small amount of income (7% of median equivalent income)
from this source. In Sweden a smaller group (48%) receives on average
an amount equal to 11 percent of the median, In the United Kingdom 42

49

percent of elders receive income-tested benefits which amount to 17 percent of median income.

The net effect of these benefits is to move a few more people who were still poor on the basis of their pension income out of poverty. In Denmark, Sweden and the United Kingdom the effect is greater - though in the end the United Kingdom and Denmark have relatively high elder poverty rates and Sweden a much lower one.

There are important variations in the role of pensions and income-tested programs for single elders versus couples. Pensions have almost all of the effect of transfers on poverty rates of couples; income-tested programs play an almost insignificant role. But, for single men, and even more single women, the addition of income-tested sources reduces poverty by large amounts in the three countries where these programs are fairly large - Denmark, Sweden and the United Kingdom.

PART 2

FAMILY POVERTY

2.1 The cost and benefits of children

Bernard M.S. van Praag and Erik J.S. Plug

1. Introduction

It is received wisdom among economists that children cost money. However, when asked how much, there is a host of methods which yield different outcomes. One of the basic presumptions of such calculations is that utility of money depends on income y and family size fs, and that the utility $U(y, fs)$ increases in income and falls in family size. The cost $\Delta_u y$ of an additional child is found from the equation

$$U(y + \Delta_u y, fs + 1) = U(y, fs) \tag{1.1}$$

An uneasy point is the result that getting children reduces welfare when income is kept constant. This observation runs counter to all practical experience, where people get children all the time out of their free will. This paradox is the subject of this paper. The proposed solution runs along the following reasoning. We assume that the decision to take a child is influenced by a calculation where additional benefits are compared with the additional costs. Just like a firm compares the additional revenue with additional costs and stops there where the difference between the two, net profit, is maximal, we assume that families get children as additional benefits outweigh additional costs and that they stop getting children if this is no longer the case.

In this paper we shall make an attempt to disentangle and to estimate the two concepts, viz., benefits and costs of additional children. In Section 2 we consider in a bird's eye view various approaches to estimate children costs. In Section 3 we focus on the Leyden approach. In Section 4 we consider the concept of well-being and its operationalization. In Section 5 we combine the two concepts and define and estimate the two concepts of costs and benefits. Section 6 concludes.

2. The literature on the cost of children

The literature on this subject is extensive. For a survey we refer to Van Praag & Warnaar (1997). The problem was brought to the fore as part of the 'social question' where poor households with many children got government support. In that respect estimates were made. The early pioneers are König (1882), Engel (1895), Sydenstricker & King (1921). These methods were based on the observation of those household expenditures which could be earmarked as being for children, for example school fees, additional food expenditures, etcetera. The need for norms was also caused by the question of 'who is poor'. If the 'poverty line' depends on the number of children, we have to know what this dependency is. However, above the minimum level households get some choice between spending part of the household budget on children or on other things. That is, the choice between buying a toy for a child or cigarettes for the parents. Costs could no longer be identified by looking at specific discretionary expenditures. The solution was to define a proxy for welfare of the parents, say $U(y, fs)$, and to define costs by equation (1.1). The welfare proxy was operationalized by Rothbart (1943), Nicholson (1947, 1976), Henderson (1949, 1950) and Deaton & Muellbauer (1986) by specifying specific 'adult goods' (like tobacco consumption, the barber, cinema) and identifying the welfare proxy as expenditures on 'adult goods'. A different approach is based on the food ratio as a welfare proxy. Families of different sizes would enjoy an equal level of welfare when they have the same amount of expenditures on adult goods or if they would have the same food ratio (see Engel (1895), Orshansky (1965)). The main objection to these methods is that it is unclear whether food ratio or expenditures on adult goods is representative for the household or parental welfare level and that the practical definition of what is food or an adult good entails many arbitrary decisions.

A more sophisticated approach is based on complete demand systems operationalized by Barten (1964), Deaton & Muellbauer (1980), Jorgenson, Lau & Stoker (1981). A utility function is specified

54

$U(x_1,...x_n; fs)$ where $x_1,...x_n$ are expenditures on commodity categories. The demand pattern depends on family size. It follows that we
can find the household cost function

$$c = c(u, fs) \qquad (2.1)$$

which yields a family equivalence scale and is an estimate of the additional costs for each utility level

$$c(u, fs+1) - c(u, fs) \qquad (2.2)$$

The fundamental critique on the approach, firstly formulated by
Pollak & Wales (1979) is that the function U describes the decision on
expenditures but not on getting children. Children is no dimension of the
commodity space. The impact of family size on demand patterns may be
estimated but the impact of family size on welfare can not be retraced.
Hence, the equivalence scales derived from complete demand systems
are strictly speaking invalid.

3. A different approach: the Welfare Function of Income (WFI)

As the previous approaches based on observing realized behavior appears to fail, in Van Praag (1971) a first attempt was made to establish
utility values straightforwardly by a direct questioning approach. The
basic instrument is a question module, the so-called Income Evaluation
Question (IEQ), which runs as follows:

Which monthly household after tax income would you in your circumstances consider to be very bad? Bad? Insufficient? Sufficient? Good? Very
good?

About $.......very bad.
About $.......bad.
About $.......insufficient.
About $.......sufficient.
About $.......good.
About $.......very good.

55

The number of levels distinguished is now mostly fixed at six, although in the first publications we used eight or nine levels; recently five or four levels have been used as well. Let the answers of the IEQ be denoted by c_1, c_2, c_3, c_4, c_5 and c_6 (or $c_1, \ldots, c_k$ for k levels) and let us define

$$\mu = \frac{1}{6} \sum_{i=1}^{6} \ln c_i \qquad (3.1)$$

and

$$\sigma^2 = \frac{1}{5} \sum_{i=1}^{6} (\ln c_i - \mu)^2 \qquad (3.2)$$

The first basic presumption is that the verbal labels "very bad", "good" and so on, convey the same emotional meaning to all respondents. This assumption is actually the corner stone of a language community; words should mean or are assumed to mean the same to each member of that community. It is well-known from everyday life and from semantic and psychological research that this is not exactly true, however deviations are assumed to be corrected by the error term.

For practical purposes, the verbal labels are translated into numbers on a zero-one scale, and more precisely the first (worst label) is identified with 1/12, the following with 3/12.. and the sixth label with 11/12. This presupposes that verbal qualification may be translated into a numerical scale and that we use equal intervals. Both assumptions are always used in school evaluations but also in other tests like ice-skating or commodity tests by consumer unions.

In Van Praag and Van der Sar (1988) and Van Praag (1991, 1994) it was shown that the Equal Interval Assumption holds approximately very well by asking people directly whether they would translate words into numerical evaluations. A different more theoretical argument for this assumption has been proposed by Van Praag (1971) and Kapteyn (1977).

For theoretical arguments, (see Van Praag (1968)), we proposed a lognormal specification $\Lambda(u; \mu, \sigma)$ where μ and σ are the previously defined parameters, which may differ for individuals. It was found from a multitude of large-scale samples that this lognormal specification was empirically acceptable, although Kapteyn and Van Herwaarden (1979) showed that other functional specifications did also perform fairly well. The logarithmic specification did even slightly better, but it was discarded for the reason that it yields an unbounded function which is psychologically less credible. This paradigm has been developed at Leyden University by Van Praag, Kapteyn, Hagenaars and others. Although none of the authors is still working at Leyden, it is sometimes referred to as the Leyden school. All these assumptions were heavily criticized by Seidl (1994). In a reaction by Van Praag and Kapteyn (1994) it was shown that Seidl's critique was ill-founded and can be discarded. The resulting function has been called the (Individual) Welfare Function of Income (WFI). The interesting point of the concept lies in its applications with respect to family equivalence scales, poverty, income inequality and so on.

The parameter μ is found to vary over individuals in a very consistent way. For most West-European countries we estimated the following equation

$$\mu = \beta_0 + \beta_1 \ln fs + \beta_2 \ln y_c \qquad (3.3)$$

Where y_c stand for current income. Surprisingly good and stable outcomes of about

$$\mu = \beta_0 + 0.10 \ln fs + 0.60 \ln y_c$$

have been generated. On the contrary the attempts to explain σ have met with only limited success. So in most analyses σ is taken to be randomly varying over individuals. The resulting welfare level U corresponding to an arbitrary income level y is found by standardization to be

$$U = N\left(\frac{\ln y - \mu}{\sigma}; 0,1\right)$$

resulting into

$$U = N\left(\frac{\ln y - \beta_0 - \beta_1 \ln fs - \beta_2 \ln y_c}{\sigma}; 0,1\right)$$

Assuming σ to be constant, an alternative (ordinal) welfare index is

$$\ln c = \ln y - \beta_2 \ln y_c - \beta_1 \ln fs - \beta_0 \qquad (3.4)$$

It follows that the individual welfare evaluation of any income level y depends on fs and current income y, say $U(y; y_c, fs)$. A specific welfare level α is reached by realizing that

$$N\left(\frac{\ln y - \mu}{\sigma}; 0,1\right) = \alpha \qquad (3.5)$$

This corresponds to

$$\ln y = \mu + u_\alpha \sigma \qquad (3.6)$$

where u_α is the (normal) α-quantile and where μ varies over individuals. Hence,

$$\ln y = \beta_2 \ln y_c + \beta_1 \ln fs + \beta_0 + u_\alpha \sigma \qquad (3.7)$$

may be interpreted as a household cost function where u_α is an ordinal utility index (see Van Praag and Van der Sar (1988)). In Van Praag (1991) it is shown how this concept can be linked to an ordinary indirect utility function in which prices appear. Here we only observe that μ must be first order homogeneous in prices and σ zero-homogeneous in prices.

Family equivalence scales can be derived by evaluating current income y_c in welfare terms as

$$U(y_c; y_c, fs) = N\left(\frac{(1-\beta_2)\ln y_c - \beta_0 - \beta_1 \ln fs}{\sigma}; 0,1\right) \quad (3.8)$$

It follows that a change from fs_1 to fs_2 has to be compensated by

$$\ln y_2 - \ln y_c = \frac{\beta_1}{1-\beta_2}(\ln fs_2 - \ln fs_1) \quad (3.9)$$

It follows that

$$\frac{y_2}{y_c} = \left(\frac{fs_2}{fs_1}\right)^{\frac{\beta_1}{1-\beta_2}} = \left(\frac{fs_2}{fs_1}\right)^{0.25} \quad (3.10)$$

if we accept the previously mentioned values for β_1 and β_2. We notice however that the value $\beta_1/(1-\beta_2)$ varies over countries; in America it reaches about 1/3 (Dubnoff, Vaughan & Lancaster (1981) speak of the "cube law") and in Greece, Portugal, Poland, Czechoslovakia still higher values in the range of 0.40 and 0.50 have been found. It indicates that scales are different over countries and that they are steeper, the less developed child support in the specific country is. The value of about 0.25 suggests a rather flat scale (see also Buhmann, Rainwater, Schmauss & Smeeding (1988)).

The Leyden approach points always to the result that having children reduces welfare.[1] This is not so by assumption, but that it is an empirical fact since β_1 is estimated to be positive. The consequence is that the Leyden welfare function is not the criterion which is used to decide on children. For, if that were true, the only valid conclusion would be that households would optimize their size by staying childless. Notice that the Leyden scale is independent of base. It also does not depend on the lognormal (cardinal) specification.

Our conclusion is that there must be a missing dimension. To get the benefits of children in the picture we need an operationalization of the concept well-being, say $W(y, fs)$ This concept does not focus only on the financial aspects, i.e. income evaluation, but on the quality of life as a whole. It is by no means clear whether W is monotonically increasing or decreasing in family size. Rather, we assume there is an optimal family size, indicating that W is first rising and than falling in family size. Actually, W a balance between benefits and costs. Consider again the equation

$$W(y+\Delta_w y, fs+1) = W(y, fs) \qquad (3.11)$$

Now $\Delta_w y$ may be positive, which implies that the net balance of children benefits and costs is negative, while a negative $\Delta_w y$ implies a positive net balance. Notice, as the case of adoption children is evidence for, that individuals may spend a lot of money to get a child. Brazilian or Korean children may 'do' more than $20,000 for initial investment.

If $\Delta_w y$ derived from equation (3.11) stands for the money value of the net balance, say the value of benifits minus the value of costs, and if $\Delta_w y$ derived from equation (1.1) and identified in equation (3.9) stands for the value of costs, it is obvious that

$$\Delta_w y + \Delta_u y \qquad (3.12)$$

is the value of the *gross* benefits of children. In the next Section we operationalize the well-being concept.

4. A new approach: welfare and well-being

The method of direct questioning may have been rather unusual or even suspect for economists at the time (1971) it was originated, in other behavioral sciences this approach is fairly standard. Cantril (1965) devised what we shall call the Cantril-question:

> Here is a picture of a ladder, representing the ladder of life. The bottom of this ladder, step 0, represents the worst possible life while the top of this ladder, step 10, represents the best possible life.

> Where on the ladder do you feel you personally stand at the present time?

Obviously this question tries also to measure something but "it" is much wider than satisfaction derived from income: it is *satisfaction from*

60

life as a whole. From now on we call the first (Leyden) concept *welfare* and the second concept *well-being*. It is tempting to explain the responses to the Cantril question as well. We refer to Plug and Van Praag (1995) and Plug (1997) for more details.

It is obvious that both welfare and well-being are metaphysical concepts. Just like other concepts, they can be coupled with a physical (measurable) counterpart by defining a measuring experiment and an operational definition of how to measure the concept. The physical counterpart is thus defined.

In the physical sciences a measurement method is accepted as yielding a successful operationalization of a metaphysical concept, if the operationalized concept matches our expectations as variation resembles what we expect from the metaphysical pre-scientific concept, (cf the definition of an operational temperature concept by a thermometer).

In a similar way we operationalize the metaphysical concept well-being. Notice that the Cantril respondent responds with a number W on a zero-ten scale. In order to stretch the explained variable on a $(-\infty, +\infty)$ range we replace the responses by $w = N^{-1}(W; 0,1)$ where N stands for the standard normal distribution function. In order to test whether W and U as measured by Cantril and the IEQ respectively measure the same or different concepts, Plug and Van Praag (1995) tried the same set of explanatory variables on both variables w and μ and it was found that for the explanation of w we needed a much larger set than μ. Hence, we concluded that Cantril and IEQ were totally different concepts indeed. In view of the following Sections we present different specifications.

Looking at the μ-equation we see that there is a considerable age-effect as μ rises with increasing age up to a maximum at the age of about 47 year after which income evaluation falls again with age. This implies that need for income increases first and falls later in life. It may also be reworded as that the same income level becomes less satisfactory first, while satisfaction rises again after the age of 47 has been reached.

The w-equation depends on a much richer set of variables. This is evidence for the conjecture that the Cantril question and the IEQ definitely do not measure the same concept. First we notice a family size squared and interaction terms of family size with income and the dummy representing two-breadwinner families. It follows that Cantril equivalence scales are not IB as they depend on income and that they differ for two-breadwinners. The fs^2-term indicates that there is an optimal family size which varies with income and the breadwinner variable. Second we see a U-shape relation with age. We find that well-being is falling with age up to about 37 years and is then rising with age.

Table 2.1.1 Equations

The μ Equation (3.3)			Variables related to		
	Estimate	t-Value	Health	0.15	11.89
Constant	1.81	4.31	Family	0.12	7.85
ln fs	0.05	7.71	Work	0.11	8.28
ln y	0.60	95.19	Partner	0.18	11.59
ln a	1.12	4.78	Sleep	0.08	5.62
ln^2 a	-0.14	-4.55	Drugs and Alcohol	0.08	4.33
			Neighborhood	0.18	17.13
N	8447.00		Parents	0.02	1.12
$R2$	0.53		Government	0.07	6.68

The Cantril Equation			N	8447.00	
	Estimate	t-Value	R^2	0.19	
Constant	4.224	2.212			
ln fs	-1.526	-1.928			
ln y	0.278	3.181			
ln y ln fs	0.175	2.438			
ln^2 fs	-0.131	-1.907			
D_{tw} ln fs	-0.032	-1.931			
ln a	-4.066	-4.098			
ln^2 a	0.564	4.162			
D_{work}	-0.074	-2.563			
Female	0.117	5.448			
Religion	0.040	3.875			

Furthermore, in this survey respondents were asked whether they had problems with drugs, the family, how positive they felt about the quality of government, their own health, their neighborhood, their parents, their relationship with their partner, whether they had problems with sleeping and their work. The "problem" variables have been rescaled by applying the inverse normal distribution function on the bounded scales, differentiated into subgroups according to age, gender, employment status and education. Finally we include dummies for having a job or not and gender of the respondent. Nearly all these variables were significant and had the "right" sign. In this paper we shall not consider all variables in detail, but we shall focus on the fs-variable. It is noticed that

$$\frac{\delta w}{\delta \ln fs} = \gamma_0 + 2\gamma_1 \ln fs + \gamma_2 \ln y_c + \gamma_3 D_{tw} \qquad (4.1)$$

where the γ's read as respectively -1.526, -0.131, 0.175 and -0.0327. In Figure 1 its shape as a function of $\ln fs$ is sketched for various rising income levels y_1, y_2 and y_3. It follows that the sign of the derivative is not unambiguous. It rises with income. It follows that there is an *optimal* family size for the various income levels reached. For low income it is always negative, implying that that family would prefer to be childless. The more income one receives, the higher the optimal family size. It turns out that the optimal family size of 3 is reached for a one-breadwinner family at an annual net income of Dfl 33,345.

5. Costs and benefits of children: a combination of both welfare concepts

Table 2.1.2 Optimum family sizes and corresponding income levels

fs	3	4	5	6
one-earner	33,345	50,712	70,436	92,269
two-earner	39,946	60,890	84,677	111,007

In section 3 we demonstrated how to derive family equivalence scales in a simple and elegant way from the IEQ results. In this Section we shall compare this with results from a similar analysis on the basis of the Cantril-module. The analysis in this Section is mostly based on Van Praag and Plug (1993). Given the results for the Cantril equation of well-being it is also possible to derive family equivalence scales for well-being, but the results will be rather unusual in the sense that their sign is not unique.

Defining a shadow price Δy for the $(fs+1)$ family member by solving

$$U(y, fs) = U(y + \Delta y, fs + 1) \qquad (5.1)$$

we get shadow prices for additional family members. We restricted the sample to two-adult households. Hence fs equals 3 indicates two adults and one child. For the IEQ it is easily seen that the shadow price is always negative. Individuals have to get a positive additional income Δy to feel equal welfare after the "$fs+1$"th has arrived. If we replace U by W and do the same exercise, we find the corresponding shadow prices for the well-being concept and they turn out to be rising with fs and rising with income. A negative shadow price implies that a child is desired, but the price of a marginal child falls. Both types of shadow prices are tabulated in Table 2.1.3.

At first sight this difference is striking, until we realize that both question modules and the concepts derived from it measure different metaphysical concepts.

The first focuses on *income* and hence on monetary costs. The second (Cantril) concept focuses on the quality of life (as a whole), say *well-being*. For life as a whole an additional child means less purchase power but probably also family blessing. In short there are non-monetary yields to be derived from having a child which are beneficial for most families. The Cantril shadow prices cover the benefits and the pure cost aspects. More precisely a child may cause

a. a monetary cost increase;
b. a non-monetary benefit.

The non-monetary benefit may also be negatively valued for those who are child-haters. Referring to the Greek μηδέν αγαν "of nothing too much", any family will finally at the arrival of the nth child exclaim "no more". For families with a very low income even the non-monetary benefit of the first child may be negative. In the case of a negative non-monetary benefit we speak of *non-monetary costs*.

64

Table 2.1.3 Shadow prices

	Shadow prices according to IEQ			
Income	1st child	2nd child	3^{d} child	4th child
20000	906	680	544	453
30000	1360	1020	816	680
40000	1813	1360	1088	906
50000	2266	1700	1360	1133
60000	2720	2040	1632	1360

	Shadow prices according to Cantril. One breadwinner			
Income	1st child	2nd child	3^{d} child	4th child
20000	1686	1518	1549	1492
30000	245	1256	1564	1639
40000	-1098	709	1367	1619
50000	-2756	-49	1012	1474
60000	-4662	-978	513	1230

	Shadow prices according to Cantril. Two breadwinners			
Income	1st child	2nd child	3^{d} child	4th child
20000	1632	1833	1784	1676
30000	941	1728	1916	1916
40000	-170	1338	1836	1988
50000	-1595	736	1597	1935
60000	-3270	-34	1233	1783

It follows that the Cantril price tabulated in Table 2.1.3 may be identified as B-A while we assume that the Leyden price stands for A only. It follows that subtracting the first part of Table 2.1.3 from the second and third part we calculate the monetary counter value of the non-monetary benefits (or costs). Using an infinitesimal approach we define the shadow prices as

$$A: \quad \Delta y = -\left(\frac{U_{fs}}{U_{yc}}\right)\Delta fs$$

monetary cost

$$B: \quad \Delta y = -\left(\frac{V_{fs}}{V_{yc}}\right)\Delta fs$$

total shadow price

$$B - A: \Delta y = \left(\frac{U_{fs}}{U_{yc}} - \frac{V_{fs}}{V_{yc}}\right)\Delta fs$$

non-monetary benefits

In Table 2.1.4 we tabulate the value of those non-monetary benefits as the result of this subtraction.

We notice that the pure benefit value of a child after correction for monetary costs is not extremely large except for the first two children in the well-to-do families. On the other hand this is an annual benefit, which when discounted, say at a 10% discount rate yields a capital value of ten times as much. This amount conforms pretty well to adoption costs where children are "imported" into the household from the own country or from abroad.

Table 2.1.4 Money value of non-monetary child benefits

Income	1st child	2nd child	3d child	4th child
		One breadwinner		
20000	-262	-838	-1005	-1039
30000	1114	-236	-748	-959
40000	2911	651	-279	-713
50000	5023	1749	348	-341
60000	7383	3018	1100	130
		Two breadwinners		
Income	1st child	2nd child	3d child	4th child
20000	-726	-1153	-1240	-1223
30000	419	-708	-1100	-1236
40000	1983	22	-747	-1082
50000	3871	964	-237	-802
60000	5990	2074	399	-423

We also see that for richer persons the net benefits are positive. For instance, a one-earner household with Dfl 40,000 income per year after taxation would like to pay -1098 to have a first child, while the shadow prices for the first two children become positive from Dfl 50,000 onwards. This raises the politically relevant question why the state should pay family allowances to richer families. For low income families we see that it would be optimal to have no children at all. For two-earner families the shadow-prices for children are larger than for one-earner families. This may be explained since the care for children in such families is more difficult than for those families where the housewife has no outside job.

6. Conclusions

The main point of this paper is that we are able to operationalize in money terms both concepts of benefits and costs related with children. In this paper we highlight the following issues.

- From a methodological point of view, we observe that there are more welfare concepts than one. At least well-being and welfare are to be distinguished.
- Secondly, we observe that after suitable equation 2.1 operationalization these concepts are measurable by means of questioning methods.
- That the two welfare concepts welfare and well-being are utilized as ordinal concepts in this paper, in the sense that all calculations of money amounts do not depend on monotonic transformations of the well-being and welfare concepts.
- And that the concepts of welfare and well-being functions mostly depend on the own situation as a point of reference. For the IEQ the evidence is that the evaluation of arbitrary income levels depends on own current income. In Van Praag (1971) this phenomenon is called preference drift.
- Finally, it may be useful to exploit two or more welfare concepts simultaneously to split up balances of two or more effects into their components.

From a policy point of view we stress that this is advisable and defensible to restrict the structure of family allowances to specific income classes and to differentiate with respect to the number of the rank of children.

Obviously our analysis in this paper is not authoritative in the sense that no other operationalizations or explanations of welfare concepts are possible. However, it is not true that there is only one all-embracing concept. Concepts may compete in the sense that both claim to reflect the same metaphysical concept. For the coming time it does not seem a first priority to defend claims for different concepts. That is a luxury problem. The first priority is to exploit this way further, because as the list of variables in Table 2.1.1 demonstrates the Cantril concept covers a multitude of aspects.

As this paper gives evidence for, welfare or well-being is not an exclusively economic concept. It is a concept which has to do with income, but also with a lot of traditionally non-economic variables as well. May be, the Cantril-concept and the IEQ may serve as a linking-pin between economic science and their social sister-sciences.

Note

1. We assume that welfare experienced by the head of the household is representative for the household as a whole. The motivation can be found in Plug and Van Praag (1998) where it is argued that both spouses in one-earner families share their opinion on family income

References

Buhmann, B. & L. Rainwater & G. Schmauss & T.J. Smeeding. 1988. Equivalence scales, well-Being, inequality and poverty: sensitivity estimates across ten countries using the LIS data base. *Review of Income and Wealth*, 34, 115-142.

Cantril, H. 1965. *The Pattern of Human Concern*. New Brunswick, Rutgers University Press.

Deaton, A.S. & J. Muellbauer. 1980. *Economics and Consumer Behaviour*. Cambridge, Cambridge University Press.

Deaton, A.S. & J. Muellbauer. 1986. On measuring child cost: with applications to poor countries. *Journal of Political Economy*, 94, 720-745. Cambridge, Cambridge University Press.

Engel, E. 1895. Die Lebenskosten Belgischen Arbeiter-Familien früher und jetzt. *International Statistical Institute Bulletin*, 9, 1-124.

Henderson, A.M. 1949, 1950. The cost of children. *Population Studies* 3/4, 130-150, 267-298.

Jorgensen, D.W. & L.J. Lau, & T.M. Stoker. 1981. Aggregate consumer behavior and individual welfare. In Currie & Nobay & Peel, editors, *Macro Economic Analysis*, London, Croom-Helm.

Kapteyn, A. 1977. A Theory of Preference Formation. PhD. Leyden University, Leyden.

König, J. 1882. Prozentische Zusammensetzung und Nahrgeldwert der menschlichen Nahrungsmittel.

Nicholson, J.L. 1947. Variations in working class family expenditure. Journal of the Royal Statistical Society, 112, 359-411.

Nicholson, J.L. 1976. Appraisal of different methods of estimating equivalence scales and their results. *Review of Economics and Health*, 2, 1-12.

Orshansky, M. 1965. Counting the poor: another look at the poverty profile. *Social Security Bulletin*, 28, 3-29.

Plug, E.J.S. 1997. *Leyden Welfare and Beyond.* PhD thesis. Tinbergen Institute Research Series. University of Amsterdam.

Plug, E.J.S. & B.M.S. van Praag. 1995. Family equivalence scales within a narrow and broad welfare context. *Journal of Income Distribution*, 4, 171-186.

Plug, E.J.S. & B.M.S. Van Praag. 1998. Similarity in response behavior between household members: An application to income evaluation, *Journal of Economic Psychology*, forthcoming.

Pollak, R.A. & T.J. Wales. 1979. Equity; the individual versus family. Welfare comparisons and equivalence scales. *American Economic Review*, 69, 216-221.

Rothbarth, E. 1943. Note on a method of determining equivalent income for families of different composition. In Madge, editor, Wartime patern of saving and spending. Oxford, Oxford University Press.

Seidl, C. 1994. How sensible is the Leyden individual welfare function of income? *European Economic Review*, 38, 1633-1659.

Sydenstricker, E. & W. King. 1921. The measurement of the relative economic status of families. *Quarterly Publication of the American Statistical Association*, 17, 842-857.

Van Herwaarden, F.G. & A. Kapteyn. 1981. Empirical comparison of the shape of welfare functions. *European Economic Review*, 15, 261-286.

Van Praag, B.M.S. 1968. *Individual Welfare Functions and Consumer Behavior*. Amsterdam, North-Holland.

Van Praag, B.M.S. 1971. The welfare function of income in Belgium: an empirical investigation. *European Economic Review*, 2, 337-369.

Van Praag, B.M.S. 1991. Ordinal and cardinal utility: an integration of the two dimensions of the welfare concept. *Journal of Econometrics*, 50, 69-89.

Van Praag, B.M.S. 1994. The relativity of the welfare concept.In Nussbaum & Sen, editors, *The Quality of Life*. Oxford, Clarendon Press.

Van Praag, B.M.S. & A. Kapteyn. 1973. Further evidence on the individual welfare function of income: an empirical study in the Netherlands, *European Economic Review*, 4, 33-62.

Van Praag, B.M.S. & N.L. Van der Sar. 1988. Household cost functions and equivalence scales, *Journal of Human Resources*, 23, 193-210.

Van Praag, B.M.S. & E.J.S. Plug. 1993. Kinderbijslag en kindervreugd. *Economisch Statistische Berichten*, 78, 720-723.

Van Praag, B.M.S. & A. Kapteyn. 1994. How sensible is the Leyden individual welfare function of income? A reply. *European Economic Review* 38, 1817-1825.

Van Praag, B.M.S. & M. Warnaar. 1997. The cost of children and the effects of demographic Variables on consumer demand. In M. Rosenzweig & O. Stark, editors, *The Handbook of Population and Family Economics*. Elsevier, Amsterdam.

2.2 Relating inputs to outcomes: child poverty and family transfers in comparative perspective

Jonathan R. Bradshaw and Helen Barnes

1. Introduction

This chapter draws on the work of the European Observatory for National Family Policies, which from 1993 to 1996 was coordinated from the University of York. Specifically it employs some of the material collected for the 1996 Observatory report (Ditch et al 1998) and uses it to explore the relationship between child poverty (outcomes) and financial provision for families with children (inputs). Much of the comparative research on poverty and on social and fiscal policies has been undertaken separately and independently and for this reason it has not been possible to explore the relationship between inputs and outcomes comparatively. This paper represents an exploratory attempt to relate estimates of the level of child poverty derived from surveys of the population to the analysis of tax/benefit systems derived from model family matrix analysis.

2. Child poverty

There are two sources of relatively up to date data on the prevalence of child poverty in EU countries - the Luxembourg Income Study (LIS) and the European Community Household Panel (ECHP).[1]

Table 2.2.1 presents ECHP data on the percentage of households, individuals living in poor households and children living in poor households, in the EU in 1993. The child poverty rate ranges from five per cent in Denmark to 32 per cent in the United Kingdom. Across the EU as a whole, one-fifth of children live in poor households.

Table 2.2.1 Percentage of poor households[a], individuals living in poor households and children[b] living in poor households in the EU, 1993 - ECHP

Country	Households	Individuals	Children
Belgium	13	13	15
Denmark	9	6	5
Germany	13	11	13
Greece	24	22	19
Spain	19	20	25
France	16	14	12
Ireland	21	21	28
Italy	18	20	24
Luxembourg	14	15	23
Netherlands	14	13	16
Portugal	29	26	27
United Kingdom	23	22	32
European Union (12)	17	17	20

a   Poor households in any one country are defined as those with an equivalised annual net monetary income which is below 50 per cent of the average equivalised annual net monetary income of all the households in that country.

b   Children: less than 16 years.

Source: Eurostat (1997)

Table 2.2.2 presents LIS data on the percentage of children living in poor households circa 1990. In contrast to table 2.2.1, the results for three poverty thresholds are given. It is clear that the poverty rate is sensitive to the threshold used but taking the 50 per cent poverty line, the highest incidence of children living in poor households is to be found in the United States followed closely by Russia, while the Czech Republic and Slovakia both have the lowest rates. Across the current EU Member States, the poverty rate amongst children ranges from 3.8 per cent in Finland, to 24.9 per cent in the United Kingdom. Appendix 1 contains some analysis of changes in child poverty rates over time.

Table 2.2.2 Percentage of children[a] living in poor households[b], for three poverty thresholds, circa 1990 - LIS

	Poverty threshold					
	40% (ranking)		50% (ranking)		60% (ranking)	
Belgium	2.4	(6)	5.6	(6)	13.7	(7)
Denmark	3.2	(7)	5.7	(7)	10.6	(6)
Germany	7.4	(10)	11.5	(10)	19.7	(10)
Spain	9.8	(15)	17.6	(15)	28.1	(15)
Italy	7.1	(9)	13.8	(11)	25.5	(12)
Netherlands	5.1	(8)	10.0	(8)	17.7	(8)
Finland	1.8	(3)	3.8	(3)	8.9	(4)
Sweden	2.0	(5)	3.9	(4)	8.1	(3)
United Kingdom	13.3	(17)	24.9	(17)	35.6	(18)
Norway	1.8	(3)	4.5	(5)	9.5	(5)
Czech Republic	0.9	(2)	2.3	(1)	5.6	(1)
Hungary	7.9	(12)	11.0	(9)	18.2	(9)
Poland	10.9	(16)	18.7	(16)	29.0	(16)
Russia	19.7	(19)	27.1	(18)	35.4	(17)
Slovakia	0.6	(1)	2.3	(1)	6.3	(2)
Israel	7.4	(10)	16.2	(12)	27.2	(13)
Taiwan, ROC	7.9	(12)	17.0	(14)	27.2	(13)
Canada	9.1	(14)	16.5	(13)	23.7	(11)
United States	18.3	(18)	28.0	(19)	37.5	(19)

a   Children: less than 18 years.
b   Poor households in any one country are defined as those with an equivalent income which is below 40 / 50 / 60 per cent of the average equivalent income of all the households in that country.
Source: Original analysis by Jun-Rong Chen, University of York, UK.

While a strict comparison between the results of the two analyses would not be very meaningful,[2] it is interesting to compare each country's relative performance in respect of poverty rates. This comparison, presented in table 2.2.3, demonstrates that, with the exception of Belgium the ECHP and LIS results produce broadly similar country rankings.

Table 2.2.3 Children living in poor households[a], EU - LIS and ECHP results compared

Rank order, lowest poverty rate to highest	
ECHP, 1993	LIS, circa 1990
Denmark	4
France	-
Germany	6
Belgium	3
Netherlands	5
Greece	-
Luxembourg	-
Italy	7
Spain	8
Portugal	-
Ireland	-
United Kingdom	9
	Sweden=2
	Finland=1
	Austria not included

a   LIS data: Poor households in any one country are defined as those with an equivalent income which is below 50 per cent of the average equivalent income of all the households in that country.
ECHP data: Poor households in any one country are defined as those with an equivalised annual net monetary income which is below 50 per cent of the average equivalised annual net monetary income of all the households in that country.

So far we have used only indicators of financial poverty. The ECHP survey asks a number of questions that may be useful indicators of non financial poverty. The indicators are listed at the bottom of table 2.2.4. The table presents a rank order league table of the EU contries on each of the indicators[3] together with an average rank. It can be seen that there is some variation in rank across the indicators and the average rank is rather different from that for the indicator of financial poverty derived from the same survey and given in col a) - in particular Luxembourg, the Netherlands and the UK move up the league table and Denmark and

France move down the league table when a wider range of non monetary poverty indicators is employed.

Table 2.2.4 Country rankings across all ECHP poverty indicators

Country	Poverty indicator rankings												Average ranking	Rank order
	a	*b*	*c*	*d*	*e*	*f*	*g*	*h*	*i*	*j*	*k*	*l*		
Belgium	4	3	7	8	8	8	4	5	5	4	6	4	5.5	6
Denmark	1	7	1	2	3	10	5	4	4	2	2	3	3.7	3
Germany	3	4	6	5	7	7	2	1	2	10	7	7	5.1	4
Greece	6	11	11	7	5	1	12	10	8	11	12	12	8.8	10
Spain	9	10	10	11	11	9	11	11	10	6	3	6	8.9	11
France	2	5	9	9	4	5	6	6	6	3	5	5	5.4	5
Ireland	11	6	2	4	10	11	9	8	11	8	7	10	8.1	8
Italy	8	8	8	1	12	3	7	9	7	7	10	9	7.4	7
Luxembourg	7	2	4	3	1	2	1	3	3	1	3	2	2.7	1=
Netherlands	5	1	3	6	2	-	3	2	1	5	1	1	2.7	1=
Portugal	10	12	12	12	6	4	10	12	12	12	9	11	10.2	12
United Kingdom	12	9	5	10	9	6	8	7	9	9	11	8	8.6	9

a % of children living in poor households.
b % of children living in households reporting a shortage of space.
c % of children living in households reporting a leaky roof.
d % of children living in households reporting damp walls.
e % of children living in households reporting that total housing costs are a burden.
f % of children living in households reporting that debts from hire purchases are a burden.
g % of children living in households reporting that unable to make ends meet.
h % of children living in households reporting cannot afford to keep home adequately warm.
i % of children living in households reporting cannot afford a week's annual holiday.
j % of children living in households reporting cannot afford to buy new clothes.
k % of children living in households reporting cannot afford to eat meat.
l % of children living in households reporting cannot afford to eat with friends.

3. Family policy

All welfare states have some combination of cash benefits, tax reliefs or services in kind which provide relief for parents with the costs of raising children. Together these can be described as a 'child benefit or family transfer package'. The policies that make up the package may not be conceived of as having the same purposes and neither in their origins nor current objectives may they be primarily concerned with the costs of child rearing. Nevertheless the package as a whole represents the effort that a nation makes to mitigate some of the costs borne by parents in raising children. The child benefit package is a measure of the extent to which the costs of children are conceived of as a collective or state responsibility, as opposed to a purely individual or family one. Some elements of the package in some countries may be explicitly or implicitly designed to target help on those families with children who have low or no earnings.

A "model families matrix" method has been used to allow comparisons to be made of the structure and value of the 'packages' of cash benefits, tax reliefs, services and charges that contribute towards meeting the cost of a child or supplement the income of low income families. The members of the European Observatory on National Family Policies complete a 'matrix' which summarises what a number of selected family types, in specific circumstances, with given earnings levels would receive in each country. The approach has been used for a number of comparative studies at York.[4] The results presented here relate to the situation in May 1996 and are derived from the data collected for 1996 report of the Observatory (Ditch et al 1998).

The methods employed and the assumptions made are discussed and critically evaluated in the 1994 Observatory report (Ditch et al 1996) and will not be repeated here.

In this paper the focus of the analysis is the contribution of public policy to the incomes of couples and lone parents with children who are either in low paid employment (represented by families with one earner earning on half national average male earnings) or out of employment and dependent on social assistance - on the grounds that these families are most likely to be those who are poor. Unfortunately we cannot cover the arrangements in social insurance schemes to support the dependent children of the unemployed, widowed and so forth, because data on those schemes are not collected.

To obtain the net income for the families on half average earnings income tax payable by a given family was deducted. Then the social security contributions required to be paid by a given family at those earnings was deducted, including all compulsory statutory contributions whether they fund social security entitlements, health entitlements or other things. The test is that they are required of employees by the state.

This gives post tax income. Then non-income related and income related cash benefits that may be made to a given family at that income level are added. These are mainly family allowances or child benefits but in some countries social assistance may be payable to low earners and lone parents may be entitled to child support, maintenance or alimony and this is included if there is a scheme for advancing at least some of the payments due from public funds irrespective of the compliance of the absent parent. We also make assumptions about health costs. The base line assumption is that health care is provided free of charge and that its quality and availability is equal between countries. Then we price what families might be actually required to pay for a standard package of health care. Account is also taken of the costs or value of free or subsidised pre-school provision and the costs/benefits of schooling.

Finally, account is taken of housing costs. One of the most problematic aspects of this methodology relates to the treatment of housing costs. There is no way of overcoming the fact that tenure patterns vary between countries, and that housing costs vary within countries according to a host of factors - direct and indirect subsidies, geographical location, the size and age of the dwelling, the length of occupation and many other factors. It would be easiest to ignore housing costs altogether. However, housing costs and housing subsidies are in many countries an important element of the child benefit package and to ignore them altogether would be to misrepresent the impact of that package. Because of the difficulties involved, results are presented both before and after housing costs. In addition local property based taxes used to fund local services are taken into account. Deducting net housing and local taxes, that is the amount payable after the receipt of any relevant housing benefit or rebates, gives net income after housing costs.

In the social assistance cases, national informants provide estimates of what each family on social assistance would receive, taking account of the impact of the benefits and services and housing costs in the way described for low earners. Where payments vary between local areas they are asked to nominate a "typical" municipality and follow its guidelines (see Eardley et al 1996 for a full discussion of the strengths and weaknesses of these methods).

The chart below takes one standard family type (a couple with two school age children) on a low wage (one earner at half national average earnings in ecu purchasing power parities) and shows how the the family transfer package impacts on market earnings. There are many interesting

77

features revealed in this chart and the reader may want to select a country for comparison, perhaps your own. But for the purposes of explanation of what the chart shows take Ireland. Half average male earnings in Ireland are eighth highest in the EU, just below the UK but ahead of Sweden, France and the southern European countries. Ireland does not tax this family type very heavily and in comparing after tax income it rises to third in the league table after Denmark and Luxembourg. It maintains that position after the impact of cash benefits thanks especially to an income related Family Income Supplement. After education and health costs (both free of charge at this income level in Ireland) it still lies third in the league table. After housing costs, thanks to a means tested differential rent scheme, Ireland has the highest after housing costs income. Indeed Ireland is the only country in the EU to leave this family better off after the impact of the family transfer package than they were before it.

In contrast it is worth commenting on two other countries. France has relatively low average male earnings - there is trade off between earnings and the social wage. But the social wage for families with children in France has most impact for preschool children (*assistantes maternelles*), families with three or more children (*allocations familiales*) and, particularly, the better off, larger families through its child tax benefits (*quotient familial*). For these reasons France comes lower down the league table for this two child low income family than one might have expected.

Sweden also has relatively low gross earnings (at least in ECU PPP terms). Direct taxes are high even at this earnings level. However cash benefits are still relatively generous, particularly social assistance which provides a supplement to the incomes of this family (though as we shall see the tax benefit package for families has deteriorated in Sweden in recent years). Charges do not have much impact but housing costs do and Sweden ends up much lower in the league table than one might have expected.

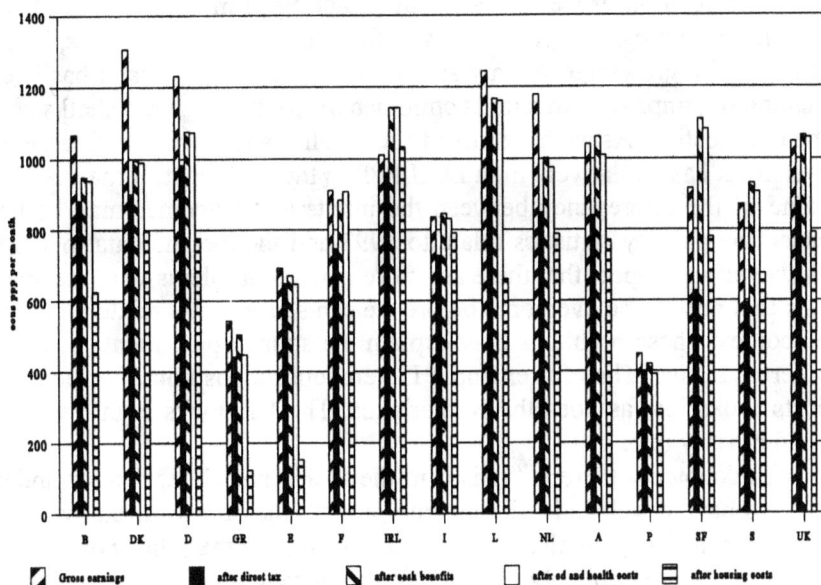

Figure 2.2.1   Couple with two school age children, One earner, 50% average male earnings

The same kind of story can be presented for each country, and we will find that the relative position of each country will vary according to the type of family chosen. This makes the overall performance of a country difficult to summarise using the matrix family method. What we have done in table 2.2.5 is to take the average income of four couples and three lone parent families with different numbers of children, with one earner earning half average earnings and the same seven families on social assistance. Thus the ranking is the product of 14 families including couples and lone parents, in employment and dependent on social assistance.

It can be seen in table 2.2.5 that the rankings vary with the income measure used. But if we take the after housing costs ranking (shadowed in the table) Germany, Denmark and Ireland come at the top of the league table. The final two columns of the table give two child poverty rankings derived from table 2.2.4. It can be seen that there is considerable variation between the input ranks and the outcome ranks, with the position of Ireland being perhaps most unexpected.

The position of Ireland is worth exploring in more detail, not least to point up some of the problems with the analysis. In recent years, in the context of a growing economy and a falling birth rate, Ireland has been making big improvements in its child benefit package - as we shall see in the next section. As we have already seen it has a relatively well targeted system. It has a relatively high ECU PPP to the Irish punt. It may be that some of the discrepancy between the inputs and outcomes may be because the poverty statistics relate to 1993 and the income data to 1996. However we suspect that there are more general problems with the analysis that need to be overcome before we can successfully relate inputs to outcomes. These problems may explain the strange placements of some other countries. Thus for example Luxembourg's position after housing costs looks low as does the Netherlands. The UK looks high given its child poverty rate.

Undoubtedly there is "noise" in the ECHP social deprivation index that we have developed - the income poverty measure is a relative one. Further sensitivity analysis is called for using other thresholds. The composite index probably calls for further development work to control for, for example, climatic variations The poverty rate is a function of the dispersion in income distribution of each country. The families chosen to represent poor families in the matrix analysis are probably not typical or representative of poor families in any country and countries vary in the balance of their poor children who living with couples and lone parents and between the low paid and social assistance recipients. In Ireland, for example, there are still very high proportions of large families and the matrix assumptions only include families with up to three children. Unfortunately the data on the characteristics of the families of poor children in different countries are not available to enable us to control for these factors.

Table 2.2.5 Average net income of 14 families on low earnings (half national average male) or social assistance ECU PPPs. Percentage difference from the mean

Net income after tax and benefits before health, education and housing costs		Net income after tax, benefits, health and education but before the deduction of housing costs		Net income after tax, benefits, health and education after the deduction of housing costs		ECHP child poverty rate below 50% average income rank order	ECHP poverty index rank order
Luxembourg	58	Luxembourg	62	Germany	57	3	4
Denmark	35	Denmark	39	Denmark	55	1	3
Germany	27	Germany	31	Ireland	43	11	8
Finland	15	Finland	21	Sweden	35		
Ireland	14	Ireland	15	Finland	34		
Belgium	13	Belgium	15	Luxembourg	33	7	1=
Netherlands	10	Sweden	14	UK	25	12	9
Austria	10	Netherlands	12	Netherlands	25	5	1=
Sweden	7	UK	8	Austria	4		
UK	-14	Austria	7	Belgium	3	4	6
France	-36	France	-4	France	-6	2	5
Spain	-40	Spain	-38	Italy	-26	8	7
Italy	-40	Italy	-42	Portugal	-52	10	12
Portugal	-50	Portugal	-53	Spain	-94	9	11
Greece	-64	Greece	-87	Greece	-137	6	10

4. Change over time

One way it might be possible to trace the link between child poverty rates and the policies designed to reduce them, and thus learn lessons about what the most effective anti poverty policies is to observe change over time. All going well eventually the ECHP survey will be able to produce a series of child poverty estimates from 1993 when it began. Since we began using the model family matrix method we have accumulated a data base on the impact of tax and benefit systems which have the potential of making comparisons over time. We have data on the situation in each EU country in 1992, 1994, 1995 and 1996. We are more confident that the assumptions on taxation and cash benefits are likely to be consistent over time than the assumptions relating to housing, health and education costs and benefits, so the comparison in table 2.2.6 is

81

restricted to the value of the tax and cash benefit element of the tax/benefit package. In these comparisons the child benefit package is expressed as a proportion of average earnings in each year. The general picture is one of remarkable consistency in the relative value of the package over time. Sweden has seen the largest reduction in the value of its package since 1994, which affected families at all earnings levels. Austria and Luxembourg have also seen a decline in value between 1994 and 1996. Significantly, given the findings earlier, Ireland nearly doubled the value of its package between 1992 and 1995 (though it fell back in 1996) - for a low wage earner on half average earnings the value of the package had doubled between 1992 and 1996.

Table 2.2.6 Changes in the value of the child benefit package over time. Child tax allowances and cash benefits only. Child benefit package as a proportion of average earnings in each year. Couple with two school age children

	One earner half average earnings				One earner average earnings				Two earners average and 0.66 average earnings			
	1992	1994	1995	1996	1992	1994	1995	1996	1992	1994	1995	1996
Belgium	13	16	16	16	14	16	16	16	14	16	17	16
Denmark	5	6	5	5	5	6	5	5	5	6	5	5
Germany	9	9	8	7	7	8	8	7	7	7	7	7
Greece	2	2	2	3	3	3	6	3	3	3	4	3
Spain	3	3	3	3	1	1	2	2	2	2	2	2
France	7	7	7	7	9	10	11	10	11	11	11	10
Ireland	9	21	18	15	5	7	9	6	4	4	3	4
Italy	6	7	2	12	3	4	3	5	1	3	1	3
Luxembourg	9	13	13	11	15	24	24	20	15	25	17	18
Netherlands	8	7	6	6	8	7	6	6	8	7	6	6
Austria		13	13	11		14	13	11		11	13	11
Portugal	4	4	4	5	6	6	6	7	6	6	7	7
Finland		20	19	17		14	13	13		16	12	10
Sweden		21	17	13		14	11	8		21	9	7
United Kingdom	14	17	12	15	8	9	7	8	6	6	6	6

5. Discussion

The family transfer package varies in the countries of the EU. Factors which might justify some variation in financial provision include variations in the costs of a child in different countries and the extent to which services are publicly subsidised. There is undoubtedly a trade-off between the level of earnings and the level of the social wage in different countries. Also countries make choices in structuring their transfer packages between arrangements which target help on the poor and low paid families with children and indeed whether they target help on families with children or the elderly or another dependent group.

The character of a welfare state is derived over a long period of time and has its roots in history, culture, political structure and economic development. Understanding how a country treats a group in its social policies at any one time, calls for the kind of historical analysis already attempted by Wennemo (1994) and forthcoming from the Mannheim project. Clearly the rankings and groupings of countries that we have found in this analysis are rather different from the welfare state regimes proposed by Esping Anderson (1990). In our previous study (Bradshaw et al 1993) we attempted to relate the relative level of the child benefit package in 1992 in 18 countries to a variety of demographic, economic and socio-political factors. We found that the most positive association with the child benefit package was social expenditure and taxation per capita and it is clear from this analysis that association still remains, though as in the case of Ireland, there are countries that buck the relationship But in general those countries that tax and spend most, that redistribute market generated income most, are the ones that are the most successful in reducing market generated child poverty rates.

It is also difficult to discern evidence of convergence in EU countries' approaches to meeting the costs of a children in poor families. There have been some changes to packages in the 1990s - for example Germany has transformed its child tax allowance into a cash benefit (a move the UK made in the 1970s); Ireland has substantially improved the level of its package, particularly for low earners; and France has cut *allocations familiales* for high incomes. So there is some evidence in some countries of a shift from tax allowances to cash benefits and the use of more income related cash benefits but these trends are far from universal (and in the 1997 budget in Britain the Government announced it was going to reintroduce an earned income tax credit for families). In fact the structure and levels of support towards the costs of children remain as different as ever. This may be *because* the institutions of the European Union have limited competence in relation to families and children: The question is: Should they have more?

Appendix 1

Changes in child poverty rates over time

In 1996 Whiteford et al published an analysis based on the circa 1985 sweep of the Luxembourg Income Survey which produced poverty rates for children for 10 countries. That analysis has been repeated on the circa 1990 sweep using exactly the same poverty threshold, equivalence scale and so forth. Unfortunately we only have data for seven countries at both circa 1985 and circa 1990. The child poverty rates are compared in table 2.2.A1. It shows that the child poverty rates have increased in the UK very much more than in any other country - by 49 per cent. In fact despite the commonly heard assertion that worldwide economic forces have been driving up poverty rates in all countries, three countries have actually seen reductions in their child poverty rates and in another child poverty rates have hardly changed.

Table 2.2.A1   Child poverty rates circa 1985 and circa 1990

Country	% below 50% threshold - c 1985	% below 50% threshold - c 1990	Change	% change
Canada	17.7	16.5	-1.2	-6.7
Germany	9.3	11.5	2.2	23.7
Italy	17.6	13.8	-3.8	-21.6
Netherlands	9.7	10	0.3	3.1
Sweden	4.4	3.9	-0.5	-1.1
United Kingdom	16.7	24.9	8.2	49.1
United States	29.6	28	-1.6	-5.4

Notes

1. The ECHP is a Community-wide multidimensional longitudinal survey. Based on a harmonised questionnaire, it provides comparable information across the Member States at both the level of the household and the level of the individual (aged over 16 years). Among the topics covered are demographic and employment characteristics, income, health, education, poverty and social exclusion, housing and migration. The first wave of the ECHP contains data on situations as at 1993 (collected in 1994), across all of the 12 Member States at that time. In total, 60,822 European households and 129,877 European individuals were interviewed in 1994.

   The LIS database consists of a set of broadly comparable income surveys, now available for three periods in time. The first 'wave' covers surveys undertaken at the beginning of the 1980s; the second wave includes surveys conducted in the mid-1980s; and the third and most recent wave is for the period circa 1990 (between 1989 and 1992). The analysis presented in the following sections is based on the latest wave, and we have included 19 countries in this analysis. Among these 19 are seven of the EU Member States as at 1990, and two subsequent members, namely Finland and Sweden. In addition it also includes a number of transitional economies, former Eastern Bloc countries. The third wave of the LIS also holds data on Austria and Australia. The former has been excluded from this analysis because of problems of reliability identified in the data. Anxieties have also been raised (Bradshaw and Chen, 1997) about the quality of some of the Italian and German data.

2. The results refer to different points in time - the ECHP results are for 1993, while those of the LIS are for various years between 1989 and 1992. Some of the definitions employed are incompatible across the two surveys. For instance, in the ECHP analysis, children are defined as less than 16 years of age, while the LIS defines all individuals under 18 years as children. Although the definitions of income employed appear to be similar, there are subtle differences in the definitions of some of the individual income components (for example, private transfers). There may also be variations in the imputation procedure adopted for missing data.

   In addition, the analyses have adopted different equivalence scales for the calculation of equivalent income. The ECHP uses the modified OECD scale (that is, 1.0 for the first adult, 0.5 for every other adult in the household and 0.3 for every child younger than 14), while the LIS uses the DSS scales by McClements (that is, 1.0 for the first adult, 0.55 for the second adult and subsequent adult(s) and 0.5 for each child). Finally, different sampling and weighting procedures may have been used..

3. Two of the indicators used in the original analysis have been excluded here: b) % of children living in households with no private car/van - on the grounds that it depends on the quality and cost of public transport whether this is a deprivation (Italy scores low and Denmark and the Netherlands score high) ; and g) % of children living in households receiving an allowance or subsidy for housing costs - on the grounds that this is an input and not necessarily an outcome of poverty (Spain and Portugal score low and France and the UK score high).

4. It was initially developed for a comparative study of child benefit packages (in 1992) in initially 15, later 18 countries (Bradshaw et al., 1993; Stephens and Bradshaw, 1995; Bradshaw and Uzuhashi, 1994). It was later adapted to compare the incentive structures facing married women engaged in housework (Shaver and Bradshaw, 1995), lone parents (Whiteford and Bradshaw, 1994) and social assistance schemes in OECD countries (Eardley et al., 1996). It was used in the 1994 report of the Observatory (Ditch et al., 1996) and in the 1995 report (Ditch et al., 1997) in the chapters on family incomes and tax/benefit policy and in the special study of lone parents labour supply undertaken alongside the 1994 report (Bradshaw et al., 1996).

References

Bradshaw, J. (1995) 'The level of social assistance in eighteen countries', *Benefits*, 16: 52-62.

Bradshaw, J. (1993) 'Developments in social security policy', in Jones, C. (ed) *New Perspectives on the Welfare State in Europe*, Routledge.

Bradshaw, J. and Chen J.R. (1997) "Poverty in the UK, A comparison with nineteen other countries", *Benefits*, 13, January 1997.

Bradshaw, J., et al (1996a) *Lone Parents and Employment: a comparison of policy in 20 countries*, London: Family Policy Studies Centre.

Bradshaw, J., et al (1996b) *Policy and the Employment of Lone Parents in 20 Countries: The EU Report*, European Observatory on National Family Policies, DGV / Social Policy Research Unit, University of York.

Bradshaw, J., Ditch, J., Holmes, H. and Whiteford, P. (1993) 'A comparative study of child support in fifteen countries', *Journal of European Social Policy*, 3, 4: 255-71.

Bradshaw, J., Ditch, J., Holmes, H., and Whiteford, P. (1993) *Support for Children: A comparison of arrangements in fifteen countries*, Department of Social Security Research Report No. 21, London: HMSO.

Bradshaw, J. and Uzuhashi, T. (1994) 'Child support in Japan', *Japanese Journal of Household Economy*, 24: 52-62.

Ditch, J., Barnes, H., Bradshaw, J.R., Commaille, J. and Eardley, T. (1995) *A Synthesis of National Family Policies 1994*, European Observatory on National Family Policies, European Commission/Social Policy Research Unit: York.

Ditch, J., Barnes, H. And Bradshaw, J. (1996) *A Synthesis of National Family Policies 1995, European Observatory of National Family Policies 1995*, European Commission/Social Policy Research Unit: York.

Ditch, J., et al (1996) *A Synthesis of National Family Policies in 1995*, European Observatory on National Family Policies, DGV / Social Policy Research Unit, University of York.

Ditch, J., Barnes, H. and Bradshaw, J. and Kilkey, M. (1998) *A Synthesis of National Family Policies 1996*, York: Commission of the European Communities.

Eardley, T., Bradshaw, J.R., Ditch, J., Gough, I. and Whiteford, P. (1996) *Social Assistance Schemes in OECD Countries: Synthesis Report*, Department of Social Security Report No. 46, London: HMSO.

Eardley, T., Bradshaw, J.R., Ditch, J., Gough, I. and Whiteford, P. (1996) *Social Assistance Schemes in OECD Countries: Country Reports*, Department of Social Security Research Report No. 47, London: HMSO.

Esping-Andersen, G. (1990) *The Three Worlds of Welfare Capitalism*, Cambridge: Polity Press.

Oldfield, N., and Yu, A. (1993) *The Cost of a Child: Living standards for the 1990s*, London: Child Poverty Action Group.

Shaver, S. and Bradshaw, J.R. (1995) 'The recognition of wifely labour by welfare states', *Social Policy and Administration*, 29, 1: 10-25.

Stephens, B. and Bradshaw, J. (1995) 'The generosity of New Zealand's assistance to families with dependent children: an eighteen country comparison', *Social Policy Journal of New Zealand*, 4: 53-75.

Wennemo, I. (1994) *Sharing the Costs of a Child*, Swedish Institute for Social Research 25, University of Stockholm.

Whiteford, P. and Bradshaw, J.R. (1993) 'Benefits and incentives for lone parents: a comparative analysis', *International Social Security Review*, 47, 3-4 94: 69-89.

2.3 Framing and reframing social policy paradigms: the case of lone parents

Nadine Lefaucheur and Martin Rein

One subject that has fascinated scholars of comparative social policy is how to classify and compare welfare state policies of different countries. Most efforts to derive a typology of types, regimes or schemes are based on cross sectional comparisons at a point in time. The patterns that emerge from such an analysis are by their nature static and presume that there is stability of policy over time. Not surprisingly, there has been a rather large body of literature, which has criticized these various efforts at developing a typology of social policy across countries. This criticism has tended to try to identify an important elision, i.e., a significant dimension that has not been taken into account, such as gender. The critics have in turn responded by developing a new classification that is based on the omitted variable. A good example is the scheme to take account of recent feminist debate, classifying countries on the extent to which they follow a strong, moderate or weak breadwinner model.

But this response is not sufficient to face what we believe is the fundamental weakness of the regime approach to comparative social policy. The assumption is that these efforts are based on a static cross sectional snapshot of prevailing policies. This approach requires the acceptance of an implicit assumption about the underlying logic of policy making, that policies are stable over time and countries can unambiguously be assigned to one type. We know these assumptions are false. The approach we want to pursue is based on different assumptions; that the quality that is most essential to social policy is that it changes over time, that actual social policies are both path dependent and resultant from current competing ideological, social and political forces, so that they are not really "intellectually and pragmatically unified packages of programs and policies, values and institutions".

As a first step in the development of a framework focused on complexity, evolution and the process of change, we propose to look at a group that is a focus of current public policy controversy - that of lone parents - and to try to identify the way in which the public response to this group has been framed and reframed over time. We will first extract the historical paradigms that have guided policy and practice towards unmarried mothers and illegitimate children and consider their current reframing and relevance with regard to debates and policies towards lone parents. Through a brief analysis of current policy change in the United States, we will then consider the internal and external forces pressing for change and how they are used by organized groups or social movements that challenge the "normatively secure" taken for granted consensus about values, means and ends and the counter movements that these initiatives stimulate.

Toward a framework for understanding complexity and change in public policies and debates relating to never-married mothers and illegitimate newborns

The early work of Nadine Lefaucheur explored the various collective responses adopted or rejected since the Middle Ages by some European countries toward the birth of illegitimate children. This is a fact that was constructed early on as a "social issue", since the centrality of the institution of marriage for the social reproduction of these countries posed for them the normative and practical question of "who has to support the fatherless children?".

The comparative approach of family policies poses numerous, and complex problems, if only because the different countries disagree about the very notion of family policy, about having adopted or not such a policy, and about what such a policy is, or would be constituted of. Nadine Lefaucheur proposed not to define *a priori* what a family policy was, but to start from an anthropologic given fact: the existence, in all societies, of newborn babies and children who have to be fed and cared for so that the society will not disappear. An anthropologic fact that, in different times, places, and groups, has given rise to different norms as far as devolution of the responsibility for supporting children.

She argued that until recently, the basic norm of the Western societies has been one that stemmed from the institutionalization of marriage, mainly by the Roman Catholic Church, around the twelfth century. This institution had a monopoly in admitting people, for life, to (heterosexual) sexual relations, conjugal cohabitation, procreation, fatherhood and legitimacy. This institution played a key role in the division of labor by gender (and age), and also for the allocation of people to socio-economic places, since this institution and inheritance lines were narrowly woven together. This institution, then, knitted together sex and gender, household and family, procreation and legitimacy, child care and child support, housework and inheritance.

There were norms for the support of children. Children had to be cared for and supported by their own mother and their own father. A child's mother was the one that carried him and gave birth to him. A child's father was, as in all "well civilized countries", according to Montesquieu thought, the mother's husband: "the one that laws, by the wedding ceremony, have declared to be such, because they found in him the one they were looking for" (i.e. to some male breadwinner) to devolve to the responsibility for supporting the child. Consequently, children who were born out of marriage had, normally, a mother but no *father*, no breadwinner responsible of supporting them and from whom they could be entitled to inherit from.

Early in European history, the birth of such *fatherless* children has been constructed as a "social issue" needing some public response. In the research mentioned above Nadine Lefaucheur concluded the investigation of the various responses given to this social issue by some European societies (namely England, France, Italy and Portugal), within the course of history, by proposing the following analytic framework.

"Supreme evil" paradigms and "lesser evil" responses

There is a limited, although rather large, set of potential responses to draw upon to deal with the birth of children outside of marriage and the subsequent absence of a *father*.

Some of the responses are preventive, and aim at avoiding the occurrence of illegitimacy: social control of the sexual behavior and relations of unmarried women, suppression of fornication and adultery, social and legal pressure into marriage on the unmarried genitors, legalization of contraception, abortion, and/or sterilization, etc.

With regard to the "father", some of the potential responses aim at applying to these deviant situations the general norm that devolves the responsibility for supporting the child of the mother's husband. These can be carried out in a restrictive way, by exempting, if not forbidding, the putative father to support the child (banning on paternity suits), or, on the contrary, in an extensive way, by devolving on him all or part of the responsibility for supporting the child that would have fallen on him if he had married the mother (paternity suits, alimonies, child support, etc.).

With regard to the mother, the potential responses can devolve on herself (and/or her own family) the whole burden of the support of the child, in particular through the banning of paternity suits and abandonment. Or, on the contrary, they can totally relieve her of this burden and transfer it to the community or to other families to protect her and her families' "honor". This response also protects the social order, when it is unacceptable to society that unmarried mothers openly bring up their illegitimate children. Examples include giving them the possibility of a secret or anonymous delivery followed by the abandonment of the newborn bastards, by creating foundling hospitals or orphanages, or by promoting fosterage or adoption, etc.

Last, some other potential responses are aimed at compensating for the absence of a father (i.e., a mother's husband) and at sharing the burden of supporting the fatherless children between their mother, eventually their putative father (through paternity suits and alimonies or child support pensions), and some local or state welfare authorities or social insurance systems (through special benefits, fiscal deductions, vouchers, childcare facilities, training programs, admission to homes for unmarried mothers and their children, casework, and so on).

Some of these potential responses that violate the norm where children have to be supported by their "father" can be given jointly. Some cannot. In specific contexts, some responses can be seen as "lesser evils" that society is willing to accept, compared with some others that appear as "supreme" or "worst evils" that need to be avoided.

Major organizing paradigms draw the line between potential responses that, at a given time and place, are rejected because they are perceived to belong to a moral or social supreme evil sphere, and the potential responses that are or could be chosen because, by comparison, they are seen as lesser evils. Each paradigm can be characterized by the content of its own supreme evil sphere, giving definition to what potential responses can be considered as lesser evils within its framework.

Within the frame of a paradigm, choosing what lesser evil responses have to be implemented creates dilemmas, since a "lesser (of two) evils" is nevertheless an evil. These dilemmas are about values and moral issues. They can also arise from practical issues, like an unexpected inflation of the number of beneficiaries (and then of the cost) of a given lesser evil response or some estimated "perverse" or (dis)incentive effects of such a response. Debates about the policies that have to be implemented can be very intense and bitter. But, there are no "intractable controversies" within a given paradigm, because within its framework, disagreements concern the means - the lesser evil responses - that are the more suitable to prevent or fight the supreme evils, of which there is a general agreement.

A paradigm can be hegemonic or highly dominant at certain periods and/or in certain countries. It runs into a crisis when a growing part of the public opinion, of the experts, of the academics and/or of the policy-makers consider the responses, or at least at some of the responses that they used to perceived to be lesser evils in the framework of this paradigm, to subsequently belong to the supreme evil sphere. This change in the definition of the content of the supreme evil sphere indicates a shift from the frame of the formerly dominant paradigm, which can then be challenged by others with differing definitions of the supreme evil sphere. The shift can arise from reasons that are endogenous to the formerly dominant paradigm, for example, inflation in the number of recipients and the associated costs and/or (dis)incentive effects of some formerly lesser evil responses: when they come to appear unbearable, they move towards the supreme evil sphere. But, for a paradigm to change, the move has to be supported by some exogenous reasons. Paradigms are indeed part of large constellations of ideas and values and have special and mutual links with specific areas of knowledge, and specific scientific or political theories. Thus, a revolution in paradigms usually corresponds with a revolution in the political regimes, main changes in power, and/or with religious, scientific or ideological revolutions.

Policies referring to different paradigms give rise to intractable controversies, since their disagreements on which responses should be implemented concern not only the means but also, and more deeply, the ends: the supreme or worse evils that have to be prevented or fought.

Fatherless children, from angels to citizens: four paradigms

From the construction of the social issues of motherhood out of wedlock and the support of fatherless children, four major paradigms can be extracted from the historical data concerning the various responses adopted or rejected by some European countries.

The first (and oldest) paradigm has been labeled *christian angelism,* or *canonical angelism* by Nadine Lefaucheur, as it is especially related to theology and canonical law, in the field of ideas and knowledge. Within its framework, the sphere of the supreme evil is filled with all that infringes both on the Commandment "Thou shalt not kill", regarding fetuses and newborn babies, and the canonical institutionalization of marriage, prescribing that sex and procreation should occur only inside marriage and never "against nature". Thus, the worse responses within this framework are abortion and infanticide.

To fight these supreme evils, there is a set of potential lesser evil responses, starting with social pressure for marriage. During the centuries when this paradigm dominated, the family of a pregnant unmarried woman and/or her community could try to normalize her situation by pressing the putative father to marry her if he was not already married, a monk or a priest (possibly by taking him to ecclesiastic, common law, or civil courts). The putative father could be condemned to pay for the delivery costs, and/or for some child support if the pregnant girl was still a virgin when he "seduced" her, and if he could not, or refused to marry her. He could even be condemned to pay her some damages and possibly a dowry to help her with finding another husband. These sentences punished the sin or fault of fornication, adultery, rape or seduction, that he had committed. But, as he was not the mother's husband, he did not become the *father* of the child. The child remained illegitimate, did not legally enter, and could not inherit from the putative father's family.

As the Catholic Church viewed the institution of marriage as a sacrament based on the basic assumption of mutual and free consent, dilemmas arose from these pressures against putative fathers, especially those to "redressing weddings" imposed by the courts on pain of prison. But the main dilemmas were posed by the foundling hospitals (or other institutions taking the foundlings into care). These dilemmas emerged from moral and practical issues: was such a solution morally closer to the sphere of the supreme evil or to the sphere of the lesser evil ? Was the cost of these institutions affordable ? Were not their (dis)incentive and "perverse" effects worse than the true evil that they aimed to alleviate ? The option that they gave to unmarried pregnant women to give birth and/or leave their offspring secretly, or even anonymously represented indeed "the lesser of two evils". This option reduced the risk these women would seek a secret abortion or commit infanticide to uphold their own honor and that one of their family, preserving their social and matrimonial chances. (In the 19th-century, a French priest who advocated the foundling hospitals, said that it didn't matter that the infant mortality rate of the fatherless children increased dramatically in, and because of these hospitals, since such an institution could prevent some abortions or infanticides and since "thousands of deaths on a battlefield are morally preferable to one murder"). But, in another respect, this option that covered up the offsprings and even the traces of sexual misconduct, could also constitute an incentive to "vice" and to "recidivism" that challenged the norms of sexual and matrimonial good behavior. Another unintended by-product arose, due to the rules and devices that were used to guarantee the secrecy or anonymity of both mothers and abandoned children. Some legitimate children could also be unduly abandoned, undermining the norm of the *father*'s responsibility to support their children, and increasing unduly the number of foundlings and the public cost of their support.

This paradigm reigned in the Western countries without almost any contest about the supreme evils that had to be prevented or fought by the policies until the Reformation. It continued to dominate policies in the Latin catholic countries for at least two centuries, until it was challenged, at the time of religious, political, ideological and/or scientific revolutions, by other paradigms that finally took precedence over it. But even though, traces of the *christian* paradigm are still visible to-day in Western policies, they seem to be emerging again in the debates of some countries, not only in Latin or Catholic countries.

Within the frame of *christian angelism,* the public support given to foundlings, by congregations, hospitals, local or state authorities that seemed to be a lesser evil, although not without any dilemma, belonged, on the contrary, to the supreme evil sphere within the frame of the paradigm called *malthusian angelism.* This second paradigm arose in regions or countries where, according to poor laws or customary laws, local authorities or institutions used to support totally or partially foundlings and even poor fatherless children, and where communities came to rail and struggle against "avoidable dependency". It developed alongside the economic and demographic thought and within the "liberal" and "free-market" universe of ideas. Within the frame of this paradigm, the social issue of fatherless children is actually not equated so much with the birth of children out of wedlock, but with the birth of children whose genitors do not have the means or the will to support them, and their subsequent dependency and calls to society to partially or totally support them.

Thus, within this framework, restrictions on the right of the poor to get married, the tolerance or even the promotion of abortion for to the poor or the unwilling pregnant women, especially unwed women, moved from the supreme evil sphere to that of the lesser evils. As for the issue of fatherless children, the main dilemma concerns paternity suits that historically, under *christian angelism,* were rather favorable for "seduced" women. Within the frame of *malthusian angelism,* it also appears legitimate not to allow the genitors, especially the seducers, to escape the responsibilities that they should have taken for their offsprings, or place such a responsibility onto society. But, if marriage is a contract that has to be freely established, can paternity that derives from it be forced? Also, allowing some women who gave themselves to a man without any guarantee of the support contract that marriage offers, to "get the man to pay" the consequences of their "gift"could be seen as providing a strong incentive for all women to surrender to the supreme evil of procreating children that they cannot support. As the number of pregnancies out of wedlock and paternity suits had increased after the 17th century, such a paradigm seems to have commanded the "masculine reaction" that in the 18th and 19th centuries has severely controlled and limited the right of women to sue the putative fathers for damages and/or child support. (For example, England passed in the New Poor Law, some bills about illegitimacy forbidding such suits. Following France, several European countries adopted civil codes that severely restrict the opening of paternity suits).

Neither *Christian* nor *Malthusian angelists* really deplored the abnormally high rates of infant mortality pervasive amongst fatherless children, especially the foundlings, until at least the early 20th-century. The *Christians* thought the most "saving" solution for the budgets of the foundling hospitals and for the souls of these sinners' children was their "natural" and rapid death and their transformation into little angels in the Heaven. The *Malthusians* thought there was no room around the table - and no food - for them at the "banquet of life". Within the *angelist* paradigms, to be sure, their premature death was considered to be a lesser evil.

The same was not true within the framework of the paradigm that can be called *healthy citizenship*. In this paradigm the "angelist" response to the issue of supporting fatherless children moved closer to the sphere of the supreme evil, alongside with contraception, abortion and infanticide (all responses that undoubtedly belong to the supreme evil sphere within *Christian angelism*, yet on the contrary are potentially lesser evils in *Malthusian angelism*).

Whereas *Malthusian angelism* has been fueled in the late 18th-century England with a political and economic concern about overpopulation and underproduction, the paradigm of *healthy citizenship* arose most likely in the France of Enlightenment, around the mid-18th-century, from a political and economic concern about depopulation and degeneration. This paradigm has been especially dominant in France - where it is still very influential - as well as in Southern Europe, under the republican regimes of the late 19th-century and early 20th-century, and also under the totalitarian regimes of the mid-20th-century. Within the *healthy citizen* framework, all of the potential responses that prevent the birth or the survival of sane, fit and healthy children, even if fatherless, belong to the supreme evil sphere. Yet, by comparison, all types of *welfare* support for unmarried deserted mothers that enable them to save the life and preserve the fitness of their children are potentially lesser evils. Looking at *welfare* as a lesser evil is, of course, in complete opposition to *Malthusian angelism*. Within that paradigm the lesser evil alternative either to desertion by the putative father, or to foundling hospitals, was "to have the unmarried mothers pay" and not "to pay the unmarried mothers for taking care of the children that are needed by the state, the country, the army, the navy, the colonies, the farming, the industry...".

As in *Christian angelism*, the potential response given to unmarried mothers to give birth and abandon their newborn babies secretly or anonymously (an option that is generally called in France *accouchement sous X*) poses a dilemma for *healthy citizenship*. Such an option indeed comes close to the supreme evil sphere when the absence of maternal breast-feeding can be equated with an increased risk of infant mortality, as that was the case until about the mid-20th-century. But on another hand, if this option could deter some women from resorting to abortion or committing infanticide, it would save some lives and help to increase the population or to alleviate its decline. Eugenic responses, for example,

97

aborting or sterilizing the (so-called) feeble-minded unmarried pregnant women or mothers, can also pose some particular dilemmas within such a framework. Lesser evils of preventing the birth of possibly unfit children are nevertheless worse evils when also possibly preventing the birth of some fit children.

Thus, the concern of the *healthy citizen* paradigm is not for the rapid creation of *angels*, but alternately, for making *numerous* and *healthy citizens*. With regard to special links with particular fields of knowledge and social practices, the *healthy citizen* paradigm appears hence closer to demography, medicine (especially pediatrics and obstetrics), eugenics, socio-economics and social work.

The main concern of the fourth paradigm, called *proper citizenship*, is not so much about the number of the *citizen* or the survival and the health of fatherless children, but about their social behavior and their potential to become *good* and *proper citizens*. Within the frame of this *proper citizen* paradigm, the supreme evils are personality disorders, anti-social behavior and, especially, juvenile delinquency that supposedly stem from the absence of a father within the family. If one can see some heralding signs of its development before the Enlightenment, it is at that time when, alongside with the paradigm of the *healthy citizen,* it started to pose a threat on *christian angelism.* Nevertheless, it fully developed in the late 19th-century, at the same time that the fields of knowledge and social practice developed, from which it derived its main sources of legitimization; namely educationalism, criminology, psychiatry, psychology, psychoanalysis, child guidance, and the treatment of juvenile delinquency. This evolved at the same time that the life expectancy of fatherless children started to increase, drawing a growing part of the policy-makers' (and policy-thinkers') attention away from the social issues of the feeding, caring for and supporting newborn fatherless babies, and towards the social issue of controlling of the behavior of fatherless teenagers.

Within such a framework, eugenic responses such as sterilization, contraception and abortion, are potentially lesser evils, since they can prevent the birth of unfit children or of children whose unmarried mothers would not be able to socialize correctly and would grow up to become anti-social individuals and criminals. As for the living fatherless children, there were different potentially lesser evil choices. A *welfare* and education policy can either help unmarried mothers support and raise their fatherless children, or promote the abandonment or fostering of

98

fatherless children, taking them into care. When this last option is considered a lesser evil, one can try to substitute the missing *father* (and, at the same time, the unmarried mother) of the fatherless children by transferring these children to adoptive or foster families. Or, it can try to compensate for fatherless children's distorted socialization with a special educational process in orphanages or reformatory schools.

The main dilemmas within *proper citizenship* take their roots in the very conception of the role of the family that informs this paradigm. Most of the French Revolutionaries thought, and as the modern "psys" uphold that "it is impossible to become a good citizen if one has no family ties, if one does not learn in this small republic that the family is how to behave in the largest Republic that the country is". If it is the incompleteness or the absence of the family that causes the risks of personality disorders and anti-social behavior among fatherless children, which option is of greater risk : to leave the fatherless children in *their* fatherless family, or to take them *out of* their family ? If opting to take fatherless children out of their incomplete-then-incompetent family, what is the lesser evil: providing them with a substitute *family* by fostering or adoption, or trying to give them a *non-family* "reforming" education within specialized institutions?

All of these four paradigms are still competing to-day in Western countries. They have different relative weights and influence on the issues related to never-married mothers - and also on the issues related to a larger category of the lone parent families, since unmarried motherhood is often used in a metonymic way when considering lone parenthood. The issues related to lone parenthood are posed, and now need to be reframed in the current context of what we can call "demarriage".

Demarriage and lone parenthood

The institution of marriage as it had been set up in the Western countries by the Catholic Church had been attacked by the Reformation, by the rise of non-ecclesiastical courts and civil legislation, and by the adoption by several countries of civil laws of marriage for religious minorities or for the general population, and of (restrictive) divorce laws. Nonetheless, even in a reformed or secularized way, it continued to knit tightly together sex, household, family, male authority, fatherhood, legitimacy and inheritance.

All of this has been unknitted for the three last decades in the Western countries, in laws as well as in social practices. The changes have been more or less rapid and intense from country to country, and manifest themselves in the same: increasing rates of unmarried cohabitation among couples, births out of wedlock, and divorce, through the decriminalization of sexual relations out of marriage (even of same-sex relations) and of abortion, through the introduction of divorce by mutual consent, of equality between spouses, of equal sharing of parental authority between fathers and mothers, and more fundamentally, abolition of the illegitimacy statuses and equality of children regardless of their parents' relations and matrimonial situation. Following this abolition (or quasi-abolition), fatherhood is now largely dissociated from marriage. The mother's husband is no longer automatically her children's *father*. The putative father who did not marry the mother of his child, whether being unmarried or married to another woman himself, can be (and ought to be) registered as the *father* of this child.

One of the main consequences of this "demarriagization" of the Western societies is a big change in the category of the now-called lone parents. Since around the mid-1970s in most Western countries, divorced, separated and never-married (often ex-cohabitant) lone parents are a growing and predominant part of the population, while the proportion of widows and widowers, who used to make up at least 50% of lone parents, decreased to represent usually less than a quarter. Thus, children who live in lone-parent households now tend to have *two* living legal parents, one with whom they constitute a lone-parent household, usually their mother, and one, usually their father, with whom they don't live every day, but who still shares the parental authority and the obligation to support them. Thus, even if the father is an "absent" parent from the *one-parent household*, he is still a member of his *children's family*, that becomes for the children, not a lone-parent family, but a two-parent/two-household family. And, if the lone parent gets remarried or cohabitates with a new partner, children can now have a step-father *at the same time* as a father, not *after* or *instead of* a father.

The main issues about lone-parenthood are currently less about how and if to oblige the putative father to marry the mother and/or to support the *fatherless* child, but how to redefine after the separation or the divorce, the obligation to support the children of the never-married, separated or divorced *fathers,* and if and how to enforce them.

It appears that, slightly reframed, the same paradigms that have been extracted by Nadine Lefaucheur from the historical data concerning *fatherless* children and *unmarried* mothers apply to the construction of the social issues and policies concerning *"demarried"* (lone) parents and children with *two separated* parents (formerly married or not). Not the slightest reason being that, as said above, unmarried motherhood is often used as a metonym of lone motherhood, which is also generally used itself as a metonym of lone parenthood. Such metonymic use goes along with different ways of categorizing and treating lone parents through social policies. Within the reframed paradigms that use the figure of the *unmarried* mother as a metonym of all lone parents, all lone parents are usually more or less treated in the same way. Also, while within the paradigms that use this figure (if not that of the *black teenage never-married* mother...) as a metonym of all *demarried* lone parents, the widowed ones are more likely to be treated differently, and usually better.

From unmarried mothers to lone parents: reframing the paradigms

From Christian angelism to an "anti-demarriage" (or "moral") paradigm

At the time of *demarriage,* besides the former supreme evils of sex and procreation out of marriage, contraception, abortion and infanticide, the supreme evil sphere can be filled with *demarriage* itself, i.e. all of the responses that can be seen as incentive - or not disincentive enough - to divorce and/or cohabitate. Whereas one can use the never-married mothers as a symbol of amorality (and a metonym) for all the *demarried* lone parents, the widowed lone parents, who did not "demarry", are not supposed to be treated in the same way as the divorced, separated or never-married ones.

From Malthusian angelism to an "anti-dependency" paradigm

Joined in the supreme evil sphere of this reframed paradigm are lone parents who separated or divorced while they were unable to support their lone-parent household, as well as the "absent" parents who did the same, or worse remarried or re-partnered, bringing in step-children and/or new children of their own when unable to afford the support of

101

two households, with the unmarried people who begot newborn babies that they had not the means or the will to support and who make claims on society to provide for themselves and/or their offspring. The dependent poor (if not also teenage and black) never-married mother on *welfare* are symbolic and metonymic of all of the (possibly) dependent lone parents. Nevertheless, within this frame, the poor widowed lone parents that did not willingly get into such a dependent condition should usually be treated better than the divorced, separated or never-married lone parents, who more or less chose their situation.

From the healthy citizen to the "anti-poverty" (or "anti-(social/gender) inequality") paradigm

As infant mortality is no longer such a big issue, and as the children involved in the separation or the divorce of their parents are not usually newborn infants, the main concern within the frame of the *healthy citizen* has moved from creating and saving babies to the higher risks of poverty amongst the households headed by lone parents, especially lone mothers, and the associated handicaps and inequalities that the children (and the parents) living in such households are confronted with (for example health and education). The poor unmarried mother and her children can be looked at as a symbol and a metonym of all lone mother households - or even of all lone parent households. This is because they are most likely to be the poorest. But, as the supreme evil sphere of this paradigm is filled with the threats on human resources that stem from social inequalities between parents and between children according to their family situation, all lone parents have to be treated equally - or equitably - within its frame, according to their needs and not to their matrimonial status or to their gender.

From the proper citizen to the "anti-absent father" paradigm

Since the *proper citizen* paradigm had developed to reduce the risks of personality disorders and anti-social behavior stemming not only from the absence of *a* father, but also from the absence of *the* father, it is not reframed by the current trend towards *demarriage*. (If not for symmetry, it could still be named the *proper citizen* paradigm...). Also, since there is no agreement about what are the worse or the lesser evils - i.e. the death of *the* father, the absence of *a* father, the absence of *a/the* (step-)father within the household, the absence of relationships with the father, the bad relationships with the father, or even the presence of a *bad* (step-)*father* within the household - there are no clear assessments on if and where a boundary has to be drawn for policy matters between the different types of lone mother households.

How (reframed) paradigms work

The case of France

Paradigms and their rationale are referred to in social policy debates and can be seen behind social programs and laws. As an illustration, we will first examine three examples out of the French system of family benefits and fiscal law:

An *allocation d'orphelin* (orphan allowance) was created in 1970 for *fatherless* (and/or motherless) children of whom both parents were deceased or unknown (full benefit) or of whom one parent was deceased or unknown (part benefit). It was reframed in 1975 to become available to children of *"demarried"* parents, living in *one-parent* households, when the absent parent "manifestly abandoned" them, that is, did not pay any child support. This first reframing happened at the same time as an important reform in law occurred, which permitted divorce by mutual consent. The passing of this law was followed by a large increase in the divorce rate and indirectly increased the number of recipients of *allocation d'orphelin*. Consequently, the cost of this allowance for the family allowance funds increased. Then, another reframing occurred in the mid-1980s. The allowance was renamed *allocation de soutien familial* (family support allowance) or ASF, and defined different scenarios:

- If the absent parents are deceased or unknown (they did not recognize legally their children and were not sued by the other parent to do so), ASF is said *non recouvrable* (un-retrievable). According to the rationale of the *healthy citizen* that has been reframed in an *anti-poverty* one, ASF is paid as before to the lone parents for their *fatherless* (sometimes motherless) children.
- If the *"demarried"* absent parents - either unmarried (but having legally recognized their children), or separated or divorced - do not pay any child support, ASF is said *recouvrable* (retrievable). The

103

lone parents in this case can receive ASF from the family allowance fund as an advance on child support, provided that they entitle the fund to sue the absent parents to retrieve the advanced amounts. The absent parents can be estimated by the fund to be *hors d'état de payer* (unable to pay) and exempted from repayment. To manage such a case, the rationale of the *healthy citizen-antipoverty* paradigm, based on income and the needs has still been used, but has been partly combined with the *malthusian* rationale of the *anti-dependency* paradigm, which deems that the absent parent has to support the child before the community.

If the lone parents refuse to sue the absent parents or to entitle the family fund to do so, they do not get ASF (unless it is estimated that it would be dangerous for them to sue the absent parents since they are violent and/or abusive). When they are entitled to some guaranteed minimum income, the amount of an *ASF fictive* (a fictitious ASF) can be deducted from this guaranteed income. In this case, the *malthusian* rationale reframed in an *anti-dependency* paradigm is adopted completely.

The creation of the *allocation de parent isolé* (lone parent allowance) or API, gives an example of the reframing of and of the competition between the rationales of different paradigms in social policy debates. This allowance subsidizes the income of lone parents up to a guaranteed level of about 53% of SMIC (the guaranteed minimum wage) for a pregnant lone woman to about 71% of SMIC for a lone parent with one child, plus 18% of SMIC for each additional child. It was created in 1976 at a time when there was not awareness of the big changes occurring in the lone-parent population (that was still mainly composed of widowed and unmarried mothers of *fatherless* children) as well as in the economy (the increase in unemployment was still limited and attributed to a temporary "oil crisis"). At the very beginning, API had been designed for *recently widowed lone mothers* to help them to get organized with their new family situation and find a job to (self)support their household. It was intended to last for one year after the decease of the late husband - according both the rationale of the *healthy citizen* paradigm, with regard to the guarantee of a minimum income, and the rationale of the *malthusian* paradigm, with regard to the limitation in time. Even before it was discussed in Parliament, it was reframed as a *recent lone mother* allowance, intended also for never-married and deserted married lone mothers, according to the *healthy citizen* paradigm, partly reframed in an *anti-poverty* paradigm. At that tie, it was not considered that "non deserted" *demarried* lone mothers could claim for this benefit, or that large numbers of them would do so.

When the proposal of AMI *(allocation de mère isolée)* - lone *mother* allowance - came under discussion in Parliament in 1976, the deputies first extended the eligibility to lone fathers and renamed the benefit API *(allocation de parent isolé)*, lone *parent* allowance. This was in accordance with the rationale of the *healthy citizen* reframed in an *anti-poverty/anti-inequality* paradigm, (arguing in favor of a policy that would not be discriminatory against men and poor recent lone fathers). Second, they extended the eligibility to pregnant lone women. As abortion had been decriminalized by law the year before, the anti-abortion deputies pleaded - according to a very strong *christian angelist* reframed in a very strong *anti-demarriage* paradigm, partly supported by an *healthy citizen pro-natalist* rationale - for such an eligibility that could prevent some abortions that would be sought out by impoverished women. Deputies also extended the length of eligibility when there were children under three. According to the *proper citizen* reframed in an *anti-absent father* paradigm, some estimated that young children age needed their mother at home, especially when their father was "absent", in order to avoid becoming anti-social teenagers and adults. According to the rationale of the *healthy citizen-antipoverty* paradigm, the same deputies estimated that lone parents with very young children had particular handicaps going into the labor market and should be entitled to API until their children reach the age to attend *école maternelle*. But the *malthusian* rationale reframed in an *anti-dependency* paradigm prevailed against the deputies that opposed time-limits on eligibility for API that would guarantee it as long as lone parents did not have a job.

Following a *healthy citizen* rationale reframed in an *anti-poverty* paradigm, the French fiscal law grants special deductions in income tax to lone parents and even to former lone parents. But for the last few years there have been some attacks on these deductions. Some of them, following this same rationale, led to some means-tested (at a rather high level) limitations of these deductions. But the main attacks were based on the rationale of the *anti-demarriage* paradigm which emphasized the "perverse effects" of deductions that the cohabitant parents could use to pay less income tax than if they had been married. These attacks won partially, as the maximum amount of these deductions has recently been lowered again. But family movements and pressure groups using the *healthy citizen-antipoverty* rationale succeeded, at least for a while, in restoring the deductions for the "true" lone parents or formerly lone parents. As is often the case in France, it is the *healthy citizen-antipoverty* paradigm that overcame...

The case of the United States

The United States does not have a policy for lone parents as exists in France. It has no children or family allowance, and the tax systems provide no privileged position for lone mothers. Indeed a single parent with two children who made less than the official poverty line for a family of three pays income taxes in half the states and is exempt from income tax in the other half. There is, however, a special provision for lone mothers which is part of the social security system. But this privileged position for the children of lone mothers is restricted to widows and to women who have cohabited for many years. This is indeed an important program. The aggregate spending for children in social security is actually larger than the total spending for the AFDC program. Young people are considered to be children until the age of 25 and the Social Security system pays benefits while they attend higher education. But aside from social security programs, the major public debate about lone parents is focused on the welfare program known as Aid to Families with Dependent Children (ADFC). It is this program that has undergone the most turbulent re-framing of its mandate since it was created in the Social Security Act of 1936.

External shocks. First, the composition of the welfare caseload by and large shifted from a benefit for orphaned children whose fathers had died, to fatherless children whose mothers were never married. Of course, this change was largely due to the dramatic change in the family structure in which children reside. In 1995, among mother headed families, 2/5 of black women, 1/3 of Hispanics and 1/5 white mothers had never been married. In the same year 23% of all children reside in a lone parent household and half of all black children. For white women, the figures are not dramatically different than those in France and other European countries. What makes the American experience distinctive is the role that minority and black mothers play in the politics of welfare, since the public perception of the program was that it largely serves

106

unmarried black mothers. Thus the American Welfare program, unlike the experience of other countries, is uniquely identified with the politically charged issue of race.

The second major context change is the volatility of the caseload which has kept welfare reform in the center of the political stage. When the program first began in 1940 only 1 in 83 families received AFDC, but by 1960 the numbers increased to 1 in 38, still the numbers were very small. But from the mid 1960s to the mid 1970s the caseload more than doubled and so too did the numbers of female headed families with children. These numbers ignited an intense political response, stimulated by Conservative academic who saw in the figures a dramatic transformation of American family life as the anti-dependency and anti-fatherless family frames became the dominant political discussion. (This trend will be discussed further under challengers). Liberal academics soon responded by pointing out that between 1973 and 1984 the trend had virtually disappeared. The welfare caseload increased from 3.2 million to only 3.7 million, while the number of female headed families with children increased from 4.6 to 6.8 million and the value of welfare benefits in real terms had declined from $204 to $169 per recipient. Thus the effort to link welfare with the rise of mother headed families no longer had a firm empirical foundation. But the story does not end here. Between 1988-1994 the welfare caseload once again began to increase precipitously from 3.7 million to over 5 million. Again welfare reform was back on the political agenda leading to a period of state welfare reform legislation and then to the passage of the Personal Responsibility and Work Opportunity Reconciliation Act (PRWORA) of 1996. In anticipation of the new legislation which transformed welfare into a temporary program with time limits the welfare caseload between 1994 and 1998 decreased by almost half.

Obviously the size and growth rate and composition of these programmatic changes were an important source of the political disquiet that animated the controversy over welfare. But two other external factors also contributed to setting the terms of the debate. There was a quite remarkable shift in the working behavior of married mothers. While women always worked, the earnings of mothers was an important part of the income package of working class families. Mothers who headed their family always had little option but to work, since there were few available public resources that such families could draw on. But after WWII, what sharply changed was the working behavior of wives who were also mothers with young children. While wife-mothers participated in the shadow economy of taking in boarders to help stretch income, now a new pattern emerged. More than two-thirds of mothers with young children had entered the paid labor force. This was an important norm shift that had an obvious spill over on fatherless families. If wives with young children worked, why shouldn't solo mothers be expected to do the same? In addition to the norm shift brought about by working wives, the political demand for welfare reform was also triggered by a concern with questions of fairness as issues of equality between the working and non working poor families surfaced.

Internal Moral Dilemmas and the Challengers. The major internal moral dilemmas that surfaced from the debate was whether rising caseloads were linked to the growth of mother headed families. Welfare legislation in the original Social Security Act was designed to make sure that children were not separated from their parents solely for reasons of poverty. The program made available, largely to widowed mothers, an unrestricted cash grant to enable a poor mother to take care of her own child in her own home without working. The anti-poverty frame was accepted as the best guarantor of the development of healthy children. However the program was not intended to increase the number of poor mother headed families, instead it was seen as a way of alleviating the economic plight of these mothers and their children. But conservative academics like Glazer, Murray and Mead argue that the unintended effects of doing good lead to a perverse situation where the programs to alleviate poverty perpetuated it by creating the very conditions it sought to relieve. The image of marriages dissolving to enter welfare, or illegitimate children were being conceived so that young women can enter welfare was aggressively asserted by conservative scholars who tried to influence public opinion with a disturbing symbol of a welfare system cast adrift in a sea of good intentions which led primarily to negative byproducts. Liberals rejoined with the argument that "We have seen that this theory, while plausible, was ultimately wrong: significant numbers of low income, female heads - black and whites - were there all along". They argued that what had changed in the liberal climate of generosity and compassion in the period between 1960 and 1973 when the caseload rose from 0.8 million to 3.2 million, was administrative practice norms of acceptable behavior. Access to the welfare system had opened as more people applied (a norm change) and of those who applied more were accepted (administrative practice). We can appreciate that the argument about whether welfare causes family breakup was not the only issue that the public was responding to, it was the view that welfare, especially for the black family had become a way of life. The average black family *entering* welfare during the 1970s, would remain on the rolls 5.3 years, while all those *receiving* welfare at a point in time, would remain on welfare for an average of 10.2 years.

A variety of legislative strategies were followed to try to reverse the trend and to decrease the size of the welfare case load. Briefly, personal social services were pursued as the first such strategy, when in 1964 it was argued that caseloads could be decreased by providing welfare clients casework to women who needed help to improve their personal functioning. The use of social work as a strategy for decreasing case loads failed as welfare continued to increase. Faith is a service approach continued, instead of social work services what was proposed, was training and job placement assistance. This was followed by an incentive program known as "thirty and one-third" designed to provide economic incentives to make it attractive for women to leave welfare and work. Recipients were permitted to keep the first 30 dollars that they earned, and one third of the remaining earnings up to a ceiling. But neither penalties, nor services nor incentives proved to be a viable approach for dealing with the rising case loads. What followed then was an administrative reform designed to reduce the caseload by decreasing the error rate of administering the programs. But the search for new approaches to tame the unwieldy fluctuations in caseloads continued unabated.

The most recent welfare reforms were based on an interpretation of lone mother on welfare as a problem of moral hazard. The new legislation mandates that women work within two years and that they could only receive five years of welfare during their lifetime. The new direction of welfare policy represents a sharp break with the past. It may be useful to try to clarify the logic underlying these changes. The new legislation views the problem of welfare as a moral problem, where lone mothers create the conditions necessary to assure their entitlement to benefits. Moral hazard can always be expected in insurance or guarantee programs, although even here the pervasiveness of the problem remains an open empirical question. In the case of welfare programs, the moral hazard can range from participants who actively exploit rules of the system to those who simply search less hard for employment to those who fail to report supplementary income. Most liberals now concede that lone mothers must find a way of augmenting their income from boyfriends, or relatives or contributions from the child's father or irregular and illegal work. Moral hazard issues can be explored in three areas, first, the evolution of political views and conflicts concerning it; second, an assessment empirically of its extent; third, the redesign of programs to meet better the multiple goals of welfare programs.

Politically, there are deeply divided opinions and values concerning moral hazard. Consider three views. There are those who perceive moral hazard as the main reason contributing to spurts of growth which have periodically occurred in welfare programs. They have tried to redesign welfare programs to eliminate it. Others are concerned primarily with the decline of opportunity for low-skill workers. They believe that lone mothers who are workers should work only in good jobs with good pay or should not work in order to take care of their children. These observers would overlook moral hazard if the welfare programs allow people to avoid bad jobs. A variant of this view is that the moral hazard does not even exist – that it amounts to blaming the victim for the lack of opportunity.

Corresponding to the division of opinion about the policy weight to attach to moral hazard is a lack of information on its extent. Now with a substantial change in American welfare programs, it is possible to reassess the magnitude of moral hazard. It is now generally conceded that most lone mothers even with young children can work, if they are required to do so. The new debate now centers not on whether these lone mothers on welfare can get a job, in the tight American labor market of the 1998, but whether they are motivated and have the skills to hold a job that they manage to get. Anecdotal evidence suggests that the recent welfare reform has been associated with a substantial change in work and work attitudes by welfare recipients. Of course, the reform has been implemented in a time of prosperity and job creation. But the experience seems to suggest that the changes are getting people to work who had previously avoided it.

If moral hazard is empirically a significant phenomenon, then it is worth rethinking the design of welfare programs. Suppose that current welfare reforms aimed at restricting participation are more powerful in getting people to work than earlier work incentives. This leaves the problem of people working, but still receiving low income. The policy options in this area are not new, but there may be new ways to incorporate them into a now reformed American welfare system. The option we

110

have adapted in practice is income supplementation conditional on work. This approach is more like the Swedish model, where entitlement to a range of benefits from vacations to unemployment depends on being at work. Benefits are work conditioned, entitlement depends on having and holding a job, rather than on the basis of current economic need. One form of this has, indeed, become a major feature of the American system through the Earned Income tax Credit, but there may be other possibilities. Work comes first and it is then supplemented by other benefits which make it possible for those at work not to be poor.

Another option involves training to get people into jobs with higher pay. However, training organized by the welfare system has itself had moral hazard problems. It raised expectations about jobs without necessarily delivering, perhaps inducing participants to remain longer on welfare. In the politics of welfare work comes first, and training is available only after receiving a job, and then only on a limited basis for short term training. The changes introduced in the American welfare system are forcing all parties to rethink the way welfare "ought" to be designed.

Conclusion

The welfare reform policy in the United States illustrates the power of the "anti-dependency" paradigm as the overwhelming dominant theme for dealing with lone mothers. Conservatives made a determined effort to make the "anti-demarrage" paradigm the central initiative of public policy for lone mothers. This was a conflict largely among conservative sponsors. A coalition of religious organization in concert with conservative think tanks argued that the single largest threat to society was the problem of illegitimacy and the weakening of the institution of marriage as the appropriate setting for sex and child rearing to be addressed by a family cap, which cut mothers off welfare if they had a second illegitimate child. The problem of long term dependency and the failure of welfare recipients to work was only a lesser evil. They launched an aggressive campaign which in the end failed to be accepted on the national agenda. The story of a contest that did not lead to dominance is interesting and worth briefly recounting here.

Illegitimacy was a particularly divisive issue within the Republican party. For some conservatives illegitimacy was the most serious threat to society. Why? Because it was interpreted as the root cause of welfare

111

dependency, crime and violence. Hence "illegitimacy, not mandatory work, needed to head the Republican on welfare reform". (Haskins 1998, p 30) This was the worse evil that needed to be addressed. The sponsors of this competing frame included organizations like the Christian Coalition, The Family Research Council, The Heritage Foundation and many others. Of course, the private, philanthropic foundations sponsored research designed to show that AFDC contributed to and was associated with illegitimacy. Liberal researchers responded by showing that an association between two variables cannot be interpreted as empirical evidence of a causal link. But the argument does not depend on resolving the scientific and technical debate about causality, since the underlying issue was without doubt a moral question. It is wrong to have sex outside of marriage and to give birth to children that the parents could not afford to support. The preservation Christian morality about sexuality and marriage was the central issue, even if this position ran against changing norms and behavior by young people.

But the more difficult question was what specific action to remedy the situation should be proposed. What was the lesser evil that needed to be accepted to resolve the supreme evil of illegitimacy. Charles Murrray who wanted to make illegitimacy as the central issue in the welfare debate, advocated the most radical solution to combat this supreme evil. He wanted to "cut children off all welfare benefits for the duration of their childhood". This proposal for welfare reform came to be know as the "family cap". This solution was rejected, perhaps largely because it seemed to harsh a penalty to impose of children, who were victims of the environment in which they were born. While compassion may have receded in the new balance between personal responsibility and social obligation, but as the family cap debate shows, it was not totally out of fashion. But if the family cap was not accepted, no one knew any other less stringent policies "that were capable of increasing sexual abstinence as the way to reducing pregnancy, or promoting marriage" (Haskins p 31 and p 11).

Nevertheless the new legislation does contains a host of provisions, that make it clear that the issue of de-marriage has by no means died on the political agenda. Consider only a partial list of the numerous programs in the new legislation designed to provide performance bonus to states for reducing illegitimacy, abstinence education which rejects the safe sex message and, perhaps most important, continued experimentation by state, already 20 states have introduced experimental "family caps" which were rejected by the national legislation. There is little doubt that Christian morality with its definition of de-marriage as the worst evil is still alive and thriving, even if it did not rise to displace the dominant frame of work comes first in the American welfare reform.

Why did the anti-illegitimacy fail to win national support. A partial answer is that the moral position would have created a serious split between law and public opinion; and the scientific argument to support the moral position created a serious split among the community of scholars. For the sponsors of this frame the only morally correct position is abstinence. The problem, of course, is that this position conflicts with the prevailing social norms, which maybe ambivalent about the moral question, but clear that from the perspective of behave, pre-marital sex, contraception and abortion are acceptable. The changing social norms undermined a serious moral debate in the public sector.

The intellectual justification was provided by policy intellectuals and entrepreneurs based in conservative think tanks. There are three main elements in the argument they advanced. First, illegitimacy is the root cause of dependency, and other problems such as , drugs, crime, delinquency. Whatever is the scientific evidence the argument appealed to the general public who could readily accept the intuition that guaranteed and generous contributed to illegitimacy. Second, white illegitimacy is now approaching the rate that blacks held twenty five years earlier. Hence there is a social threat that a white underclass is emerging. Charles Murray developed this argument in a very influential op-ed article that appeared in the Wall Street Journal. The argument was exported to Britain where it also had a significant impact on a receptive conservative audience, sympathetic to the position. Third, lone parenting has a negative effect on the cognitive development of young children.

It is important to say that the "anti-demarriage" paradigm only failed to lead to become the dominant frame, but it did indeed lead to a reframing and in a significant way it became an important component of the lesser evil anti-dependency frame. Many provisions in the final welfare law were designed to combat rising illegitimacy.

There are perhaps three main reasons why the contest did not lead to reframing of the anti-dependency definition of the worse evil. First. there was a conflict between morality and compassion. The family cap may have contributed to a reduction in illegitimacy, but it would have challenged an equally important value of compassion for the children who would have lost economic resources, that is central to the "anti-inequality" paradigm. There is an obvious conflict of aims in trying to alter the behavior of the mother, but also protecting the interest of the child. Secondly, the intellectual justification depended on an academic debate, which favored the liberal position. There is no scientific doubt that there is only a statistical association between dependency and illegitimacy but no causal relationship. But conservatives were not concerned about the lack of consensus in the social science literature as they advanced their strong claim about the evils of illegitimacy. The conservatives rested their justification for the emphasis on illegitimacy largely on public judgment and on weak evidence of a negative impact of illegitimacy on mothers and children. So both the value and intellectual arguments were ambivalent and weak and this contributed to the failure to achieve a dominant reframing from dependency to illegitimacy.

Welfare policy for lone mothers is based on the premise that work first before training, the emphasis being on finding a job rather than waiting for a good job. The work-first feature is one of the interesting innovations in the welfare reform plan, although it is too early yet to see the results.

While the two-year time limit is part of the work requirement, there is also a five-year lifetime limit, which is intended to deal with long-term welfare dependency. Lone mothers on welfare have not yet reached their five-year limits. It is still too early to tell how serious a problem it will be to cut lone mothers off welfare when the limit is reached. If there is a crisis states may revise their policies. Thus, the outcome concerning the future treatment of lone mothers without economic resources will depend on an implementation process that is not yet complete.

References

Goodin, Robert & al. *The Real Worlds of Welfare Capitalism*. Cambridge University Press, 1999, p. 6.

Johnson, David Cay, "3 More States Stopped Taxing Poorest Families in '97 , Study Says". *The New York Times*, April 13, 1998.

Lefaucheur, Nadine, "Qui doit nourrir l'enfant de parents non mariés ou démariés?" & "La société française et le traitement des naissances hors mariage: de l'angélisme au patriotisme", in Nadine Lefaucheur & Claude Martin (eds). *Qui doit nourrir l'enfant dont le père est "absent"? Rapport de recherche sur les fondements des politiques familiales européennes (Angleterre, France, Italie, Portugal)*. Research funded by the Caisse nationale d'allocations familiales, Paris, 1995, pp. 9-44 & 125-143.

Levy, Frank, *The New Dollars and Dreams: American Incomes in the Late 1990's*. The Russell Sage Foundation, 1998.

Montesquieu, *De l'esprit des lois*, Paris, Flammarion, 1979, p. 106.

Schon, Donald A., & Martin REIN. *Frame reflection. Toward the Resolution of Intractable Policy Controversies*. New York, Basic Books, 1994.

Thery, Irène, *Le démariage: justice et vie privée*. Paris, Odile Jacob, 1993.

2.4 Work incentives in single parent families

Katja Forssén and Mia Harkovita

Introduction

In the past twenty years there has been a significant growth in the number of single parent families in all OECD countries (Bradshaw et al 1993; Whiteford and Bradshaw 1994; Duncan and Edwards 1997; Lewis et al 1997). The increasing diversity of family life puts greater pressure on the capacity of families to earn an income and to provide social care. This development has been associated with a shift in the composition of the low income population, and has posed new challenges to systems of social security. The number of single parent families has increased in parallel with transfers spent on this group. This has led in some quarters to questions about the effects of the benefit system on single parents' incentives to participate in the labour market, as well as incentives for individuals to become or stay single parents. (Whiteford and Bradshaw 1994.) In the liberal welfare states and in particular in the US, people hold strong views about the possible disincentive effects of taxes and transfers. At the time of the latest recession in Europe, the rhetoric of work disincentives and welfare dependency started to gain support also in the Scandinavian countries among some politicians and citizens.

Single parent families have very often been taken as an example of a group which tends to be dependent on state income support. This dependency of single parents on state welfare is seen as pathological by those who defend the so called dependency culture theory (Hernnstein and Murray 1994; Murray 1984). According to this theory dependency results from free and deliberate choices of the claimants and, therefore, if somebody is to be blamed for the situation it is the beneficiaries themselves. However, many reasons can be identified for the economic problems of single parent families. The head of the single parent family is often young, poorly educated and female, which makes the family more vulnerably to social risks. Poorly educated and young people are often in a weak position on the labour market. Women's incomes are also lower than men's. Changes in employment patterns tend to widen the gap between the incomes of dual-earner, one-earner and no-earner households. The clearest link between changes in family structure and the development of new forms of poverty lies in the circumstances of single parent families. Single parent families run a very high risk of poverty (Burkhauser et al 1988; Smeeding et al 1988; Millar 1992; McLanahan et al 1993). Single parents can be viewed as a highly disadvantaged group in terms of their resources which include money, time and social networks (Hobson 1994).

The problem of work disincentives is very often strongly associated with family policy. The main task of family policy is to provide benefits for families with children. This leads easily to situations where single parent families are economically better off when on welfare rather than working. However, modern family policies have also other than just economic aims. In the Scandinavian countries family policy has to a great extent focussed on enabling parents to combine the care of their children with working life. (Kamerman et al 1994; 1978; 1981.) This has been made possible by offering day care services for children, home care support for parents with children under 3 years and a child allowance for all children.

The aim of this article is to study work disincentives and their implications for single parent families. In this study we will answer the following questions: Have high income taxes and high day care fees been a disincentive to work? What are the effects of different transfer programmes on single parent families? The majority of previous studies have concentrated on hypothetical calculations. In addition to these calculations we investigate how single parents really behave in work disincentive situations. The outline of the paper is as follows. First we present an overview of theories dealing with work incentives and single parenthood. Then we will present our data. The empirical analysis is aimed at testing the work disincentive hypothesis by using data from Finland which has a Nordic type welfare state. The analysis is preceded by a brief description of the current family policy system in Finland. The empirical analysis will make use of micro-simulations and data from the

118

Finnish Living Conditions Survey (1994) in order to address the above questions. In the concluding section, the results are discussed on a more general level.

Two approaches to the welfare state, work incentives and single parenthood

Single parents are an interesting group from both an economic and a moral point of view. They are the focus of some of the most difficult issues faced by the modern welfare state, including theories on the relation between welfare benefits and work incentives. Concern has been expressed that welfare state benefits discourage people, especially single parents who are dependent on social provisions, from working.

It has been said that single parents are better off living on welfare and that due to lavish welfare provisions it does not pay to work. Economic dependency on public agencies is a prominent political issue particularly in the US and the UK. This discourse is linked to the underclass debate, which has its origins in conservative ideology.[1] It is argued that a certain proportion of the population deliberately choose passive dependence on benefits rather than self support. Single parents are seen as active agents in the creation of this underclass. They are said to choose to have children in order to gain benefits and when supported by the state, they choose not to work. (Murray 1984.) This so-called work disincentive approach assumes that the higher the level of social provision, the lower the incentives for an individual to become employed. A common thread running through this issue is the discussion on welfare dependency. 'Welfare dependent' is used as a synonym of 'welfare recipient', when it is assumed that recipients become dependent on the state by obtaining welfare. Although, the term dependency is nothing more than a synonym of long-term welfare use, it often has a pejorative connotation. Those who are dependent are inactive, ineffectual and even irresponsible in the eyes of the many. (Bane and Ellwood 1994; Gans 1995.) Yet, Murray (1984) argues, that the dependency on social security is due to the poor themselves. Dependency is a deliberate choice probably enhanced by the welfare state that somehow is an incentive to fail.

The issue of single parents in Nordic welfare politics in not the same as in the UK and the US (Stoltz 1997; Björnberg 1997). This re-

119

flects the way in which single parents are addressed in the legislation of these countries (Lewis et al 1997). As a result of gender neutral social legislation and the general aim of social policy, namely treating women equally regardless of marital status, stigmatization of single parenthood is rare in the Nordic countries. Instead of blaming single parents for their situation, they are portrayed as a social problem.[2] They do the best they can to make their living in unfavourable circumstances and they need help. Single parents need to be enabled to obtain paid work and to escape poverty and state dependency. (Duncan and Edwards 1997.) According to this approach, the incentives for single parents to enter the labour market go hand in hand with extensive public day care services and as well as with benefits linked to labour market activity (Lewis et al 1997). Therefore, the role of the welfare state as an incentive to supply labour is twofold. First, the welfare state has created work opportunities especially for women. Second, subsidised child care services have enabled women and single parents to enter the labour market. (Esping-Andersen 1990.) However, despite a relatively high level of employment among single parents, many of them receive public support in order to cope with daily living. This need for support is related to the low incomes of single parents.

Single parents are seen an instrumentally rational agents such as the ones that appear in neo-classical economic theory as utility maximizers. It is assumed that single parents make life decisions by calculating benefits: they examine the options they face, evaluate them according to their tastes and preferences, and in deciding which course of action to choose among those available, they are assumed to usually do what they believe is likely to have the best monetary outcome (see Elster 1989). Needless to say, this does not provide full understanding of the labour market behaviour of single parents. First, this approach is timeless. Decisions are made only for one period and there are no repercussions for the future. In reality, people usually assess their decisions in the long run. Second, values can be pursued just as rationally as any material interest (Hechter 1994; Hedström and Swedberg 1997). That is to say, people may behave irrationally from the economic point of view, but they may put more emphasis on values in their decision making. Thus, values are important factors affecting people's decisions concerning labour market participation. We can point out two aspects that are relevant in this context. On one hand, financial considerations are not the most important ones in making decisions regarding working. People work because their jobs are fulfilling in their own right, providing social esteem and a sense of social integration (Jahoda 1992; Gershuny 1994). On the other hand, the economic approach also offers little insight into the question of alternative rationality and women's right to choose caring activities. The combination of single motherhood and paid work is not easily understood through using economic rationality as a primary basis for human actions. Also, social and individual understanding of what is best and morally right are fundamental issues. (Edwards and Duncan 1996; 1997.) Every time a single parent thinks about returning to work, she has to consider whether she will earn enough to compensate for the costs of childcare and whether the work will still enable her to spend quality time with her children to compensate for the hours she will have to spend away from home. As Ford (1996) points out it must be accepted that some single parents will choose not to work despite any incentive provided to work. Ford found out that the biggest reason given for not working was that the children of single parents were young and needed a mother at home. From this point of view, in taking care of their own children, single parents may make a rational choice in the light of their individual preferences. Single parents give primacy to the moral benefits of caring for children themselves over the financial benefits of undertaking paid employment and their behaviour can be understood through 'gendered moral rationalities' (Edwards and Duncan 1996). Taking up paid work is seen as morally wrong and this is linked to male breadwinner ideology in the society.

Predictions about the impact of policy choices differ dramatically depending on what the origins of the problem are understood to be. The liberal view emphasises the importance of the economy and jobs, and conservatives the disincentive effects of the welfare system (Bane and Ellwood 1994). In many countries the concern for the incentive effects of welfare programmes has resulted in the introduction of policies designed to ensure that financial rewards from work are higher than the benefits that can be received outside the labour market. The welfare states are developing incentives for single parents to take up paid work as well as disincentives to stay on public support (Eardley et al 1996; O'Connor 1996). In the UK the earning disregards for single parents have been increased and also the eligibility criteria for benefits paid to those in work have been extended (Lewis 1997). In the Netherlands similar legislation has been passed and there are also prescribed sanctions for non-compliance with work seeking requirements (Eardley et al 1996). If it is

121

because of the welfare benefits that single parents are not working, then the elimination of financial aid would increase their labour force participation and eliminate dependency of social benefits. On the other hand, if welfare recipiency is a symptom of background disadvantages that lead to poverty and dependency, then reducing financial aid would not help much.

Data

This study focuses on work incentives and their implications for single parent families. We test the work disincentive hypothesis which assumes that the higher the level of social provision, the lower the incentives for an individual to get employed. In testing this hypothesis we will take Finland as an example. According to the work disincentive hypothesis, Finnish single parent families should be a good example of a group which faces the disincentive problem because of the universal and multiple family policy system that will be described in the next section. Provided that people are driven by financial utility calculations, we can expect to find a low labour force participation rate among single parents because of the high quality of benefits. The better the welfare benefits, the lower the work participation rate. This would support the work disincentive hypothesis according to which welfare systems increase the recipient's willingness to leave the welfare system because of the availability of state support.

We also study the effects of transfer programmes on single parent families. First, we locate possible disincentive traps. For this we use micro-simulations. Have high income taxes, income deductible housing benefit and high day care fees created work disincentives? The second aim of the article is to investigate how single parent families really behave in work disincentive situations. Do they work or do they live on the dole if that is economically more rewarding? Or does work have some value in itself? For this purpose we use data from the Finnish Living Condition survey collected in 1994 by the Central Statistical Office of Finland. The data was gathered from interviews and tax registers which were used mainly for income data. The sample size of the survey was 8650 Finns. First, we cross-check single parents' possible disposable incomes against what they would earn by working or by living on social benefits. To do this we use a special micro-simulation model. By using the Finnish Living Condition Data we check how single parents have actually behaved in those work disincentive situations. To what extent are they working or not? Single parents will be clustered in different groups according to their position in labour market and their disposable incomes.

Micro-simulation offers an analytical tool for assessing the redistributive potential of social security systems. At the same time, simulation has its limits. First, it is based on the model family approach and therefore it has involved collecting of information on a set of hypothetical family circumstances. However, the information micro-simulation gives us is used to compare the entitlements of families receiving benefits with the incomes of families in paid work. Second, the results of micro-simulation models can never explain the human behaviour effects brought about by the welfare benefits. Therefore in this study we have used both micro-simulation and the Living Conditions Data to find out how social security might have influenced single parents' labour market behaviour.

Family policy and work disincentives in single parent families

By introducing family policy systems during the twentieth century the state has in the Western countries to an increasing extent taken responsibility for the financial cost of children. These family policy systems consist of three ingredients - family legislation, social services and tax and transfer benefits - and each country has its own combination of cash benefits, tax reliefs or services in kind that provide support for families rearing children. (see Bradshaw et al 1993; Wennemo 1994.) Family policy is concerned both with the effects of all types of activities on the family and with the efforts to use the well-being of families as an objective or as a source of goals and standards in developing public policy. Family policy may be defined as a field in which certain objectives regarding the family are established and various policies and measures are developed to achieve these goals (Kamerman and Kahn 1978).

The way in which family policies have been developed in different countries depends partly on ideological backgrounds. There is a divide among the countries with regard to the issue of supporting families with children. In the Scandinavian countries, families with children are supported not only through income transfers but also through comprehensive social services. In the liberal and corporatist welfare states the standard of family policies is distinctly lower than in the Scandinavian countries. The notion that the responsibility for children's welfare belongs to the family has survived in both liberal and corporatist countries. This is reflected in tough means-testing of benefits and services and scarcity of individual social rights.

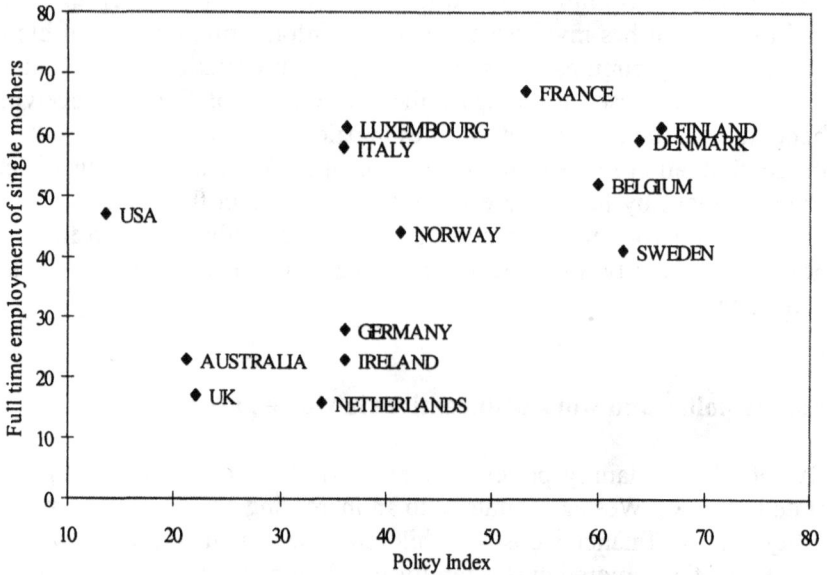

Figure 2.4.1   The level of benefits that enables single mothers to work full time

Source: Policy Index, Gornik et al 1998. Index that measure family benefits enabling the employment of mothers with children under three years old. Index value is structured by 0.50 [legislated job protection + (coverage) * (paid maternity leave)+ wage replacement rate + coverage + 0.50(paternity benefits)] + tax relief for child care + guaranteed child care coverage (0-2) + percent children (0-2) in publicly funded child care.

The number of authors have pointed out the effects of family policy on women's labour supply and employment patterns. There is some connection between womens' employment rates for women and family policy. In countries where family policy supports employment of women by producing services and in-work benefits the employment rates of single mothers are high. Figure 2.4.1 shows these cross-national differences in the family policies and single mothers' labour force participation rates.

As displayed in figure 2.4.1, there seems to be a positive correlation between benefit level and labour force participation. The higher the level of welfare benefits, the stronger the commitment to work (r=.88). This analysis therefore supports the work incentive theory: the better the benefits and services for single mothers the higher the labour force participation. The results indicate that in countries where benefits are generally generous single parents are more likely to participate in the labour market. All countries clustered in the upper right section have combined generous maternity benefits and legislative mandate to provide care for children (Gornik et al 1998). In France the importance of the commitment to family policies has promoted the employment of single parents (Martin 1995).

The evidence presented here, does not support the simple disincentive hypothesis. Welfare state benefits rather encourage work than cause unwillingness to work, because in countries with high quality social protection single parents tend to work. In other words, in countries with citizenship based benefits and services, single parents are likely to enter to the labour market. They are allowed to package incomes for other sources too and it reduces the barrier to work.

Presenting international comparisons at macro level many produce a distorted picture of the real situation at micro level. Moreover, it is hard to detect the process that create the association at macrolevel. Therefore, it is interesting to see, if the general patterns found at macro level operate at the micro level as well. In order to tackle these issues specific country studies are needed to unravel the possible poverty traps and work (dis)incentives built in the social security system. Here we focus on the Finnish experience. The Finnish case is interesting in two reasons. First, welfare provisions are rather extensive and this can be expected to have an impact on single parents' choices regarding welfare and work. Second, Finland displays a rather high female and also single parents' labour force participation rates. Therefore, Finland provides an interesting test case.

The structure of Finnish family policy

The family policy goal in the Nordic welfare state model is social integration, sought by maintaining high-quality public services that are reasonably priced and available to all who need them. Basic security is typically at a reasonable level, the state has a central role as a provider, and benefits are universal. All citizens are covered by the social security programs. A reasonable level of benefits is determined by minimum security on the one hand, and income-relatedness on the other hand. The state has a multi-faceted regulating role in society; it is used as an instrument that creates equality and social rights. In addition to the goal of equalizing the cost of having children across population groups, family policies are aimed at supporting the combination of work and family responsibilities and making it possible for women to work.

In order to provide the reader with a basic understanding of the institutional context where single parents are acting and making their decisions, we give a cursory account of the different benefit systems upon which parents can rely. The Finnish case is interesting in the sense that the country provides rather high welfare provisions which can thus be expected to have an impact on single parents' choices regarding welfare and work.

Finland has established a policy of obtaining gender equality and a better balance between work and family life. Young child policy is targeted overwhelmingly at children with working parents. The policy package assumes employment of parents, both as a source of eligibility for a rich package of benefits and as the basic source of income, once children are older than 3 years. (Kamerman and Kahn 1994.) Single parents' high labour market participation rate is one result of the above-mentioned principles of family policy. In the Scandinavian countries social benefits have been quite important in lifting single parents from pre-transfer poverty and improving the economic well-being of those above the poverty line (Smeeding et al 1988; Danziger et al 1995; Forssén 1998a), because benefits supplement rather than replace earnings.

The principal characteristic of family policy in Finland has been a strong commitment to improving and expanding the scope of care arrangements for young children. Children under eleven months are typically taken care of by their own mothers because mothers can take a rather long maternity leave with earnings-related compensation. *Mater-*

126

nity cash benefits represent a compensation for the costs arising from childbirth. Since 1985, the period for which the system compensates about 80 % of income loss, has been 263 days. Some collective bargaining agreements require that employers continue to pay wages to workers during part of the maternity leave. Although both parents are eligible for such benefits, the dominant share of days goes to mothers.

After maternity leave there are two alternative policy options available for families with children under three years: a public day care system or home care allowance. *Publicly provided day care* is organised and financed mainly by local authorities. Public involvement in child care has increased steadily in Finland during the last decades. The modes within the public day care system are the day care centres and family day care. The fees for public day care are income-related and parents pay fees based on rates decided upon in each municipality. In 1994 the daycare fees were divided into five different cost brackets: 385, 550, 825, 1100 and 1430 FIM per one child/ a month.[3]

The child home care allowance is aimed at facilitating the arrangement of day care for a child under three years of age. Child home care allowance is often paid to a mother who stays at home to take care of the child(ren). It is intended as an alternative to municipal day care. Home care allowances consists of three different parts: basic payment, additional means-tested payment and sibling supplement. The child home care allowance is taxable income. The basic payment is available to all families and additional means-tested payment is paid to families whose income falls below a specified level. When there are two or more children under school age in the family, the sibling supplement is received.

The other benefits for families with children are universal child allowance, maintenance allowance and income-tested housing benefits. *Child allowances* are paid for every person up to the age of 17. Its rate depends on the number of children eligible for child allowance in the family. The allowance is increased for each child in single-parent families. The child allowances are not subject to income tax. *The maintenance allowance*, also paid by the government, ensures child support payments to single parents in the absence of the other parent or other parent's failure to fulfil the maintenance obligation. *Housing benefits* are income-tested and are not subject to income tax. The housing benefit covers most of the housing costs when there is only one parent in a family.

In addition to these benefits which are targeted to families with children, there are other universal benefits for all citizens such as *unemployment benefit* and social assistance. Unemployment allowance is payable under two different schemes: the basic unemployment allowance scheme and the earnings-related unemployment allowance scheme. Basic flat-rate unemployment benefits are designed to ensure a minimum standard of living during unemployment. The earnings-related unemployment insurance funds are run by trade unions and benefits are paid only to fund members. This unemployment insurance is voluntary for individual employees in Finland. The benefits are calculated on the basis of previous earnings and the replacement rate for an average worker is usually 60 per cent of gross earnings.

A person or a family not receiving any kind of salary or social security benefits (or only very low compensation) may apply for *social assistance*. According to the law, all persons with a low income who cannot make ends meet in any other way are eligible for social assistance. This is a means-tested transfer, that has its historical roots in poor relief. The typical recipient of social assistance is a young adult or a single mother. Taking into account all households in the country, single parent families constituted the category which had the highest proportion of social assistance recipients: one third of all single parent households received social assistance in 1994. Time-series studies show that the rate of unemployment strongly affects the rate of social assistance recipiency. Social assistance also seems to act as a substitute for unemployment insurance benefits (Living allowance 1994).

Disincentive traps in the system

The level of incomes and benefits of single parents can be measured in a number of ways. This analysis has looked at the disposable incomes and replacement ratios in single parent families. Disposable incomes consist of total earnings and social transfers from which taxes have been deducted. By using micro-simulation we have inspected how the income tax and social security contributions and social service fees provide disincentives for single parents to participate in the labour market. Incentives have been evaluated by comparing earned income and in-work benefits with the benefits paid outside the labour market. At the intervals where the marginal change of disposable income is negative or constant, the family might face a work disincentive situation. In evaluating work incentives, replacement ratios are also good indicators. Benefit replacement rates are usually calculated by comparing the levels of out of work benefit income with some measure of income from work (Esping-Andersen 1990; Eardley et al 1996; Whiteford and Bradshaw 1994). Benefit replacement rates indicate what percentage of earnings is replaced by benefits. One measure used to detect potential incentive problems is the relation to the gross replacement rate, that is, the benefits received in relation to the income before tax when working. The net replacement rate is a more realistic approach because housing benefits and child care costs are also included in the calculations. Replacement rates close to or above 100 per cent indicate an incentive problem where living on welfare benefits gives the same income level as working.

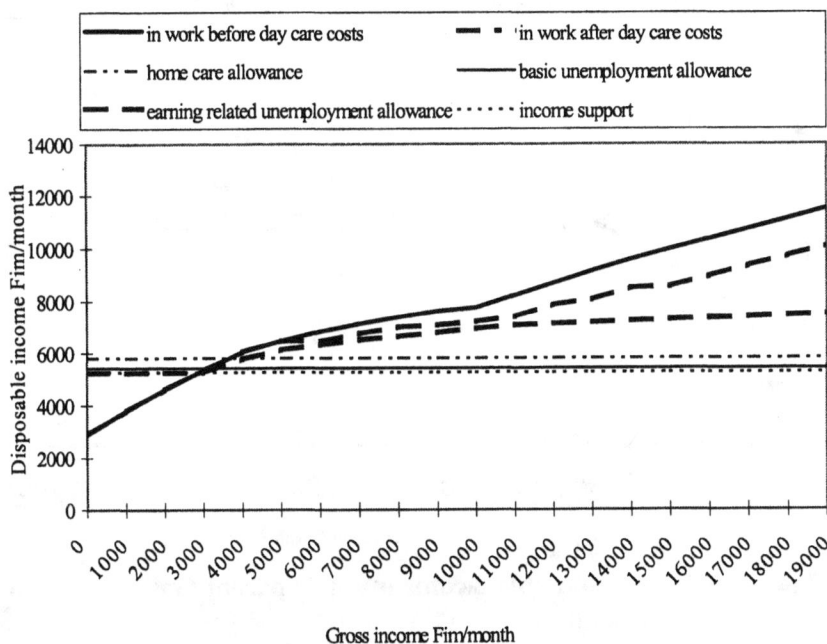

Figure 2.4.2   Disposable income in single parent family with one child

In single parent families with one child under three years of age, the disposable income when receiving income-related unemployment cash benefit, basic unemployment benefit or home care allowance is higher in low income level than disposable income from work (see figure 2.4.2). After taking into account the day-care fees paid as a consequence of higher earnings, the level of income at which it is financially worth working increases. If a working single parent has to pay for child care, the social security system provides disincentives to work even at very high income levels. The combined effect of extra taxes paid and benefits lost as a result of an increase in income leads to a poverty trap. The poverty trap arises from the interaction between the income test, other means-tested forms of assistance and the personal income tax system.

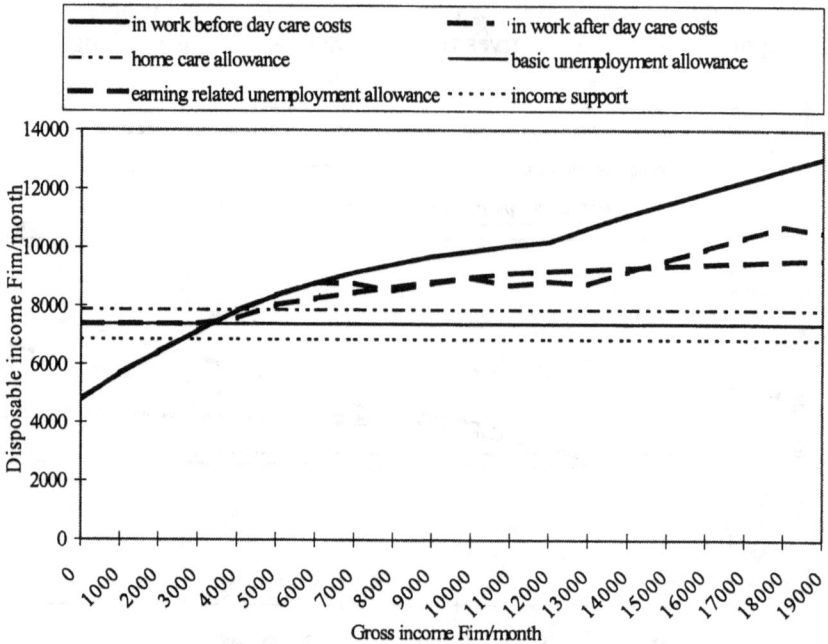

Figure 2.4.3   **Disposable income in single parent family with two children**

Figure 2.4.3 shows the situation of a single parent with two children under three and seven years of age. It is not financially worth working even at a very high gross income level. To gain the same disposable income from earnings rather than from earnings-related unemployment benefit, the gross income has to be twice as much as the average income of women, if the day care payments are taken into account. In the lower level disposable incomes do not increase because losses of the income deductible housing allowance and higher day care fees paid as a result of increase in income. It seems that taking into account the child care payments in middle income families, disposable income will actually decrease if the parent begins to work. Earnings-related unemployment cash benefits bring the strongest disincentives to both types of single parent families. This is due to the high level of compensation of housing costs through housing allowances for unemployed single parents. Housing subsidies are a significant component of the benefit package of unemployed single parent families and a move from unemployment to work can bring a sharp increase in the proportion of the rent which they have to pay and this acts as a disincentive to work. The effect of the size of the day care fees might indicate their distinct role in producing disincentives. This means that the day-care payments alone put middle income families in an income trap situation where any additional post-tax income will go directly to increased day-care payments. In many situations lack of co-ordination between income transfers and service fees creates a "perverse" situation where an increase in income causes in the end financial losses to the income earner. Also, the interaction effects of social security and taxation and the social services fees at the microlevel can lead to people being trapped in unemployment or recipiency of social benefits.

Replacement ratios are also used as indicators of potential income effects of benefits systems. These replacement rates tend to rise with the number of children. For single parent families with one child the replacement rates are lower than for a family with two children. Figure 2.4.4 contains the net replacement rates for single parent families with two children on different welfare benefits. Those net replacement rates are potentially high, being almost 100% in middle and high income families when unemployed and in receipt of earnings-related unemployment benefit. In low income families the highest replacement rates are on home care allowance.

As mentioned above, modern Scandinavian family policy has several, often contradictory functions. Family policy packages have distinct and explicit objectives. Some are clearly related to education, housing, health and child care policy. Others are more generally related to a vision of family life or the role of women in the labour market. Because the functions are varied and sometimes contradictory, disincentive situations can be found when regarding the system as whole. Income-based benefits together with income-tested housing allowance, income based day-care fees and home care allowance can very easily lead to disincentive situations. This disincentive problem occurs especially in single parent families.

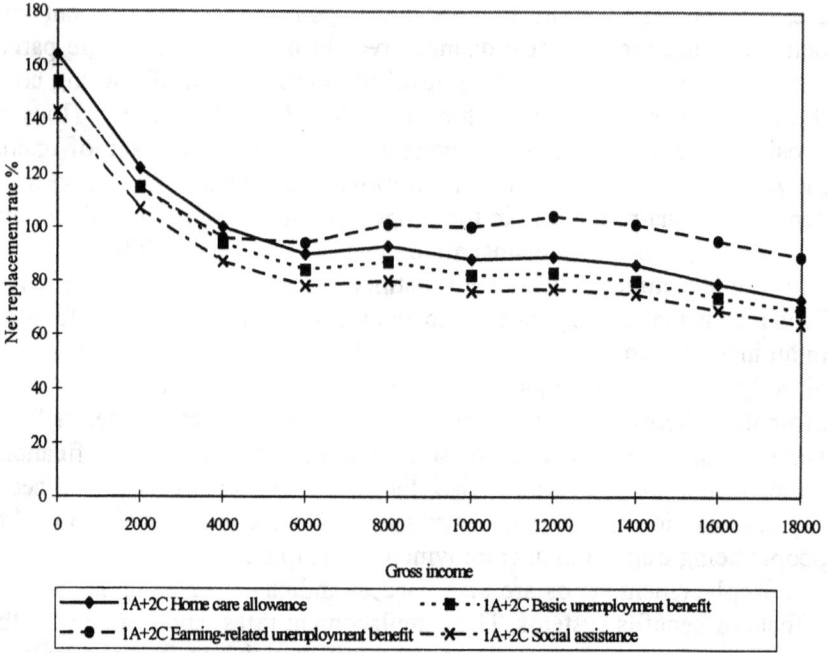

Figure 2.4.4   Net replacement rates in single parent family with two children

1A+2C One adult and two children, one under 3 years of age, other under 7 years of age

Work chosen despite better benefits

In the previous chapter we have described the social security scheme and how it in theory produces disincentives to work for single parent families. The central issue regarding welfare benefits and labour market behaviour is also an empirical one. Benefits might have effects which are negative with regard to the income level in the labour market and evidence is needed to determine the effects on the labour market behaviour of single parents. The question is: do welfare benefits have an effect on labour market behaviour? The mere existence of social provisions that act as a disincentive to work does not imply that persons entitled to such benefits do not work

Table 2.4.1 Relation of the number of children, age of the youngest child, family type, age of parent and vocational training to percent of social transfers out of households' disposable incomes (Multiple Classification Analysis)

	N	Eta Unadjusted deviations	Beta Adjusted deviations
Grand mean		28.88	28.88
Number of children***		0.07	0.02
1	1244	-1.38	-.61
2	1221	-1.82	-.46
3 or more	584	6.73	2.26
Age of the youngest child***		0.29	0.29
0 - 2 –years	808	22.09	22.04
3 - 6 –years	726	-3.78	-3.29
Over 6 years	1515	-9.97	-10.18
Family type***		0.06	0.09
Two parent family	2797	-.90	-1.22
Single parent family	252	10.00	13.53
Age of parent*		.17	0.08
15-24 years	66	46.52	22.86
25-44 years	2309	1.05	-1.11
Over 44 years	674	-8.14	1.57
Vocational training***		0.13	0.13
Vocational school	1118	2.88	2.37
Vocational college	685	-.57	-1.28
University	441	-13.89	-13.35
No vocational training	805	4.10	5.12
Multiple R^2			0.113

A positive deviation from the grand mean indicates increasing amount of social transfers out of households' disposable incomes. Asterisks indicate the statistical significance of the differences. *p < 0.05; **p < 0.01; ***p < 0.001.

In this chapter we will test the work disincentive hypothesis. How do single parents really behave in different work incentive /disincentive situations? We begin by showing how social transfers are targeted at different groups and by indicating the groups in which the disincentive

133

problems are strongest. After that we will examine this group's work behaviour and within this group we will make comparisons between different family types and between those who are working and those who are unemployed.

Table 2.4.1 shows groups at which social transfers are mostly targeted. The mean of the amount of social transfers as a proportion of child households' disposable income is about 29 percent. The groups that have most social transfers as a proportion of disposable income are families with children under 3, young parents and single parent families. This indicates that the work disincentive problems occur most probably in these groups. In figure 2.4.5 we have compared single parents' and two parent families' unemployment rates because unemployment is one of the most obvious factors which increases the use of social transfers. The unemployment rate for single parents with at least one child between 3 and 6 years is three times higher than the unemployment rate among two parent families. The unemployment rate for two parent families is almost the same in spite of the age of the youngest child; on the other hand the unemployment rate for single parents is first very low, the rate increases when the child is 3-6 years old, and decreases remarkably when the child starts school.

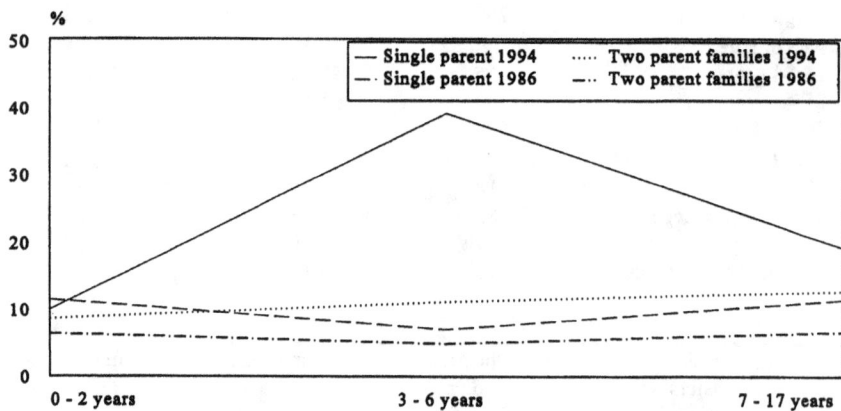

Figure 2.4.5   **Unemployment of single parents and two parent families in 1986 and 1994**

Both two parent families and single parents with a child under 3 years of age behave differently in the labour market than families with children over 3 years because of the home care allowance. The majority of single parents with children under 3 years of age (52 %) are at home, 35 % are economically active and 10 % are unemployed. This can be explained by the principal tasks of our family policy. One of the main principles of family policy is to make it possible for parents to choose between employment and taking care of the child by themselves. The result is that almost half of the single parents choose to stay at home. This indicates the attractiveness of home care allowance. The popularity of home care allowance implies that married as well as single mothers tend to stay at home when the children are under three years of age. This trend is also evident in labour force statistics. In the case of women aged 20-39 the labour force participation rates have dropped and the number of women engaged in household duties has increased (Ilmakunnas 1997).

As regards data for 1994, the fact that the unemployment rate among single parents' is four times higher when the youngest child is 3 - 6 years old can indicate that this group is behaving as the work disincentive hypothesis assumes. The families with children over three years of age are no more eligible to the home care allowance and parents have to decide whether they will return to the labour market. This assumes that single parents go on the dole because it is economically a better solution than going to work and paying high day care fees. There are other explanations, too. High unemployment rate among single parents with children over three years of age indicates that at the time of the high unemployment there were no work opportunities available to poorly educated single parents. Single parents had to be registered as job searchers, but work opportunities were minimal. This explanation is further supported by the Living Condition Survey from 1986. At that time the unemployment rate in Finland was low. In the 1986 data there were no statistically significant differences in unemployment rates with regard to family structure and the age of children. In 1986 single parents' unemployment rate was 11,4 % when the child was under 3 years old, 6 % when the child was 3 to 6 years old, and 10 % when the youngest child was over six years old. There were no significant differences in unemployment rates between family types. This finding affirms that single parents constitute one of the groups that suffered from the economic recession more than others. They can be said to be victims of the recession. It seems that the higher unemployment risk of single parent families with small children is connected more generally to problems of life cycle, together with problems caused by the lack of the other parent in the family. It is said that single parents with young children are discriminated against by employers because the risk that they are absent (because of children's sickness) is greater than with employees from two parent families' and because they are not able to be work flexible hours.

According to calculations based on micro-simulation, single parents are very often in work disincentive situations. Single parents' wages are lower than the average because of their young age and low education level. In our data only 14 % of employed single parents had a higher income level than what they would have got when unemployed. This means that most (86 %) of the employed single parents are working despite the fact that the same or higher disposable income could be received through benefits. One could say that these persons are behaving irrationally from an immediate economic point of view. On the other hand they might be behaving rationally if we evaluate their behaviour in the long run. As the work incentive hypothesis assumes, earnings-related welfare benefits encourage people to work and people are motivated to work in order to qualify for better benefits.

Single parents' higher unemployment risk is analysed in detail by comparing unemployed single parents with other family types by demographical variables and variables connected to values held. In table 2.4.2 we have first compared single parent families with two parent families and there are clear differences between these two family types. Single parent families are less educated, have fewer children and live more often in urban areas and in rented flats than two parent families. The importance of family seems to be greater to two parent families. Only 65 % of single parents named their family as the most meaningful area in their lives; 27 % indicated work to be the most meaningful area in their lives. Work means more to single parent families than to mothers in two parent families, even though conception of work seems to be similar in both groups. The high value of work explains single parents' interest in participating in the labour market even in situations where work disincentives are very strong.

Single parents' unemployment risk is not concentrated in certain groups because unemployed and employed single parent families do not differ from each other at all. Because of unemployment, unemployed single parents are in a worse economic situation than employed single

136

parents. Comparison between unemployed single parent families and employed two parent families gives the same result as comparison between single parent and two parent families as a whole. It seems that the bulk of the differences is connected more often to family structure than to unemployment. The fact is that unemployment affects more often single parent families (occurrence of unemployment is higher among them) and especially those single parent families which have children under school age.

All in all it seems that results do not give strong support the work disincentive hypothesis. Our study identified a number of cases where there are some incentive problems in the Finnish social security system. Although there are quite a few work disincentive traps, single parents prefer to work. The majority of employed single parents are working, in spite of the fact that their disposable incomes would be the same or even higher if they were unemployed. Unemployment has not hit any special group among single parent families particularly hard, except single parents with children between the ages of three and six. The fact that the unemployment rate is four times higher in this group than in other groups can be explained by the effects of the recession. The economic recession reduced the number of vacancies and jobs requiring only primary level of education (Education and Earnings 1994). It is also said that employers discriminate against single parents with small children because they have a higher risk of being absent than other employees (Ford 1996).

These findings indicate that single parents are not 'voluntarily' unemployed, that is to say that they prefer to work but there are no work opportunities available to them. In other words, this group is not behaving as the work disincentive hypothesis assumes. Reasons for their higher unemployment rate are connected to structural factors within the society and to the effects of the recession.

Table 2.4.2 Comparison between unemployed single parent families and other family types in life satisfaction, values of life and some background variables

	Single parent family	Two parent family
Vocational training		
No	36.2 (90)	25.8 (630)***
School	36.7 (91)	36.9 (901)
College or university	27.1 (68)	37.2 (910)
Age		
Below 35	38.8 (96)	33.3 (814)
35 or more	61.2 (152)	66.7 (1627)
Number of children		
One	59.5 (148)	39.8 (971)***
Two or more	40.5 (100)	60.2 (1450)
Type of municipality		
City or town	75.2 (186)	60.7 (1482)***
Small municipality	24.8 (62)	39.3 (939)
Type of housing		
Owns a house or an apartment	42.8 (106)	81.5 (1971)***
Lives in rented flat	57.2 (142)	18.5 (450)
Life satisfaction		
Economic situation is worsen	50.2 (124)	49.9 (1216)
Lack of money to buy food	62.8 (154)	32.2 (780)***
There has been some negative life events	40.1 (99)	19.0 (464)***
I am satisfied with my life	89.5 (222)	93.6 (2279)*
Description of work		
I work just to get money	12.4 (19)	11.5 (206)
My work has no variety	8.1 (13)	8.5 (154)
My work is light	54.4 (84)	63.8 (1154)*
I cannot use my skills at work	4.2 (6)	5.1 (91)
My work is never too difficult	97.9 (152)	93.6 (1697)
The value of family		
Home means family children and love	44.7 (111)	67.3 (1642)***
Home means a place of safety	35.2 (87)	14.4 (352)***
Family is the most meaningful thing in my life	64.8 (97)	81.6 (1433)***
Work is the most meaningful thing in my life	27.2 (41)	14.0 (246)***

Asterisks indicate the statistical significance of the differences.
* $p<0.05$
** $p<0.01$
*** $p<0.001$

Unemployed single parent family	Employed single parent family	Employed two parent family	Unemployed two parent family
38.0 (23)	31.3 (49)	23.2 (418)***	32.6 (96)
45.1 (27)	36.5 (57)	35.8 (645)	45.6 (135)
16.8 (10)	32.1 (49)	41.0 (740)	21.7 (65)
43.4 (26)	33.7 (52)	27.8 (502)**	39.9 (118)
56.6 (34)	66.3 (103)	72.2 (1302)	60.1 (177)
66.6 (39)	56.7 (88)	39.7 (716)***	38.1 (112)***
33.4 (20)	43.3 (67)	60.2 (1087)	61.9 (183)
80.0 (47)	72.6 (113)	39.6 (715)***	41.4 (122)**
20.0 (12)	27.4 (42)	60.4 (1088)	58.6 (173)
22.4 (13)	54.8 (85)***	86.1 (1553)***	71.6 (212)***
77.6 (46)	45.2 (70)	13.9 (250)	28.4 (83)
51.4 (30)	52.2 (81)	46.9 (846)	65.3 (192)
85.8 (50)	53.0 (82)***	26.1 (467)***	52.0 (151)***
42.3 (25)	38.4 (60)	18.3 (330) ***	24.5 (72)**
87.9 (52)	88.7 (138)	95.7 (1723)**	83.1 (243)
..	12.4 (19)	11.6 (206)	..
..	8.1 (13)	8.5 (154)	..
..	54.4 (84)	63.9 (1149)	..
..	4.2 (6)	5.0 (90)	..
..	97.9 (152)	93.6 (1687)	..
44.7 (26)	43.8 (68)	67.8 (1222)***	61.5 (181)**
41.6 (25)	32.8 (26)	13.0 (235)***	20.8 (61)**
..	64.8 (97)	81.6 (1433)	..
..	27.2 (41)	14.6 (1246)	..

Discussion

Two contradictory theories of the impact of welfare state programs on the willingness to work have been presented. The work disincentive theory maintains that if the state assumes responsibility for the economic well-being of single-parent families, parents will assume less responsibility. Higher incomes from welfare benefits will reduce the incentives of single parents to work and increase their reliance on public welfare. The other work incentive theory assumes that social policy is not constructed to violate the work ethic, but on the contrary was designed to promote labour market participation.

In this study, we have compared the financial incentives facing single parents which may influence their decisions to work. We have illustrated the issues by taking Finland, a member of the Nordic welfare state regime, as an example. Choosing Finland as a case study is justified on the grounds that the Finnish system of family policy covers a wide area and offers benefits and services of a high standard and level of generosity (Gornick et al 1996). Due to the broad range and coverage of Finnish family policies, they should serve as a good illustration of the dependency-creating and disincentive effects of welfare put forward in the discourse in the countries belonging to the liberal welfare regime. As pointed out in this study the relationship between the structure of the benefit system facing single parents and their individual behaviour is clearly not straightforward. Despite the generous welfare benefits in Finland, single parents are working even if they would receive higher disposable incomes through benefits. Many single parents benefit only slightly from working; this is especially true for many single parent families burdened with day care payments. These findings are in contrast to the widely held popular opinion that the welfare state has seriously damaged work incentives.

Single parents prefer work (see also Evanson 1998), but they might be unable to take up paid work, because of the poverty traps in the social security system. Therefore, the mechanism for delivering social welfare is an important factor affecting the labour market behaviour of single parents. Earnings-related welfare benefits encourage people to work because part of the welfare benefit is paid out in proportion to the recipients' prior earnings and people are motivated to work in order to qualify for better benefits. Earnings-related unemployment compensation as opposed to means-tested assistance may provide some incentives for individuals to go back to work so that they will be covered by social insurance also during the next period of unemployment (Atkinson and Micklewright 1991; Aronsson and Walker 1997).

Table 2.4.3 The economic situation of single parent families in different countries in 1990

Country	Amount of means tested benefits in single parents' income package	Single parents' dependency on social assistance	Index of welfare dependency*	Relative poverty rates for single parent families
Sweden	12	70	0.8	41
Finland	10.4	70.3	0.7	43
Denmark	17.7	66.7	1.2	87
Netherlands	43.7	68.5	3	255
Germany	18.1	33.9	0.6	197
United Kingdom	53.4	78.6	4.2	409
Australia	40.5	69.8	2.8	515
USA	37.9	62.7	2.4	583

(Amount of means tested benefits) (dependency on social assistance)/1000
Source: Luxembourg Income Study

However, income from employment is only part of the story. Despite the high labour force participation of single parents in the Nordic welfare states, single parents are dependent on social transfers, too.

Although poverty is relatively low among single parents in the Nordic countries as compared with other countries, dependency of single parents on means-tested benefits is common in all welfare regimes (table 2.4.3). This is due to a number of reasons: first, one income is usually not sufficient to guarantee a decent standard of living in a family with children. Second, most single parents are women and women are often engaged in low paid employment which means that their income is small. Third, single parent families in particular have been affected by increased flexibility on the labour market and by the proliferation of new forms of ("untypical") work (Evason 1998). This may mean interruptions in receiving wages, and higher expenditure on child care. These factors are a partial explanation of the heavy dependence of single parents on last resort social assistance in all welfare regimes.

This study which concentrates on the Finnish case has falsified the argument that social security makes the recipients passive and discourages them from working. It can be expected that these results would be obtained in all Scandinavian countries due to the very similar social security systems and high labour force participation rates among women. The discussion on the disincentive effects of social security has been particularly prominent in countries belonging to the liberal welfare regime. It is reasonable to assume that the debate should have been most acute in the Nordic countries where the level of social security is highest and the forms of family policy are most diverse. This, however, has not been the case. The nature of the debate is then probably more strongly linked to the ways in which social security has developed in different countries. As is evident from table 2.4.3, the combinations of benefits and incomes received by single parents are very different in different welfare states. In the US, the UK and Australia, over 40 percent of the incomes of single parents consist of means-tested benefits. The corresponding percentage for the Nordic countries is under 20. This may be the starting point for the differences in the discussions on the disincentive effects of welfare. When the social security system is based almost completely on means-tested benefits with a carefully selected recipient population and with most people not receiving any benefits, the functioning of the system is easy to criticise and the recipients are often stigmatized. In the Nordic countries, universal social security benefits guarantee everybody a decent livelihood as protection against social risks. In liberal welfare regimes, the conditions for receiving benefits are such that single parent households constitute the majority of benefit recipients. This fact has contributed to the focus on single parents and on the misuse of social security benefits by single parents.

The position of single parents in particular in countries with a liberal welfare regime is problematic. Single parents prefer to work, but earnings from work alone are not sufficient and they have to combine income from work and benefits in order to reach a reasonably high standard of living. On the basis of previous studies (Kahn and Kamerman 1983; Bradshaw et al 1993; Sainsbury 1996; Lewis et al 1997) it seems that single parents are likely to be best off where benefits for single parent families and children are on the whole generous. Single parents' welfare is greatest where they are allowed to combine income from work and social transfers.

Nevertheless, it must be accepted that some single parents will choose not to work despite the hardship they may experience or the incentives to work provided by the system (Ford 1996; Evanson 1998). They consider their role as a mother to be more important than their role as a worker for instance because they feel that their children need a mother at home. Single parents are also faced with a difficult balancing act between the demands of the labour market and child care.

Notes

1. The underclass theory posits that low income families live in spatially segregated areas where welfare dependency, female headed families, male joblessness and dropping out of high school are common. People in these families are assumed to suffer from behavioural deficiencies and to operate outside the mainstream of commonly accepted values. (Wilson 1987; see Roseneil and Mann 1996; Edwards and Duncan 1997).

2. Duncan and Edwards (1997) have divided the discourse on lone parenthood into four categories: lone motherhood as a social threat, as a social problem, as part of the lifestyle change, and as an escape from patriarchy.

3. The cost of childcare for families has increased substantially in the 1990s. In 1990, municipalities were given the power to decide the income limits for different income brackets for all but the so-called zero payment bracket. At the same time, the determination criteria were changed to being based on gross income rather than net income. As a consequence of this decentralization, 99 % of municipalities tightened their income brackets. (Forssén 1998b.)

References

Atkinson, A.B. - Micklewright, J. 1991. Unemployment Compensation and Labour Market Transitions: A Critical Review. *Journal of Economic Literature Vol. 24, 1679-1727.*

Aronsson, T. - Walker, J.R. 1997. The Effects of Sweden's Welfare State on Labour Supply Incentives. In Freeman, R.B.- Topel, R.- Swedenborg, B. (ed.) *The Welfare State in Transition. Reforming the Swedish Model.* The University of Chicago Press. Chicago.

Bane, M.J. - Ellwood, D.T. 1994. *Welfare Realities. From Rhetoric to Reform.* Harvard University Press. Cambridge.

Björnberg, U. 1997. Single Mothers in Sweden: Supported Workers who Mother. In Duncan, S. - Edwars, R. *Single Mothers in an International Context: Mothers or workers?* UCL Press. London.

Bradshaw, J. - Ditch, J. - Holmes, H. - Whiteford, P. 1993. *Support for children: a comparison of arrangements in fifteen countries.* HMSO. London.

Bradshaw, J.- Kennedy, S. – Kilkey, M. – Hutton, S. – Corden, A. – Eardley, T. – Holmes, H. – Neale, J. 1996. *The Employment of Lone Parents: A Comparison of Policy in 20 Countries.* Family Policy Studies Center. London.

Burkhauser, R. - Smeeding, T. - Merz, J. 1988. *Relative Inequality and Poverty in Germany and the United States Using Alternative Equivalence Scales.* Luxembourg Income Study. Working Papers No 117.

Danziger, S. - Smeeding, T. - Rainwater, L. 1995. *The Western Welfare State in the 1990's: Toward a new Model of Antipoverty Policy for Families with Children.* Luxembourg Income Study. Working Papers No 128.

Duncan, S. - Edwards, R. 1997. Introduction: A Contextual Approach to Single Mothers and Paid Work. In Duncan, S. - Edwards, R. (ed.) *Single Mothers in an International Context: Mothers or workers?* UCL Press. London.

Eardley, T. - Bradshaw, J. - Ditch, J. - Gough, I. - Whiteford, P. 1996. *Social assistnce in OECD-countries: Synthesis Report. Department of Social Security.* Research Report No. 46. HMSO. London.

Edwards, R. - Duncan, S. 1996. Rational Economic Man or Lone Mothers in Context? The uptake of paid work. In Bortolaia Silva, E. (ed.) *Good Enough Mothering? Feminist Perspectives on Lone Motherhood.* Routledge. London.

Edwards, R. - Duncan, S. 1997. Supporting the Family: Lone Mothers, Paid Work and the Underclass Debate. *Critical Social Policy 53, 29-49.*

Elster, J. 1989. *Nuts and Bolts for the Social Sciences.* Cambridge University Press. Cambridge.

Esping-Andersen, G. 1990. *The Three Worlds of Welfare Capitalism.* Princenton University Press. Princenton.

Evanson, E. 1998. Lone Parents in Northern Ireland: The Effectiveness of Work Incentives. *Social Policy & Administration (32)1, 14-27.*

Ford, R. 1996. *Childcare in the Balance. How Lone Parents Make Decisions about Work.* Policy Studies Institute. London.

Forssén, K. 1998a. *Child Poverty and Family Policy in the OECD-countries.* Luxembourg Income Study Working Paper, No 178.

Forssen, K. 1998b. Decentralization of Decision-making The case of Payment Policies for Children's Daycare. *Scandinavian Journal of Social Welfare (3) 7, 277-287.*

Gans, H.J. 1995. *The War Against the Poor: the Underclass and Antipoverty Policy.* New York Basic Books. New York.

Gershuny, J. 1994. The Psychological Consequences of Unemployment: An Assessment of the Jahoda Thesis. In Gallie, D. - Marsh, C. - Vogler, C. (ed.) *Social Change and the Experience of Unemployment.* Oxford University Press. New York.

Gornik, J. - Meyers, M. - Ross, K. 1998. Public Policies and the Employment of Mothers: A Cross-National Study. *Social Science Quarterly 1(79), 35-54.*

Hechter, M. 1994. The Role of Values in Rational Choice Theory. *Rationality and Society. 3(6), 318-333.*

Hedström, P. - Swedberg, R. 1997. Rational Choice, Empirical Research and the Sociological Tradition. *European Sociological Review 2(12), 127-146.*

Hernnstein, R. - Murray, C. 1994. *The Bell Curve. Intelligence and Class Structure in American life.* The Free Press. NewYork.

Hobson, B. 1994. Solo Mothers, Social Policy Regimes and the Logics of Gender. In: Sainsbury, D. (ed.) *Gendering Welfare State.* Sage Publications. London.

Ilmakunnas, S. 1997. *Female Labour Supply and Work Incentives.* Labour Institute for Economic Research. Studies 68. Hakapaino. Helsinki.

Jahoda, M. 1992. Sociala och Psykologiska Effekter av Arbetslöshet på 1930-talet. In Edwards, R. - Burawoy, M. - Jahoda, M. - Elster, J. (ed.) *Ideer om arbete.* Tidens

144

förlag. Stockholm.

Kahn, A.J. - Kamerman, S.B. 1983. *Income Transfers for Families with Children*. Temple University Press. Philadelphia.

Kamerman, S. - Kahn, A. 1978 (ed.). *Family Policy: Government and Families in Fourteen Countries*. Columbia University Press. New York.

Kamerman, S.B - Kahn, A.J 1981. *Child Care, Family Benefits and Working Parents. A Study in Comparative Policy*. Columbia University Press. New York.

Kamerman, S. B. - Kahn, A. J. 1994. Family Policy and the Under-3s: Money, Services and Time in a Policy Package. *International Social Security Review 47 (3-4), 31-43*.

Lewis, J. 1993. Introduction: Women, Work, Family and Social Policies in Europe. In Lewis, J. (ed.) *Women and Social Policies in Europe*. Edwar Elgar. Aldershot.

Lewis, J. and Hobson B. 1997. Introduction. In Lewis, J. (ed.) *Lone Mothers in European Welfare Regimes*. Jessica Kingsley Publishers. London.

Living allowance 1994. Statistics Finland . Helsinki.

Martin, C. 1995. Father, Mother and the Welfare State. Family and Social Transfers after Maritial Breakdown. *Journal of European Social Policy (5)1, 43-63*.

McLanahan, S.S. - Garfinkel, I. 1993. Single Mothers, the Underclass and Social Policy. In Wilson W.J. (ed.) *The Ghetto Underclass. Social Science Perspectives*. Sage. Newsbury Park.

McLanahan S.S. - Sandefur, G. 1994. *Growing up with a Single Parent. What Hurts, what Helps*. Harvard University Press. Cambridge.

Millar, J. 1992. Lone Mothers and Poverty. In Glenningar, C. - Millar, J. (ed.) *Women and Poverty in Britain the 1990s*. Harvester Wheatsheaf. Hertfordshire.

Murray, C. 1984. *Losing Ground. American Social Policy 1950-1980*. Basic Books. New York.

O'Connor, J. 1996. From Women in the Welfare State to Gendering Welfare State Regimes. *Current sociology (44) 2, Summer 1996*.

Roseneil, S. - Mann, K. 1996. Unpalatable Choices and Inadequate Families. Lone Mothers and the Underclass Debate. In Bortolaia Silva, E. (ed.) *Good Enough Mothering? Feminist Perspectives on Lone Motherhood*. Routledge. London.

Sainsbury D. 1996. *Gender Equality and Welfare States*. University Press. Cambridge.

Smeeding, T. - Torrey, B. 1988. *Poor Children in Rich Countries*. Luxembourg Income Study, Working Papers No 16.

Stoltz, P. 1997. Single Mothers and the Dilemmas of Universal Social Policies. *Journal of Social Policy (4) 26, 425-443*.

Wennemo, I. 1994. *Sharing the Cost of Children. Studies on the Development of the Family Support in the OECD-countries*. Akademitryck. Stockholm.

Whiteford, P. - Bradshaw, J. 1994. Benefits and Incentives for Lone Parents: A Comparative analysis. *International Social Security Review (47) 3-4, 69-89*.

Wilson, W.J. 1987. *The Truly Disadvantaged. The Inner City, the Underclass and Public Policy*. The University of Chicago Press. Chicago.

145

PART 3

PENSION REFORM AND DISABILITY POLICY

3.1 Reforming social security: how, why and so what?

Estelle James

Over the next 35 years, the proportion of the world's population that is over age 60 will nearly double, from 9% to 16% (figure 3.1.1). Due to rapid increases in life expectancy and declines in fertility rates, populations are aging much faster in developing countries than they did in industrial countries. As young working-age people near retirement - around the year 2030 - 80% of the world's old people will live in what today are developing countries. These countries will be shifting from systems of informal to formal old age security and, given their rapid aging, it is essential that they get this right from the start. At the same time, industrialized countries are trying to reform their existing systems to make them more sustainable and less costly.

Cross-sectional analysis shows that public spending on formal pension plans increases exponentially as populations age. It now exceeds 15% of GNP in some industrialized countries and will do so in many more countries as the demographic transition proceeds (figure 3.1.2). With such large sums involved, how this money is generated and spent can affect the entire economy, by influencing factor supplies, productivity and therefore the size of the GNP pie. For example, high payroll taxes can lead to lower employment in the formal labor sector, while pre-funding pension expenditures can be part of a plan to increase national saving. As another example, countries with higher private pension spending and assets have lower public spending, and these two types of spending may have different effects on the broader economy (figure 3.1.3). Therefore, two over-arching criteria should be used to shape and evaluate these programs: they should protect the old (in an equitable way) and they

149

should promote (or at least not hinder) economic growth - which is important both for the old and the young.

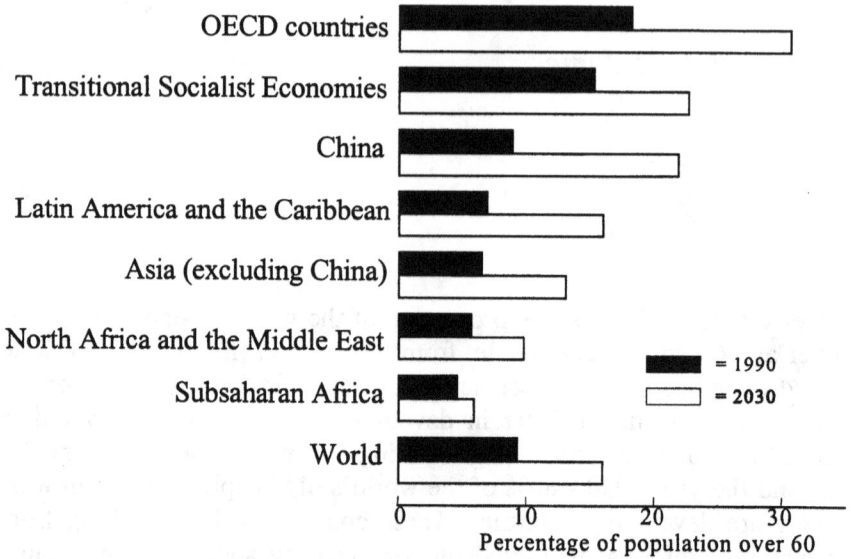

Figure 3.1.1   **Percentage of the population over 60 years old, by region, 1990 and 2030**

In the past, most old age security systems established by governments were pay-as-you-go (PAYG) systems - taxing workers today to pay pensions to old people today. This paper argues that growing old is a predictable life experience that most of us will have with a high probability, so a large part of old age security can instead be provided by self-insurance - people saving for themselves, shifting consumption from their younger productive years to their older years when consumption exceeds income. Myopia among workers may require that retirement saving be mandatory. But relying to some extent on self-insurance and saving may reduce many of the incentive problems associated with tax and transfer PAYG systems, thereby having a positive impact on the over-all economy.

However, another part of old age security systems requires pooling risks and insuring or redistributing across individuals - because some people, due to factors beyond their control, will retire early with disabilities, die young and leave dependents, live longer than average and run out of resources, or earn very low lifetime incomes which are insufficient to support them both for their working and non-working lives. This is the rationale for providing old age security through a combination of mandatory self-insurance and insurance across individuals - in a multi-pillar system that puts greater emphasis on saving, has separate financing and managerial mechanisms for redistribution and saving, and shares responsibility between the private and public sectors.

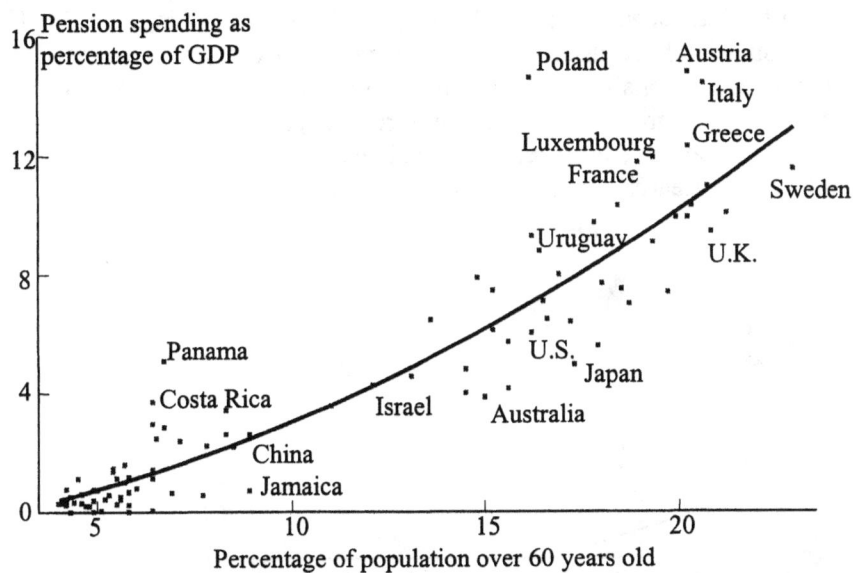

Figure 3.1.2   **Relationship between percentage of the population over 60 years old and public pension spending**

Over the past few years, many countries have indeed been adopting multi-pillar old age security systems. Although structural change is always difficult, the experience of these countries shows that it is possible, that it takes somewhat different forms in different places and it usually involves transition costs that are spread over several generations. Preliminary empirical evidence suggests a positive impact on efficiency and growth. But it also brings to the fore new problems - concerning high administrative costs and regulatory regimes that distort investment decisions - that remain to be solved.

Section 1 of this paper briefly describes the almost universal problems in traditional systems and sets forth a recommendation for the systems of tomorrow. Section 2 contrasts three structural reform models that are now being implemented - the Latin American model in which workers decide how their savings will be invested, the OECD model in which employers and/or union representatives control the investment strategy for an entire enterprise or occupation, and the Swedish model in which workers have large notional accounts, possibly supplemented by small funded accounts with real savings and investments in them. Methods countries have used for covering transition costs are discussed in section 3. Sections 4 and 5 examine empirical evidence on the positive efficiency and growth impact of these reforms, as well as the major new problems that have emerged. The final section summarizes these recent policy and research developments.

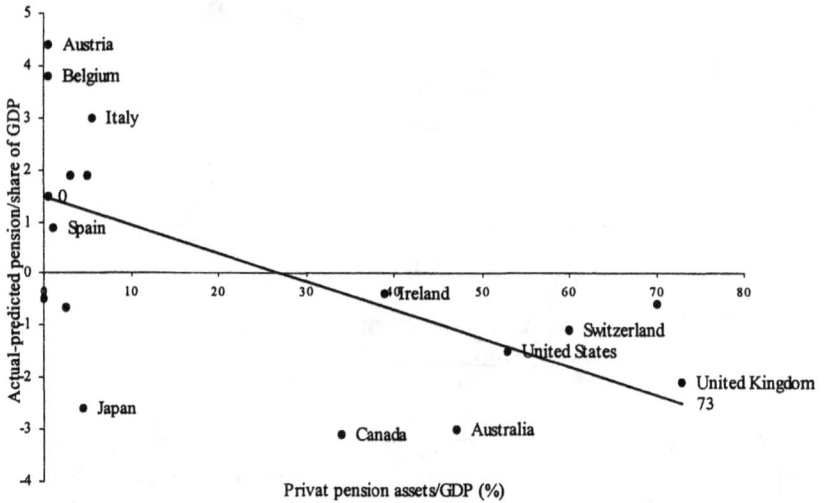

Figure 3.1.3　　　**Relationship between public pension spending and private pension assets**

Source:　Robert Palacios

152

1. Problems in old systems and recommended new systems

Most formal systems of old age security today are publicly managed, pay "defined benefits" according to a formula based on the worker's earnings and years of service, and are financed by payroll taxes on a pay-as-you-go (PAYG) basis - meaning that the contributions made by today's workers are used to pay the pensions of those who have already retired. However, it is now widely recognized that these systems generate many problems, including:

- high and rising payroll tax rates that may increase unemployment;
- evasion and escape to the informal sector, where productivity is lower;
- early retirement, which reduces the supply of experienced labor;
- misallocation of public resources, as scarce tax revenues are used for pensions rather than for education, health or infrastructure;
- lost opportunity to increase long term saving;
- failure to redistribute to low income groups;
- unintended inter-generational transfers (often to high income groups);
- and the growth of a large hidden implicit public pension debt, which makes the current system financially unbalanced.

As a result, existing systems have not always protected the old, they especially will not protect those who grow old in the future, they often have not distributed their benefits in an equitable way, and they have hindered economic growth. In addition, they are simply not sustainable in their present form.

Now, each of these problems is not found in every country, but they are found in most countries, both developing and industrialized. This suggests that these problems are not accidental, but rather they are inherent in the economics and politics of PAYG defined benefit schemes, which make it easy for politicians to promise short run benefits at the expense of large long run costs.

To avoid these dangers, the World Bank has been recommending and many countries have been moving toward a system that is partially defined contribution, funded and privately managed, rather than fully defined benefit, PAYG and publicly managed. Specifically, these new systems contain three pillars:

153

- a mandatory publicly-managed tax-financed pillar for redistribution;
- a mandatory privately-managed fully funded pillar for saving;
- a voluntary pillar for people who want more protection for old age.

The first pillar resembles existing public pension plans but it is smaller and focuses on redistribution - providing a social safety net for the old, particularly the old whose lifetime income was low. The benefit formula can be flat (uniform for everyone or related to years of covered employment, as in Argentina and the U.K.), means- and asset-tested (as in Australia) or provides a minimum pension guarantee (as in Chile). The last alternative is obviously cheaper while the first provides additional co-insurance and redistribution to lower middle class workers. In some cases (Australia, Chile) this pillar is financed out of general revenues rather than a payroll tax. Because of its limited scope and broad tax base, tax rates to support this pillar are much lower than the public system requires in most countries today.

The second pillar differs dramatically from traditional systems. It links benefits actuarially to contributions as in a defined contribution (DC) plan, it is fully funded and privately competitively managed. (In a DC plan the contribution rather than the benefit is defined and the future pension depends on accumulated contributions plus investment returns. In a fully funded system assets are always sufficient to cover future liabilities.) Essentially, people are required to save for their old age, and this pillar handles their savings.

A third pillar, voluntary saving and annuities, offers supplemental retirement income for people who want more consumption in their old age.

The second pillar is the most innovative and controversial of the three, so it is worth examining the rationale for its characteristics. This rationale takes into account the behavioral reactions of workers, savers and politicians to incentives posed by alternative social security systems.

Why mandatory? The rationale here is myopia - a significant number of people may be shortsighted, may not save enough for their old age on a voluntary basis, and may become a burden on society at large when they grow old.

Why defined contribution (DC)? The close link between contributions and benefits in a DC plan should discourage evasion, escape to the infor-

154

mal sector and other labor market distortions, since people are less likely to regard their contribution as a tax. And those who do evade bear the cost in the form of lower benefits rather than passing the costs on to others and undermining the financial viability of the scheme. Since the pension is acquired on actuarially fair terms given the age and accumulation of the worker, DC plans are likely to deter early retirement and to raise the normal retirement age automatically as longevity increases - without a collective decision that is often difficult for politicians to make.

Why fully funded? First, pre-funding makes costs clear up front so countries won't be tempted to make promises today that they will be unable to keep tomorrow. Second, it avoids large payroll tax increases that are needed in a PAYG system as populations age. Third, it prevents large inadvertent inter-generational transfers from young people to older workers. Once an unfunded system is set in motion, inter-generational transfers occur automatically as a result of the aging and maturation process, sometimes in ways that people did not expect and would not have chosen after an open discussion. For example, the early generations to be covered (including its rich members) gain, while later generations (including its poor members) lose - even though they did not even have a chance to participate in the political decision that produced this inter-generational contract. Full funding eliminates such undesirable transfers.

Third, funding may be used to help build long term national saving. These savings can enhance the productivity of future workers, they can be imbedded in consumer durables that provide a stream of future services, and they can be invested abroad, then redeemed to finance an inflow of consumer goods. Thus, saving can be an important ingredient of a long run strategy for providing additional domestic consumption when the dependency rate increases.

Why privately managed? This maximizes the likelihood that economic rather than political objectives will determine the investment strategy, thereby producing the best allocation of capital and the highest return on savings; and it helps countries (especially middle income countries) develop their financial markets. Empirical data show that publicly managed pension reserves typically earn low, even negative returns - largely because public managers are required to invest in government securities or loans to failing state enterprises, at low nominal interest rates that

155

become negative real rates during inflationary periods. The hidden and exclusive access to these funds makes it easier for governments to run large deficits or to spend more wastefully than they could if they had to rely on a more accountable source of funds.

Competitively managed funded pension plans, in contrast, are more likely to be invested in a mixture of public and corporate bonds, equities and real estate, thereby earning a higher rate of return. Private pension funds can enjoy the benefits of investment diversification, including international diversification, that enables them to increase their yield and reduce their risk, by protecting them from inflation and other country-specific risks. They build constituencies that help them resist political manipulation. They spur financial market development, by creating a demand for new financial instruments and institutions. But three caveats: countries must have at least rudimentary capital markets before they can put the funded pillar in place; considerable government regulation and regulatory capacity are need in order to prevent fraud and excessive risk; and if this regulation is excessive or misdirected, financial markets and investment policies will not be optimal.

All three pillars co-insure against the many risks that old people face, in particular, against the generalized risk stemming from uncertainty about the future economy or polity - such as breakdowns of the government or the market, changes in relative prices of labor and capital, deterioration in the position of a particular country - by diversifying across types of management (public and private), sources of finance (from labor and capital) and investment strategies (equities and bonds, domestic and international). Risk diversification is especially important given the long time periods and great uncertainty involved. Whatever unpredictable disasters occur in the future - as they surely will - this diversified system is most likely to continue providing protection for the old, according to the old adage - don't put all your eggs in one basket. (See World Bank 1994 for more details about the problems of old systems and the recommended new system. For a quantification of the welfare gains from diversification see Pujol 1996).

2. How have countries reformed?

During the past decade, with the pace accelerating during the past five years, several countries have adopted variations on this multi-pillar system. The three major variations are the Latin American (individual account) model, the OECD (employer-sponsored) model and the Swedish (notional DC) model. We have learned from this experience that pension reform is possible, even in democracies, but it takes somewhat different forms in different countries, as a result of their different initial conditions and political economies.

For example, these different conditions led Argentina to choose a relatively large public pillar while in Peru there is no public pillar at all, at present. They led Chile and Australia to choose a much larger private pillar than Mexico and Argentina. They led the UK and Switzerland to build upon a history of employer-sponsored plans, Australia and Denmark to build upon widespread union-negotiated plans. And they led Sweden and Italy to adopt a DC plan in their structural reform, but to keep it largely PAYG.

Table 3.1.1 Implicit pension debt during the early 1990s

	IPD/GAP for 4% discount rate	% of population over 60 years old
Senegal	27	4.3
Mali	26	4.9
Burkina Faso	15	5.0
Venezuela	30	5.6
Peru	37	5.8
Cameroon	44	5.8
Congo	30	6.1
Brazil	187	6.7
Turkey	72	7.1
Albania	67	8.1
China	63	8.9
Uruguay	214	16.4
Croatia	350	17.8
Ukraine	141	18.7
Hungary	213	19.3

Source: Finance and Development/June 1996, Robert Palacios for Albania, Cheikh Kane for Burkina Faso, Congo and Mali p. 38.

One of the most important initial conditions that influences the shape of the reform is the implicit pension debt (IPD) - the present value of the pension promises that are owed to current pensioners and to workers according to their years of participation in the old system. The IPD is inherent in PAYG systems, where workers expect to get a specified pension in return for their contributions, but assets are not accumulated to cover this; instead the obligation is covered by implicit IOU's of the government. The IPD exceeds the conventional explicit debt (backed by government bonds) in many countries and exceeds 200% of GNP in some cases (table 3.1.1). It is especially large in countries with high coverage, generous benefits and older populations. Although this debt is not always legally binding, it tends to be socially and politically binding; governments cannot easily renege on these obligations. Reform often converts (part of) the IPD into explicit debt, which creates a barrier to reform in countries that do not want to make their debt transparent. Most developing countries have small IPD's because of their low coverage rates, and are therefore in the enviable position of being able to change their systems to partial funding before the debt becomes unmanageable.

The Latin American versus the OECD models

Choice of investment manager: individual choice versus group choice. The Latin American model was pioneered by Chile in 1980 and, bolstered by its initial success, was closely followed by Argentina, Peru, Colombia, Mexico, Uruguay and Bolivia in the 1990s. It has just been adopted by the first countries outside the region, Hungary and Kazakhstan. It is now under consideration in Nicaragua and El Salvador and is one of three options proposed by the Social Security Advisory Committee in the United States. In this model, each worker chooses the investment managers of their own individual DC retirement accounts.

By comparison, the OECD model built on the widespread existing employer-sponsored pension plans and made them the foundation for the second pillar. These plans simply became mandatory instead of voluntary in Australia, Switzerland, Denmark (and de facto by collective bargaining in the Netherlands) or an optional alternative to the state plan in the U.K. In this model the employer or a combination of employer and union trustees choose the investment manager for each company or occupational group as a whole. This enables them to benefit from economies of scale and financial expertise, and possibly to minimize marketing costs (although this has yet to be proven). However, in DC plans it introduces the principal-agent problem - where employer or union representatives choose the investment manager but workers bear the risk, the choice may not be in the worker's best interest and may not maximize net returns. For this reason, workers may ultimately demand more individual choice in OECD countries; they have already been given this choice in the UK and Australia.

Add-on versus diversion of contributions and size of the public pillar. As another important difference between the Latin American and OECD models - most of the OECD countries cited above had a modest public pillar with a small IPD and with little or no payroll tax financing when they started their new system, so they could simply retain it, often as a flat benefit, and start the second pillar on top of that. They had no trouble financing the transition because accrued rights were small and/or contributions to the second pillar were added on, rather than being diverted from the first pillar.

For example, Australia had a means- and asset-tested first pillar, financed out of general revenues, to which it simply added a mandatory occupational funded pillar financed out of payroll contributions. Denmark's flat benefit in the public pillar (now being downsized) was also financed out of general revenues. In the U.K. the state earnings-related pension had just been started a few years earlier, when Thatcher decided to end it by encouraging employers and workers to opt out; the accumulated rights were still very small. Most workers in the U.K. are now simply eligible for the basic (flat) benefit. In Switzerland, employer-run plans that already existed in many firms became mandatory, on top of a compressed earnings-related public pillar which remained.

In contrast, the Latin American countries had bloated and often regressive benefit promises in public pillar to start out. Thus, to create space for the second pillar, the first pillar had to be greatly downsized and redesigned. In many cases (Chile, Bolivia, Mexico) it was given a very subsidiary role - providing a minimum pension guarantee to low income workers whose personal accumulations fell below a specified amount.

When a worker switched to the new system, he was given credit for his past service under the old system, while part of his future contributions were diverted to the new second pillar. These countries had to find the money to continue paying the promised benefits to current pensioners

159

and older workers (the IPD) under the old system, while part of the payroll tax flowing in was diverted to funded individual accounts - a problem that has become known as "financing the transition". Most countries that reform in the future will have to solve this problem. (For further details on the Latin American and OECD reforms, see Bateman and Piggott forthcoming, Cerda and Grandolini 1997, Hepp forthcoming, Johson forthcoming, Mitchell 1996a, Rofman and Bertin 1997, von Gersdorff 1997, Palacios and Rocha 1997, Valdes-Prieto forthcoming and Queisser 1998).

The Swedish model: notional DC plans

What is the NDC? Many countries with large public pillars and implicit pension debts have found it exceedingly difficult to make the transition to a partially funded system with a mandatory private pillar - in part because of the financing problem but also because of the political interests associated with existing institutions. This explains the third group of reforming countries - those that feature notional defined contribution plans.

A notional defined contribution (NDC) plan is one in which the worker has an individual account that is credited with his contributions plus interest. However, the accumulation is notional rather than actual, since the money paid in by workers is immediately paid out to pensioners rather than being invested; i.e. the system remains PAYG. Upon retirement, the notional accumulation is converted into a real annuity, supposedly on actuarially fair terms. Thus the NDC plan is essentially a reform of the first (PAYG public) pillar, although it is sometimes accompanied by a second (funded) pillar.

The notional account system was developed by Sweden, although it has not yet been implemented there. It was adopted shortly thereafter by Italy, but with a long transition period. In both cases, the first pillar will be converted into a notional DC plan, buttressed by a redistributive or guaranteed pension. This will be supplemented by a small (2.5%) funded pillar in Sweden. The system is also being implemented by Latvia, which hopes to save enough money from reducing evasion and early retirement to eventually start a funded pillar. Poland plans to have a new system with a first pillar that is NDC and a second pillar that is funded, with investment managers chosen by the individual workers. Outside of Europe, China has a notional defined contribution system, de facto. While in principle China wants to start a second pillar made up of funded individual accounts, many cities have been unable thus far to finance the transition, so the individual accounts remain largely notional.

Labor market and equity effects. The NDC system was designed to capture some of the advantages described above of linking benefits closely to contributions within each cohort. Most important, it reduces idiosyncratic intra-cohort inequities and labor market distortions, including incentives to evade - providing the notional interest rate is close to the market interest rate. For example, early and late years of contributions receive the same rate of return and workers with flat and steep age-earnings profiles receive the same rate of return, while this is not true of most defined benefit systems, Most people would consider this more equitable. In addition, this pattern induces younger workers and workers with flat age-earnings profiles to stay in the system rather than trying to evade. In addition, it makes the system more sustainable since it avoids the selection problem that occurs when low return people evade and high return people remain in the system.

Further, the notional defined contribution system discourages early retirement and avoids its negative impact on system sustainability, because workers automatically receive lower benefits if they choose to retire early; the costs are internalized rather than being passed on to others. For the same reason, it automatically adjusts the retirement age for increased longevity, thereby avoiding the difficult political decision to raise the retirement age that is periodically necessary in defined benefit plans.

However, the notional defined contribution system is not inherently redistributive, so it does not accomplish the crucial first pillar task of protecting low earners. For this purpose, a redistributive "0 pillar" must be added, creating a potential conflict with the NDC. If the redistributive component is large it may override the linkage between contributions and benefits that is responsible for these labor market improvements. In Sweden, for example, given the level of the guaranteed pension in the "0 pillar", the DC component will be irrelevant for many workers, including the majority of women.

Absence of funding and financial market effects. A bigger failing is that the NDC does not capture the benefits of funding, since there are no funds. That is, it serves as the first (PAYG) pillar, and may crowd out the opportunity for a large funded pillar. Inter-generational transfers remain, saving is not augmented and financial markets do not develop. Most important, as the dependency rate increases, the contribution rate would have to increase for newer cohorts, to keep the system solvent in the absence of pre-funding. These younger cohorts may have to "save" for their old age a much larger amount than is optimal for them, in order to cover benefits promised to older cohorts. In that case, the incentives for evasion and escape to the informal sector would be strong.

Sweden plans to build a buffer fund to reduce the need for large tax increases as its population ages. But this buffer fund will be a publicly managed overlay, since the individual accounts remain notional. This raises all the problems (summarized earlier) concerning political manipulation and poor allocation of publicly managed funds.

Choosing the notional interest rate and conversion rate to annuities. A key factor in NDC plans is - how are the notional interest rate and the conversion rate of notional capital into annuities determined? If the notional interest rate is higher than the market rate, it will be a costly guarantee to the government. If it is less than the market rate, the contribution is more likely to be regarded as a tax so labor market distortions reappear and pressures may arise for an increase. Typically the interest rate is set equal to some exogenous rate, to insulate it from such political manipulation; nevertheless, the possibility remains that a future government will discard this connection and arbitrarily change the rate.

Most commonly thus far, the notional rate has been tied to the growth in the per capita wage (possibly Poland), the total or covered wage bill (Sweden and Latvia) or GDP (Italy) - supposedly an equilibrating device. If the wage bill increases so too do contributions and therefore the ability to impute interest will be high. However, this means that when the working age cohort is large and growing (e.g. the baby boomers) the imputed interest rate is high and the IPD increases rapidly, but when the working age cohort declines (generation X) so too does the notional interest rate. This generation must then pay a high contribution rate to cover the IPD and will receive a low notional interest rate - fertile grounds for evasion and questionable from the viewpoint of inter-generational equity. Thus, using wage bill growth as the notional interest rate does not appear to be an equilibrating device as the dependency rate changes (see Schwarz and Valdes 1998).

The conversion factor into annuities supposedly depends on expected longevity upon retirement. However, because the process is notional, it too is highly subject to political manipulation. For example, the government can decide to grant notional credit for non-contributing years (a common problem in old PAYG DB systems), it can impute a low or a high future interest rate into the calculation, and it can fail to adjust the conversion factor when life expectancy increases. In the absence of market discipline, implicit taxes or subsidies can creep in and interfere with the labor market efficiency effects of the new system. Since both the conversion factor and the interest rate are set by the government, the NDC may be thought of as a PAYG DB in which the DB is defined in a new way.

In sum, the notional defined contribution system is attractive to countries that have very large implicit pension debts, especially those that are unwilling to incur an explicit fiscal deficit to finance the transition and will therefore end up with a large earnings-related first pillar. In this context, it may be a politically convenient way to reduce benefits in inflated programs and to equalize the retirement age for men and women. This may lay the groundwork for savings that eventually enable the growth of a funded second pillar; but until that happens it should be recognized as a reform of the first pillar rather than an introduction of a multi-pillar system. (For details on the Swedish reform see Sunden 1998, on Latvia see Fox 1998, on Poland see Rutkowsky 1998, on Italy see Hamann 1997. For another comprehensive summary of recent structural and piecemeal reforms see Demurgic-Kunt and Schwarz 1997).

3. Financing the transition

If countries with a large PAYG pension debt shift to a multi-pillar system that includes a funded component, some of the contribution usually is shifted to the individual accounts. This creates a financing gap between the remaining PAYG revenues and the expenditures needed to cover the IPD; some other revenue source must be found to cover this gap. Countries following the Latin American model have faced this transition cost problem, while those following the OECD model have not (because they had small public pillars and did not divert contributions) nor did the NDC countries (because they remain largely PAYG). How did the Latin American countries finance the transition? Three types of basic methods have been used: reducing the value of the IPD and the financing gap, finding alternative revenue sources to pay it off, and, finally, resorting to the general borrowing and taxation powers of the treasury.

Reducing the value of the IPD and the financing gap

1.   Before making the transition, reform the old system by downsizing benefits, raising retirement age and penalties for early retirement, tightening eligibility for disability benefits, and changing the indexation method to price indexation, so the outstanding debt, whether implicit or explicit, will be smaller. Chile, Argentina and Uruguay followed this strategy, which may be indispensable to a good pension reform. This cuts the benefits that must be paid to those who stay in the old system, it also cuts the compensation owed to those who switch to the new system, and it increases the probability that they will switch. Otherwise, you run the risk of casting in stone benefit promises that never should have been made in the first place, and making it more difficult for the government to escape from these promises.

2.   Issue a recognition bond (as in Chile) or promise of a compensatory pension (as in Argentina) to each worker who switches to the new system, that acknowledges the value of the pension that he has earned thus far. This postpones the day when cash will be needed, since the recognition bond cannot be cashed until the worker retires and the compensatory pension is gradually paid off over the entire retirement period of the worker. Besides extending the pay-off period, the issuance of the recognition bond provides another opportunity to reduce the debt. Since it is a legally binding piece of paper it gives the worker greater certainty that the pension debt will eventually be repaid, and in return for reducing uncertainty the government can downsize the face value of or interest rate on the bond (as in Peru). The face value can be further reduced if workers have much more faith in the new than the old system; they (especially young workers) will then be willing to switch even with little compensation for their past service. By choosing the minimum terms that are needed to convince the desired number of workers to switch, a government can substantially downsize the recognized debt and save considerable money in its transition costs (as in Hungary).

164

3. Keep some workers, and their contributions, in the old system. This may be accomplished by excluding some workers, such as the military or the police, from the new system (as in Chile), or by giving all workers a choice but making the new system attractive mainly to young workers (as in Argentina). Colombia has kept the old system operating side-by-side with the new and workers are permitted to switch back and forth. In Uruguay the new funded pillar is made compulsory only for rich and young workers, voluntary for the others. Since those remaining in the old system continue to contribute to it, this reduces the financing gap. The serious danger is that, in order to solve a short run cash-flow problem, these countries have increased their long term implicit debt by keeping participants in a financially unsound PAYG system; this solution may turn out to be non-sustainable.

4. Retain a large PAYG component in the new system, so that some of the revenue in-flow continues to the public pillar. Argentina followed this strategy, by utilizing a flat benefit in its new public pillar, rather than the narrower minimum pension guarantee as in Chile. In Argentina, about 60% of the total contribution flows into the public pillar. In addition, workers can choose between a funded and a PAYG option for the second pillar. The inflow of funds to the first pillar and the PAYG second pillar helps to pay current pensioners and, eventually, the compensatory pension. But if the public pillar or PAYG second pillar offer benefits that are too generous (actuarially unsound), the reform will not be sustainable in the long run - a danger that Argentina faces.

Finding alternative revenue sources

5. Build a pre-existing primary surplus in the general treasury, that can be used to pay off part of the pension debt. Chile did this but most other countries are burdened with fiscal deficits rather than surpluses.

6. If there is a pre-existing surplus in the social security system, use it to pay off part of the debt. While the Latin systems generally did not have a surplus, the U.S. social security trust fund could be used in this way, if the U.S. were to make a transition.

7. If public enterprises are being privatized, use some of the proceeds to pay off the pension debt - a cancellation of long term assets

against long term liabilities. This strategy is being followed by Peru, considered by Poland and Bolivia is also using privatization assets for pension reform. An existing unfunded pension debt generates uncertainty that reduces the market value of enterprises in the process of privatization, so paying off the pension debt may enable a higher price as public enterprises are privatized.

8. Reduce evasion and increase coverage, thereby increasing system revenues. This was part of Argentina's plan; however, the reduced evasion has not yet materialized. China is considering financing the transition by bringing all workers at township and village enterprises, a rapidly growing group, into the new partially funded system. Such coverage expansion would help to pay off the old IPD but simultaneously would create a new IPD, as the newly covered workers will eventually demand their pensions. If future benefits are generous, the short run gain comes at a high long run cost while is promised benefits are low and the cross-subsidy is high, evasion will be encouraged among the newly covered workers. Thus, this strategy is most useful as a temporary financing device if the PAYG part of the new system is small and the newly covered workers will be maaking most of their contributions to and getting most of their pension from their individual accounts.

Using general borrowing and taxation

9. Issue general treasury debt to cover the remaining cash gap in the short run. Because of the fungibility of money we do not know to what extent resources for pension reform have come from debt versus other general revenue sources, but government borrowing has usually increased in the early years of the reform. In countries with a large IPD use of temporary debt finance is almost inevitable so that a heavy double burden of taxation is not imposed on the transition generation of workers. Since young and future workers will benefit most from the reform, it is appropriate that they should also pay part of the cost.

Some of this debt may be sold to the pension funds in the new second pillar; government debt and bank deposits have been the largest initial investments of the new pension funds. An important proviso is that the pension funds should not be compelled to purchase government bonds; bond sales should be open, transparent and should pay the market interest rate. However, all Latin American countries limit international diversification of pension fund investments, which virtually ensures large investments in government bonds.

Is this temporary debt finance problematic? Financial markets might react negatively if they were not previously aware of the size of the implicit pension debt, if they believed the obligation to repay it was "soft" and has now become "hard" and if this increases the expected default risk on regular bonds. Two pieces of evidence suggest that, so far, the financial market response has been positive. First, the IMF recently adopted the position that debt finance earmarked for a pension transition should be allowed beyond the permissible ceiling for other debt, because it is a swap of implicit for explicit debt in the short run and is intended to reduce the over-all debt, hence to improve fiscal solvency, in the long run. Second, Hungary's credit rating from Moody's improved after it adopted its pension reform, even though this required an increase in the explicit debt, for much the same reasons.

10. Eventually pay off this debt through taxation, or the object of increasing national saving will not be achieved (additional private saving will be offset by additional public dissaving if the implicit debt is simply changed to an on-going explicit debt). The redemption of the debt through tax revenues can be spread over a long period of time - but the longer the pay-off the slower the country will receive the benefits of increased national saving for productive investment.

The kind of tax that is used can greately affect the benefits of the transition (Kotlikoff 1996). In general, a consumptin or value-added tax will be lest distortionary and most growth-enhancing; but it may also be the most difficult to implement in developing countries and is prblematic brom an equity point of view if coverage is incomplete. As discussed above, frequently the payroll tax paid to the public pillar us used to finance part of the transition. It has been estimated that if half the current PAYG system were converted to a funded system the financing gap would be paid off by a payroll tax rate of about 1.5% for 70 years in the U.S (Gramlich 1996) and a roughly similar amount in China (Friedman, et al 1996).

Some of these measures have also been used to mitigate political opposition to reform. Bureaucrats and unions that helped to run the old system often do not want to phase it out. Maintaining a large PAYG pillar in the new system not only reduces transition costs, it also serves to palliate opponents of pension reform and therefore may facilitate passage of reform legislation. Borrowing to finance the transition reduces the costs to and therefore the opposition of middle-age workers. But a consequence is that the benefits of a full reform are not received and sustainability of the new system may be undermined. This conflict between pragmatism and principle, short run and long run, has been faced in almost all the reformingn countries.

4. Efficiency and growth effects of reform: how large are they?

The chief theoretical argument for the recommended multi-pillar system is that it will have a positive effect on efficiency and growth, because the old system introduced or failed to remove distortions that will be eliminated by the reforms. A secondary argument is that it will enhance the financial sustainability of the old age system and thereby provide better protection for the old in the long run. And still a third argument is its better distributional effects, especially on inter-generational equity.

Efficiency and growth effects are notoriously difficult to quantify and prove, in part because relatively little experience and data are available and in part because, even if we had the data, it would be difficult to build models that capture all the complex dynamic interactions; that is, it is difficult to specify the counter-factual. Pension reform has several different potential efficiency effects; usually studies focus on one of these while ignoring or holding the others constant. For example, general equilibrium models that analyze labor supply effects often assume perfect capital markets and thereby limit the predicted increases in saving, and vice versa. In this section I summarize the limited empirical research that has been done on these topics, concentrating on the simulated effects in countries that have been considering structural reforms and econometric estimation of the actual effects in Chile, the main country that already has a track record. In general, the beneficial labor market effects come from the shift from defined benefit to defined contribution, the beneficial impact on saving comes from the shift from PAYG to funding and the financial market impact comes from private management of these funds.

168

First a brief comment on the distinction between efficiency and growth. Greater efficiency, for example, due to a reduction in labor market distortions, increases the level of output. If some of the increased output is plowed back into investment, as would often be the case, it also increases growth. Growth can also be increased without an increase in efficiency. For example, an increase in saving (and consequently growth) may simply indicate an inter-generational or life cycle redistribution that does not increase efficiency because it does not make (or have the potential to make) everyone better off. However, such an increase is efficiency-enhancing if the initial saving rate was sub-optimal due to public or private myopia or to a tax wedge between private and social returns to investment. Both of these conditions are usually alleged as a justification for mandatory retirement saving plans, in which case they would expand both efficiency and growth. In the following pages I discuss both efficiency and growth effects, focussing on the former in the case of labor markets and the latter in the case of saving and financial markets. While measuring these effects is problematic, the available evidence indicates that they are positive, possibly large, and undoubtedly the financial sustainability of the system has improved.

Reduced labor market distortions: early retirement and informal sector

One problem in PAYG defined benefit (DB) systems is the possibility that the high payroll tax will lead to labor market inefficiencies (stemming from distorted decisions about labor force participation, hours worked, age of retirement, choice of job and location, degree of effort, form of compensation, etc.), while in a defined contribution (DC) system the contribution may be regarded as saving rather than as a tax. We have only fragmentary evidence about the effect of pension reform on most of these actions.

Perhaps most important, Wise shows that the age of retirement is very sensitive to the implicit social security tax on labor, stemming from the absence of actuarial penalties on early retirement. The loss of generous DB benefits during years when older men continue working induces most men to stop working before the age of 60 (Wise, 1997). Countries that have a larger actuarial adjustment in their systems, hence a lower implicit tax on labor, have higher labor force participation rates of older men. Funded DC plans automatically build in this actuarial adjustment, so, by extension, should deter early retirement and its negative impact on GNP and financial solvency of the scheme.

The distortionary labor market effects of traditional systems on younger workers may be larger in developing than in industrialized countries because escape to the informal sector is easier there, both for workers and employers. Productivity in the informal sector may be lower because firms have less access to product and credit markets, or because technological change is embodied in capital in the formal sector and has an external effect on labor productivity throughout the economy (as in the endogenous growth literature). In addition, regulations that set a minimum wage and other benefits in the covered sector may lead to a wedge between wages and productivity in the formal versus the informal sectors. In simulations for a representative economy, Corsetti and Schmidt-Hebbel (1997) show that a payroll tax rate of 20% could cause a massive (47%) shift to the informal sector, thereby reducing the economy-wide growth rate by over 1% annually. In many Latin American countries the informal sector and small firms in the quasi-informal sector do indeed absorb more than half of the labor force (ILO 1996). Although many other forces are, of course, at work, a shift to a DC system might reduce these incentives for informality, because it closely links benefits to contributions.

What light is thrown on this issue by actual experience in Chile? Between 1980 and 1990, a period when the average share of informal employment in Latin America increased from 26% to 31%, this share dropped from 36% to 31% in Chile. Unemployment fell and wages rose. Edwards (1997) shows that, given reasonable assumptions about the elasticity of labor demand in the two sectors, the pension reform was responsible for a decline of 2.2%-3.6% in unemployment and a 5-8% increase in wages.

In evaluating these numbers and their applicability to other countries, it is important to realize that a shift to DC may not always have this salutary effect. For example, myopic workers may continue to evade contributions because they will not be able to access their mandatory savings for many years. In periods when investment returns are low, workers may be especially tempted to evade, preferring to consume or to invest in education, housing or consumer durables. In Chile, returns have been high (over 12% real during the first 15 years), encouraging compliance.

170

As another example, if the payroll tax for pensions is only a minor part of a large total payroll tax, the incentive to escape to the informal sector may remain strong. Indeed, this seems to be the case in Argentina, where the over-all payroll tax is high (Valdes-Prieto forthcoming). In contrast, a careful study in Chile, where the total payroll tax is relatively small, found that evasion had dropped to only 5% of potential contributors (Chamorro 1992, Schmidt-Hebbell 1997). (Chile does not even attempt to cover the self-employed, who are the biggest evaders in other countries). It is difficult to be conclusive about this, because it is hard to separate evasion from normal labor force withdrawals and exogenous shifts into self-employment.

If escape to the informal sector occurs in a funded DC plan it does not have the same negative effects on system sustainability that it does in a PAYG DB plan, since the costs are simply borne by the evader in the form of lower benefits, rather than being passed on to others in the form of a higher contribution rate. This is a big plus. Nevertheless, it still creates the same problem for labor allocation and productivity and an even greater problem for the financial security of the evading workers who may not have an adequate pension and may become a charge on the public treasury when they grow old. So, while the initial evidence is encouraging, we need to analyze the data on evasion, wages and employment carefully, as other countries reform their systems, to determine how robust and generalizable are these results.

Increased long term national saving

A major rationale for pension reform that emphasizes fully funded plans is that it will increase long term national saving. This is important because empirically we observe that most savings stay in the country of origin and most of a country's productive investment comes from its own saving, despite the global capital markets that supposedly prevail.

When a country without a prior PAYG system institutes a multi-pillar system, consumption will decrease and saving will increase if the mandatory saving rate exceeds the voluntary rate. When a country with an existing PAYG system replaces it with a multi-pillar system, national saving increases if benefits are cut or taxes are increased, usually to cover transition costs. In both cases, putting part of the contribution into the worker's own mandatory saving account may be more politically acceptable and less economically distortionary than increasing saving

171

through a high tax rate that goes into the general treasury. As mentioned above, this increase in saving is likely to enhance both efficiency and growth in many cases.

But again, there are reasons why this increased saving might not materialize. For example, mandatory saving may not increase total private saving if individuals find ways to offset them against other voluntary saving or accumulated assets. In that case, capital may accumulate and returns increase in the mandatory pillar, but they may commensurably decrease in the voluntary pillar. With perfect capital markets, private saving will not increase at all, since people will simply borrow against their mandatory pension saving. A positive saving effect ultimately depends on the assumption that voluntary long term saving and assets are small and borrowing opportunities limited for substantial groups within the population. The low asset condition probably holds for most slow-growing economies, the limited borrowing condition for most developing countries, and both hold for low income households in most countries.

Public as well as private saving matter. On the one hand, pension reform may decrease public dissaving as governments no longer need to borrow to cover escalating pension costs, but on the other hand, it may increase public dissaving if the build-up of pension reserves relaxes fiscal discipline and makes it easier for governments to run large deficits. If the transition is fully financed by borrowing, government dissaving will offset private saving, and the expected increase in national saving will simply not transpire. But if it is financed through taxes or cutbacks in other government expenditures, public saving increases national saving further. Estimating the impact on public saving therefore requires modeling government behavior - how governments will behave after pension reform and how that might have behaved in the absence of reform.

A number of simulations have been run projecting the impact on saving of a shift to a fully funded scheme. Not surprisingly, the results turn out to be highly dependent on the assumptions, especially the assumptions about the crowd-out of voluntary by mandatory saving and the method of financing the transition. Underlining the importance of the former, simulations of a "representative economy" indicate that a tax-financed transition to a fully funded system in the presence of credit constraints (implying low crowd-out) will increase output by 22% and

172

welfare by 16% in the long run, while the gain is only 2% without credit constraints (Cifuentes and Valdes-Prieto 1997).

In planning its mandatory occupation scheme, Australia assumed 50% crowd-out and higher for workers who already were covered by voluntary occupational plans. This implied that, in the long run, when the contribution rate reached 12%, national saving would increased by 1.5% of GDP, thereby almost doubling the current net national saving rate which is 2.2% of GDP. (The gross national saving rate is about 15% of GDP). Australia, of course, had the advantage that the government did not have to borrow to pay off a pension debt since the second pillar was an add-on rather than a diversion of previous contributions. Although initially the tax-deductibility of contributions was projected to cause some government dissaving, in the long run the decreased burden on the means-tested public pension is expected to reduce government dissaving. One of the main effects of the reform may be to shift the allocation of private saving away from home ownership, which is now the predominant form because of investment, and toward other more productive forms (Bateman and Piggott forthcoming).

In his simulations for Mexico, Ayala (1996) assumes a 30-40% rate of crowd-out. If the transition is tax-financed or if it is debt-financed and Ricardian equivalence holds (so that private saving goes up to offset public dissaving), total saving goes up .4%-2.1% of GDP, a similar magnitude to that expected in Australia. But if the transition is debt-financed and Ricardian equivalence does not hold, the impact on total saving is much smaller, even negative in some years, although positive over-all during the next 30 years.

The only country that has had a mandatory saving plan long enough for saving effects to be estimated is Chile. Data from Chile are problematic and the savings ratio is erratic, complicating this analysis and making the results highly sensitive to the starting date for comparisons. According to Corsetti and Schmidt-Hebbel (1997), private sector saving as a percentage of GDP increased from almost zero in 1979-81 to 17% in 1990-92 while private consumption decreased commensurably. Their reduced-form two-stage-least-squares regressions attribute half of the decline in the private consumption ratio to the growth of Chile's funded pension plans and correlated developments such as capital market deepening. Time series regression analyses by Haindl Rondonelli (1996) indicate that pension reform accounts for 6.6 of the 9.9 percentage point increase in the national saving rate in Chile (from 16.7% of GDP 1976-

80 to 26.6% 1990-94). Of the 6.6% increase, 3.1% was due to the direct impact of pension saving, 4.2% was due to the financial market deepening impact of pension fund size on other private saving, and a crowd-out effect of -0.7% was due to borrowing constraints. Using an error correction model, Morande (1996) also finds a significant positive effect of a pension fund dummy on private saving, 1960-95. He speculates that the financial market deepening caused by pension reform may have made voluntary saving less likely to be crowded out by and therefore less sensitive to fluctuations in foreign saving; and made the country's supply of investable resources less dependent on foreign capital.

Agosin, Crespi and Letelier (1996) are more skeptical because they find that the main source of increased private saving was private corporations, whose saving gradually jumped from 6% of GDP in 1978-85 to 23% in 1994 - a response, they believe, to the non-availability of foreign credit and the privatization of public enterprises. (Of course, privatization was itself facilitated by the pension reform, illustrating the complex interactions among these variables). Voluntary saving of households was negative (about 4% of GDP) throughout this entire period, indicating consumer dissaving or borrowing. However, forced saving through the new pension system gradually grew to almost 4% of GDP, and this was not offset by greater voluntary dissaving (presumably because credit constraints had already been exhausted). This 4% magnitude is roughly consistent with the findings of Bosworth and Marfan (1994), that the pension reform increased saving 3% of GDP. The risk remains that the growth of consumer credit, possibly fueled by the pension reform, could increase consumer dissaving and offset some of these gains in the future (Holzmann 1996).

While these analyses focus on enhanced private saving, other studies emphasize the impact of pension reform on public saving and dissaving. Chile had to finance a pension transition, in part through deficit finance - which decreased national saving. The fiscal costs of the transition may have canceled out the positive effect on private saving initially (Agosin et al 1996). Observing that the pension-related deficits of the government (payments to pensioners left over from the old system plus redemptions of recognition bonds for new pensioners who had switched) were larger than the inflows to the new pension funds until 1989, Holzmann concludes that during the 1980s the new pension system had a negative effect on national saving. However, he appears to overlook the fact that redeemed recognition bonds became part of private pension saving and were not immediately consumed. Correcting for this point alone generates a positive savings effect as early as 1985.

More important, a simple accounting exercise neglects the disciplining impact that pension reform might have had on government behavior, particularly other taxes and expenditures. Chile ran an increasing surplus over this period, possibly to help cover the transition costs. Since 1987 the consolidated government budget has been in surplus, which quickly exceeded 5% of GDP. In addition, Chile accumulated a large budgetary surplus ex ante in preparation for the reform, thereby reducing its need for deficit finance. While we do not know how large the current or past surplus would have been otherwise, to the degree that the pension reform was financed by increasing general taxes, cutting other public spending or accumulating a prior surplus, transition costs did not decrease public saving. Moreover, the transition costs are short run while the increased private saving may persist in the long run. As a result of all these factors, total national saving in Chile is currently much higher than it was pre-reform.

Thus, preliminary evidence indicates that pension reform can have beneficial effects on long term national saving and capital formation - increasing it by 10 to 30% of the ex ante gross rate and even more of the ex ante net rate - especially if it is accompanied by a broader set of policies designed to constrain consumer and government borrowing.

Financial market development

One reason for favoring private management of pension funds is that this will develop a set of financial institutions - investment managers, insurance companies, and banks - that are essential for economic development. On the one hand, a funded pillar cannot get started without some minimum financial market capacity, but on the other hand, the funded pillar, if competitively managed and well-regulated, can be instrumental in enabling the financial market to grow in safety, size, depth and complexity. In developing countries, where private saving is already high, one of the main effects of a funded pillar may be to shift these savings out of land and jewelry and into long term financial market investments that are better for the broader economy, because of the development of these financial institutions.

Even in Australia it is expected that the financial market will grow as a result of the mandatory second pillar. For example, as noted earlier,

175

some private saving may be redirected out of owner-occupied housing into the financial markets. Insurance companies are expanding, developing a new line of products, including annuity products, to meet the anticipated demand stemming from pension funds (Bateman and Piggott forthcoming). In Switzerland also, growth of the life insurance industry, investment companies and mutual funds, have been spurred by mandatory funded pension plans. And corporate governance has been gradually changing, as institutional investors have demanded disclosure and better performance (Hepp forthcoming). All these changes are efficiency-enhancing.

But the strongest evidence for this expected growth effect comes from Chile. During the five years preceding the adoption of its new system, Chile prepared the groundwork by organizing a primary market for treasury bonds, reforming its laws governing mutual funds, corporations and securities, privatizing banks, authorizing a price-indexed mortgage bond market and liberalizing the provision of insurance and reinsurance (Valdes-Prieto 1997). After the new system was introduced, this process continued - financial markets became more liquid as the number of traded shares on the stock market and their turnover increased; demand was created for the equities of newly privatized state enterprises; information disclosure and credit-rating institutions developed; the variety of financial instruments including indexed annuities, mortgage and corporate bonds grew; and asset pricing improved. In several of the studies summarized above, financial market deepening associated with pension reform was given credit for the observed increase in private saving. Econometric analysis suggests that financial market efficiency induced by the reformed pension system (and other factors with which this was closely correlated) increased total factor productivity 1% per year, or half of the increase in total factor productivity, in Chile (Holzmann 1996).

Summary

In sum, a small but growing body of empirical evidence indicates that pension reform has produced positive efficiency and growth effects. That is, the impact on saving, productivity, output and welfare may be high relative to exogenous sources of growth and other policies available to increase growth.

176

Several caveats are essential in interpreting this evidence. First, given the high correlation between pension reform and other reforms that are often simultaneous, the controversy surrounding the determinants of private saving and labor supply (e.g. which variables are endogenous?), the even greater uncertainty about the determinants of public saving (e.g. what is the counter-factual?), and the difficulties in modeling feed-back effects, all these econometric and simulation results are highly sensitive to model specification and the topic clearly requires additional evidence and research. In particular, the econometric analyses for Chile are subject to omitted variable bias and the simulation results depend heavily on assumptions about crowd-out, transition costs and rates of return. Second, the growth impact also depends on key policy decisions in setting up the new system, such as the question of how high the required contribution rate will be, what proportion of the multi-pillar system should be funded and DC, and how the transition will be financed. While debt finance may be necessary for political purposes, partial tax finance may be necessary to meet the economic objective of increased saving, and of course some taxes have better efficiency properties than others. Third, it is important to remember that, even if it claims to use a general equilibrium model, each study typically deals with only one possible source of growth, so many of these results are partially additive - the total growth effect is the sum of the separate effects on labor market distortions, early retirement, escape to the informal sector, capital accumulation, financial market development and other sources of growth. So if each separate effect increases GNP in amounts ranging from 1-10%, their sum may increase GNP much more.

5. New problems and issues for further research

While many efficiency gains seem to have been achieved, the new systems have also created new problems that remain to be solved and related research that needs to be done. The major problems that have surfaced so far concern high administrative costs and financial market distortions due to regulations. A third area needing further study involves the distributional effects of pension reform. Finally, the analysis of annuities markets will become increasingly important as workers begin to retire under the new systems.

177

The big advantage of private over public investment is the likelihood that it will produce a better allocation of capital, therefore higher returns for the fund and growth for the economy. However, decentralized systems also may charge high administrative fees, partly due to high marketing costs in competitive industries. In some cases marketing costs produce important side-benefits of consumer information and increased compliance, but this does not appear to be the case in most countries that have recently reformed.

Preliminary evidence indicates that workers are ill-informed, do not make decisions based on investment returns, and pension funds incur high sales commissions and other marketing costs to attract them. In Chile and most other Latin American countries fees are front-loaded, meaning that workers pay a one-time fee on new contributions rather than an annual fee based on assets. (This system was probably adopted because the new system had no assets initially). Specifically, this one-time fee is about 2 percent of wages, or 15-25 percent of new contributions, in virtually all cases, and about one-third of this is for marketing.

These numbers appear very high. To understand their impact on net returns, it is necessary to convert these one-time charges on contributions into their equivalents in terms of annual charges on assets, a conversion which depends on how large the assets are relative to the contributions. Obviously, for accounts that have small accumulated assets (young workers with few years of contributions), this fee will be high relative to assets. However, for accounts that have built up substantial assets over the years, the fee will be small relative to assets.

Simulations show that if the current fee schedule is maintained, the average Chilean worker who contributes for 40 years will pay the equivalent of less than 1 percent of assets per year. This is approximately the same amount mutual funds charge for voluntary retirement savings accounts in the U.S.; it is not excessive from the lifetime point of view, in comparison to a competitive market retail price for individuals. Moreover, it is not excessive in comparison to a less expensive system that produces much lower gross and net returns (e.g. publicly managed reserves in Singapore and the U.S. social security trust fund).Competition may bring costs down further in the long run.

However, this fee structure is an apparent problem in the early years of a new system, when all accounts are small. It is a real problem for workers who will be in the system for only 20-30 years, such as workers who were relatively old upon the date of reform; simulations show that these workers pay a much higher lifetime fee as a percentage of assets. It is a problem for transient workers who move in and out of the labor force, such as women, especially if their contributions are concentrated in their later years. The higher lifetime fee as a percentage of assets and hence the lower net return received by these groups is a matter of concern on equity grounds in a mandatory system. In addition, for workers who are very risk-averse, it is questionable whether to compel them to incur these costs with certainty while the benefits are uncertain. Besides the equity consideration is the practical consideration that high costs may lead these groups to evade. Moreover, it would be desirable to find ways to increase administrative efficiency for all workers, since this would increase their rates of return and replacement rates.

Some analysts believe that administrative costs would be lower under a group plan and hence favor choice by the employer or union. Such group plans may be better positioned to benefit from economies of scale in decisionmaking, greater financial expertise, and lower marketing costs. (On the existence of scale economies see James and Palacios 1995, Mitchell 1996b). This is one rationale given for employer and/or union choice of the investment manager in OECD countries. However, because employers or union representatives make the investment decision while workers bear the risk, such plans can also open the door to financial abuse and principal-agent problems: employers might choose investment managers or strategies that benefit them even if this implies lower returns for their workers.

For example, lower "wholesale" charges appear to be available for large group [401(k)] plans in the U.S. but not all employers have gone to the effort of obtaining these rates. In Switzerland employers tend to place retirement funds at banks with which they have had long-standing financial relationships, without exploring other options carefully (Hepp forthcoming). One of the worst cases of employer abuse of worker retirement funds was the Maxwell scandal in the U.K.; but individual choice also led to a scandal in that same country, as uninformed workers were induced to abandon their employers' plans and purchase financially disastrous policies by unscrupulous insurance company salesmen (Johnson 1997). Basing the second pillar on occupational plans is especially a problem for mobile workers, who may end up with many small costly accounts unless these can be consolidated in one personal account -

179

problems which weighed heavily in Australia and the new Hong Kong scheme.

Thus we have anecdotal evidence about costs and returns to group choice versus individual choice and a careful empirical study has yet to be done. Meanwhile, the principle-agent problem makes it likely that political pressures will develop to give workers the right to opt out of employer pension plans into their own personal retirement savings plan in most mandatory systems, and this has already happened in the U.K. and Australia.

A third alternative may be desirable in small countries whose markets cannot support many pension companies efficiently due to economies of scale, countries with undeveloped financial markets that want to attract investment expertise and minimize start-up costs, and countries with low contribution rates to the second pillar. Instead of open entry, the government might auction off operating rights to a limited number of investment companies, among whom workers then choose. The contract could specify the maximum risk, offer a reward for high returns, and choose the winners based on who charges the lowest administrative fees.

The voluntary Thrift Saving Plan for U.S. federal employees uses a competitive bidding process to choose its money managers, at a total cost of less than 10 basis points (.1%). An auction process was recently used in Bolivia, which expects to have much lower administrative costs than Chile as a result. Or instead of letting the fee be determined in an auction for a pre-specified number of winners, an alternative is to set a low fee ceiling and open entry to all qualified pension fund managers willing to abide by that limit. Sweden will use a variation on his theme for its new second pillar - centralized collection and record-keeping, while workers choose among mutual funds that have reached an agreement on fees with the central agency.

The dangers here are the difficulties in insulating the auction and investment process from political manipulation, corruption and collusion, and the importance of incorporating incentives for good performance, when entry and price are limited. Otherwise, while these mechanisms may feature lower marketing expenditures, they may also feature lower investment returns, less consumer education and service. The advantages are that much lower costs, allowing a substantial increase in rates of return and replacement rates, can be achieved, if the process is well-handled.

Summing up: one could construct a continuum with considerable choice, competition, political insulation and relatively high administrative cost on one end (Chilean AFP's, UK, Australia, voluntary IRA's in the U.S.), with limited choice, competition and lower costs on the other end (Bolivia, Sweden, U.S. federal employees Thrift Saving Plan), each arrangement having different implications for political insulation, rates of return and other kinds of service. Countries could then choose which mix of costs and benefits they prefer. Many additional measures can be and are being considered to economize on costs and their effects should appear over the next decade. The impact of alternative institutional arrangements on administrative costs in the second (decentralized funded) pillar has heretofore received little attention. We could certainly benefit from careful analytic and empirical studies in this area.

Financial market distortions

Multi-pillar systems have justifiably been given credit for stimulating the growth of financial markets in middle income countries where this is an important ingredient of the recipe for economic growth. However, as these systems have been implemented, we also observe ways in which they have distorted the operations of financial markets.

This problem stems from the fact that policy-makers want workers to make investment decisions and bear the corresponding risk, but they also want to limit this risk to avoid a disaster. Relatedly, the government must set certain investment constraints and offer guarantees in order to overcome political opposition to reform. The contradiction here can potentially lead to malfunctioning markets, particularly if the pension funds are relatively large players in the market.

As examples of this ambivalence: In Chile and several other Latin American countries pension funds (AFPs) are heavily penalized if they deviate more than 2 percentage points from the group mean. This has been accused of leading to herding behavior, as each AFP tries to look very much like the others. Rather than having a choice of different points on the risk-return frontier, stemming from differing asset allocations - as would be the case in a well-functioning financial market - workers have the much less meaningful choice among companies that provide the same asset allocation and risk-return mix. Also, workers are required to invest in one AFP instead of diversifying among several and thereby reducing their risk; of course, given the lack of meaningful portfolio differences among the AFP, the gains from diversification would be small in any event.

In Mexico all workers are required to enter the new system but those currently in the labor force are given the right to return to the old pay-as-you-go system upon retirement if this allows them to fare better. This insurance scheme was included to acknowledge the "acquired rights" of workers and therefore avoid a legal challenge to the reform efforts. However, it creates an obvious moral hazard problem - workers have an incentive to gamble with their pension funds, accepting too much risk, since they are substantially protected from loss. The Mexican authorities have avoided the moral hazard problem by greatly limiting the AFORES' choice of investment strategies: at least 65% of all assets must be invested in government bonds (currently the AFORES are 99% in bonds) and international investments are proscribed. Since workers have no real choice of portfolios, moral hazard is avoided; but the flow of funds through the AFORES to the financial market and the private sector is also avoided.

Bolivia initially intended to invest most of its revenues from privatization (targeted for pension reform) abroad, to protect it from excess government borrowing and other country-specific risk. However, in order to overcome union opposition to these reforms, the government had to take on the responsibility for paying off the implicit debt of the complementary pensions that unions had negotiated in the past. To cover these and other expenditures, the final arrangements decreed that initially almost all of the privatization assets would be invested domestically, in government bonds. In Uruguay, to help cover transition costs, AFP's are required to put at least 80 % of their assets into special issue government bonds. While the risk-reducing benefits of international diversification and diversification into private sector securities is one of the rationales for pension reform, in fact most Latin American countries require or strongly encourage almost exclusive domestic investments, with a heavy concentration in government bonds.

Regulations in Switzerland require a 4% nominal guaranteed rate of return in their second pillars, thereby leading to a very conservative investment strategy, consisting largely of bonds. Until recently, providers of second pillar pensions for civil servants in the Netherlands faced little competition, again leading to low rates of return that might have been off or at a corner of the risk-return frontier.

These distortions should not be exaggerated, because the guarantees and limits on competition and portfolio diversification are likely to fall through time, as the schemes mature. Chile started with rigid restrictions but has gradually opened up the system to greater diversification, including international investment. Mexico is now considering allowing each AFORES to offer more than one type of portfolio, together with worker diversification among different portfolios. Along similar lines, pension funds might be allowed to differentiate their asset allocation strategies and corresponding benchmarks (if available), applying different risk limits depending on type of portfolio chosen. For example, portfolios might be offered that concentrate in bonds, stocks, and international investments, with different degrees of risk implied by each (as in the U.S. federal employees Thrift Saving Plan). This would allow workers to choose their preferred point on the risk-return frontier and should help the financial markets to operate better, but it also requires substantial worker education as well as greater diversity of financial instruments than exists presently in many developing countries.

The distributional impact of pension reform

Although this paper has focused on the efficiency and growth impact of pension reform, an equally important topic is the impact of reform on equity. Because traditional pension systems are typically both inefficient and inequitable, they offer an opportunity to improve both. However, we do not know whether or the extent to which multi-pillar system have actually succeeded in achieving a better distributional outcome. Closer examination suggests that the devil is in the details and some of the results may be surprising.

For example, in Chile's public pillar, workers are eligible for a minimum pension guarantee of about 27 percent of the average wage after 20 years of contributions, meaning that the government tops up the benefits of these workers to the guaranteed point if their own accumulation does not suffice. The main beneficiaries here will be low earners who worked only 20 years, disproportionately females, who have limited labor market attachment, while workers who remain in the formal sector for a full career are unlikely to receive this subsidy. In contrast, in Argentina a flat benefit of about 28 percent of the average wage is paid to all workers who have at least 30 years of contributions (plus an additional 1 percent for every year above 30 up to 45). The main recipients will be workers who spent most of their adult lives in the formal labor sector and (in sharp contrast to Chile) women are unlikely to qualify. In the U.K., which pays a flat benefit that is about half the size of Argentina's (as a proportion of the average wage) but does not set a required number of contributory years, the big gainers are people who work few years and live long lives, such as women. Switzerland's public pillar is earning-related and hence appears less redistributive than that in Argentina, but the payroll tax which finances it is levied on all earnings (that is, there is no ceiling on taxable earnings as there is in Argentina), which works in the opposite direction.

The setup of the second pillar also has distributional consequences. If flat fees per account are permitted, this reduces net returns for low earners more than for high earners. Flat fee were charged by Chilean AFP's initially but the unfavorable publicity they encountered was one factor leading them to drop this practice; it is now used by some AFORES in Mexico. If low income workers tend to choose more risk-averse investment strategies than high income workers, this will lead them to have lower replacement rates in the future. The distributional issue is explored further in a separate paper (James 1997) and certainly merits additional empirical research.

6. Conclusion

Averting the Old Age Crisis (World Bank 1994), argued that old age security systems with a large funded defined contribution component, decentralized competitive management of these funds, and a social safety net, are most likely to promote economic growth, provide acceptable income to the old, and reduce risk by diversification. During the past five years, the move toward multi-pillar systems has accelerated. With the aging of the global population, it has become increasingly important to choose a reliable and cost-effective method of old-age support. As economic growth slows and financial markets open, it has become increasingly important to raise productivity through improved incentives in the labor market and through the accumulation of capital which is then allocated to its most efficient uses. As income disparities have widened, it has become increasingly important to provide additional protection to low wage-earners who have grown old. A multi-pillar system that includes a mandatory publicly managed tax-financed defined

184

benefit pillar for redistribution, a mandatory privately managed funded defined contribution pillar to manage peoples' retirement savings, and a voluntary pillar for people who are willing to pay for more security, has seemed to many countries most likely to accomplish these objectives.

Thus several Latin American, OECD and transition countries have already adopted multi-pillar systems, and they are under serious consideration in many more. Preliminary evidence from Chile, the only country that has had this system for long enough for empirical studies to be conducted, supports the existence of a positive growth effect, stemming from increased labor market efficiency, mobilization of long term saving and financial market development. This suggests that the reward may be worth the effort of a carefully planned reform that takes into account its impact on the broader economy.

It may be surprising to find so much variety among the countries that have adopted multi-pillar systems of old age security - indicating substantial room for country-specific conditions. It should not be surprising to find that the new solutions have created new problems, in this case high administrative costs and restrictions on financial market flexibility. Countries that are on the verge of reforming their social security systems can learn from the experience of the first-movers and make the late reforms even better.

References

Agosin, Manuel R., Gustavo Crespi T., and Leonardo Letelier S. 1996. "Explicaciones del Aumento del Ahorro en Chile". Centros de Investigación Económica, Santiago, Chile: Banco Interamericano de Desarrollo.

Ayala, Ulpiano. 1996. "The Savings Impact of the Mexican Pension Reform". Green Cover Report 16373ME Mexico Country Dept. World Bank.

Bateman, Hazel and John Piggott forthcoming. "Mandatory Occupational Pensions in Australia". *Annals of Public and Cooperative Economics.*

Bosworth, Barry and Manuel Marfan. 1994. "Saving, Investment, and Economic Growth". In Bosworth, Barry, Rudiger Dornbusch and R. Laban, eds., *The Chilean Economy: Political Lessons and Challenges.* Washington D.C.: Brookings Institution.

Cerda, Luis and Gloria Grandolini. 1997. Mexico: The 1997 Pension Reform. EDI Conference volume.

Chamorro, C. 1992. "La Cobertura del Sistema Chilean de Pensión". Ph.D. Dissertation. Catholic University, Santiago, Chile.

Cifuentes Rodrigo and Salvador Valdes-Prieto 1997. "Transitions in the Presence of Credit Constraints". in *The Economics of Pensions: Principles, Policies, and Interna-*

185

tional Experience, ed. Salvador Valdes-Prieto. Cambridge: Cambridge University Press.

Corsetti, Giancarlo. 1994. "An Endogenous Growth Model of Social Security and the Size of the Informal Sector". *Revista de Análisis Económico* 9, 1, 57-76.

Corsetti, Giancarlo and Klaus Schmidt-Hebbel 1997. "Pension Reform and Growth". in *The Economics of Pensions: Principles, Policies, and International Experience*, ed. Salvador Valdes-Prieto. Cambridge: Cambridge University Press.

Demurgic-Kunt, Asli and Anita Schwarz. 1997. "Taking Stock of Pension Reforms Around the World". EDI Conference volume.

Edwards, Sebastian. 1997. "Chile: Radical Change Toward a Funded Pension System". Paper presented at Kiel Week Conference, University of Kiel, Germany. UCLA and NBER, processed.

Fox, Louise. 1998. "The Latvian Pension Reform". World Bank, Washington D.C.

Friedman, Barry, Estelle James, Cheikh Kane & Monika Queisser. 1996. "How Will China Care for Its Aging Population?" World Bank PRD Discussion Paper.

Gramlich, Edward. 1996. "Different Approaches for Dealing with Social Security". *Journal of Economic Perspectives*, 10, 3, 55-66.

Haindl Rondanelli, Erik. 1996. "Chilean Pension Fund Reform and its Impact on Saving". IBC Discussion Paper 96-2. University of Miami, International Business Center, Coral Gables, Florida. Processed.

Hamann, A. Javier. 1997. "The Reform of the Pension System in Italy". IMF Working Paper WP/97/18.

Hepp, Stefan. forthcoming. "The Swiss Multi-Pillar System". *Annals of Public and Cooperative Economics*.

Holzmann, Robert. 1996. "On Economic Usefulness and Fiscal Requirements of Moving from Unfunded to Funded Pensions". University of Saarland Working Paper, Saarbrucken, Germany.

ILO (International Labor Organization). 1996. PANORAMA. Geneva.

James, Estelle and Robert Palacios 1995. "Costs of Administering Public and Private Pension Plans". *Finance and Development*. 32:12-15.

James, Estelle. 1997. "Pension Reform in Latin America: Is There an Efficiency-Equity Trade-off?" In Nancy Birdsall, Carol Graham and Richard Sabot, eds., *Beyond Trade-offs: Market Reforms and Equitable Growth in Latin America*. Inter-american Development Bank and Brookings Institution. Washington, D.C.

Johnson, Paul forthcoming. "Pension Reform in the United Kingdom". *Annals of Public and Cooperative Economics*.

Kane, Cheikh and Robert Palacios. 1996. "The Implicit Pension Debt". *Finance and Development*. 33:38-41.

Kotlikoff, Larry. 1996. "Privatizing Social Security At Home and Abroad". Discussion paper.

Mitchell, Olivia 1996a. "Social Security Reform in Uruguay". Pension Research Council WP 96-20. Univ. Penn.

Mitchell, Olivia 1996b. "Administrative Costs in Public and Private Pension Systems". NBER Working Paper.

Mitchell, Olivia and Annika Sunden. 1994. "An Examination of Scoial Security Administration Costs in the United States". Pension Research Council WP 94-7. Univ. Penn.

Morande, Felipe G. 1996. "Savings in Chile: What Went Right?" Inter-American Bank Working Paper Series 322a.

186

Office of the Government Plenipotentiary for Social Security Reform. 1997. "Security through Diversity: Reform of the Pension System in Poland". Warsaw.

Palacios, Robert and Roberto Rocha. 1997. "The Hungarian Pension System in Transition". EDI Conference Volume.

Pujol, Thierry. 1996. "Some Considerations on Pay-As-You-Go vs. Fully-Funded Schemes". World Bank.

Queisser, Monika. 1998. *The Second-Generation Pension Reforms in Latin America.* OECD Development Centre Studies, Paris.

Reid, Gary and Olivia Mitchell. 1995. "Social Security Administration in Latin America and the Caribbean". World Bank Working Paper.

Rofman, Rafael and H. Bertin. 1997. "Lessons From Pension Reform: The Argentine Case". EDI Conference volume.

Schmidt-Hebbell, Klaus. 1997. "Pension Systems: From Crisis to Reform". EDI Conference volume.

Schwarz, Anita and Salvadore Valdes. 1998. "Notional Accounts: An Analytic Framework". World Bank, Washington, D.C.

Sunden, Annika. 1998. "The Swedish Notional Account System". Working Paper, World Bank, Washington D.C.

Von Gersdorff, Hermann. 1997. "The Bolivian Pension Reform: Innovative Solutions to Common Problems". World Bank Working Paper.

Valdes-Prieto, Salvador, forthcoming. "Pension Reform in Latin America: Transition and Implementation Problems". *Annals of Public and Cooperative Economics.*

Whitehouse, Edward. 1998. "Pension Reform in Britain". Social Protection Discussion papeer 9810, World Bank, Washington D.C.

Wise, David. 1997. "Retirement Across Decades, Across Nations (using HRS data)". presented at Conference on Economics of Aging, International Health and Retirement Surveys Conference, Amsterdam, processed.

World Bank 1994. *Averting the Old Age Crisis: Policies to Protect the Old and Promote Growth.* Washington DC: World Bank and Oxford University Press.

3.2 Pension policies for ageing populations: labour market policies, funded and mixed systems

Colin Gillion

The objective of this paper is to say something about the policy responses of different countries to the prospect of ageing populations: in particular, to the question of providing pensions to a larger group of older people in the population. It also draws on this discussion to comment on the general design of pension systems. The issue is by now a well known one and has been discussed many times. But the debate has not led to any commonly agreed approach. Some commentators consider that by moving to funded schemes the pensions of a larger cohort of retired people can be financed in advance and the accumulated savings used to pay pensions when the population ages. Other commentators, including myself, do not agree that this will help the situation, at least at the national level, and prefer to place emphasis on increasing the average age of retirement and increasing the employment and earnings of women. This would simultaneously reduce the number of dependents requiring support and increase the number of contributors. In addition, some increase in contribution rates and reduction in benefit rates might be required.

The view taken in this paper is that the question of providing support for inactive persons needs to be seen in broad terms: that is, in terms of providing support for dependents of all kinds - children, students, non-working wives, the disabled and the unemployed as well as the retired - and that the cost of providing support should be viewed in aggregate, and not simply counted in terms of the contribution or saving rates used for pensions. This means that all sources of benefits for dependents and all sources of revenue should be counted: intra-family transfers, income from savings, earned income from employment, unearned income from capital, as well as public and private pensions.

The paper falls into four main sections.

Section 1 briefly reviews the demographic outlook in seven main OECD countries: Japan, France, Germany, Norway, the United States, Austria and Italy.

Section 2 discusses the effect on contribution rates of increasing male retirement age, increasing female employment and a 10 per cent reduction in benefit rates.

Section 3 examines the consequences of moving to funded pension schemes.

Section 4 discusses the broad objectives of pension schemes - as seen by the ILO - and comments on the risks associated with funded schemes and the benefits of mixed systems.

The paper is also accompanied by a number of tables and figures. These might appear rather overwhelming to a first time reader, although they are not especially complicated. Those who seek a simplified version could concentrate on the figures and on tables 3.2.7 and 3.2.8.

As far as conclusions are concerned, there are three main messages, broadly corresponding to the discussion in sections 2, 3 and 4.

First, labour market policies which increase the retirement age of men and increase the participation rate of women are broadly sufficient to cope with the affects of ageing populations. Indeed, if they are combined with a small reduction in benefit rates for all dependents, they would leave contribution rates in 2035 at about the same or lower levels than in 1995.

Second, funded schemes do not help to provide pensions for ageing populations any better than Pay-As-You-Go ones. In part this is because it is not possible to carry over consumption goods from one year to the next, so that resources for this year's pensioners must be drawn from the incomes of this year's workers. In part because the ageing population will need to sell its financial assets to active workers in order to finance its pension.

Third, there are important risks associated with funded pension schemes which make it impossible to guarantee the replacement rate of contributors. These risks are large, probably of the order of 30 per cent or more. They become acceptable only if they form part of a multi-tiered pension structure in which the basic guarantees are provided by a defined benefit scheme of the public, PAYG, type.

1. The comparative demography

Figure 3.2.1 displays the historical and projected old age dependency rates for Japan, North America and Europe from 1950 up to the year 2050. They show that Japan and the other two regional groupings are experiencing rapid growth in their population 60 and over as a proportion of population of working age (15 to 60). For Japan this ratio has increased from 7 per cent in 1950 to 17 per cent in 1995 and is expected to rise to 40 per cent by the year 2035. For North America the comparable rises are from 12 per cent to 16 per cent to 30 per cent in 2035. For Europe the figures are respectively 11 per cent, 15 per cent to 31 per cent. For all three the increases stem mainly from earlier declines in fertility, although they have also been influenced by increases in life expectancy at the age of retirement. In Japan, fertility levels have fallen sharply from 2.75 in 1950 to 1.48 in 1995. In North America the decline over the same period was from 3.48 to 1.93 and for Europe from 2.56 to 1.45. But the Japanese decline was the largest, the earliest and the most rapid. Additional figures are given in table 3.2.1 which shows the population structure in two years, 1995 and 2035, for the seven countries of the comparison, for men and women separately, and in terms of the main age groups.

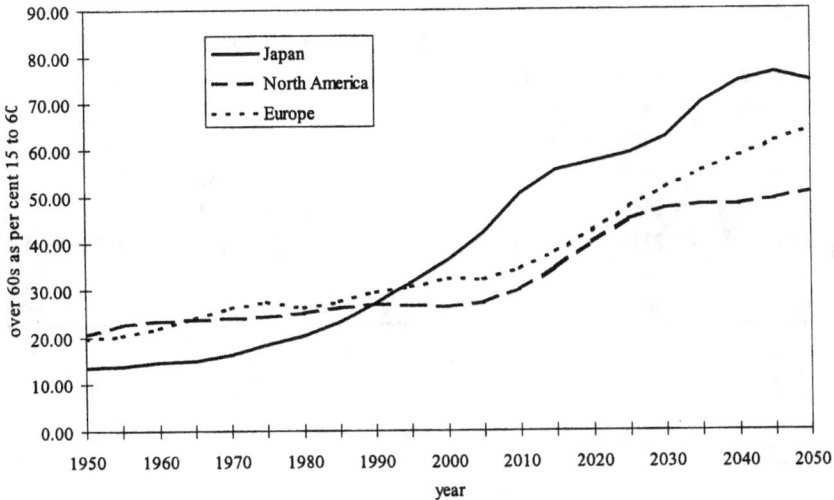

Figure 3.2.1   Old age dependency rates

Table 3.2.1 Demographic projections: 1995 and 2035

	Japan	France	Germany	Norway	USA	Australia	Italy
Population age groups in 1995 (000's)							
Men							
under 15	10379	5772	6737	430	30259	736	4406
15 to 19	4418	1981	2320	137	9087	249	1899
20 to 24	5101	2162	2649	163	9090	287	2255
25 to 54	26702	12095	18631	949	58992	1837	12269
55 to 59	3885	1387	2891	95	5525	228	1698
60 to 64	3583	1371	2112	86	4874	168	1552
65 to 69	2944	1245	1776	86	4592	162	1377
70 to 74	1917	990	1219	83	3902	125	1118
75 to 79	1260	548	609	60	2707	66	544
over 80	1217	751	855	58	2572	81	692
Total	61405	28303	39800	2148	131600	3938	27812
Women							
under 15	9863	5508	6389	409	28881	690	4161
15 to 19	4198	1893	2171	130	8683	230	1804
20 to 24	4865	2080	2425	156	8773	268	2158
25 to 54	26442	12070	17658	901	58308	1741	12251
55 to 59	4037	1442	2932	97	5793	238	1821
60 to 64	3844	1517	2256	91	5312	188	1747
65 to 69	3368	1496	2210	96	5341	200	1662
70 to 74	2718	1324	2187	104	4985	218	1542
75 to 79	2013	837	1273	88	3941	133	855
over 80	2316	1634	2294	114	5498	201	1391
Total	63663	29800	41793	2185	135515	4108	29392

Table 3.2.1 Demographic projections: 1995 and 2035 (continued)

Population age groups in 2035 (000's)

Men

under 15	8691	5031	5267	448	32832	579	2879
15 to 19	2807	1685	1867	148	11126	203	999
20 to 24	2978	1673	1883	144	11085	204	1049
25 to 54	19819	10570	14477	855	63699	1459	7987
55 to 59	4163	1852	2679	131	9433	282	1811
60 to 64	4626	1931	2697	148	8831	297	2069
65 to 69	3804	1795	3108	146	8641	321	2074
70 to 74	3151	1576	2730	120	8487	284	1806
75 to 79	2596	1292	1820	91	6853	194	1311
over 80	4259	1677	1659	97	6827	174	1596
Total	56893	29082	38187	2329	167814	3998	23582

Women

under 15	8247	4797	4996	424	31288	548	2711
15 to 19	2669	1612	1770	140	10617	192	941
20 to 24	2836	1605	1786	137	10593	194	990
25 to 54	19034	10238	13269	817	61985	1364	7592
55 to 59	4066	1830	2428	127	9429	254	1760
60 to 64	4633	1975	2526	147	9118	275	2068
65 to 69	4006	1962	3167	151	9349	317	2180
70 to 74	3529	1907	3060	134	9739	305	2028
over 75	3161	1742	2387	116	8722	243	1633
over 80	7101	3058	3449	173	12051	338	2856
Total	59283	30726	38837	2366	172892	4031	24759

Old age dependency ratios

1995	31.6	33.4	32.5	32.9	26.6	30.4	34.5
2035	70	60.9	66.2	53	47.2	66.3	84.8

Source: *Population projections, 1996.* United Nations

193

These projections are relatively robust, at least for the next forty years or so. People who will be 65 in the year 2035 are now aged 18: those aged 40 in 2035 have just been born. Their numbers will not be affected by future changes in birth rates. On the other hand, those who will be 15 in the year 2035 will not be born until the year 2020, so that about half the labour force will be affected by the fertility rates of the next 25 years. Fertility rates are the most volatile element of the projections, but it would take a very dramatic change appreciably to affect the projections of dependency rates. Changes in life expectancy will also alter the number of pensioners in 2035. Such changes in the past have developed along a trend which has grown relatively slowly and is reasonably predictable. After 2035 the population projections become progressively less reliable. But barring some major catastrophe or some very abrupt change, we must accept the idea that old age dependency rates - give or take a few percentage points - will develop along the lines shown in figure 3.2.1 and table 3.2.1.

2. The retirement age for men, the employment of women and the adjustment of benefit rates

In most developed countries only about half the population is actively employed at any one time. Children under the age of 15 or 16 are compulsorily at school, and many of them continue in full time education into their mid twenties. Participation rates for men aged 25 to 55 are much higher, of the order of 90 per cent. But even so some of them are unemployed, others are disabled and cannot work. From the age of 55 onward men begin to retire, gradually at first but in increasing numbers, until by the age of 70 very few are still left in the labour force. Participation rates for women are lower than those for men at all ages. There are cultural and historical reasons for this many of them linked to the low provision of education for young women which existed in the 1950s and 1960s and their subsequent difficulty in finding employment. But in addition to these social factors many women withdraw from the labour force for several years to look after young children. And when it comes to retirement, many wives who are younger than their husbands by two or three years, wish to retire at the same time. All this group of non-active people constitute a body of dependents who must be supported, one way or another, from the incomes of the economy as a whole - chiefly from the incomes of the active population.

Details of these participation rates are shown in table 3.2.2, which also calculates the implied dependency rate for the different countries. The overall dependency rate for Japan in 1995 was just under 50 per cent: higher than in Norway and in the United States, but significantly less than in France, Germany, Austria or Italy. Table 3.2.2 also calculates the dependency rates for the year 2035, using the participation rates for 1995 but applying them to the projected population structure for 2035. Obviously, because population structures are ageing, the dependency rates increase: to around 56 per cent in the case of Japan but with comparable increases for the other countries.

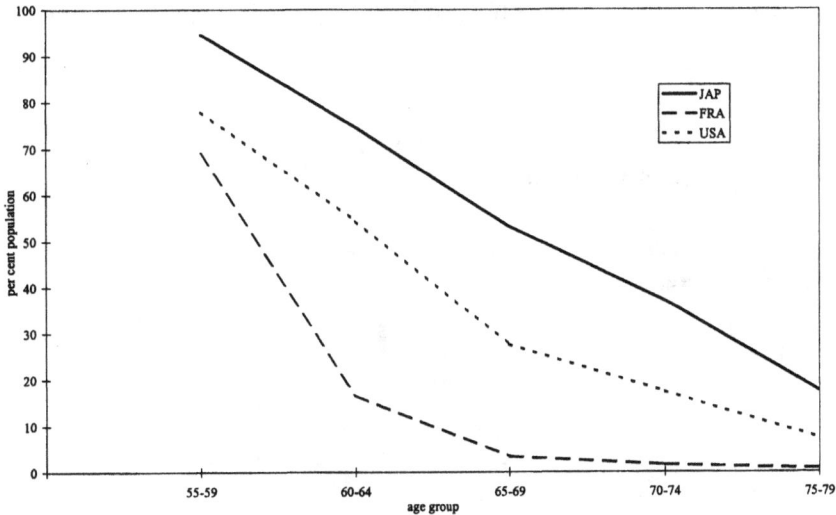

Figure 3.2.2   Participation rates of older men in 1995

Table 3.2.2 also calculates the estimated contribution rates associated with this dependency. This is done by applying an arbitrary replacement rate of 60 per cent to the estimated GDP per active person in order to arrive at the estimated income per non-active person and hence the contribution rate to be levied on the incomes of active persons. The assumption clearly requires a bit of explanation. In the first place, the contribution rate is one which applies to incomes of all kinds and is applied to all dependents. It is therefore much higher than would normally be associated with the contribution rates used only to provide pensions for retired persons. Second, there is very little information about the appropriate level. Recent evidence from the OECD[1] suggests that the relative income of pensioner households is around 90 per cent of that for other households, assessed in terms of equivalent incomes per person which weight children at 25 per cent and retired persons at 75 per cent of working age adults. Given the mix of dependents in the calculation a replacement rate of around 60 per cent across all dependents seems plausible, especially if the cost of education is included in the support of children. But little is known about cross country differences, hence the uniform assumption across all the countries in the sample. This is clearly something which needs to be worked out more carefully. But it is not critical to the main argument used here and in a later (6) the assumption is varied.

Table 3.2.2 Demographic and labour market assumptions: no change scenario

	Japan	France	Germany	Norway	USA	Australia	Italy
Participation rates in 1995 (per cent)							
Men							
15 to 54	64.9	50.6	56.6	76.5	74.9	52.3	51.7
55 to 59	946	68.9	73.9	83.2	77.9	63.7	60.2
60 to 64	74.5	16.5	28.7	62.5	54.3	16.7	30.9
65 to 69	53.1	3.3	6.8	25.3	27.5	7.0	11.1
70 to 74	37.0	1.5	4.1	5.0	17.3	4.8	5.0
75 to 79	17.5	0.7	1.9	2.2	7.3	1.9	2.4
Women							
15 to 54	42.5	39.6	40.2	66.0	59.3	35.4	29.2
55 to 59	58.1	50.8	50.5	68.3	59.8	25.4	19.9
60 to 64	39.0	14.6	11.3	48.9	38.2	8.7	7.7
65 to 69	27.0	2.7	3.3	16.0	17.2	3.8	2.7
70 to 74	165	0.8	1.6	2.0	8.8	2.0	1.4
75 to 79	6.3	0.4	0.6	1.0	3.1	1.0	1.2

Table 3.2.2 Demographic and labour market assumptions: no change scenario (continued)

	Japan	France	Germany	Norway	USA	Australia	Italy
Outcomes in 1995:							
Number of actives	53105	16904	27627	2113	119659	2369	15588
Number of inactives	52525	30132	42203	1509	89788	4401	33273
Dependency rate (over 15's)	49.7	64.1	60.4	41.7	42.9	65.0	68.1
GDP ($ billion; current PPP's)	2594	1112	1602	95	6650	162	1068
GDP per active ($000 at current PPP's)	48841	65771	57975	45095	55573	68514	68539
Replacement rate (per cent)	50	50	50	50	50	50	50
GDP per inactive ($000 at current PPP's)	24421	32885	28987	22548	27786	34257	34270
Contribution rate (per cent)	**33.1**	**47.1**	**43.3**	**26.3**	**27.3**	**48.2**	**51.6**
Outcomes in 2035:							
Number of actives	44102	15355	21871	2032	142027	1974	10667
Number of inactives (000'S)	55135	34625	44891	1790	134559	4928	32083
Dependency rate (over 15's)	55.6	69.3	67.2	46.8	48.6	71.4	75.0
GDP ($ billion; current PPP's)	2154	1010	1268	92	7893	135	731
GDP per active ($000 at current PPP's)	48841	65771	57975	45095	55573	68514	68539
Replacement rate (per cent)	50	50	50	50	50	50	50
GDP per inactive ($000 at current PPP's)	24421	32885	28987	22548	27786	34257	34270
Contribution rate (per cent)	**38.5**	**53.0**	**50.6**	**30.6**	**32.1**	**55.5**	**60.1**

Sources: Yearbook of international labour statistics, 1997; ILO. Medium term population projections, 1996; United Nations. National Accounts 1996; OECD

What will happen between now and the year 2035 if participation rates change? In particular, if the average age of retirement were to increase and/or female participation rates were to increase. And what will happen if the replacement rate were to be reduced by around 10 per cent.? The answers to these questions are shown in tables 3.2.3, 3.2.4, 3.2.5 and 3.2.6 and the results summarised in table 3.2.7.

In table 3.2.3 the male retirement age for all countries is increased to the 1995 levels in Japan, which has the highest participation rate for older male workers. In table 3.2.4 the participation rates for women are increased to the 1995 levels in Norway, which has the highest female participation rate. In table 3.2.5 both changes are applied simultaneously. And in table 3.2.6 both these changes are combined with a 10 per cent reduction in replacement rates, from 60 per cent to 54 per cent. Although the tables are fairly large ones, the outcomes are readily understood and not difficult to follow from the summary in table 3.2.7. The main features are the following:

1. The overall contribution rates for 1995 are higher than those which would apply only to pension schemes, simply because they must provide support for dependents of all kinds, as well as just pensioners. Equally important, they embody all kinds of income, including intra-family support for children and non-working wives. This does not invalidate the argument: the support must be provided one way or another. But it does lead to higher overall figures.

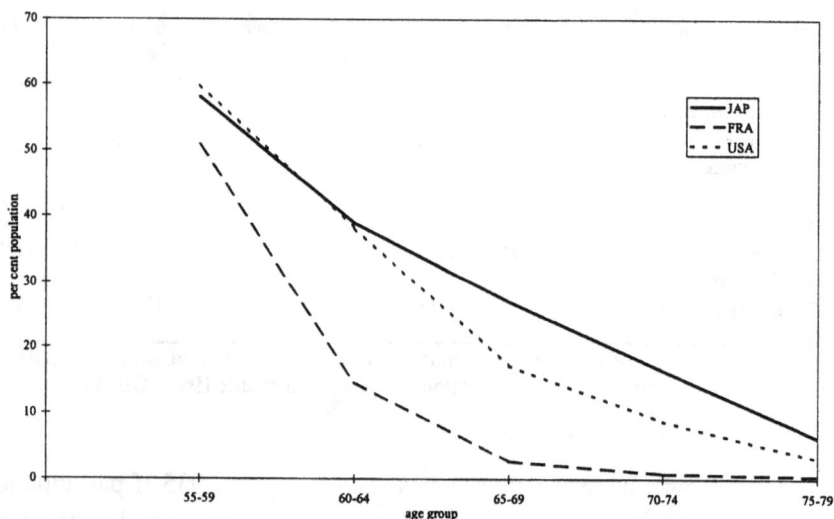

Figure 3.2.3   Participation rates of older women in 1995

198

2. The increase in overall contribution rates on a no-policy-change basis (table 3.2.2) are much less frightening than might be expected simply by looking at the expected changes in the old-age dependency rate (figure 3.2.1 and table 3.2.1). Old-age dependency rates are expected to increase sharply between 1995 and 2035 (for example Japan by 26 percentage points, Italy and the US by 23) and pension contribution rates follow suit. But the corresponding overall contribution rates increase by much less (9 points in Japan, 8 points in the US, 10 points in Italy). Other countries experience similar increases.

3. There are significant differences between countries, in both 1995 and 2035 in the no-change scenario. For 1995 the overall contribution rate varies between 35 per cent in Japan to over 50 per cent in France and Italy. For 2035 the overall contribution rate varies between 43 per cent in Japan to 60 per cent in Italy. It is worth noting that in both cases Japan has the lowest contribution rate. Dependency rates show a similar variation.

Table 3.2.3 Demographic and labour market assumptions: increased retirement age

	Japan	France	Germany	Norway	USA	Australia	Italy
Participation rates in 1995 (per cent)							
Men							
15 to 54	64.9	64.9	64.9	64.9	64.9	64.9	64.9
55 to 59	94.6	94.6	94.6	94.6	94.6	94.6	94.6
60 to 64	74.5	74.5	74.5	74.5	74.5	74.5	74.5
65 to 69	53.1	53.1	53.1	53.1	53.1	53.1	53.1
70 to 74	37.0	37.0	37.0	37.0	37.0	37.0	37.0
75 to 79	17.5	17.5	17.5	17.5	17.5	17.5	17.5
Women							
15 to 54	42.5	39.6	40.2	66.0	59.3	35.4	29.2
55 to 59	58.1	50.8	50.5	68.3	59.8	25.4	19.9
60 to 64	39.0	14.6	11.3	48.9	38.2	8.7	7.7
65 to 69	27.0	2.7	3.3	16.0	17.2	3.8	2.7
70 to 74	16.5	0.8	1.6	2.0	8.8	2.0	1.4
75 to 79	6.3	0.4	0.6	1.0	3.1	1.0	1.2

Table 3.2.3 Demographic and labour market assumptions: increased retirement age (continued)

	Japan	France	Germany	Norway	USA	Australia	Italy
Outcomes in 1995:							
Number of actives	53105	21442	32471	2049	116070	2960	20036
Number of inactives	52525	25595	37359	1573	93377	3809	28826
Dependency rate (over 15's)	49.7	54.4	53.5	43.4	44.6	56.3	59.0
GDP ($ billion; current PPP's)	2593.7	1111.8	1601.7	95.3	6649.8	162.3	1068.4
GDP per active ($000 at current PPP's)	48841	51852	49328	46504	57291	54822	53325
Replacement rate (per cent)	50	50	50	50	50	50	50
GDP per inactive ($000 at current PPP's)	24421	25926	24664	23252	28646	27411	26662
Contribution rate (per cent)	**33.1**	**37.4**	**36.5**	**27.7**	**28.7**	**39.2**	**41.8**
Outcomes in 2035:							
Number of actives	44102	20613	27795	2025	141378	2738	15163
Number of inactives (000'S)	55135	29366	38967	1797	135208	4164	27586
Dependency rate (over 15's)	55.6	58.8	58.4	47.0	48.9	60.3	64.5
GDP ($ billion; current PPP's)	2154	1069	1371	94	8100	150	809
GDP per active ($000 at current PPP's)	48841	51852	49328	46504	57291	54822	53325
Replacement rate (per cent)	50.0	50.0	50.0	50.0	50.0	50.0	50.0
GDP per inactive ($000 at current PPP's)	24421	25926	24664	23252	28646	27411	26662
Contribution rate (per cent)	**38.5**	**41.6**	**41.2**	**30.7**	**32.3**	**43.2**	**47.6**

Sources: Yearbook of international labour statistics, 1997; ILO. Medium term population projections, 1996; United Nations. National Accounts 1996; OECD

4. It is immediately apparent from table 3.2.7 that the different alternatives - increased retirement age, increased female participation rates, reduced replacement rates - would each result in a significant reduction in contribution rates. So much so that in combination they would result in contribution rates for France, Germany, Austria and

Italy which in 2035 would be substantially below their 1995 levels. For Japan the reduction would be small, for the United States minimal, and for Norway, which already has high participation rates for both men and women, there is a very slight increase over the 1995 level. The gains from taking these measures in comparison with doing nothing are striking, especially for the main European countries. In effect, labour market policies of these kinds, together with a relatively small adjustment of benefits can completely wipe out the adverse consequences of ageing populations.

Table 3.2.4 Demographic and labour market assumptions: increased female participation rates

	Japan	France	Germany	Norway	USA	Australia	Italy
Participation rates in 1995 (per cent)							
Men							
15 to 54	64.9	50.6	56.6	76.5	74.9	52.3	51.7
55 to 59	94.6	68.9	73.9	83.2	77.9	63.7	60.2
60 to 64	74.5	16.5	28.7	62.5	54.3	16.7	30.9
65 to 69	53.1	3.3	6.8	25.3	27.5	7.0	11.1
70 to 74	37.0	1.5	4.1	5.0	17.3	4.8	5.0
75 to 79	17.5	0.7	1.9	2.2	7.3	1.9	2.4
Women							
15 to 54	66.0	66.0	66.0	66.0	66.0	66.0	66.0
55 to 59	68.3	68.3	68.3	68.3	68.3	68.3	68.3
60 to 64	48.9	48.9	48.9	48.9	48.9	48.9	48.9
65 to 69	16.0	16.0	16.0	16.0	16.0	16.0	16.0
70 to 74	2.0	2.0	2.0	2.0	2.0	2.0	2.0
75 to 79	1.0	1.0	1.0	1.0	1.0	1.0	1.0

Table 3.2.4 Demographic and labour market assumptions: increased female participation rates (continued)

	Japan	France	Germany	Norway	USA	Australia	Italy
Outcomes in 1995:							
Number of actives	61544	22221	35419	2113	125410	3336	23503
Number of inactives	44065	24865	34462	1509	84038	3486	25414
Dependency rate (over 15's)	41.7	52.8	49.3	41.7	40.1	51.1	52.0
GDP ($ billion; current PPP's)	2594	1112	1602	95	6650	162	1068
GDP per active ($000 at current PPP's)	42144	50034	45222	45095	53025	48645	45459
Replacement rate (per cent)	50	50	50	50	50	50	50
GDP per inactive ($000 at current PPP's)	21072	25017	22611	22548	26512	24322	22729
Contribution rate (per cent)	**26.4**	**35.9**	**32.7**	**26.3**	**25.1**	**34.3**	**35.1**
Outcomes in 2035:							
Number of actives	49622	20199	28018	2032	148421	2767	16173
Number of inactives (000'S)	49615	29781	38744	1790	128166	4134	26576
Dependency rate (over 15's)	50	60	58	47	46	60	62
GDP ($ billion; current PPP's)	2091.2	1010.6	1267.0	91.6	7870.0	134.6	735.2
GDP per active ($000 at current PPP's)	42144	50034	45222	45095	53025	48645	45459
Replacement rate (per cent)	50	50	50	50	50	50	50
GDP per inactive ($000 at current PPP's)	21072	25017	22611	22548	26512	24322	22729
Contribution rate (per cent)	**33**	**42**	**41**	**31**	**30**	**43**	**45**

Sources: Yearbook of international labour statistics, 1997; ILO. Medium term population projections, 1996; United Nations. National Accounts 1996; OECD

5. In *economic* terms, the policies proposed are eminently feasible: they amount to no more than persuading countries to adopt the best practice measures already in place in Japan and Norway. Their implementation would be helped by the relatively long period - around 40 years - during which they could gradually be put in place.

Increasing life expectancy, especially increases in life expectancy in good health, will make later retirement age easier to adopt. There is already a strong trend towards greater female participation rates which would reinforce expanded employment of women. And reasonable economic growth will make a small downward adjustment of replacement rates easier to accept: a growth rate of only 1.75 per cent per annum from now on would imply that average incomes in the year 2035 will be double those in 1995.

Table 3.2.5 Demographic and labour market assumptions: increased retirement age and female participation rates

	Japan	France	Germany	Norway	USA	Australia	Italy
Participation rates in 1995 (per cent)							
Men							
15 to 54	64.9	64.9	64.9	64.9	64.9	64.9	64.9
55 to 59	94.6	94.6	94.6	94.6	94.6	94.6	94.6
60 to 64	74.5	74.5	74.5	74.5	74.5	74.5	74.5
65 to 69	53.1	53.1	53.1	53.1	53.1	53.1	53.1
70 to 74	37.0	37.0	37.0	37.0	37.0	37.0	37.0
75 to 79	17.5	17.5	17.5	17.5	17.5	17.5	175
Women							
15 to 54	66.0	66.0	66.0	66.0	66.0	66.0	66.0
55 to 59	68.3	68.3	68.3	68.3	68.3	68.3	68.3
60 to 64	48.9	48.9	48.9	48.9	48.9	48.9	48.9
65 to 69	16.0	16.0	16.0	16.0	16.0	16.0	16.0
70 to 74	2.0	2.0	2.0	2.0	2.0	2.0	2.0
75 to 79	1.0	1.0	1.0	1.0	1.0	1.0	1.0

Table 3.2.5 Demographic and labour market assumptions: increased retirement age and female participation rates (continued)

	Japan	France	Germany	Norway	USA	Australia	Italy
Outcomes in 1995:							
Number of actives	61544	26759	40262	2049	121820	3928	27950
Number of inactives	44065	20327	29619	1573	87627	2894	20966
Dependency rate (over 15's)	41.7	43.2	42.4	43.4	41.8	42.4	42.9
GDP ($ billion; current PPP's)	2594	1112	1602	95	6650	162	1068
GDP per active ($000 at current PPP's)	42144	41549	39782	46504	54587	41318	38225
Replacement rate (per cent)	50	50	50	50	50	50	50
GDP per inactive ($000 at current PPP's)	21072	20775	19891	23252	27293	20659	19113
Contribution rate (per cent)	**26.4**	**27.5**	**26.9**	**27.7**	**26.5**	**26.9**	**27.3**
Outcomes in 2035:							
Number of actives	49622	25457	33942	2025	147772	3531	20670
Number of inactives (000'S)	49615	24523	32821	1797	128814	3370	22079
Dependency rate (over 15's)	50	49	49	47	47	49	52
GDP ($ billion; current PPP's)	2091.2	1057.7	1350.3	94.2	8066.4	145.9	790.1
GDP per active ($000 at current PPP's)	42144	41549	39782	46504	54587	41318	38225
Replacement rate (per cent)	50	50	50	50	50	50	50
GDP per inactive ($000 at current PPP's)	21072	20775	19891	23252	27293	20659	19113
Contribution rate (per cent)	**33**	**33**	**33**	**31**	**30**	**32**	**35**

Sources: Yearbook of international labour statistics, 1997; ILO. Medium term population projections, 1996; United Nations. National Accounts 1996; OECD

6.   There are of course significant difficulties, mainly of a political and social kind. In the first place, many European countries have delib-erately pursued policies of early retirement in order to alleviate the

high and growing levels of unemployment which they have experienced over the last twenty years. Early retirement has also been linked to invalidity pensions which in a number of countries have in turn been linked to labour market conditions as well as physical and mental handicaps. These policies would need to be reversed. In most countries early retirement involves a reduced pension, both on the part of public schemes and also by occupational schemes. In France and the United States, pensions are reduced by about 6 per cent for every year of early retirement: In Germany the figure is around 3.5 per cent. But the amount by which pensions have been reduced has been insufficient to prevent large numbers of older workers choosing early retirement, and the corresponding additional rewards for postponing retirement beyond the official age have not induced many workers to continue. Clearly both the rates and conditions for early and late retirement do not reflect their *social* cost (as distinct from their individual and actuarial cost) will need to be tightened. This is unlikely to be popular with electorates, especially if older workers continue to find it difficult to get a job. Similarly, the trend towards higher levels of employment for women will need to be promoted, through the provision of child care facilities and a reduction in the gender bias towards female employment. In this case measures to increase employment of women would be reinforcing an already strong trend. Finally, any reduction, even a small one, in benefit rates is likely to be resisted. But these difficulties are not insuperable and in the long run are easier to face than the corresponding increases in contribution rates.

7.   Finally, it should be noted that the overall picture presented here disguises some reallocation of contributions and benefits between different categories of dependents. To maintain pension benefits for the elderly may require smaller tax benefits for children and non-working wives and perhaps some tighter conditions and slightly lower benefits for the unemployed - although this is a tricky and separate matter.

Table 3.2.6 Demographic and labour market assumptions: later retirement, higher female participation, lower benefits

	Japan	France	Germany	Norway	USA	Australia	Italy
Participation rates in 1995 (per cent)							
Men							
under 15	0	0	0	0	0	0	0
15 to 19	18.4	18.4	18.4	18.4	18.4	18.4	18.4
20 to 24	97	97	97	97	97	97	97
25 to 55	97.7	97.7	97.7	97.7	97.7	97.7	97.7
55 to 59	94.6	94.6	94.6	94.6	94.6	94.6	94.6
60 to 64	74.5	74.5	74.5	74.5	74.5	74.5	74.5
65 to 69	53.1	53.1	53.1	53.1	53.1	53.1	53.1
70 to 74	37	37	37	37	37	37	37
75 to 79	17.5	17.5	17.5	17.5	17.5	17.5	17.5
over 80	0	0	0	0	0	0	0
Women							
under 15	0	0	0	0	0	0	0
15 to 19	41.7	41.7	41.7	41.7	41.7	41.7	41.7
20 to 24	68	68	68	68	68	68	68
25 to 54	81.8	81.8	81.8	81.8	81.8	81.8	81.8
55 to 59	68.3	68.3	68.3	68.3	68.3	68.3	68.3
60 to 64	48.9	48.9	48.9	48.9	48.9	48.9	48.9
65 to 69	16	16	16	16	16	16	16
70 to 74	2	2	2	2	2	2	2
75 to 79	1	1	1	1	1	1	1
over 80	0	0	0	0	0	0	0

Table 3.2.6 Demographic and labour market assumptions: later retirement, higher female participation, lower benefits (continued)

	Japan	France	Germany	Norway	USA	Australia	Italy
Outcomes in 1995:							
Number of actives	65945	28812	43542	2159	132194	4191	30161
Number of inactives	59123	29291	38051	2174	134921	3855	27043
Dependency rate (all ages)	47.3	50.4	46.6	50.2	50.5	47.9	47.3
GDP ($ billion; current PPP's)	2594	1112	1602	95	6650	162	1068
GDP per active ($000 at current PPP's)	39331	38589	36785	44148	50303	38725	35423
Replacement rate (per cent)	54	54	· 54	54	54	54	54
GDP per inactive ($000 at current PPP's)	21239	20838	19864	23840	27164	20912	19129
Contribution rate (per cent)	**32.6**	**35.4**	**32.1**	**35.2**	**35.5**	**33.2**	**32.6**
Outcomes in 2035:							
Number of actives	50299	25496	34919	2007	145909	3600	21251
Number of inactives (000'S)	65877	34312	42106	2688	194798	4430	27089
Dependency rate (all ages)	56.7	57.4	54.7	57.2	57.2	55.2	56.0
GDP ($ billion; current PPP's)	1978	984	1285	89	7340	139	753
GDP per active ($000 at current PPP's)	39331	38589	36785	44148	50303	38725	35423
Replacement rate (per cent)	54	54	54	54	54	54	54
GDP per inactive ($000 at current PPP's)	21239	20838	19864	23840	27164	20912	19129
Contribution rate (per cent)	**41.4**	**42.1**	**39.4**	**42.0**	**41.9**	**39.9**	**40.8**

Sources: Yearbook of international labour statistics, 1997; ILO. Medium term population projections, 1996; United Nations. National Accounts 1996; OECD

Table 3.2.7 Dependency rates in 2035 under alternative scenarios

	Japan	France	Germany	Norway	USA	Australia	Italy
1995 base level	47.0	63.8	54.1	53.3	51.9	54.5	62.5
2035:							
no change scenario	56.2	69.9	64.1	60.9	60.0	65.5	71.5
higher retirement age for men	56.2	63.9	57.4	57.2	56.5	58.0	63.7
increased female participation	56.7	63.3	61.3	60.9	60.7	62.7	63.9
both	56.7	57.4	54.7	57.2	57.2	55.2	56.0
both plus lower replacement rates	56.7	57.4	54.7	57.2	57.2	55.2	56.0
1995 base level	34.7	51.4	41.4	40.6	39.3	41.8	50.0
2035:							
no change scenario	43.5	58.2	51.7	48.3	47.4	53.2	60.1
higher retirement age for men	43.5	51.5	44.7	44.5	43.8	45.3	51.3
increased female participation	44.0	50.9	48.8	48.3	48.1	50.2	51.5
both	44.0	44.7	42.0	44.5	44.5	42.5	43.3
both plus lower replacement rates	41.4	42.1	39.4	42.0	41.9	39.9	40.8

3. Funding pensions: the individual and the economy

The fallacy of composition

It is frequently thought that pensions can be funded in advance: that by saving and building up financial assets pensions can later be paid by drawing down on the funds. In addition, it is thought that the process of saving will enable higher levels of investment to be achieved, which in turn will increase future GDP and permit higher pensions to be paid. If this view is correct it clearly opens possibilities for coping with the consequences of ageing populations. Pension funds can be accumulated when the population structure is relatively young. When the population structure becomes older the funds can be reduced to pay for the increased number of pensioners without increasing the burden of support required from younger workers.

For individuals, the way this works is the following. People who wish to save for their own retirement may do so either as individuals or as part of some group arrangement, often in a funded occupational scheme to which their employer also contributes. The mechanism is a simple one. During the individual's working life contributions are paid into an account which accumulates interest and builds up capital in the form of financial assets. On retirement, when there are no more earnings, this account is run down to provide for current consumption: either directly, or through the purchase an annuity which will provide a regular stream of income until the individual dies. Both imply the sale of the financial assets to someone else in the economy. Obviously, the higher the rate of interest, the larger the contributions, or the longer the working life, the larger will be the capital on retirement and the higher the ultimate pension. There are risks. The rate of return is not known in advance, and the individual may end up saving more or less than he or she needs. Neither is the growth of real wages known in advance, and individuals' perception of what they need is likely to be based on a comparison between incomes in retirement and incomes in work: i.e. the replacement rate. The individual may also die earlier or later than expected. But on average, and over a lifetime, the individual accounts can be expected to be in balance, with withdrawals in retirement matching savings during the active life.

Collectively however, and at the level of the whole economy, things do not work this way. Even if funds of financial assets have been established in advance, it is not possible - except on a very limited scale - to carry over consumption goods from one year to another or to ensure that they are directed uniquely at pensioners. The point is illustrated in table 3.2.8 which shows how the annual national accounts might look for a hypothetical population of 100 persons (25 retired, 75 active) and a total Gross Domestic Product and National Income of 10000. In this highly simplified example the economy is pictured as running a small balance of payments deficit which is funded by an equal volume of transfers from abroad. The income of active persons is set at 91 per cent of National Income and includes both earnings and profits. The income of retired persons is set at 9 per cent of National Income, includes no earnings and on a per capita basis is only one quarter of that received by active persons. But the per capita consumption of retirees is nearly three quarters of the per capita consumption of active persons. It must be financed by dissavings on the part of retirees: something they are able to do by selling their stock of financial assets to active persons. Active persons must save 24 per cent of GDP: sufficient to provide not only for investment in fixed assets and stocks (here pictured as 15 per cent of GDP) but also to purchase the financial assets sold by retired persons (an additional 9 per cent of GDP).

Table 3.2.8 The fallacy of composition: Example of the economy of a hypothetical population

Expenditure on Gross Domestic Product		Incomes Generated by Gross Domestic Product	
Personal consumption expenditure by retirees	1600	Wages and salaries of active persons	7800
Personal consumption expenditure by actives	6700	Profits received by active persons	1300
Total personal consumption expenditure	8300	Total income of active persons	9100
Government consumption expenditure	400	Wages and salaries received by retired persons	0
Gross fixed investment	1400	Profits received by retired persons	700
Increase in stocks	100	Total income of retired persons	700
Exports minus imports	-200	Transfers from abroad	200
Gross Domestic Product	10000	**Gross National Income**	10000
Population of retirees	25	Savings by actives	2400
Population of actives	75	Dissavings by retirees	-900
Total population	100	Total net savings	1500
Per capita consumption of retirees	64	Per capita income of retirees	28
Per capita consumption of actives	89	Per capita income of actives	121
Ratio of per capita consumption	0.72	Ratio of per capita incomes	0.23

The balance is clearly a fragile one. If the proportion of retirees in the population increases (from say, 25 to 30 per cent) or if their consumption relative to that of active persons increases (for example, because interest rates increase) something has to give. The number of options is limited:

- stock building might be reduced: but this option provides very limited resources;
- gross fixed investment might be reduced: but this will reduce future GDP and economic growth;
- government consumption might be reduced: but this may result in reduced services such as education, health or defence;
- the current external balance may be widened: but this is not a long-term option;
- the per capita consumption of retirees - and the implied replacement rate -might be reduced: but this would break the implicit contract between retirees and active workers.

None of these options appears particularly palatable, optimal in terms of economic development, or feasible in terms of the economic and political instruments which might be brought to bear.

Three features of this framework are important.

In the first place, the level of GDP is fixed. It is a consequence of the total productive capacity of the economy, which in turn will have been influenced by past levels of investment. But it is not influenced by what happens in the current year.

Second, the ability of retirees to dissave will be made easier if they have previously built up financial assets, which they can later sell to active persons. But this sale of financial assets does not in itself result in additional new real resources in the current year.

Third, it is not possible to make room for more retirees without either reducing other components of GDP or by reducing the implied per capita replacement rate. Since the implied pension contract, between actives and non-actives, is framed in terms of *relative* standards of living, this amounts to breaking the contract and risks offending people's sense of equity and justice about promises made some considerable time earlier.

Thus for all practical purposes, and at an aggregate level, funded pension schemes operate as Pay-As-You-Go schemes under which the consumption of today's pensioners is drawn from the consumption of today's workers.

Obviously there is a conflict between the perception of individuals and the macro-economic constraint just described. How are the two to be reconciled, and what happens to the money which individuals save for their retirement? There are at least two possibilities, depending on whether or not the additional savings result in increased gross fixed investment.

If the retirement savings of individuals do not result in higher fixed investment, what will occur is an inflation of asset prices. The volume of money seeking a financial investment will increase relative to the (unchanged) level of real fixed assets with the result that asset prices will increase. There will be no increase in GDP resulting from an increase in real fixed capital, but instead the rate of return on financial investments will decline. Pensioners and active persons will end up sharing the same total level of consumption and for one or other of them to increase their level of consumption will mean a reduction in the level of consumption of the other. Or an adjustment in the other components of GDP will be required, in the manner just described.

If the retirement savings of individuals result in higher real investment, it can be expected that the capital stock, and hence future GDP will be increased. Both profits and wages will be increased. If they are increased in the same proportion there will be no change in the capacity of the economy to provide for a higher replacement rate for the same number of pensioners or to provide for more pensioners at the same replacement rate. If the profits received by pensioners increase proportionately more than the profits plus earnings received by active workers then pensioners may be able to increase their share of total consumption. But only by reducing the relative share received by active workers. What matters here is not the size of GDP and total consumption, but the share of both which flows respectively to pensioners and active workers: that is, the overall replacement rate. To increase the share flowing to pensioners means that the share flowing to active persons must be reduced.

Of course there is the possibility that pension funds will invest abroad, with the implication that the country will operate a deficit on capital account and a surplus on current account. These flows would be reversed when the funds were drawn down and the country began to import more than it exported. This transfers the problem from a national to a global scale, and would clearly be most advantageous if the pension funds from ageing populations were invested in countries whose populations were younger (provided there were some assurance that profits could be repatriated when they were needed). But the problem does not go away simply by being globalized.

Another possibility is that the process of increasing asset prices would lead to financial speculation about their further increases, and hence fuel additional increases in asset prices. This might alter the share of profits - especially in the form of capital gains - flowing to pensioners. But ultimately the bubble would burst, especially when pensioners wished to cash in their assets in return for pensions, and the consequent reversal of asset prices would be correspondingly more abrupt.

The arithmetic

Some of the implications both of the participation rate analysis in section 2 and of the discussion above on the fallacy of composition can be illustrated with reference to a stylised comparison of the different reactions to PAYG schemes and Mandatory Retirement Savings (MRS) schemes to different levels of interest rates, dependency ratios, retirement ages and age at death. Formally the structure of such calculations is set out in table 3.2.9, but for those who prefer a more intuitive approach, the results are illustrated in figures 3.2.4, 3.2.5, 3.2.6 and 3.2.7. The argument runs as follows.

Consider a worker who becomes employed at the age of twenty, earns the same real income throughout his working life, contributes to a pension scheme throughout his career, retires at sixty and lives until he is eighty. If the pension scheme is a Mandatory Retirement Savings (MRS) scheme, a simple calculation tells us that if he saves and invests 15 percent of his earnings and if he receives a real rate of return of 2.5 per cent per annum on his savings and investment, then his income in retirement will represent a replacement rate of 60 per cent of his final earnings. As an alternative, suppose the same worker participates in a Pay-As-You-Go (PAYG) scheme for which the ratio of pensioners to contributors (all of whom earn the same) is a constant 25 per cent and which stipulates a replacement rate of 60 per cent. Then he will be required to contribute 15 per cent of his earnings throughout his 40 year working life.

Table 3.2.9 Basic simulation

	Parameters		
	Independent parameters		
15.00	MRS Contribution rate (%)	MRSCR	15.00
2.30	Interest rate (%)	IR	2.30
60	PAYG Replacement rate	PYGRR	60
60	Retirement age	AR	60
80	Age at death	AD	80
1.00	Reference earning period(yrs)	REP	1.00
0.00	Earnings growth (per cent p.a.)	EG	0.00
0.00	Age-earnings profile	EA	0.00
0.00	Inflation rate	CPI	0.00
-0.80	Population age adjustment	PADJ	2.00
	Independent variables		
	Insured population	POP	86291.93
	Dependent parameters		
50	Passivity ratio (%)	PR	50
58	Dependency ratio (%)	DR	58
9896	MRS Capital at retirement	KR	9896
0	MRS Capital at death	KD	0
1000	Reference earnings	REF	1000
17257	PAYG Benefits	PAYGB	17257
49627	PAYG Earnings base	PAYGC	49627
34.8	PAYG Contribution rate (%)	PYGCR	34.8
60.9	MRS Replacement rate (% REF)	MRSRR	60.9
0.0	PAYG Surplus/Deficit	SURP	0.0
-12.8	MRS Net New savings	SAVE	-12.8
60.0	PAYGRR at retirement	PYGRT	60.0
60.9	MRSRR at retirement	MRSRT	60.9
	Total capital stock (MRS)	KTOT	4.4

Table 3.2.9 Basic simulation (continued)

	Basic Parameters					Outcomes MRS		PAYG
Age	RI	NI	TI	CPI	POP	C/B	K	C/B
20	1000	1000	1000	1.00	1000	150	153	348
25	1000	1000	1000	1.00	1090	150	975	348
30	1000	1000	1000	1.00	1167	150	1896	348
35	1000	1000	1000	1.00	1162	150	2928	348
40	1000	1000	1000	1.00	1295	150	348	348
45	1000	1000	1000	1.00	1427	150	5379	348
50	1000	1000	1000	1.00	1298	150	6830	348
55	1000	1000	1000	1.00	1338	150	8456	348
60	1000	1000	1000	1.00	1431	-609	9501	-600
65	1000	1000	1000	1.00	1539	-609	7384	-600
70	1000	1000	1000	1.00	1527	-609	5012	-600
75	1000	1000	1000	1.00	1270	-609	2355	-600
80	1000	1000	1000	1.00	1111	0	0	0
85	1000	1000	1000	1.00	694	0	0	0
90	1000	1000	1000	1.00	407	0	0	0

RI =   Average real income
NI =   Average nominal income
TI =   Total real income
CPI =   Consumer price index
POP =   Total population
C/B =   Average contributions (+) or benefits (-)
K =   Accumulated capital (MRS)

The two stylised cases above yield the same results in terms of contribution rates and replacement rates, and have been constructed so that they do so.[2] But they are sensitive to different parameters. In the first case (MRS), the replacement rate is the dependent variable and depends on the contribution rate, the rate of return, and the ratio of years in retirement to years of contribution (the passivity ratio). In the second case (PAYG), the contribution rate is the dependent variable and is sensitive to the replacement rate and the ratio of pensioners to contributors (the dependency ratio).

What will happen to the pension system and the worker as these initial assumptions are varied in respect to different interest rates, different dependency rates, different retirement ages and different life expectancies ?

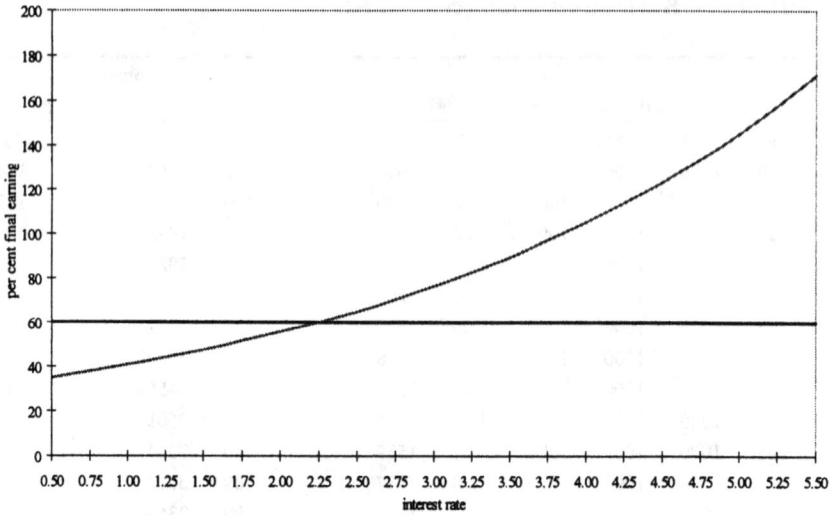

—— PYGRR = Pay-As-You-Go replacement rate

········ MRSRT = replacement rate in a Mandatory Retirement Saving scheme

Figure 3.2.4a   Replacement rates as a function of interest rates

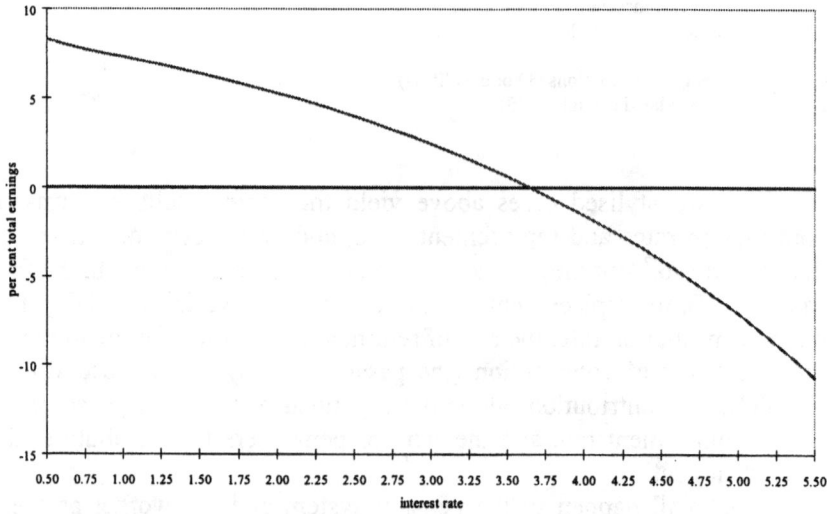

—— SURP = surplus under a Pay-As-You-Go scheme

········ SAVE = net new savings generated by a Mandatory Retirement Saving scheme

Figure 3.2.4b   Net new MRS savings as a function of interest rates

Interest rates

A comparison of the two possibilities, corresponding to different rates of interest, is provided in figure 3.2.4. Broadly what this shows, on the particular assumptions used above and for this simplified case, is that for rates of interest above about 2.5 per cent per annum, the MRS provides a higher replacement rate (or correspondingly, a lower contribution rate for the same replacement rate) than the PAYG scheme. Since dependency ratios of around 25 per cent, passivity ratios of around 50 per cent, and long-term real interest rates of around 2.5 per cent all appear within the range of recent experience, it is this kind of comparison which has lead some authors[3] to prefer MRS pension systems over defined benefit PAYG schemes, especially since ageing population structures imply substantial future increases in dependency ratios. The gains in replacement rate are in fact substantial. If the cross-over point between the two regimes occurs at a (real) interest rate of around 2.5 per cent, then doubling this rate will more than double the replacement rate to be expected under an MRS scheme. Conversely, a decline in the interest rate from around 2.5 per cent to around 0.5 per cent brings the MRS replacement down from around 60 per cent of final earnings to less than 40 per cent. But these gains have a cost. As replacement rates under the MRS scheme increase, net new savings decline, turning from positive to negative at an interest rate of about 3.75 per cent. Net new savings are here defined as the difference between total contributions to the pension scheme and total benefits, expressed as a percentage of the total earnings of all workers. What starts off as a savings rate of about 8 per cent of earnings when interest rates are 0.5 per cent and replacement rates just under 40 per cent becomes a dissaving of around 7 per cent of earnings when interest rates are 5 per cent and replacement rates 140 per cent of final earnings. Clearly what is happening is that the higher replacement rates must be paid for somewhere, and in the case of the MRS scheme they are drawn from the other savings of the population. The PAYG scheme is insensitive to interest rates: the contribution rate is set so that the scheme is always in aggregate balance and this is reflected in the straight line across the graph.

In fact of course, interest rates are volatile, especially over a period of 40 years or so, and neither the accumulated capital on retirement nor the annuity which it can purchase can be guaranteed. One of the tests which countries contemplating MRS schemes should apply is to examine

217

the historical movement of interest rates over a long period, and its effect on capital accumulation, and also to examine the extent to which new pensioners are exposed to interest rate risk at the time of their retirement. This is discussed in more detail in section 4.

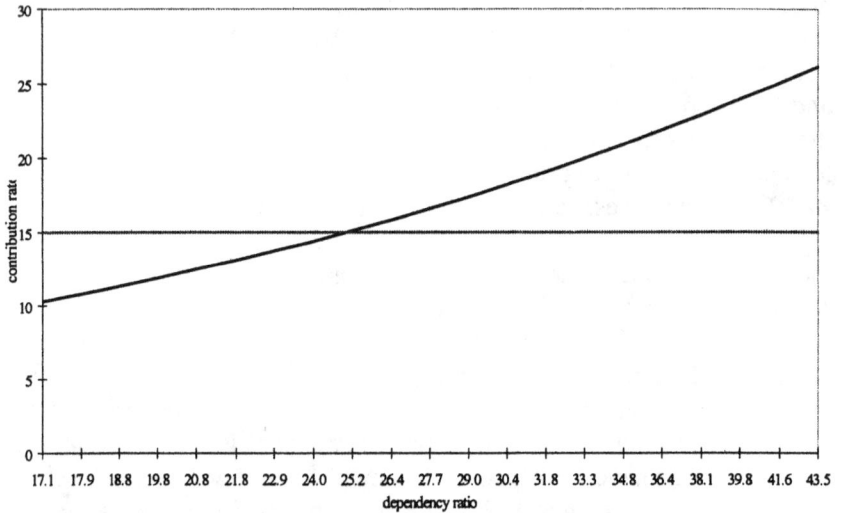

Figure 3.2.5a   Contribution rates as a function of dependency ratios

Dependency ratios

One of the concerns facing pension planners is the prospective increase in the proportion of old people in the population. In most countries this is occurring because of previous declines in fertility rates coupled with increases in longevity as the health status of the population improves. Obviously this has implications for pensions, with different implications for PAYG as compared to MRS schemes.

218

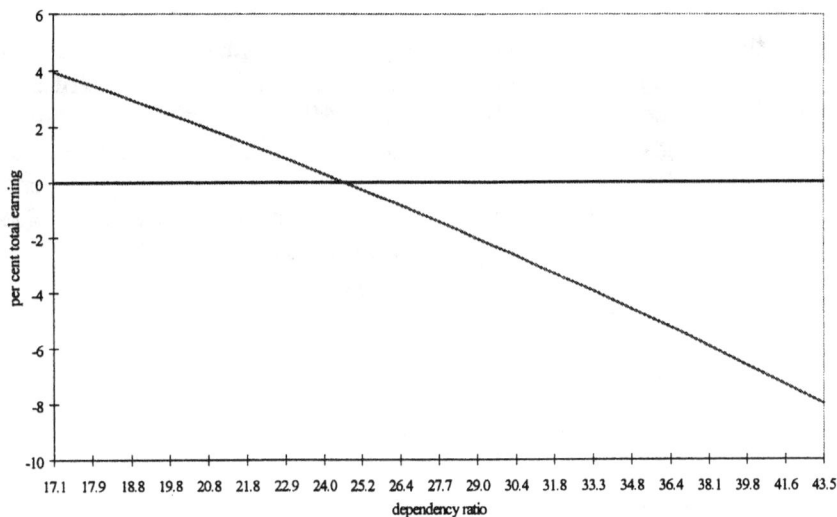

per cent total earning

dependency ratio

SURP = surplus under Pay-As-You-Go scheme
SAVE = net new savings generated by a Mandatory Retirement Saving scheme

Figure 3.2.5b   Net new savings as a function of dependency ratios

Under a PAYG scheme, which guarantees a predetermined replacement, the increased cost of pensions will be absorbed by increases in contribution rates. This is shown in figure 3.2.5. With a dependency ratio of around 10 per cent, the PAYG contribution rate is low: in the simplified model used here (no earnings growth, no inflation) it might be as low as 8 per cent. This alters rapidly as the population ages, to the point where at a dependency ratio of around 27 per cent the contribution rate increases to 20 per cent. This is obviously a major increase, especially if it needs to be taken together with other social charges, for example health care, unemployment compensation or other social services. It can be avoided if an MRS scheme is adopted. An MRS scheme is insensitive to changes in the dependency ratio, since contributions are accumulated in individual accounts and do not respond to collective pressures from the ratio of total pensioners to total contributors. So as in the previous example, the MRS contribution rate is shown in figure 3.2.5 as a straight line (a fixed 15 per cent) which intersects the PAYG contribution rate at the previous point of balance, around a dependency rate of 25 per cent. But also as in the previous example there is a cost to this advantage.

219

Whereas the PAYG scheme is, by definition, always in aggregate balance, the MRS scheme moves into aggregate imbalance as the dependency ratio increases: more individuals are in the spending phase of their lives than are contributing. Total net new MRS savings decline: from a positive saving of around 7 per cent of total earnings when the dependency ratio is 10 per cent to a dissaving of 1 per cent when the dependency ratio reaches 27 per cent. This dissaving must be drawn from elsewhere in the economy, most likely from the savings which individuals undertake in the form of housing or financial assets.

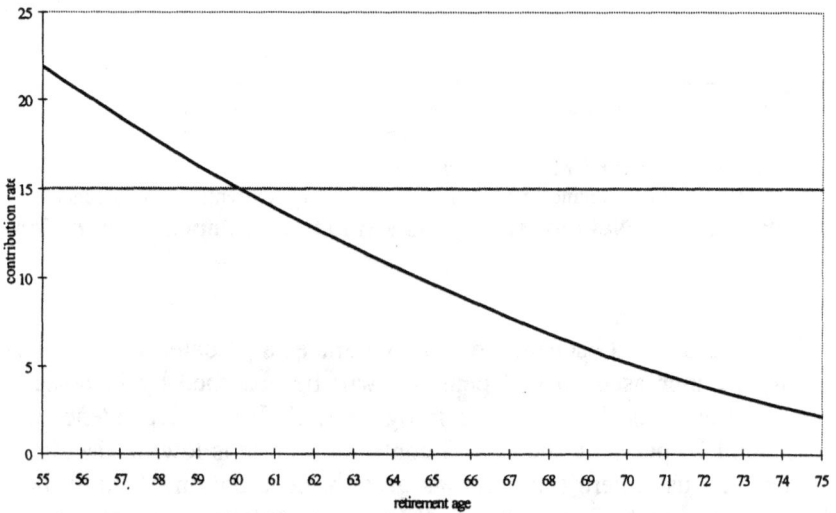

— PYGCR = Pay-As-You-Go contribution rate
MRSCR = contribution rate in a Mandatory Retirement Saving scheme

Figure 3.2.6a   Contribution rates as a function of retirement age

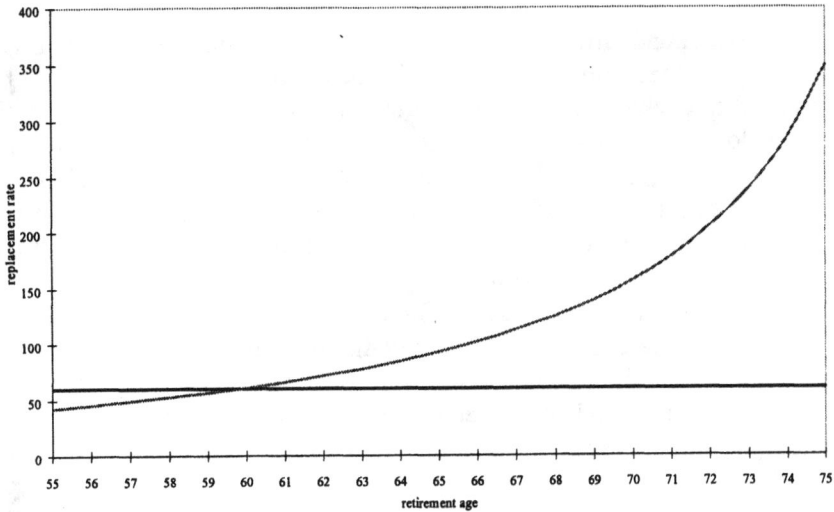

Figure 3.2.6b   Replacement rates as a function of retirement age

Retirement age

Normal retirement age in most OECD countries is 65 for men, 60 for women, although most OECD countries are also gradually bringing the retirement age for women into equality with that for men. One approach to overcoming the ageing problem might be to contemplate an increase in retirement age. This would have the double advantage of reducing the number of pensioners at the same time that it increased the number of contributors. Some of the implications are shown in figure 3.2.6: but on the assumption that the age of death remains the same (80) for both men and women; that the PAYG replacement rate remains unchanged (60 per cent); and that the MRS contribution rate and interest rates are not altered (15 per cent and 2.5 per cent respectively). Again there are differences between the two regimes. PAYG contribution rates are substantially affected. An increase of 10 years in the retirement age, from 60 to 70, could reduce the PAYG contribution rate by 10 percentage points, from 15 per cent to 5 per cent. This would go a long way to meeting the additional costs of an ageing population. But it would also represent a major change in the parameters of the scheme and one which other countries have found difficult to achieve politically and one which might require long lead times: a transition period of ten or more years might be required to enable existing contributors to adjust to the idea of a significantly longer working life. For the MRS scheme contribution rates are assumed to remain unchanged, but as retirement age approaches the expected age at death, replacement rates increase exponentially: in the (hypothetical) example shown here from around 60 per cent of final earnings when the retirement age is 60 to close to 150 per cent of final earnings when retirement age is 70 (still on the assumption that the age of death is 80). But in this case, savings patterns are unaffected: it is simply the case that the accumulated savings of contributors are spread over a shorter period of retirement with the consequence that benefit rates per annum can be increased. PAYG replacement rates are unaffected.

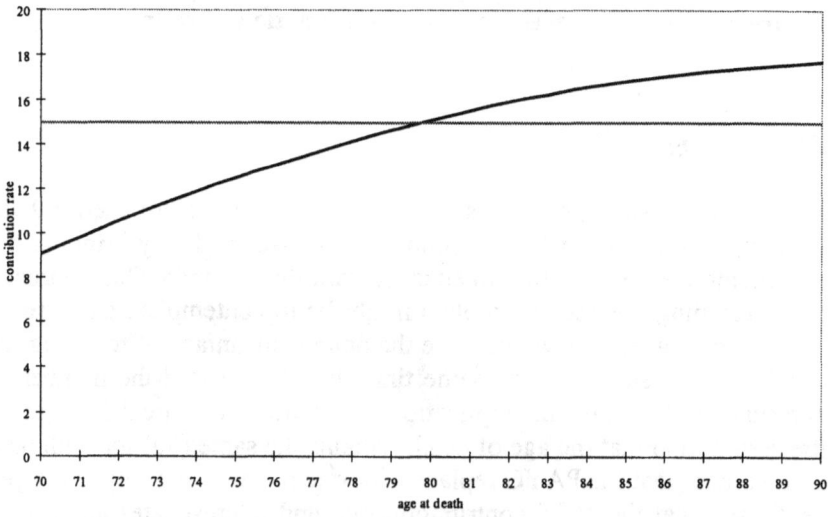

PYGCR = Pay-As-You-Go contribution rate
MRSCR = contribution rate in a Mandatory Retirement Saving scheme

Figure 3.2.7a   Contribution rates as a function of age at death

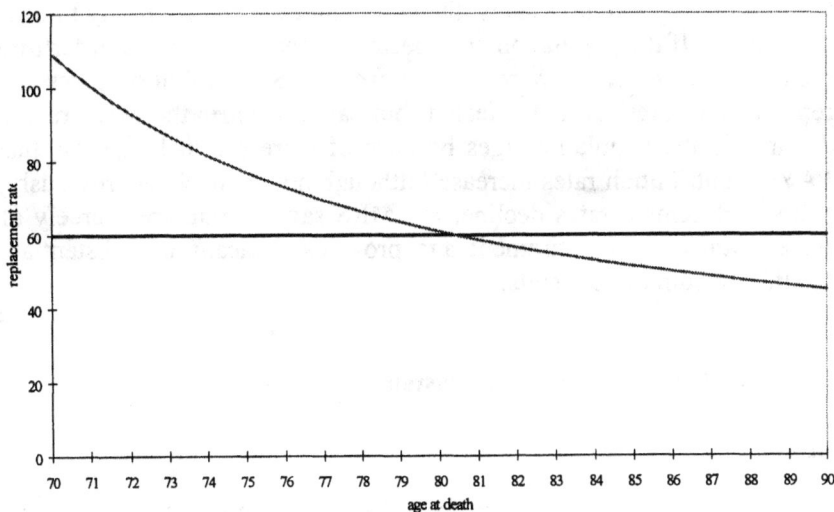

▬ PYGRR = Pay-As-You-Go replacement rate

⋯ MRSRT = replacement rate in a Mandatory Retirement Saving scheme

Figure 3.2.7b   Replacement rates as a function of age at death

Life expectancy

An alternative way of looking at the same issue is to ask what would happen if the passivity ratio, the ratio of years in retirement to years in work, were to increase. The basic simulation assumes that the ratio is 50 per cent: 20 years of retirement in relation to 40 years of work. Figure 3.2.7 shows the consequences of increasing this ratio by increasing the expected age at death while holding the retirement age constant, at 60. All the other parameters of the basic simulation remain unchanged.

What happens is what one might expect. It is necessary to increase PAYG contribution rates, to cope with a longer expected period of retirement. Conversely, the replacement rates provided by the MRS system decline, under constant contribution rates, again to spread the accumulated benefits over a longer retirement. There is very little change in the savings ratio generated by the MRS scheme. The significance of this set of variations lies in its relationship to the two previous ones. For most countries the ageing of the population is the outcome of at least two factors: previous declines in fertility rates and increases in life expec-

223

tancy. And as the figures show, the two regimes react differently to these two causes. If the population ages because of earlier declines in fertility, then PAYG contribution rates increase, MRS contribution rates and replacement rates are not affected, but savings under the MRS regime decline. If the population ages because of increases in longevity, then PAYG contribution rates increase (although not as much as previously). MRS replacement rates decline, but MRS savings rate are scarcely affected. Raising the retirement age provides a means of substantially modifying both these results.

4. Risks, objectives and mixed systems

Risks

One of the features of defined contribution, fully funded pension schemes concerns the risk to the individual that his accumulated lifetime saving may not be sufficient to fund an adequate pension. This may occur either because the growth of his earnings is greater than he or she expected at the beginning of the career, or because interest rates are lower than expected. Conversely, earnings growth may be lower and/or interest rates may be higher than expected, with the result that the individual may end up saving more than necessary and will have consumed less than he or she might have done during the working life. Since the working life is a relatively long one over which to make projections, this is a very real consideration in setting what level of savings or mandatory contributions is the right one. What is the order of magnitude of such risks? Are they small in relation to the final pension, or are they large?

An attempt to examine these questions has been made by Lawrence Thompson[4] in a number of numerical experiments applied to four OECD countries: Germany, Japan, the United Kingdom and the United States. It is assumed that all workers earn the average wage over a 43 year working life, from 1953 to 1995, and that their target during their working life was to accumulate sufficient assets to provide a pension which would amount to 50 per cent of the average wage. The experiment consisted of examining the actual growth of wages and the actual interest rate over this period to see whether the individual would undershoot or overshoot his target requirement on the basis of contribution rates set in terms current wages and interest rates. Clearly this depends not only on the actual trend and fluctuations in wages and interest rates but also on the ability of individuals and the government to predict them. Various decision rules are applied and the experiments are run both forward and backward: once using the actual sequence of interest rates and wage increases in the order in which they occurred; the other reversing the sequence of interest rates over the 43 years, on the argument that trends could have gone either way. The reader is referred to the original article for details.

Table 3.2.10a   **The contribution rate required to produce a 50 per cent replacement rate: for wage growth and interest rates corresponding to different periods**

	Germany			Japan			United Kingdom			United States		
	W	I	CR	W	I	CR	W	I	CR	W	I	CR
First 21 years (1953 to 1974)	7.1	3.8	48.5	8.5	4.6	54.2	5.4	1.7	53.5	2.2	0.3	33.4
Second 22 years (1974 to 1995)	2.6	4.0	12.9	1.8	3.0	14.0	1.8	1.9	19.0	-0.1	4.1	5.1
Full 43 years (1953 to 1995)	4.8	3.9	25.5	5.0	3.8	28.1	3.6	1.8	32.2	1.0	2.3	13.5

Table 3.2.10b   **The ratio of simulated actual balance to target balance at retirement for contribution rates based on different decision rules (per cent)**

	Germany			Japan			United Kingdom			United States		
	W	I	CR	W	I	CR	W	I	CR	W	I	CR
Simulation 1	Contribution rate set at level appropriate for long term (43 year) trend											
Actual sequence		137			132			140			138	
Reverse sequence		88			80			73			80	
Simulation 2	Contribution rate set at level appropriate for first 21 years											
Actual sequence		261			255			233			342	
Reverse sequence		41			40			43			40	

The results are startling, and are given in summary form in table 3.2.10. They depend not only on the actual variation in interest rates and wages but also on the decision rules adopted concerning contribution rates and the ability to forecast them and their sequencing. If it were possible to accurately predict the long-term (43 year) trend of interest rates and wages, but not their year-to-year variation and to embody this estimate into a long-term rate of saving or contribution, then individuals would have ended up saving 30 to 40 per cent too much for their pension. If the same experiment were repeated, but the order of interest changes reversed, individuals would have saved 20 to 25 per cent too little. If contribution rates were set on the basis of the first 21 years, and continued unchanged into the second 22 years, then individuals would have saved between 150 per cent and 240 per cent too much. But if this sequence also is reversed, the ultimate pension would be 60 per cent below target. An experiment in which contribution rates are adjusted every 10 years would lead to intermediate results. It should be noted that each of these outcomes involves considerable variation in contribution rates, ranging from an implausible level of over 70 per cent (the United Kingdom for the years 1953 to 1962) to just over 5 per cent (the United States for the years 1973 to 1982). In these simulations the difference between the growth of real wages and the real interest rate plays a critical role. When wage growth is significantly higher than interest rates a high contribution rate is required. If this is continued into a period when wage growth is lower than interest rates, substantial overshooting occurs. And vice versa when interest rates are higher than real wage growth. But both wages and interest have varied considerably over the 43 years of the simulations, and have also differed across countries, and cannot be easily predicted.

Objectives

Uncertainties of this magnitude conflict with the objectives of pensions schemes - at least as seen by the ILO - and it is time to say something about them, although without elaborating on them in any detail.

Over the years the ILO has developed a number of general principles for the creation and development of systems of old age pensions. These principles have been consecrated in a number of International Labour Standards and reflected in a number of international declarations. They have thus acquired the support of the international community. There are four main principles which are:

1. Pension schemes should include a basic minimum pension as an anti-poverty tier, perhaps means tested and available to all old people regardless of their contributions.

2. Individuals whose incomes and contributions lie above this minimum should receive a moderate but guaranteed replacement rate in old age - possibly subject to a ceiling - in return for their contributions.

3. There should be provision for individuals to supplement their pension through a savings scheme - which might be voluntary or mandatory and which might be privately managed - and organised on either on an individual basis or through collectively agreed occupational schemes.

4. Both pensions and retirement savings should be indexed against inflation.

There are a number of other principles, including the need for equal treatment, compulsory affiliation, democratic management of the schemes and the responsibility of the State to ensure that pensions are provided (although this last does not mean the State has to provide them directly, only that it should ensure that it is done and regulate the schemes).

The difficulty arises with the guarantee of a reasonable pension in return for contributions, up to a ceiling, embodied in the second of these principles. It is clear from what has been said earlier in this part of the paper that the risks associated with defined contribution fully funded schemes are too great for fully funded schemes alone to provide the necessary guarantee. A pension which turns out to be 30 per cent too high or 30 per cent too low reflects an unacceptable degree of uncertainty and may also imply too great a variation in the associated contribution rate. The simulations shown in table 3.2.10 suggest that the variation may be greater than 30 per cent, depending on the decision rules used to set contribution rates, and that the implied sensitivity of contribution rates takes them well beyond what is politically feasible. This is especially the case for workers in middle- to late- career whose opportunities for correcting their position are limited, even if they could accurately forecast the future movements of interest rates and wages.

Mixed systems

One suggested compromise is to combine the needs for a basic minimum pension for low income workers, a guaranteed but limited pension for middle income workers and the opportunity for a supplement in a three tier system of the following type:

1. A basic minimum anti-poverty tier, means tested but financed from general taxation. Benefit levels would be set above the poverty line, but not too far above.

2. A social insurance, Pay-As-You-Go defined benefit pension scheme which would provide a guaranteed pension on retirement equal to around 40 per cent of previous earnings on the basis of contributions during the working life. This would be subject to an earnings ceiling, say three to four times average earnings.

3. A retirement savings scheme, possibly also mandatory, which would supplement the PAYG social insurance scheme by providing an expected additional 30 to 40 per cent of previous earnings, but which for the individual would be subject to risks concerning the course of wages and interest rates.

A mixed system of this type would embody a number of advantages.

In the first place it would include an absolute guarantee of a minimum basic pension to all those on low incomes, including individuals whose contributions were either non existent or too low. It would be financed out of general revenues, but the expenditure would not be especially great and would be closely similar to the amounts needed to provide social assistance benefits to poor people, including for example the disabled or the long-term unemployed.

The second tier would provide the necessary guaranteed, but relatively modest, replacement rate to workers in the middle range. Risks concerning population ageing, economic growth, wages and interest rates would be borne collectively, by an adjustment of the contribution rate to whatever was necessary to pay this year's pensions. It would mean accepting the idea that some distortion of capital and labour markets might be inevitable, although the extent would not be too great. But it would meet the requirements set out in International Labour Standards of pro-

228

viding a guaranteed pension for average workers. It would avoid any perverse redistribution from poor to rich. And it would be self financing without requiring contribution rates which might become unacceptably high.

Under the third tier, risks would be borne by the individual but would be applied only to that part of the pension which supplemented the second tier. The individual would be exposed to the risk that wage growth and interest rates might turn out differently from expected. The individual would also carry the risk associated with increasing life expectancy after retirement. But the individual would not be exposed to the risk of population ageing due to previous increases in fertility. As the discussion concerning the fallacy of composition shows, that risk is one which would be borne by the community at large. Individuals with high personal incomes - that is, above the ceiling - would carry a greater degree of personal risk than those on middle- to low- incomes.

Pension issues are complex ones, and many of the complexities are beyond the scope of this paper. Many other questions affect the choice between defined contribution and defined benefit schemes besides the ones considered here. They include questions of privatisation, the interaction of labour market and pension policies, and whether it is necessary to introduce indexed bonds in the case of private schemes. There are also a number of issues not fully taken into account in this paper, including for example the cost of education for children and health care costs for the whole population. Even so, the main conclusions of the paper are clear.

In the first place, policies which alter the retirement age or which promote the employment of women are likely to have a large effect on the capacity of countries to deal with ageing populations without very large increases in contribution rates. These policies maybe difficult to implement, but they are likely to be easier than simply moving to funded pension schemes, which will not do the trick anyway.

Second, funded pension schemes do not help countries deal with ageing populations. Arithmetically and in aggregate they cannot do so without major disturbances to the composition of GDP or without destroying the implicit contract between pensioners and actives.

Third, there are substantial risks to the individual in funded pension schemes which make it dangerous to rely wholly on funded schemes to replace social insurance, Pay-As-You-Go ones. A better compromise would be to introduce a three tier system along the lines described above, which spreads the risks between the community and the individual.

Of course there are risks associated with PAYG social insurance schemes which have not been discussed in this paper. Chief of these is the danger that governments will over-promise: they will not take into account what is known about future demographic trends or may base their promises about replacement rates on unrealistic expectations about the future growth of real wages. If they do over promise, this will place future governments in difficulties: either they will have to raise contribution rates to levels which are unacceptably high in real terms; or they will have to reduce benefits, the most popular mechanism being to renege on the indexation of benefits. In developed OECD economies such political risks are much lower than elsewhere in the world, but to the extent that they exist, a mixed system would guard against them, as well as those from fully funded schemes.

Finally, a word about political trends. In the end, the standard of living of dependents - the retired as well as the non-retired - depends upon the social and political contract between them rather than upon the weight of market forces or economic power. The discussion above has provided some indications of how the two approaches interact, their equivalence, and their different allocation of risks. But there are obvious signs in most countries that the existing contract, and its institutional framework, are being reconsidered, mainly in the direction of reducing not only the guarantees which society is prepared to offer old-age dependents for their retirement income, but also the support which it provides to the unemployed and other dependents. The debate is a partly technical one and the analysis is important. But the risk for the future is that technicalities will confuse and overwhelm a process of social and political choice, already disturbed by a complex of many different interest groups and voices. What we are really talking about is the desired distribution of income, and that is a normative area where economists do not have the last word.

Notes

1. The caring world: an analysis. Annex: Tables and Figures. OECD, February 1998.

2. Although it is a moot point, in demographic terms, whether a dependency rate of 25 per cent is compatible with a passivity ratio of 50 per cent.

3. Notably the World Bank in its recent research report *Averting the Old Age Crisis: policies to protect the old and promote growth.*

4. Lawrence Thompson. *Predictability of individual pensions.* Paper to the joint ILO-OECD workshop on the development and reform of pension schemes, December 1997. To be published in a forthcoming book from the ILO on pension reforms around the world.

3.3 Social security reform and inter-generational transfers: simulation results for Switzerland

Stefan Felder

1. Introduction

Old age security in Switzerland is generally referred to as the 'three-tier-system'. The 1st tier, introduced in the early 1960s is state-run and works according to the pay-as-you-go method. Employees' contributions towards the 1st tier amount to 8.4% of their wages. The 2nd tier obliges employers and employees alike to pay into a capital funded savings account. After retirement a monthly payment is paid out until the employee's death. The 2nd tier has been in operation since 1985. The 3rd tier is the tax-deductible form of savings, either via tied benefit schemes (tier 3a) or via untied saving (tier 3b). With tied savings, the saved capital and the interest are paid out in full after retirement. The decision to implement the 2nd tier in 1985 and the 3rd tier in the early 1990s was by no means accidental, as by that time the inadequate long-term prospects of the pay-as-you-go system had become apparent. But even with the capital-funded complements will the declining number of new-borns combined with a rising life expectancy and reduced growth rates undoubtedly result in a marked increase of pay-as-you-go contributions. As a result, old age pension is on the Swiss policy agenda again. Among the proposals made by an expert panel to the Swiss government was the recommendation to raise VAT rather than wage contributions in order to keep the pay-as-you-go system running in the decades to come. This proposal is unique in one aspect: it asks for a contribution of pensioners as well. This is meant to partly reimburse the young for the increase in inter-generational transfers that they will experience in the course of the ongoing double ageing of the population. Raising VAT instead of wage contributions will also lessen the financial burden on future generations because it will help bring down the public debt entailed in the "contrat social" between generations.

This paper investigates on the effect this recommendation will have on the distribution between current and future generations. Part 2 offers an introduction into the generational accounting method. This is seen as the basis for calculations of the inter-generational distribution effects resulting from government decisions. Part 3 describes the institutional set-up of the Swiss old age pension system and outlines two of the proposals. A possible alternative would of course be the immediate abolishment of the pay-as-you-go system, with acquired pension entitlements to be paid directly from the general budget. Part 4 presents the result of both scenarios on the social security's implicit public debt and the inter-generational distribution as given by the simulations. Part 5 concludes.

2. The generational accounting method

Just like private households, governments are subjected to an intertemporal budget constraint. If the government decided to borrow today and the budget were to be balanced in the long run, this would imply higher taxes in future. As a general rule, government budgets only account for the annual deficit at a given point in time but do not reflect future liabilities. This is true for old age pension in particular. *Kotlikoff et al.* (1991) have introduced generational accounts as an alternative. These accounts make transparent the result of government decisions on the inter-generational distribution. At a given year, a generation's account will show the present value of all net payments to the government during the residual life time. Even though other payments could well be taken into account, we will limit the scope of this paper on old age pension exclusively.

The starting point of the analysis is the intertemporal budget constraint which needs to hold for old age security:

$$\sum_{s=0}^{\Omega} N_{t,t-s} + \sum_{s=1}^{\infty} N_{t,t+s} + W_t = 0 \qquad (1)$$

The term $N_{t,k}$ stands for the present value of all net payments (with year t as reference) to old age security paid by the generation born in year k. Index s in the first term in equation (1) runs from age 0 to Ω, the longest possible life span. The first term, then, equals the sum of all present values of the net payments made by all generations alive in year t. The second term represents the combined net payments of all generations born in year $t+1$ or later. Finally, W_t are the net assets of old age security in period t. The term $N_{t,k}$ in equation (1) is defined as:

$$N_{t,k} = \sum_{s=\max(t,k)}^{k+\Omega} T_{s,k} P_{s,k} \left(1+r\right)^{t-s} \tag{2}$$

$T_{s,k}$ is the average net payment made in year s by a member of the generation born in year k. $P_{s,k}$ stands for the number of persons in generation k that will survive to year s. For generations born before year t, contributions will be taken into consideration from this year on. For all generations born at a later date ($k>t$), contributions will be taken into account starting in year k. Payments will be discounted with t as the reference year, at a base of an exogenous real interest rate r. The balance of the financial burden of generation k will be expressed in per-capita units:

$$GA_{t,k} = \frac{N_{t,k}}{P_{t,k}} \tag{3}$$

Payments and transfers, differentiated according to age, sex and nationality, will be indexed to an (arbitrarily) chosen 'base generation'. We consider 100 overlapping generations living at any period of time, and differentiate between male (M), female (F), as well as between Swiss citizens (CH) and foreigners living in Switzerland (A). The reference generation are the 65-year-old male Swiss. The reference generation's contributions and pensions received are derived from the total payments of type i in the year 1995 divided by the total population expressed in terms of the base generation:

$$h_{B,t}^{CHM} = \frac{H_{i,t}}{\sum_{a=0}^{D}\sum_{z}I_{a,i}^{z}P_{t,t-a}^{z}}, \quad z = \{MCH, FCH, MA, FA\} \quad (4)$$

$I_{a,i}^{MCH}$ is a vector of indices of male Swiss aged a, with $I_{65,i}^{MCH}=1$. Index vectors for female Swiss as well as foreign nationals living in Switzerland - both male and female - ($I_{a,i}^{FCH}, I_{a,i}^{MA}, I_{a,i}^{FA}$) are made compatible with the base generation, i.e. a 65-year-old male Swiss. Accordingly, for contributions and pensions in t it can be said that:

$$h_{a,i,t}^{z} = h_{B,i,t}^{MCH}I_{a,i}^{z} \quad (5)$$

Contributions to the pension scheme are assigned the index 1 and result in a positive value for $h_{a,1,t}$. All transfers received from the system however are indexed $i=2$, which makes $h_{a,2,t}$ negative. Net contributions in time s are defined as:

$$T_{s,k} = h_{s-k,1,s} + h_{s-k,2,s} \quad (6)$$

Public debt entailed in the pay-as-you-go system corresponds to the aggregated net position of the today's generations, i.e. the sum of (weighted) accounts of generations alive in period t plus the value of financial assets of old age insurance. Public debt are the total of liabilities that future generations inherit from the current generations. Since the intertemporal budget constraint holds (see equation (1)), the net position of current generations exactly corresponds to the net position of future generations. Hence, we have for public debt in period t:

$$D_t = \sum_{s=1}^{\infty}N_{t,t+s} \quad (7)$$

3. Reforms of old age security

The burden imposed by old age security on today's and future generations depends on two parameters: the institutional set-up of the pay-as-you-go system and future developments in the number of both employed and early retirees. In our analysis, we make use of the prognosis on developments of the birth rate, death rate and migration as published by the Swiss Federal Statistics Office (1991). The crude birth rate rises from 1.58 in 1991 to 1.64 and drops again to 1.62 in 2040. Life expectancy in the interval from 1991 to 2010 will rise from 74.0 to 78.4 years for men and from 80.8 to 85.5 years for women and remains constant thereafter. The migration balance will remain positive up to 2010, becomes negative for the 17 years to follow, only to rise to 0 again after 2027. The resulting immigration surplus is responsible for the rise in population to 7.5 million in 2010. Population will continuously fall in the remainder of the 21st century and reach 6 million in 2100.

The Swiss Federal Office for Social Security supplied data covering all four groups of the population (*MCH, FCH, MA, FA*): contributions to the pay-as-you-go system in relation to age and average pensions paid in relation to the marital status. The distribution of marital status in different age groups has been used to determine pensions in relation to age. This led to an estimated 19.74 billion Swiss Francs paid out in pensions in 1995. Contributions were estimated to be 16.70 billion Swiss Francs in the same year. Pensions and contributions were then adjusted in such a manner as to fit the numbers published by the Swiss Federal Office for Social Security (18.69 billion Swiss Francs in paid out pensions - excluding the transfer from the government budget - and 18.31 billion Swiss Francs in contributions). In 1995, transfer payments from federal and state governments amounted to 19.625% of total expenses in the pay-as-you-go system, of which the federal government paid 16.625% and state governments contributed 3%. Total government transfers have risen to 20% of expenses in 1996, a figure we have used for all following periods.

In addition, net assets of the pay-as-you-go system were valued at 23.266 billion Swiss Francs in 1994 and used to cover future deficits in all scenarios. The base reference assumes a real interest rate of 2% and a 1% rise in labour productivity.[1] We tested our results for sensitivity using interest rates of 3 and 4% as well as 1.5 and 2% growth rates in labour productivity.

We distinguish three different scenarios:

Base case: (future deficits financed through rise in wage tax)

In the Swiss pay-as-you-go system a so-called mixed index is used to calculate pensions. This is to say that pensions rise at a rate determined by the arithmetic mean of inflation and real growth. With the rise in labour productivity at π, pensions will grow as expressed in equation (8):

$$h_{k,2,t} = h_{s-k,2,t}\left(1+0.5\pi\right)^{s-t} . \tag{8}$$

The variable q_s defines the ratio between total income and total expenses of the pay-as-you-go system in period s:

$$q_s = \frac{\sum_{k=s-D}^{s} P_{s,k} h_{s-k,2,t}\left(1+\pi\right)^{s-t}}{\left(1-y\right)\sum_{k=s-D}^{s} P_{s,k} h_{s-k,1,t}\left(1+0.5\pi\right)^{s-t}} , \tag{9}$$

where y represents the government share in total expenses. The wage tax resulting in a balanced budget of the pay-as-you-go system can be determined by multiplying the wage tax rate in 1995 (8.4%) and q_s. With y assumed to be constant, government transfers will have to grow at rate q_s as well. This holds true for contributions to the pay-as-you-go system in general:

$$h_{k,1,t} = h_{s-k,1,t}\, q_s . \tag{10}$$

Our simulations predict that today's net assets are sufficient to balance the system up to the year 2008. In 2009 already, q will reach 1.23; that is a 10.3% wage tax is needed to balance expenses and income. q reaches a maximum of 1.96 in 2032, which corresponds to a 16.5% wage tax. q will continuously fall from 2033 on and will reach 1.14 in 2100, or a 9.6% wage tax.[2]

238

Policy recommendation # 1: VAT (future deficit financed through a rise in VAT)

In scenario # 1 the deficit in the pay-as-you-go system is covered by raising VAT.[3] We have estimated representative expenditure patterns of consumers over a life cycle. As the expenditure data available did not allow for a differentiation between *MCH, FCH, MA* and *FA*, the consumption pattern is assumed to be the same for all groups. Accordingly, the absolute value of contributions under the VAT scenario was set to be a fixed proportion of wages in all groups. The VAT rate needed to cover the deficit in pensions can then be concluded to amount to 2.9 % in 2009. It will rise to 8.6% in 2032 and fall continuously thereafter to reach 1% at the end of the 21st century.

Policy recommendation # 2: "funded" (immediate transition to a funded social security system)

Scenario # 2 models an abolition of the pay-as-you-go system in period t. As a replacement, a fully capital funded system is introduced. Funded old age insurance works according to the equivalence principle; i.e. for each future generation, the sum of expected future transfers equals the sum of expected future contributions. Without loss of generality we thus set contributions and transfers equal to zero for all generations born after t:

$$h_{k,1,s} = h_{k,2,s} = 0, \quad \forall s > t \tag{11}$$

The currently living generations have entitlements on transfers from the pay-as-you-go system. Since we have no information on historic contributions of the four population groups, we base their future transfers on distribution of labour income over the life-cycle, weighted with the income share of the groups. Contributions of living generations are assumed to be zero:

$$h_{k,1,s} = 0,$$
$$h_{k,2,s} = h_{s-k,2,s}\,\alpha_k \quad \forall\ s \le t. \tag{12}$$

239

with

$$\alpha_k = \frac{\sum\limits_{s=o}^{k} h_{s,k,1}}{\sum\limits_{s=o}^{\Omega} h_{s,k,1}}. \tag{13}$$

where α_k is the share of wage income of total human wealth that is earned from age 0 to age a.

4. Public debt and inter-generational transfers: simulation results

The simulations have been run for real interest rates of 2, 3 and 4% and growth in labour productivity of 1, 1.5 and 2%. The reference case assumes a real interest rate equal to 2% and a growth rate of 1%. Table 3.3.1 displays the public debt entailed in pay-as-you-go financed Swiss old age security for all scenarios in 1995. The base case will result in a 491-billion-debt in 1995 figures. The amount is considerably smaller in a VAT-scenario, amounting to 428 billion Swiss Francs. This can be explained by the age difference between those who contribute and those who receive transfers from old age insurance: in contrast to the base case, the difference in age between contributors and retirees is less pronounced. With the implicit budget deficit depending positively on the age difference, this means a reduction of public debt under the VAT-scenario.

Finally, a transition to a funded system increases public debt to 700 billion Swiss Francs, a 40% rise against the base case. This result is a consequence of the fact that with an abolition of the pay-as-you-go system there are no more contributions, and transfers to currently living generations are financed from the government's budget.

Table 3.3.1 further present public debt of social security for varying interest and growth rates. It shows that public debt increases with productivity growth. This does not come as a surprise because, according to the pension formula (8), the growth rate accounts for 50% of the increase in transfers. Since pensions are not fully linked to productivity growth, public debt as a percentage of GDP decreases with a rise in the growth rate. Higher interest rates will dramatically reduce public debt. Doubling the interest rate from 2 to 4% cuts debt by more than half in all three scenarios.

Table 3.3.1 The public debt of the pay-as-you-go system (1995; in billion Swiss Francs)

| | | Scenarios | | |
		base case	VAT	funded
	$\pi = 0.01$	491	428	692
r = 0.02	$\pi = 0.015$	558	502	731
	$\pi = 0.02$	635	590	773
	$\pi = 0.01$	296	255	564
r = 0.03	$\pi = 0.015$	334	297	593
	$\pi = 0.02$	377	346	624
	$\pi = 0.01$	183	155	467
r = 0.04	$\pi = 0.015$	205	179	490
	$\pi = 0.02$	229	207	514

As for the financial burden to be borne by future generations in comparison to living generations, future generations will contribute to a reduction of the public deficit in accordance with their population strength and their economic performance.[4] The resulting financial burden on citizens born in 1996 or later is:

$$d_{1996} = \frac{D_{1995}}{\sum_{s=1}^{\infty} \left(\frac{1+\pi}{1+r}\right)^{s-1} B_s}, \qquad (14)$$

with B_s reflecting the number of new-borns in year s. The simulation results are collected in table 3.3.2.

Table 3.3.2 The generational account of the 1996 cohort (in 1,000 Swiss Francs)

		base case	VAT	funded
	$\pi = 0.01$	169	143	89
$r = 0.02$	$\pi = 0.015$	145	121	49
	$\pi = 0.02^a$	107	84	0
	$\pi = 0.01$	161	138	132
$r = 0.03$	$\pi = 0.015$	157	137	108
	$\pi = 0.02$	149	130	79
	$\pi = 0.01$	131	112	149
$r = 0.04$	$\pi = 0.015$	134	118	136
	$\pi = 0.02$	136	121	119

a   For $r=\pi$ the denominator of (14) diverges. In this case we set d_{1996} equal to zero.

The present value of the total (positive) net payments, which combine the net payments to the social security system and the amortisation payment for the public debt, decreases if social security is partly financed with a VAT increase. The balance of the 1996 cohort increases by 20,000 Swiss Francs on average. With an immediate transition to a funded system the payments of the 1996 cohort to old age insurance is zero, so that the balance of the generation accounts are exclusively determined by the amortisation of public debt. The burden of public debt for future generations significantly depends on the difference between interest and growth rate. With a large difference, the total present value of future birth is small (see equation (14)), resulting in a large burden for the 1996 cohort. Conversely, the financial burden decreases when the difference between interest and growth rate falls and converges to zero when interest and growth rate coincide.

The following figures show how social security reform affects the currently living male and female generations born from 1896 to 1995. Since there is no difference in the pattern of generational accounts between Swiss citizens and foreigners living in Switzerland, except that the figures for Swiss citizens are higher on average, we refrain from presenting the foreigners' accounts.

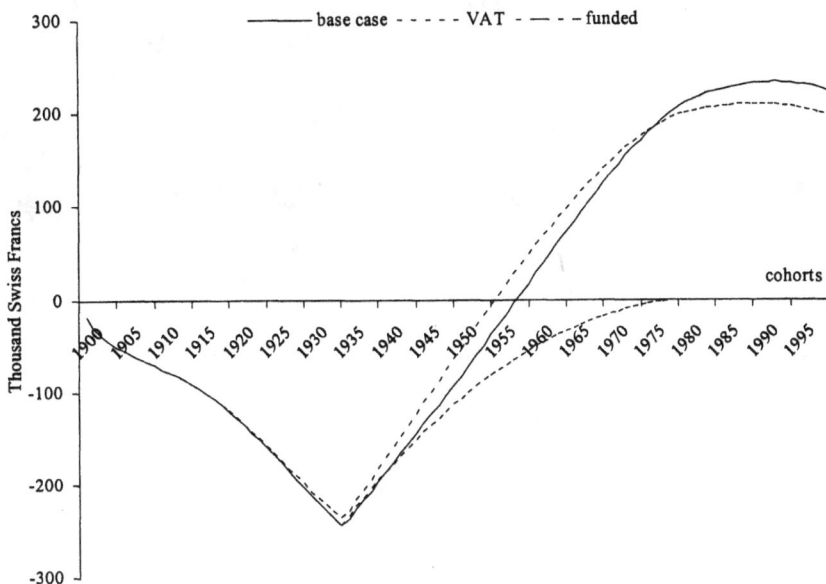

Figure 3.3.1   Generational accounts of male Swiss

The generational accounts of citizens born between 1920 and 1940 show the largest balance. For this group the current value of the balance between contributions paid and pensions received is at 150,000 for men and 230,000 Swiss Francs for women, or higher. If wage taxes were the only means of financing, people born in 1931 would have the largest balance: -250,000 Swiss Francs for men and -360,000 for women, respectively. It does not come as a surprise that of all surviving generations in 1995 people born in 1995 are worst off (with 220,000 (men) and -20,000 (women) in the VAT scenario).

The younger generations benefit from using VAT to partly finance social security. Paying contributions to social security via VAT defers payments to a higher age, hence the present value of payments decreases. A differentiation between men and women reveals larger gains for men. Compared to women, men's labour income shows a more accentuated hump shape, with a peak at age 45. Men would gain even more with a transition to a funded system, the rationale being that currently a redistribution from men to women takes place. If an abolition of the pay-as-you-go system were to remove this redistribution, men's balance would im-

243

prove. Moreover, men would benefit because they avoid paying the large contributions needed to finance the social security bill over the next 40 years.

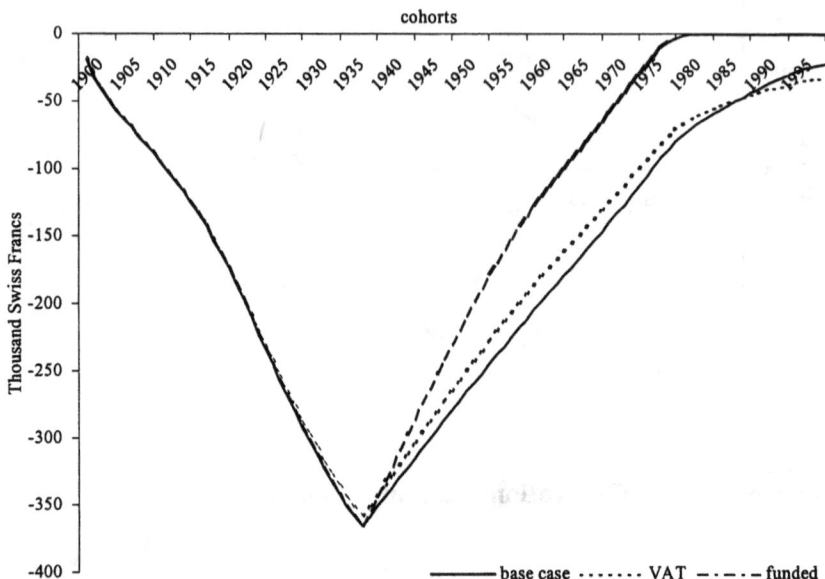

Figure 3.3.2   Generational accounts of female Swiss

5. Concluding remarks

This article introduces the generational accounting concept in the context of pension reform. The issue under debate is whether a VAT-financed reform of the Swiss pay-as-you-go system or, alternatively, a transition to a fully funded system, yields a positive result with respect to distributional effects between generations. Not surprisingly, our calculations reveal a heavy financial burden on future generations induced by the current system. The largest burden - a liability amounting to 740 billion Swiss Francs - results if the current 8.4% wage tax rate were to increase to cover future deficits stemming from both a low birth rate and an increase in life expectancy.

The first policy reform finances future deficits of the pay-as-you-go system with an increase in VAT. This reform lowers the burden for young generations because the bulk of payments is deferred to older ages, which decreases the present value of payments to the social security system. By comparison, retired individuals are worse off as they have to contribute to social security under the VAT. Future generations benefit because i) contributions are deferred, and ii) public debt of social security decreases with the reform. If deficits were financed through a rise in VAT, the financial burden would be 430 billion Swiss Francs. Spreading the implicit government debt evenly on citizens born in 1996 or later delivers an estimate for the per-capita-liability: for people born in 1996 it amounts to 169,000 Swiss Francs under the base case and to 143,000 Swiss Francs under the VAT scenario. Citizens born in 1995 - and in accordance with our assumptions not subject to the government debt - will only lose 106,000 or 89,000 Swiss Francs respectively. Financing the pay-as-you-go system though a rise in VAT and the resulting lower budget deficit yields a particularly positive result for the generational accounts of the younger generation. The surplus for people born in the 1980s amounts to an average 15,000 Swiss Francs.

The second policy reform models an abolition of the pay-as-you-go system. While the existing entitlements of retired individuals are fully respected, demands of the working population are met proportionally to their historical contributions. In particular this reform removes the subsidisation of women's pension from men's contribution. This explains why men benefit most from a funding of social security. Future generations benefit in general since the funded system, as opposed to the pay-as-you-go system, is decoupled from the demographic transition. According to our simulations a funding of social security increases public debt to 700 billion Swiss Francs, a rise of 40 %. The corresponding financial burden for future generations depends to a large extent on the relative size of interest and growth rates. A large interest rate combined with slow growth results in a marked increase of the burden borne by future generations.

A consistent application of generational accounting does of course call for an inclusion of all government programmes into the analysis. Studies for other countries have shown old age security to be responsible for the largest share in inter-generational transfers (see Boll, 1996). However, income tax and health coverage also have an impact. The inter-generational transfer induced by health insurance is assumed to be less pronounced in Switzerland than in Germany because health care is financed through per-capita-premiums rather than wage taxes.

245

The present article does not deal with the efficiency of pension reform because the reactions of households and firms to changing prices and income are not modelled. However, the extensive literature on this topic has direct implications for the reform under discussion. Breyer (1989) shows in a model with exogenous labour supply that a transition to a fully funded system will not produce an efficiency gain. This result follows from the well known theorem by Cass (1972) stating that growth paths with interest rates exceeding growth are dynamically efficient. Redistribution between generations - social security reform only affects inter-generational distribution in a world without taxes - cannot prove to be welfare enhancing. The consequence for pension reform analysed in this paper is that gains of the generations that will benefit will not be sufficiently large to compensate generations that will be worse off after the reform.

Conversely, pension reform may produce a Pareto improvement, provided taxes exist and distort the decision of household and firms. Homburg (1992) as well as Breyer and Straub (1993) and Kotlikoff (1996) have shown that pension reform may result in significant welfare gains.

Notes

1. In comparison to other industrialised countries over the past 30 years real interest rates in Switzerland were at a low level:

	1960-1970	1970-1980	1980-1990	1990-1994
yearly growth rate (in %)	4.7	1.38	2.09	0.02
real interest rate (in %)	0.71	0.17	1.30	1.78

2. The deficit develops as follows: the onset is 5 billion Swiss Francs in 2009, with a maximum of 21.7 billion in 2034. From 2035 on the deficit will drop again to reach 5.2 billion in 2100.

3. AT is at a different level for three categories of consumer goods. VAT is set at 6.5% for the majority of goods, but there are two exceptions: groceries and the like are levied with a considerably lower rate of 2 %, goods such as housing, medical and cultural services are exempt from VAT. Using the Federal Office for Statistics' (1992) consumer survey we conclude that 61.5 % of all expenses are taxed at a full rate, whereas 14% are taxed at a reduced rate and the remaining 24.5% are free of VAT.

4. In contrast to *Auerbach* et al. (1991) we refrain from calibrating generational accounts for people born in 1996+ to fit $GA_{t,t+s} = GA_{t,t+1}[(1+\pi)/(1+r)]^{s-t-1}$. In comparison to a conventional viewpoint our simulation overestimates the financial burden on people born from 1996 to 2000. This group will be hardest hit by the very high wage tax from 2025 to 2040. A conventional simulation would spread the liability evenly between all age groups born in 1996 or after (see *Raffelhüschen et al.*, 1994).

References

Auerbach, Alan J., Jagdesh Gokhale and Laurence J.Kotlikoff, (1991), Generational Accounts: A Meaningful Alternative to Deficit Accounting, in: David Bradford (Hrsg.), *Tax Policy and the Economy*, Vol. 5, NBER, MIT Press, Cambridge, 55-110.

Boll, Stefan, Bernd Raffelhüschen and Jan Walliser (1994), Social Security and Intergenerational Redistribution: A Generational Accounting Perspective, *Public Choice* 81, 79-100.

Breyer, Friedrich (1989), On the Inter-generational Pareto-Efficiency of a Pay-as-you-go Financed Pension System, *Journal of Institutional and Theoretical Economics* 145, 643-658.

Breyer, Friedrich und Martin Straub (1993), Welfare Effects of Unfunded Pension Systems when Labor Supply is Endogenous, *Journal of Public Economics* 50, 77-91.

Cass, David (1972), On Capital Overaccumulation in the Aggregate: Neoclassical Model of Economic Growth: A Complete Characterization, Journal of Economic Theory 4, 200-223.

Fehr, Hans and Laurence J. Kotlikoff (1995), Generational Accounting in General Equilibrium, *Finanzarchiv* 53, 1-27.

Homburg, Stefan (1990), The Efficiency of Unfunded Pension Schemes, *Journal of Instituional and Theoretical Economics* 146, 640-647.

Kotlikoff, Laurence J. (1996), Privatization of Social Security: How it Works and Why it Matters, in: James Poterba (Hrsg.), *Tax Policy and the Economy*, Vol. 10, NBER, MIT Press, Cambridge, 1-32.

Raffelhüschen, Bernd (1993), Funding Social Security through Pareto-optimal Conversion Policies, *Journal of Economics*, suppl. 7, 105-131.

Swiss Federal Office for Statistics (1992), Szenarien zur Bevölkerungsentwicklung der Schweiz: 1991-2040, Bern.

PART 4

HEALTH CARE POLICY

4.1 Inequality in health care access and utilization and the potential role for the public sector

Barbara L. Wolfe and David Vanness

People who are poor, single or who have no close friends are more likely to develop heart problems and die of them ... Patients with coronary heart disease were three times as likely to die within five years if they were not married and had no one in whom they could confide, Dr. Redford Williams of the Duke University Medical Center told a meeting organized by the American Psychological Association.

A 29-year study of 1,000 adults in Alameda County, California, found that the more they experienced economic hardship, the greater their risk of developing serious physical and psychological ailments, University of Michigan School of Public Health researchers told the meeting. Men and women who had incomes less than twice the poverty level were roughly three times as likely to report cognitive difficulties, health problems and depression, they said.

Dr. John Lynch of the University of Michigan said a study of 2,682 middle-aged men in Finland had found that employment in adult life reduced the risk of disease:

> Those who were born into poor families but who completed their high school education and went on to find white-collar employment had better health behaviors; they did not smoke or drink as much as someone from a poor background who did not complete high school and went on to find employment in manual blue-collar occupations.

People who were economically disadvantaged throughout their lives were less likely to be physically active, ate more high-sodium and fatty foods and had higher levels of depression, hopelessness and cynicism, Lynch said. "Dr. Wayne Giles of the Center for Disease Control and

251

Prevention told the conference that whites were more likely to be given invasive cardiac procedures after a heart attack. When other factors such as type of hospital, insurance status and disease severity were accounted for,

> procedures such as cardiac catheterization, percutaneous transluminal coronary angioplasty and coronary bypass surgery were being used less on black patients than on white patients and less on females than on males. (11 May 1998, *INFOBEAT News*)

The issue of equity in access to medical care is one that has received considerable attention from a variety of perspectives.[1] Most members of society are troubled by the type of results reported in the news stories above, stories that appeared the day I decided to look for an article in the popular press that gave an example of the issue of equity in health care. Health influences most other activities of life, from the ability to engage in everyday functions to the ability to enjoy life itself. It is therefore not surprising that societies should be concerned about varying levels of health among their members, and about the allocation of the most visible means by which health is thought to be influenced-medical care. This paper explores the potential ways that society, through social insurance, can affect health status and health care.[2]

A fundamental issue is what we mean by equity in the health sector, the subject of section 1 below. A second issue, what is required to achieve equity, according to each of these definitions is the subject of section 2. The implications of section 2 for equalization of health under alternative definitions are discussed in section 3. International evidence on the link between public insurance and use of medical care in a number of developed countries and in the United States is reviewed in section 4. Section 5 offers conclusions.

1. Equity: a matter of definition

The realm of health, perhaps more than any other, gives rise to the view that the private market should not be left alone to determine such outcomes as health status, access to health care, or the use of care, and that some form of public intervention is needed. But what do we mean when we set as our objective achieving equality in the health care area?

252

The most basic, but most difficult to achieve, objective would be to *equalize health status* itself. One version of this would mean that for all persons born in a given year, we should attempt to achieve equal health.[3] Another variant would set a goal of achieving a minimum or threshold level of health for all persons. Those who are ill would receive care to make them well again. But medical care is only one of many factors that influence health. This objective would require public interventions in many spheres beyond the allocation of medical care.

An alternative definition is *equalization of the use of health care.* By this, we mean equal use of medical care for any state of health, or ill health. For any two individuals who have a particular illness, such as first-degree breast cancer, and are otherwise healthy, the treatment that is received should be identical.[4] A third definition is *equality in access to and knowledge of medical care.* Under this definition individuals would face the same direct price for medical care and the same time and travel costs (indirect costs), and would have the same knowledge of when and where to go to receive care. It differs from the second definition in that actual equalization could differ. A fourth definition is *equality in access to medical care.* To achieve this objective, individuals would need to face the same direct and indirect costs of medical care, but equal knowledge would not be required. A fifth possible definition is *equity in terms of equalization of the direct cost of medical care.* The only requirement of this definition is that the per unit cost of care would be equal across all persons. The sixth and last definition considered here is *equity in terms of the cost of care of a limited package, or minimum package, of care.* This would restrict definition five to a package of care, which might include treatment of a life-threatening illness or prevention of illness, or some package defined according to other well-specified criteria.[5]

To explore these definitions further, let us consider a simplified system of equations that specify the determinants of health status (H) and medical care utilization (MC). We begin with a production function of H; lying behind it, although not specified here, is a utility function for each individual "whose elements" are health status and the consumption of other goods and services.

Let:

$$H = H(H°, MC, B, E, K, Y) \tag{1}$$

where

H°	represents initial or underlying true health status;
B	stands for behavioral factors that represent the choices that individuals make, such as diet, amount of time spent exercising, living arrangement (household structure), and engaging in risk-taking behaviors such as smoking, drinking or using illegal drugs;
E	stands for environmental factors such as pollution, quality of housing, safety of the workplace;
K	represents information or knowledge of health and medical care needs; and
Y	stands for a variety of indicators of income, including own income, income uncertainty, and possibly income inequality as perceived by the individual.

All or nearly all of these have been included in one or more health production functions within the existing literature.

Underlying equation 1 is a production function for H° such that $H^\circ = H^\circ$ (G, MC, B), in which G stands for genetic factors, MC refers to prenatal care received by the mother as well as care received by individuals in periods prior to the current one; and B refers both to own behavior of the individual and to the mother's behavior, especially risk taking and diet while pregnant.

The next equation of primary interest is one explaining medical care utilization. Let:

$$MC = MC\ (D^i, D^p, S^{mc}, E^{mc}) \tag{2}$$

where

D^i	refers to the individual's own demand for medical care;
D^p	refers to the demand of everyone else in the market area (or region);
S^{mc}	refers to the supply of medical care, incorporating the supply of medical doctors, nurses, and other practitioners, hospital beds, various therapies, pharmaceuticals and medical equipment;[6]
E^{mc}	refers to the efficacy of medical care, which can be measured by the quality of medical providers (the quality of S^{mc}) as well as the resources devoted to medical research.

Finally, own demand can be thought of in the following way:

$$D^i = D^i(H, P(1- \alpha), w(tr + a), P^{tr}, K, T, Y) \qquad (3)$$

where
P   stands for the full price of a unit of medical care;
$(1- \alpha)$ represents the share paid by the individual (α represents the share paid by insurance) and $P(1- \alpha)$ is the net direct cost to the consumer of a unit of medical care;
w is the value per unit of time of the individual;
tr   is the time spent in travel to the medical care provider;
P^{tr} is the direct cost of travel to medical care facilities;[7]
a   is the amount of time spent waiting for care and receiving care;
K   is again knowledge of the efficacy of medical care;
T   stands for individual tastes.

This set of equations is used to define in more detail what would be required in order to achieve equality in the health area and to analyze the potential role of social insurance in successfully achieving each of the possible objectives.

2. Equity objectives and requirements

Determinants of health status

Health status is influenced by many factors. The potential role of social insurance in influencing each of the factors included in equation 1 above is highlighted below.

Medical care is one contributor to good health, and social insurance could attempt to influence the provision of MC as a move toward equalizing health status. All members of a population would be provided appropriate preventive care, including well-baby and well-child care, all vaccinations, cancer screening, eye and ear tests, etc. Known and effective medical treatment for medical conditions and illness could be equally provided as well. But to equalize health status, we would need to go far beyond prevention and far beyond our current state of knowledge and ability to deliver effective medical care.[8] Even within the sphere of medical care there is a question of allocating resources to research in order to be able to treat or prevent diseases that we cannot currently treat. Must we not allocate resources to all research ideas that are viewed as promising in this arena? Finally, there is the role of individual demand for and compliance with medical care, discussed more fully below.

H is also influenced by a person's underlying health status, $H^°$. This reflects the individual's prior use of medical care, and it is also affected by the individual's genetic composition, behavior, and mother's behavior, especially during her pregnancy and the individual's childhood. For the current population, history cannot be changed ($H^°$ should be viewed as fixed in the short run), so $H^°$ is a limiting factor to achieving equalization of health status in the short run. In the longer run, equalization of the use of medical care, especially medical care related to pregnancies, might reduce some of the differences in $H^°$, but unless we also reduce risk-taking behaviors, such as smoking,[9] and increase genetic engineering it is unlikely that a society can fully eliminate differences in $H^°$ at birth. Differences that result thereafter are part of the overall discussion of the determinants of health status.

Equation 1 also suggests that behavior may play an important role in influencing health status. Risk-taking behavior (smoking, excessive drinking) that clearly influences health would have to be reduced or eliminated to achieve this goal.[10] Other behavioral factors that influence health include the choice of living unit, choice of diet, and amount and type of exercise. These choices are likely to reflect preferences, prices, and income constraints. Social insurance could influence such behavior by attempting to change the prices of certain "merit goods", such as subsidizing foods viewed as healthy and/or subsidizing the price of exercise activities. It could provide special nutrition for infants, children, and pregnant women. Or, moving beyond social insurance to other governmental activities, tax authorities might raise the price of certain goods that have negative externalities, such as alcohol and tobacco, and could even influence the financial gains to marriage. School systems might modify curricula so that the knowledge of school-age children and perhaps their parents on such issues as the costs of tobacco might be emphasized, and the public sector might work with the media on a campaign to influence consumption behavior. The central government might provide funding to encourage communities to establish athletic facilities and leagues. All of these are quite wide reaching, subject to other considerations, and unlikely to fully reduce differences in individual behavior that are important for health. They are also costly, and benefits would need to be weighed against costs before a full-scale effort was undertaken.

Another set of factors included in equation (1) are environmental in nature. They include pollution, quality of housing, and the safety of the workplace. Lead paint is perhaps the most commonly used example of housing quality, as it influences the mental capacity of children exposed to it. Reducing hazards to health from most or all of these environmental conditions is something most citizens and countries desire, but it is a costly goal, and we traditionally weigh the benefits against costs and determine that some level of hazards is acceptable. Social insurance may have a role to play in reducing aspects of these harmful environmental factors. In terms of housing quality, social insurance might reduce the income constraint that leads families to choose inadequate housing through housing subsidies and/or the provision of a minimum income. Social insurance also may set up a workers' compensation system that penalizes firms experiencing high rates of worker accidents in order to create a financial incentive for firms to increase the safety of their workplaces. And other agencies of government may, independently or on the advice of the social insurance system, establish a system to monitor and reduce industrial and other sources of pollution, including taxes on gasoline to reduce combustion and produce cleaner-burning engines. Ultimately, however, it is unlikely that all environmental hazards that reduce health will be eliminated, because to do so is enormously costly.

Information or knowledge of health and medical care needs are additional factors that influence health.[11] Persons with more education seem to know when and how to access the health care system, how to follow directions, obtain good sources of nutrition, and other factors that influence health status and health care utilization. These affect their health status and that of other family members. Education is publicly funded for ages 6 to 16–19 in nearly every developed country and, in some cases, for university education as well. Early (preschool) education is less universally funded, and doing so might ultimately lead to more equality in education.

The social insurance sector could be involved in the provision of health-specific education, providing educational materials on the need for preventive care, on nutrition, etc. Informing individuals where care may be obtained is easier than ensuring that individuals have equal knowledge concerning when care should be obtained. An information system, accessed easily, in which an expert provides answers to such questions as under what circumstances care should be sought might be one approach to dealing with this component.[12] Ultimately, however, innate ability, opportunities, prices, and income constraints will all play a role in determining the choice of levels of education.

Income is the final determinant of health included in equation (1). It is included because of evidence that poverty, income uncertainty, and income inequality may play a role in determining health status over and above the items included independently. For example, a recent study argues and provides some evidence that income inequality may be related to health inequalities.[13]

Social insurance can play a role in reducing income inequality and uncertainty. The economic efficiency costs to doing so will limit the ability to eliminate inequality and uncertainty, even if they were otherwise desired.

Determinants of medical care utilization

Equation (2) attempts to lay out the factors involved in medical care utilization.

The first factor is the individual's own demand for care. This is influenced by health status or health care needs, the net price of medical care to the individual, the indirect price, and knowledge regarding health and medical care, as shown in equation 3, as well as individual tastes toward the receipt of care. Because we are discussing the determinants of care utilization for individuals with the same medical problem, we focus on factors other than health status.

Social insurance could equalize the net price of a unit of medical care across all individuals. It could, for example, cover the full direct cost of medical care, so that 100 percent of the direct cost is paid by social insurance. It could require a specific copayment per unit of care, such as $5 for an ambulatory visit. It could also combine a fixed schedule of fees with a coinsurance percentage, so that an individual would pay 20 percent of the cost of a unit of care.[14]

The indirect price is more difficult to determine, because distance to providers differs, as does waiting time.[15] And the value of time clearly differs. Social insurance could act to influence the location of medical care providers,[16] could provide a voucher to cover the cost of transportation or transportation above some minimum, but the travel time cost will still differ. Time to get an appointment also frequently differs according to the demand of others, another element in the utilization equation. Social insurance can hope to influence this by influencing the availability of providers by influencing their location. However, effective demand differs sufficiently across individuals and hence areas that it is unlikely that waiting times can be fully equalized.[17] Related to this is the issue of how to take into account or eliminate any differential penalty that an employer might impose on an employee who takes time off in order to receive medical care for himself or herself or members of the family. This could be accomplished by mandating that all employers provide a certain number of hours per year for such activities.

Equalizing knowledge of medical care efficacy was discussed above. The final factor here is preferences for medical care (tastes), which are rarely discussed by economists. Even after controlling for price, income, and health status, differences in utilization remain. Whether they would remain a significant factor if there were an estimation of the fuller set of equations specified here is not known. However, language differences, differences in "home care", differences in prior experiences with medical care and in the norms of utilization may also influence effective demand.

The demand of others in the same medical market area will have influence over the actual care received by an individual. These persons compete for available resources, and their demand influences waiting time and time to get an appointment. As noted above, social insurance or the government more generally can try to influence this by influencing the location of providers. The provision of knowledge of when to seek care may reduce utilization that has little or no impact on health (inefficient utilization) and increase utilization in cases where care could be effective.

The supply of medical care influences the amount an individual receives. If supply is unequal relative to the demand in a community, differences will clearly result. The waiting time for an appointment, the wait at the appointment, and the time and resources allotted to a person's treatment will all differ according to available supply. Beyond physician time and bed availability, there may be other differences across communities, such as in the quality of education or of caring on the part of providers, etc. While some of these can be equalized, the most difficult to equalize may be the quality of care, and the ability to care for and communicate with patients.

Some interventions by the public sector to reduce these differences are noted above. In addition, the public sector could reduce education loans of providers who locate in underserved areas and allocate dollars to establish protocols for differing symptoms and diseases to standardize care.[18]

The last factor among determinants of medical care utilization is efficacy of medical care. We might include differences in availability of the latest technological equipment, beds, physical therapy, etc.[19] Social insurance can play a role in reducing inequities here by influencing the location of facilities. Yet for very expensive equipment or equipment that is used for rare diseases or diagnosis, location among heavy concentrations of persons in major urban areas may be desired, given the relevant benefit-cost calculation.

Clearly, equalizing the utilization of medical care requires far more intervention than simply modifying the direct price of care. The provision of health insurance to all residents or citizens should not be expected to lead to equalization of medical care use.

To facilitate our discussion in the next section, we combine these equations. First we substitute the determinants of own demand in the equation for medical care utilization (equation (4)) and then combine this equation into the production function for health (equation (5)).

We then have:

$$MC = MC(H, P(1 - \alpha), w(tr + a), P^{tr}, K, T, Y, D^P, S^{MC}, E^{MC}) \qquad (4)$$

$$H = H(H^\circ, B, E, P(1 - \alpha), w(tr + A), P^{tr}, K, T, Y, D^P, S^{MC}, E^{MC}) \qquad (5)$$

3. Equalizing health status under alternative definitions

Definition one refers to equalization of health status. To achieve this objective, a country through its social insurance system would attempt to equalize health status across all persons or all persons within a given cohort or bring everyone up to a threshold level. However, our discussion above makes it clear that although many of the factors that influence health can be modified so as to reduce inequality of health status, in many if not most cases, such changes would go far beyond the usual view of the role of social insurance. The greatest difficulty with this definition is that many factors beyond medical care and income inequality influence a person's health. The most severe challenge to the usefulness of this definition of equality is that it requires major changes in areas beyond the health care sector and the income transfer system.[20] This can be seen in equation (5).

An alternative definition is equalization of the use of care. By this we mean equal use of medical care for any state of health, or ill health. It would mean that there should be no detectible differences in care after a heart attack. To use the news story cited above, once disease severity has been accounted for, procedures such as cardiac catheterization, percutaneous transluminal coronary angioplasty, and coronary bypass surgery would not differ according to a person's race or economic status. This concept is similar to the concept of need as used in the medical profession. In such cases, the definition of an adequately served or underserved area is based on the number and characteristics of the population, which are used as proxies for a count of diseases and needed preventive care.[21] Equation (4) and the discussion of the factors that play a role in determining actual medical care utilization make it clear that this objective is difficult to achieve. Perhaps the public sector might achieve some equalization in the quality and quantity of medical care across areas. The requirements for success in this dimension go beyond equalization of population provider ratios, since effective demand also should be taken into account. The difficulty in achieving this objective is the nature of own demand or effective demand, whose aggregate value determines the demand of others in the community (D^i and D^p.) The individual demand function and its arguments are analyzed above under the discussion of equation (3).

The other definitions are narrower in scope and hence require less from the social insurance system to achieve their objectives. In the case of equality in access to and knowledge of medical care, important factors are the price of medical care (direct and indirect) and knowledge regarding efficacy of care. Also implied in these requirements are elements of equation 4, such as equalization of the supply of medical care and efficacy of care. The details of the requirements of achieving these and the potential role of public insurance and other components of the public sector are discussed above.

For the fourth definition, equity in access to medical care, the requirements are to equalize the direct and indirect costs as well as the supply components included in equation (4). The difference between this definition and the third is essentially the requirement of equal knowledge, which would require equalizing education regarding the efficacy of medical care. The requirement of equal knowledge of availability of care is included under this definition as well. Without such knowledge it is difficult to understand what is meant by equality in access to medical care. For the role of the public sector and particularly public insurance, see the relevant discussion above.

For the fifth definition, equity in terms of the equalization of the direct cost of medical care, the requirements are limited to components of equation (3). They include equalization of the value of $P(1-\alpha)$ for all persons for each type of care. The final objective, equality in terms of the cost of care of a minimum package, would require equalizing the direct cost of care of a limited package that might be defined in terms of type of care (prevention, curative, physical and mental) or site of care (in- and out-patient). Alternatively, certain types of care might be excluded. A classic example of this is cosmetic surgery, except in the case of major accidents.

Clearly, the narrower the definition of equality, the easier it is to be successful.[22] Hence it would be easiest to achieve definitions five and six. (The fifth is likely to be more costly and possibly to include expenditures that are viewed as frivolous and/or ineffective; this may lead to limited political support and the eventual reduction of resources for medical care and/or its equalization.) In fact, most developed countries have a system that achieves definition five or six. This is the case in all countries with a universal health insurance program.

No country has a system that fully achieves any of the other definitions. Some, however, have attempted to achieve definition four, equalization of access to medical care. The United Kingdom, for example, might be thought to have designed its system of public provision of care in order to equalize access. Canada and the Netherlands, with their limits on the ability to practice in certain regions, are another example, and the U.S. programs that forgive loans to medical students who then practice in underserved areas also attempt to equalize access across geographical regions.

A number of countries behave as though their goal is equality in use of health care, definition two. Numerous studies, such as those conducted under the auspices of the European Community, have addressed the question of equalization of use of medical care. As implemented, the definition seems to be interpreted as equalization of care within subgroups defined in terms of age, sex, and health status. The instruments under discussion are, however, generally limited to those that relate to achieving definition four, equalization of access to medical care; they include equalizing the direct and indirect price of care and possibly the location of providers and the distribution of income. The use of indicators of inequality, such as differential mortality rates by age and cause, relate to equalization of health status. Several studies in the United Kingdom, especially those by LeGrand, have used these measures to indicate the success of the National Health Care Service in equalizing health status. Yet it is difficult to see how this goal can be achieved with the measures so far employed by the public sectors of today's developed countries.

Developed countries have public sectors of very different sizes. They provide or finance medical care for all or a subset of inhabitants, and as a result may have a more equalized health care system and distribution of health status by any or all of these definitions. In the next section we review two types of evidence.

4. Equity across and within countries: does it vary according to share of the public sector?

If the public sector can play a significant role in influencing equity in the health care sector, then we would expect that those countries in which the public sector plays a larger role might have greater equality of health status. Other factors enter in, of course, in particular the overall level of economic well-being per capita.

Using the OECD database on 27 countries in 1990, we attempt to see if aggregate country-level data provide evidence that a larger public sector role in the health arena increases equality of health.[23] We use 1990 data because it is the latest year for which these data are reasonably complete.

Table 4.1.1 Private and public shares in financing health care, selected OECD countries, 1990

	Private health insurance as a proportion of health expenditures (%)	Proportion of population covered by publicly financed medical care (%)	Proportion of medical expenditures paid by public sector[a] (%)
Australia	10.8	100	70
Austria	7.8	99	84
Belgium	1.6	99	88
Canada	8	100	82
Czech Republic	n/a	100	n/a
Denmark	n/a	100	85
Finland	1.7	100	82
France	2.8	99.5	75.1
Germany	n/a	92.2	92
Greece	1.6	100	88
Hungary	n/a	n/a	n/a
Iceland	n/a	100	87.1
Ireland	n/a	100	90
Italy	0.9	100	75.9
Japan	n/a	100	87.9
Luxembourg	n/a	100	91
Mexico	n/a	55.8	n/a
Netherlands	12.8	70.7	72.4
New Zealand	3.5	100	n/a
Norway	n/a	100	90
Portugal	0.7	100	n/a
Spain	3.7	99	90
Sweden	n/a	100	93.8
Switzerland	1.8	99.5	91
Turkey	n/a	55.1	n/a
United Kingdom	3.3	100	93
United States	33.3	44	61

[a]   Among those publicly insured
n/a   not available

The first column of table 4.1.1 reports the share of health care financing that is private. The order among the reported countries is clear: the United States has the highest share of privately financed medical expenditures. The Netherlands and Australia are second and third, but lag far behind. Finland, France, Greece, Italy, Portugal, Spain, Switzerland, and the United Kingdom all have proportions below 5 percent. The next column reports the proportion of the population covered by social insurance (the public sector) for medical care. The results are generally consistent with the first column: the United States has the lowest proportion (44 percent), followed by Turkey and Mexico at about 55 percent, and then by the Netherlands at about 70 percent. All the others are at 90 percent or higher, and Germany is the only one below 95 percent. Another component of the public share is the proportion paid by the public sector for those publicly insured. As reported in the last column, the United States stands at the low end, at 61 percent. Australia is the second lowest, at 70 percent. The Netherlands is again relatively low, at about 72 percent, closely followed by France close (75 percent) and Italy 976 percent). Those with the highest proportions paid are Sweden, the United Kingdom, Luxembourg, and Germany, at more than 90 percent. Taking these data together produces this rough ordering:

- the United States has by far the smallest public role in the health care sector;
- it is distantly followed by the Netherlands and Australia, then Turkey and Mexico;
- Sweden has the highest public share, and the remaining countries are slightly below Sweden.

Table 4.1.2 provides information on additional measures of the public sector role. The first column addresses coverage for pharmaceuticals, an element not always covered by public insurance and/or covered less broadly than other costs. These results show an even wider gap between the United States and the other countries. Ireland, Mexico, Turkey, and the Netherlands rank higher than the United States. Differences among the other countries are small. Column two shows the rate of cost-sharing for pharmaceuticals, again revealing the small public sector role in the United States.

265

Table 4.1.2 Public share in financing of other aspects of health care, selected OECD countries, 1990

	Proportion of Population with Publicly Provided Health Insurance Covering Pharmaceuticals (%)	Proportion of Pharmaceutical Expenditures Paid by Public Sector[a] (%)
Australia	100	45
Austria	99	50
Belgium	93	52
Canada	n/a	33
Czech Republic	100	n/a
Denmark	100	45
Finland	100	46
France	98	58.7
Germany	92.2	50
Greece	100	75
Hungary	n/a	n/a
Iceland	100	79
Ireland	40	62
Italy	100	66.4
Japan	100	85
Luxembourg	100	84
Mexico	55.8	n/a
Netherlands	61.5	66.6
New Zealand	100	65
Norway	100	60
Portugal	100	67
Spain	99	77
Sweden	100	71.7
Switzerland	99.5	45
Turkey	55.1	85
United Kingdom	100	91
United States	12	25

[a]   Among those publicly insured.
n/a   not available.

Table 4.1.3 Health status differences in mortality, selected OECD countries, 1990

	Perinatal mortality among live and stillbirths (%)	Additional years of female life expectancy at birth as compared to male	Female life expectancy at birth, in years	Additional years of female life expectancy at 80 as compared to male
Australia	0.61	6.2	80.1	1.8
Austria	0.69	6.5	78.9	1.3
Belgium	0.89	6.7	79.1	1.8
Canada	0.77	6.6	80.4	2.2
Czech Republic	0.77	8.5	76.0	0.8
Denmark	0.83	5.7	77.7	1.7
Finland	0.62	8.0	78.9	1.4
France	0.83	8.2	80.9	1.8
Germany	0.6	6.4	79.1	1.6
Greece	1.19	4.8	79.4	0.5
Hungary	1.4	8.6	73.7	1.0
Iceland	0.63	4.6	80.3	1.6
Ireland	1.02	5.5	77.5	n/a
Italy	1.05	6.5	80.0	1.6
Japan	0.55	6.0	81.9	1.8
Luxembourg	0.69	6.2	78.5	n/a
Mexico	1.7	6.3	74.0	1.6
Netherlands	0.96	6.3	80.1	1.8
New Zealand	0.74	5.9	78.3	1.6
Norway	0.75	6.4	79.8	1.7
Portugal	1.26	7.0	77.9	1.0
Spain	0.75	7.0	80.4	1.3
Sweden	0.65	5.6	80.4	1.7
Switzerland	0.77	6.9	80.9	1.7
Turkey	n/a	4.3	68.4	0.7
United Kingdom	0.81	5.7	78.6	1.9
United States	0.91	7.0	78.8	1.9

n/a   not available.

Table 4.1.4 Health status differences in morbidity, selected OECD countries, 1990

	Low birth weights among all hospital deliveries (%)	Occurrence of Spina Bifida per 10,000 newborns	Iatrogenic (drug-related) deaths per million people
Australia	6	5.5	2.2
Austria	5.6	n/a	0.6
Belgium	6.5	8.9	n/a
Canada	5.4	n/a	1.1
Czech Republic	5.7	n/a	0.5
Denmark	5.2	n/a	n/a
Finland	3.9	0.8	2
France	5.3	4.8	12
Germany	5.7	n/a	0.8
Greece	6.0	1.6	0.4
Hungary	9.3	n/a	1.2
Iceland	3.0	n/a	n/a
Ireland	4.2	7.2	0.9
Italy	n/a	4.3	0.2
Japan	6.3	3.6	1
Luxembourg	n/a	n/a	n/a
Mexico	5.6	16.4	1.3
Netherlands	4.9	10.7	0.9
New Zealand	5.8	2.9	13.6
Norway	4.5	3.9	0.2
Portugal	5.6	5.5	1.7
Spain	5.0	4.4	1.8
Sweden	4.5	4.4	0.1
Switzerland	5.1	3.7	0.7
Turkey	n/a	n/a	n/a
United Kingdom	6.7	1.7	0.8
United States	7.0	4.2	0.7

n/a   not available.

Does a larger role played by the public sector reduce differences in health outcomes? We look at a few indicators of health differences. The first is the percentage of perinatal deaths as a share of all births. Excluding those countries that are not fully industrialized (Czech Republic, Greece, Hungary, Mexico, Portugal, and Turkey), the two countries with the highest ratios are the Netherlands and the United States, which points to an association with a smaller public role. Australia's very low rate is somewhat inconsistent, as are the higher rates in Belgium, France, and Denmark.

The difference in life expectancy between females and males is also a puzzle. The Czech Republic, Hungary, France, and Finland register the greatest differences, while Sweden and the United Kingdom have the smallest differences. The third column is provided as a reference, offering data on life expectancy of females at birth across these countries. Among fully industrialized countries, the United Kingdom ranks lowest, although the United States is not far above it. The final column, also a reference, shows the difference in life expectancy between males and females at age 80. The differential has narrowed in all countries. The largest difference, in Canada, is unexplained.

The next set of health measures reveal mixed outcomes. In regard to the share of low birth weight babies among all births, Hungary has the highest rate, followed by the United States and then the United Kingdom. Iceland and Finland have very low rates. A major birth defect is spina bifida, shown in column 2. Mexico and the Netherlands experience very high rates, while the United States has an intermediate position. In terms of the rate of premature deaths (deaths prior to age 70) due to medicinal drugs, New Zealand and France have by far the worst records, while the United States has a low rate.

The picture that emerges from these health indicators is mixed, and does not support a close link between a large public sector role and reduction in health inequalities. Perhaps other factors mitigate the public effort.

Other factors that are likely to lead to health problems are shown in table 4.1.5. In terms of butter consumption per capita, New Zealand and France are the leaders, whereas Portugal, Greece, Turkey, Spain, and the United States have the lowest levels. Tobacco consumption may also weaken the effect of public health expenditures on health status. The measure used here is grams per capita among the population 15 years and over. We find a high rate of tobacco smoking in Japan. France has a far higher rate of alcohol intake per capita than any of the other twenty countries.

Table 4.1.5 Risk-taking behavior differences, selected OECD countries, 1990

	Butter consumption kilos/capita	Tobacco consumption grams/capita 15 (Aged 15+)	Alcoholic beverage intake-consumption liters/capita (aged 15+)
Australia	2.6	1972	10.3
Austria	5.2	2329	12.6
Belgium	7.8	2462	12.4
Canada	3.4	1980	9.2
Czech Republic	n/a	n/a	n/a
Denmark	9.3	2614	11.6
Finland	5.6	1409	9.5
France	8.8	2272	16.7
Germany	6.5	n/a	13.8
Greece	1.1	n/a	n/a
Hungary	n/a	n/a	n/a
Iceland	5.1	2472	5.2
Ireland	3.4	n/a	9
Italy	2.4	n/a	10.9
Japan	0.7	3220	7.5
Luxembourg	7.8	n/a	14.7
Mexico	n/a	n/a	n/a
Netherlands	4.1	n/a	9.9
New Zealand	10.4	1957	10.1
Norway	3.3	1851	5
Portugal	1.0	n/a	9.8
Spain	0.5	n/a	13.6
Sweden	4.4	1850	6.4
Switzerland	6.1	n/a	12.9
Turkey	2.0	n/a	n/a
United Kingdom	3.4	n/a	n/a
United States	2.0	n/a	n/a

n/a   not available.

A few graphs provide evidence on the link between health and the public sector. The first plots perinatal mortality against the proportion of public expenditures among those covered. The plotted line is as might be expected, and the sign of the correlation coefficient is consistent as well. The perinatal mortality rate generally declines as the share paid by the public sector increases. A number of countries lie far off the line however: Greece, Italy, Australia, and Japan in particular stand out, the first two for their high perinatal mortality rate and the latter for their low rates. The next figure plots the proportion of low-weight births against the extent of costs paid by the private sector (insurance and direct patient payments), and it also finds the expected relationship. In this case, the United Kingdom and Finland lie farthest from the line, Finland having a lower proportion of low-weight births and the United Kingdom a higher proportion. The third graph looks at a measure of health among the older population - the rate of premature deaths among women under 70. The line again suggests a positive role for publicly provided health insurance. Figure 4.1.4 does the same for males, and finds a stronger correlation between premature deaths and public expenditure. The last figure at first seems surprising but less so upon reflection: it shows a positive association between deaths due to medicinal drugs (pharmaceuticals) and the public insurance coverage of such drugs. The last three figures together nevertheless point to a positive association between greater public coverage and better health. All of this evidence is only suggestive, however. No causal modeling is attempted, the sample size is very small, and in many cases the U.S. experience may account for much of the observed relationship.

Three things seem to emerge from this limited look at the link between the role of the public sector and health outcomes: (1) the association is weak; (2) reducing the direct price of care by increasing the share paid by the public sector does seem to reduce certain types of premature mortality, which is a form of equalization of health status; (3) the link between behavior, health, and the public sector may reflect a pattern in which individuals use publicly provided health care to reduce the consequences of poor choices. With the possible exception of a government effect on reduction of tobacco consumption, we find little evidence of success of the public sector in influencing risk-taking behavior.[24]

271

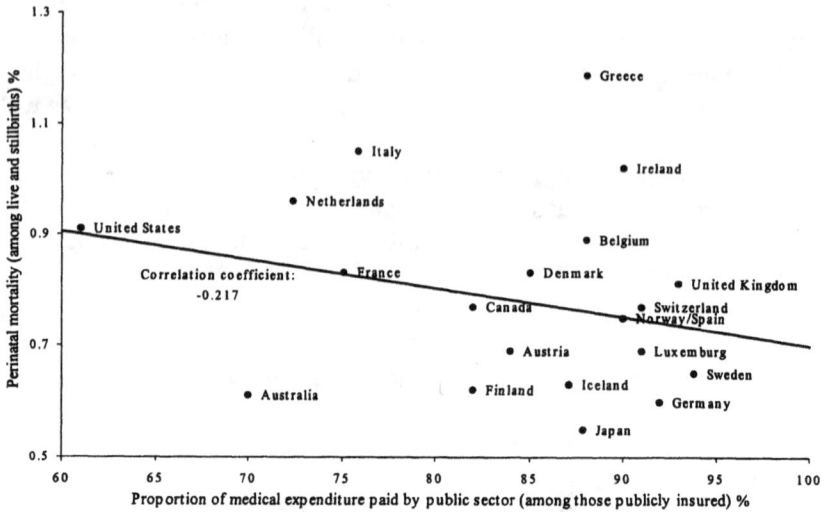

Figure 4.1.1 **Perinatal mortality rate compared to share of medical care costs paid by public insurance for those covered (OECD health data 1996)**

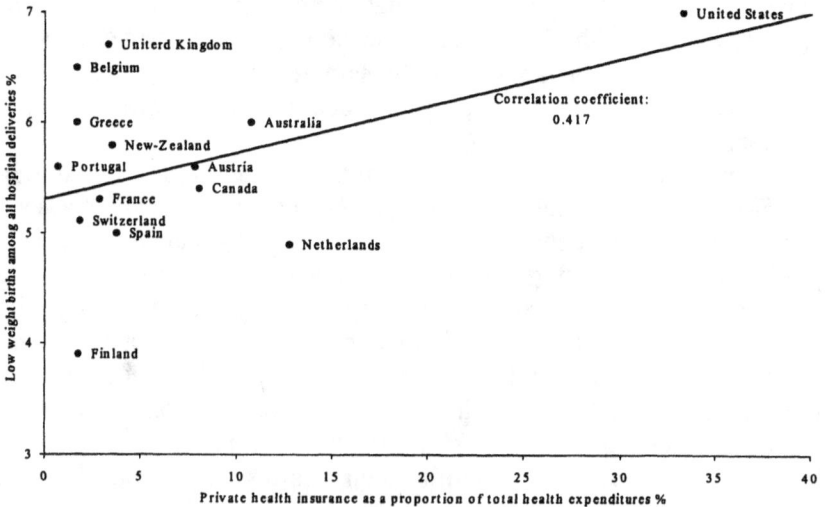

Figure 4.1.2 **Ratio of low-weight births to share of costs paid by private sector (OECD health data 1996)**

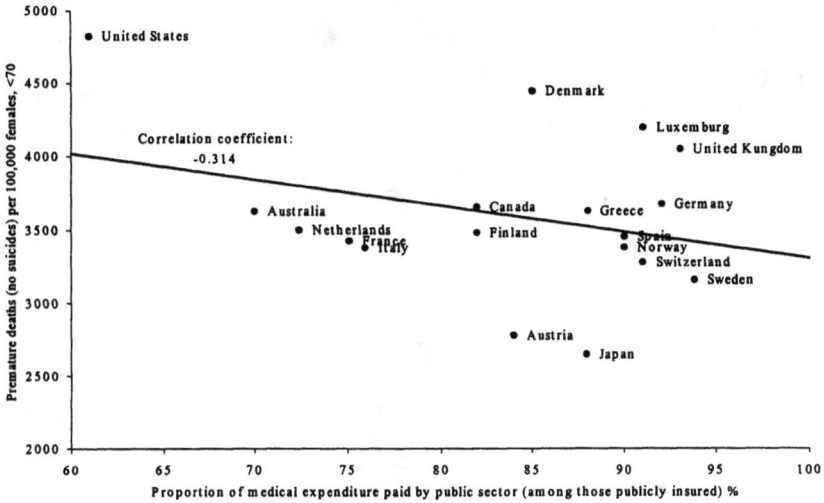

Figure 4.1.3   Rate of premature deaths for females ages < 70 compared to share paid by public insurance (OECD health data 1996)

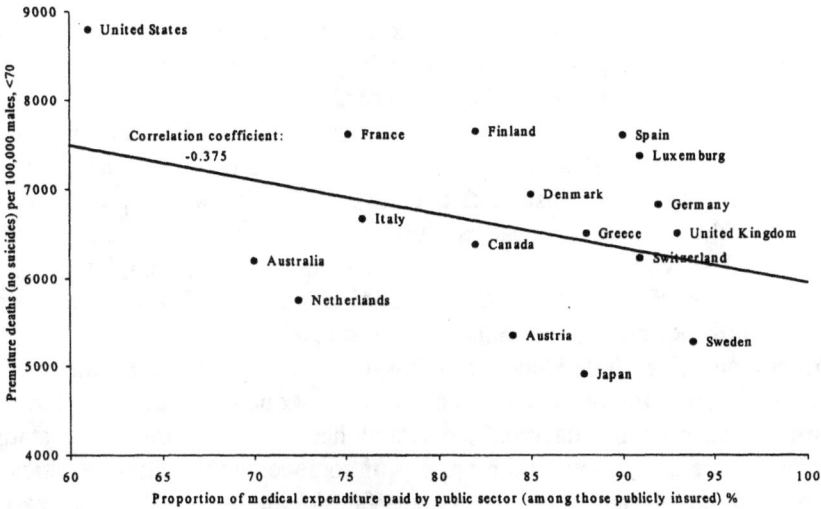

Figure 4.1.4   Rate of premature deaths for males ages < 70 compared to share paid by public insurance (OECD health data 1996)

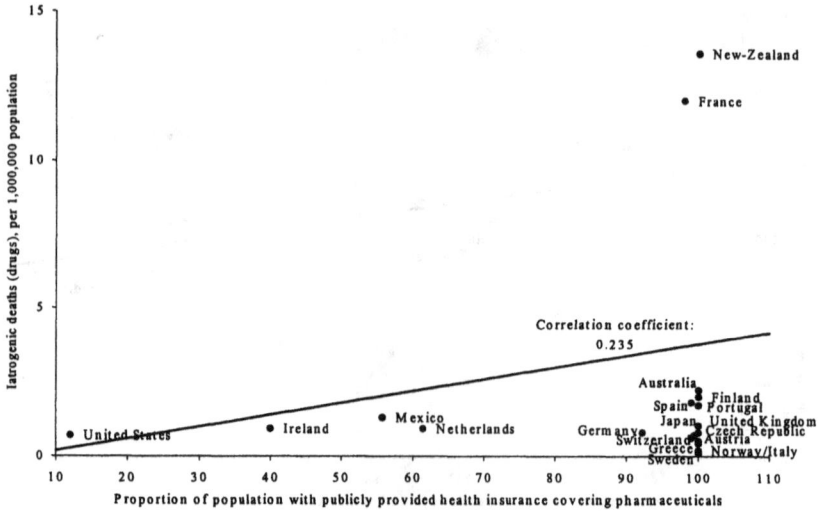

Figure 4.1.5 **Iatrogenic deaths due to drugs compared to the % of drug bills paid by public insurance (OECD health data 1996)**

Our final analysis concerns one country, the United States, in one year, 1987. We explore the role of health insurance in determining equity in the utilization of medical expenditures.[25]

The goal of this exercise is to explore the potential role of insurance in reducing inequality in utilization of medical care. We ask whether shifting from private insurance coverage or no coverage to public coverage would equalize medical care utilization.[26] The data are from a large national survey conducted in 1987, the National Medical Expenditure Survey, covering about 14,000 households interviewed four times over a 16-month period.[27] Subpopulations of special policy interest who were oversampled included poor and low-income families, the functionally impaired, and minorities. The survey was conducted by the U.S. government and contains data on individual health, health insurance status, health care utilization, and a variety of socioeconomic characteristics of the individuals and their immediate family members. Most utilization reports were verified by obtaining data from providers.

274

Table 4.1.6 Predicted expenditures and predicted expenditures under simulated alternative insurance coverage, U.S. adult population, 1987, by income

Adults	All income Mean	All income Median	Poor Mean	Poor Median	Middle Mean	Middle Median	High Mean	High Median
All adults								
Privately insured	$1133	$819	$1177	$770	$1051	$793	$1181	$864
If public insurance	1729	725	1868	986	1640	720	1756	808
Uninsured	580	244	656	313	476	167	405	164
If private insurance	1023	650	1047	620	927	675	1096	721
If public insurance	1317	677	1530	885	938	443	1017	304
Publicly insured	2744	1209	2608	1259	2604	1151	4100	1733
If private insurance	1611	893	1605	858	1576	951	715	893
Adults in poor health clusters								
Privately insured	$2457	$1601	$2376	$1332	$2441	$1580	$2501	$1765
If public insurance	5526	1906	3983	1906	4706	1342	6747	2679
Uninsured	1336	457	1412	473	NS		NS	
If private insurance	2150	1230	2121	1140	NS		NS	
If public insurance	2789	1725	2832	1984	NS		NS	
Publicly insured	5028	2470	4473	2548	NS		NS	
If private insurance	2470	1281	2527	1189	NS		NS	
Adults in good health cluster								
Privately insured	$878	$750	$845	$632	$791	$720	$949	$785
If public insurance	1000	635	1281	838	1068	680	882	505
Uninsured	418	221	430	290	415	147	371	164
If private insurance	782	590	763	564	772	630	891	626
If public insurance	1003	604	1186	742	783	376	625	187
Publicly insured	1131	742	1118	798	1303	798	NS	
If private insurance	888	758	868	714	962	895	NS	

NS   Sample size < 50

We use a nonparametric technique that makes use of data provided in the survey. We employ total medical expenditures as our measure of utilization.[28] The control or conditioning variables are age, race, sex, urban area or not, income, and insurance status. We also separately conduct estimates for subgroups defined by health that utilizes responses to several self-reported measures of health status and chronic condition prevalence.[29] (See Vanness and Wolfe, 1997, for more on the data set and the approach.)

The results for non-parametric expected expenditures by current insurance status are reported in Table 4.1.6, as are the results of simulations in which we change the insurance status of these individuals.[30] The columns represent income groups: poor, middle, and high, the groups being approximately evenly divided.[31] Three panels are presented: the first for all persons, the second for adults in the poor health groups, and the last for adults in the good health group. Figures 4.1.6 to 4.1.11 present evidence on the expected response to a change to public insurance by these groups, but provide the full probability distribution of expenditures rather than only the average.[32]

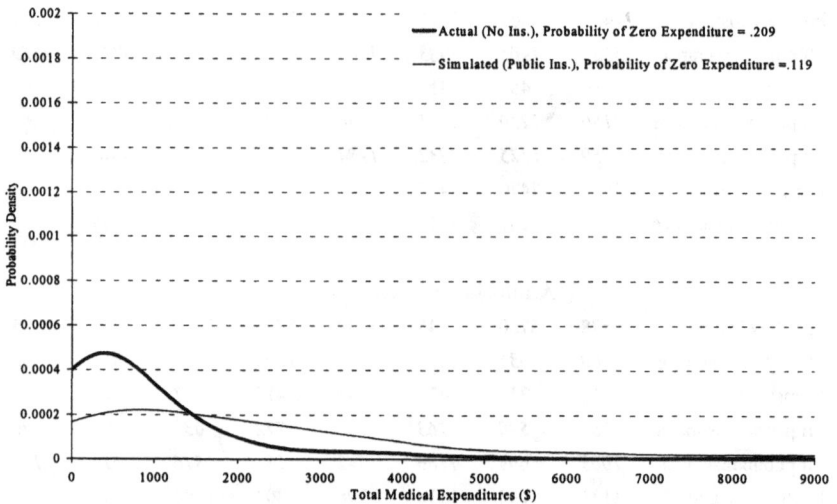

Figure 4.1.6   **Adults in poor health clusters, all income levels, no insurance. n=258. Simulation: what if they had public insurance?**

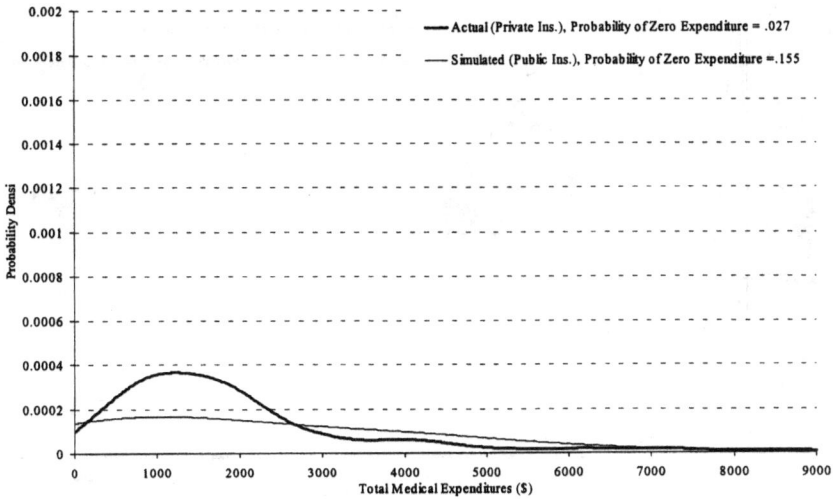

Figure 4.1.7 Adults in poor health clusters, all income levels, private insurance. n=1272. Simulation: what if they had public insurance?

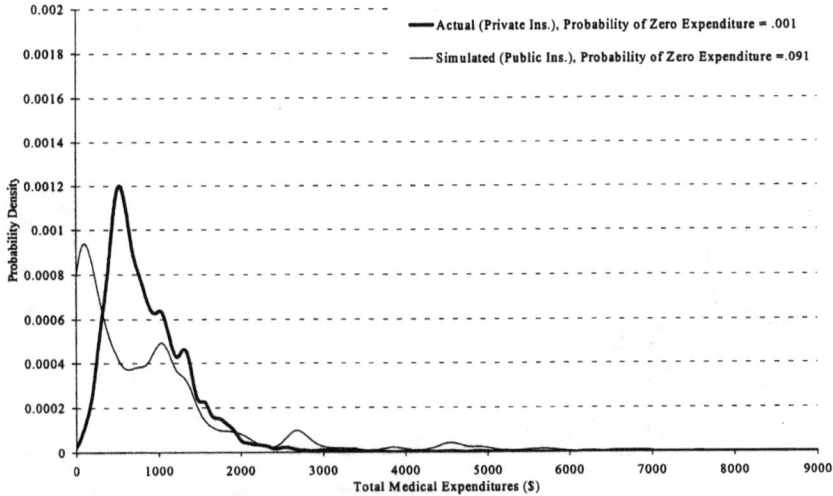

Figure 4.1.8 Adults in good health clusters, all income levels, private insurance. n=6624. Simulation: what if they had public insurance?

277

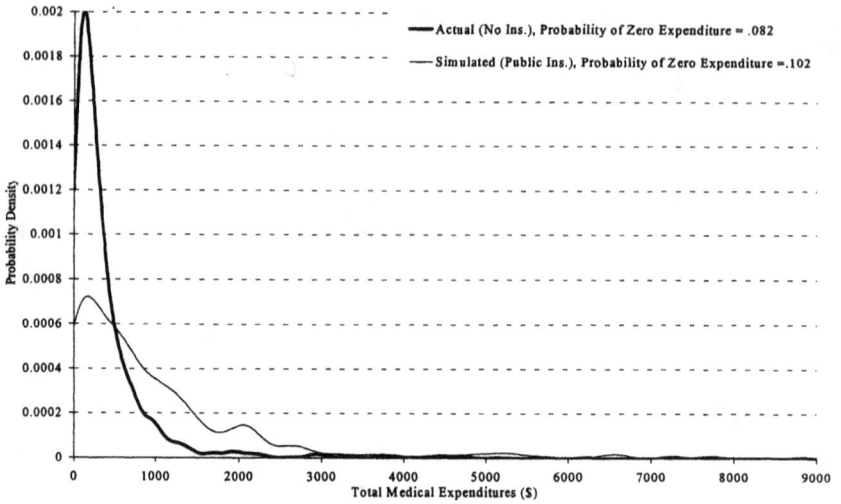

Figure 4.1.9   Adults in good health cluster, all income levels, no insurance. n=1210. Simulation: what if they had public insurance?

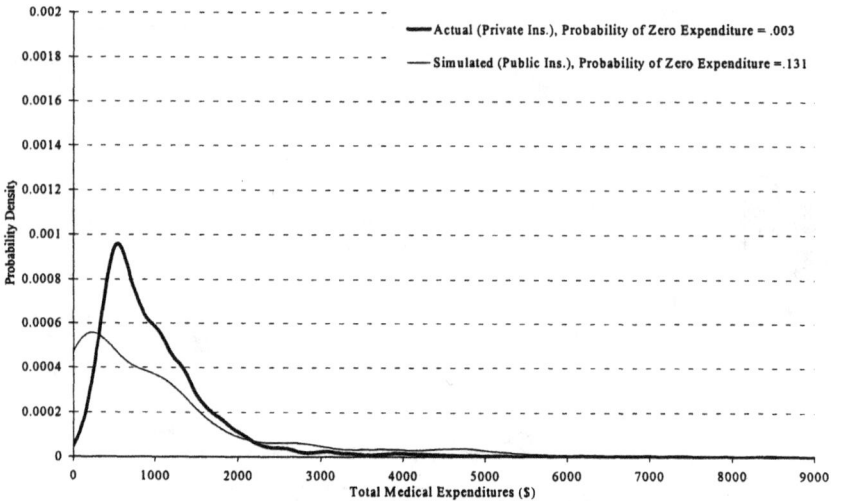

Figure 4.1.10   Adults in all health clusters, all income levels, private insurance. n=7896. Simulation: what if they had public insurance?

278

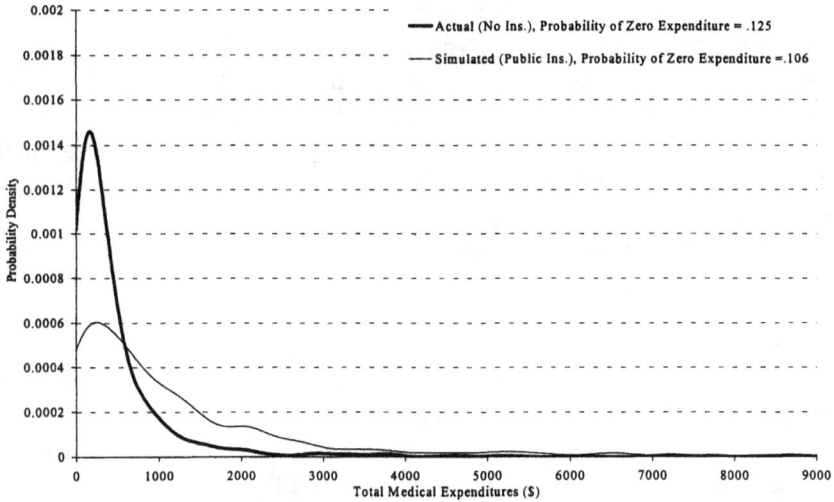

Figure 4.1.11   **Adults in all health clusters, all income levels, no insurance. n=1468. Simulation: what if they had public insurance?**

The results using the mean of the non-parametric expected expenditures indicate that among those with private insurance, there is a shallow U-shaped relationship between expenditures and income, and the middle group has lower expenditures than do the low- or higher-income groups. If these individuals were to be publicly insured, their expenditures would increase substantially, but the overall pattern would remain. If instead we use median non-parametric expected expenditure as our basis for measuring equality of use, the pattern is quite different: among the privately insured, low-income individuals have the lowest expenditures and high-income individuals, the highest expenditures. This is likely to reflect the impact of required coinsurance payments. If instead these same individuals were to be publicly insured, we predict that the low-income group would have the highest expenditures. This again suggests that copayments reduce spending on medical care disproportionately among the low-income population.

In the uninsured group, expenditures are quite low; using both mean and median expected expenditures, those who are poor have the highest expenditures, a pattern that is surprising, but may reflect poorer health. If this group were to be privately insured, the U-shaped pattern of mean

279

expenditures is as expected; if publicly insured, the expected expenditures are higher on average, which is accounted for primarily by the much greater expected expenditures of the poorest group. The high-income group is expected to have lower medical expenditures under public coverage compared to private coverage, a difference that is much greater when we compare median expected expenditures than when we compare means.

Since these patterns are likely to reflect poorer health status among the lowest-income group, we now look at the patterns by health status, a proxy for need.[33] The first rows are again for those currently privately insured, and show that on average those with more income have slightly greater expected expenditures. But comparing the lowest to the highest, the differences in mean expected expenditures are about $125, or about 5 percent; using median expected expenditures they are 32.5 percent. If this group were to be publicly insured, our simulation shows a significant increase in expenditures and a far greater difference in mean expected expenditures between the lowest and highest income groups, with a differential of 69 percent. Using median expected expenditures we see a similar pattern. Among the uninsured, poor adults in poor or fair health have somewhat higher expenditures than the overall average. If they were insured, their expenditures would increase greatly, especially under public coverage.

Turning to the final panel, which includes only those in good health, we see a U-shaped pattern in mean expenditures among those with private coverage, and a generally increasing pattern of median expenditures with income. With both measures, the greatest expenditures occur among those with the highest incomes.

Among the uninsured, we observe small average expenditures, and the lowest-income group has somewhat higher expenditures than those with more income. Providing uninsured individuals who are in good health with private coverage will lead to significant increases in expected expenditures - somewhat smaller among the lowest-income group than among those with more income. Moving these same individuals to public coverage will lead to greater increases in expected expenditures among the lowest-income group.

This simulation suggests several conclusions:

—   If copayments are required, those with the highest income are likely to use more care (have greater medical expenditures) than those

with less income. Hence, using private coverage that can impose copayments, even if mandated for all, may still result in unequal medical expenditures.
- Indirect costs seem to play an important role. The middle-income group seems especially sensitive to these costs.
- Providing public insurance without copayments would dramatically increase medical care costs. This suggests that achieving equality by across-the-board public insurance coverage is very expensive and still results in some inequality in expenditures, especially among those in poor health.

Therefore, although it may be easier to equalize utilization by providing public insurance with no or very limited copayments, the high (and probably inefficient) utilization of care that results may not be an effective or very efficient way to move toward the equalization of health status, or even of medical care use.

5. Conclusion

This paper has described many definitions of equity in the health care sector, even when only horizontal equity is considered. In the end it is doubtful that we can fully achieve the goal of equity under many of the definitions by working with the traditional tools of the public sector, especially the traditional tool of a public insurance system. What is clear is that in order to equalize health or access to medical care we must move far beyond interventions in the medical care and health insurance systems. Equation 5 makes this point very clearly.

Were we to agree on a goal and the appropriate tools, we would need to measure the outcome in order to measure progress in meeting the goal.[34] And we would need to understand the production function in order to achieve the goal most efficiently. These, however, are very difficult tasks, and neither is undertaken here.

Notes

1. Some of the best known of these include writings of Alan Williams, Alan Maynard, A. Donabedian, A. J. Culyer, Julian LeGrand. See the references in van Doorslaer, Wagstaff and Rutten (1993).

2. The paper is broad in scope but omits many other equity issues, such as the financing of health care, the financing of other expenditures that influence health and medical care, the organization of health care, and incentives for immigration.

3. This version of definition one would refer only to horizontal equity. A fuller version would also have to define goals across birth cohorts; that is, provide a definition that encompasses vertical equity as well.

4. Issues in debates on the most effective treatment are ignored here.

5. An example of this is the package of care provided under Medicaid in the state of Oregon, which was developed through several stages of effort, including obtaining opinions from citizens.

6. Also incorporated in the supply of medical care are other factors that might influence the actual supply of care provided, such as the presence of managed care, or the form of provider reimbursement (salary, fee for service, capitation).

7. The sum of $w(tr + a)$ plus P^{tr} represents the indirect cost of a unit of medical care.

8. For example, Victor Fuchs (1974, p.6) argued that "differences in health levels between the United States and other developed countries or among populations in the United States are not related to differences in the quantity and quality of medical care," and Julian LeGrand (1983, p. 41) argued along similar grounds that "the fact remains that death rates and general ill health do not seem to be greatly affected by the availability of medical care."

9. A recent study provides evidence that parental tobacco use increases low birth weight, sudden infant death syndrome (SIDS), asthma exacerbations, and fire-related injuries. See Aligne and Stoddard (1997).

10. This might be partially accomplished through a set of new laws, creation of stigma, etc. but generally lies outside of the social insurance system.

11. Wolfe and Zuvekas (1997) provide evidence on nonmarket gains from schooling and cite several studies that document the gains to own health, spouse's health, and children's health that accrue to own schooling.

12. Similar to providing information on the location of care, information on the way to obtain recommendations regarding care could be implemented.

13. See van Doorslaer et al. (1997).

14. A related definition would require that the cost of care to individuals be equalized in terms of a proportion of permanent income. Under this scenario, the cost of a unit of care, such as a short preventive ambulatory visit, might be set equal to 1/1000th of

282

the family's average monthly income. This cost could be set to include the indirect cost of time as well. This approach eliminates the uncertainty regarding how to calculate the indirect time costs, since they would be calculated in terms of a proportion of family income.

15. A recent study (Leidl, 1998) raises the question of access to care when outside of one's area (country) of residence. We do not take this issue up here, as this would represent inequality primarily if persons are treated differently (some get access while others do not); an alternative consideration, that certain individuals are out of their area of residence more frequently than others, is a dimension worthy of consideration, especially if the travel is tied to one's employment or family obligations. It is, however, not considered below.

16. Examples of the government intervening to influence location decisions of providers include limits on numbers who can practice in an area (the Netherlands, Canada, and many others) and financial incentives (the U.S. program to increase providers in rural areas).

17. The U.K. approach to this problem is to say that individuals can use care outside of their area. Few persons do so, however, because of transportation costs.

18. An example of this is the series of "Guides to Clinical Preventive Services" developed by the U.S. Preventive Services Task Force.

19. Of course a more important determinant of care will be the availability of anything that can be done for a person and the type of treatment available. I think here of the difference often mentioned between curative and simply palliative care.

20. If we were to narrow this objective to equalization of certain aspects of health status, the definition would be more attractive. For example, according to LeGrand (1983), the U.K. National Health Service has used mortality rates and reported illnesses as measures of the equalization of health status across social class. His research suggests, however, that these indicators are not very sensitive to the provision of medical care. Eddy (1998) reviews and critiques a broad set of measures in his discussion of how to measure quality of care.

21. These are generally based on guidelines of appropriate care for a given illness or condition.

22. This should not be viewed as a trivial statement that must always be true. In many cases having multiple factors that can be influenced or are subject to policy interventions increases our ability to achieve the objective.

23. *OECD Health Data 1996*, CD-ROM, using CREDES Software (Paris: OECD, 1996). OECD makes every effort to ensure that data across countries are comparable.

24. An earlier study using OECD data also suggested that health care expenditures are associated with better health once behaviors such as butter consumption and alcohol consumption are taken into account. See Wolfe and Gabay (1987).

25. This section is co-authored with David Vanness.

26. Using data from one country has the advantage of removing the impact of unobserved differences in values, other institutions, the health care system, and the age distribution from our analysis.

27. See "Sample Design of the 1987 Household Survey, National Medical Expenditure Survey, Methods 3," Agency for Health Care Policy and Research, Publication Number 91-0037 for detail.

28. The essence of this approach is to use information based on observations with a similar set of background or conditioning characteristics but to avoid imposing a functional form. We use a kernel-smoothed regression in which the kernels might be thought of as windows that allow more information from observations that are similar to the value of the conditioning variables chose than from those that are farther away. The actual results may be sensitive to the bandwidth chosen. Here we follow the Silverman rule of thumb (Silverman, 1986).

29. The NMES questions include height, weight, smoking, activity limits, self-characterized health, and presence of chronic conditions including emphysema, heart disease, arthritis, diabetes, etc. We use principal components analysis to create a smaller number of linear combinations of these responses that capture as much information as possible regarding health. We then group individuals according to these components using a partitioning clustering algorithm. Two of these clusters contained individuals with several indicators of poor health, while the third cluster contained individuals with few or no indicators of poor health.

30. Our approach ignores any endogeneity with regard to the purchase of insurance.

31. Unfortunately, we must use the categories provided by the publicly available dataset rather than actual income. Hence we cannot use the more traditional quintile or decile approach.

32. To accomplish this, we use the kernel-regression predictions of expenditures and simulated predictions as the variables of interest. We then conduct density analysis of these results using Kernel Density Estimation (see Silverman, 1986), with publicly available smoothed cross-validation bandwidth selection code (thanks to Berwin Turlach) for each income and health group.

33. Clearly, using a group that is more narrowly stratified in terms of a health condition (a measure of health care need) is critical for understanding the impact of type of insurance coverage on utilization.

34. This is the topic of a large number of studies. See van Doorslaer et al., 1993 for a set of useful references.

References

Aligne, C. Andrew and Jeffrey Stoddard. 1997. "Tobacco and Children: An Economic Evaluation of the Medical Effects of Parental Smoking."*Archives of Pediatrics and Adolescent Medicine*. July.

Eddy, David. 1998. "Performance Measurement: Problems and Solutions." *Health Affairs* 17 (4) July/August.

Fuchs, Victor. 1974. *Who Shall Live? Health, Economics and Social Choice*. New York: Basic Books.

Le Grand, Julian. 1983. *The Strategy of Equality: Redistribution and the Social Services*. London: George Allen and Unwin.

Leidl, R. ed. 1998. *Health Care and Its Financing in the Single European Market*. Amsterdam: IOS Press.

Rawls, J. 1971. *A Theory of Justice*. Cambridge, MA: Harvard University Press.

Sen, Amartya 1992. *Inequality Reexamined*. New York: Russell Sage Press.

Silverman, B. W. 1986. *Density Estimation for Statistics and Data Analysis*. London: Chapman and Hall.

van Doorslaer, E., A. Wagstaff, and F. Rutten, eds. 1993. *Equity in the Finance and Delivery of Health Care: An International Perspective*. Oxford: Oxford Medical Publications.

van Doorslaer, E., A. Wagstaff, et al. 1997. "Income-Related Inequalities in Health: Some International Comparisons." *Journal of Health Economics* 16 (1): 93–112.

Vanness, D. and Barbara Wolfe. 1997. "The Nondiscrimination Law and Health Insurance: For Whom Did It Increase Coverage?" Mimeo. December 17. Institute for Research on Poverty, University of Wisconsin–Madison.

Wolfe, Barbara, and Mary Gabay. 1987. "Health Status and Medical Expenditures: More Evidence of a Link." *Social Science and Medicine* 25 (8): 883-888.

Wolfe, Barbara, and Samuel Zuvekas. 1997. "Nonmarket Outcomes of Schooling." *International Journal of Educational Research* 27 (6).

4.2 Risk adjustment and the equity and efficiency of health care systems

Erik Schokkaert and Carine Van de Voorde

In many countries increasing health care costs have led to reforms of the health care system. Even countries where the population seems to be satisfied with the present system (like the Netherlands, Belgium and Germany and France - see Mossialos, 1997) are introducing reforms. One of the main challenges is to control expenditures without endangering the quality of care and the equity of the system. Many countries have opted for the introduction of regulated competition with risk-adjustment schemes as a possible way to achieve this balance between efficiency and equity of access to health care. In this paper we discuss some important questions which are raised by these risk-adjustment schemes.

Because there are as many reforms as there are countries or even regions in Europe, it is impossible to give an extensive overview. Each country is different from all others in its unique history, institutional settings and in its social contract between government and inhabitants. Therefore we have chosen to focus on two examples, which are close to theoretical benchmarks. Switzerland has many characteristics of a private market system, Belgium is a public and centralised system. However, recent developments have led to a moderate convergence of the two. We do not go into the Dutch situation, which since the presentation of the Dekker-plan has been extensively discussed in the academic literature (see, e.g. van de Ven, 1997). Nor do we consider national health service (NHS) systems of the British type, as we will restrict ourselves to systems with a clear insurer-provider split.

In a first section, we will briefly sketch the theoretical background to compare private and public health insurance systems and the rationale of regulated competition. In this sketch we will focus on the aspects of efficiency and solidarity. The developments in Belgium and Switzerland are described in a second section. The last section brings together the lessons we can draw from these experiences. It will be argued that the construction of risk adjustment schemes is not merely a technical matter, but raises substantial ethical questions. It is very important to avoid confusion between technical or statistical problems on the one hand and ethical or political choices on the other hand. This whole discussion has important consequences for the design of the risk adjustment formulae.

Solidarity and insurance

Since health care needs are difficult to predict and may have substantial financial consequences, health care is usually funded in large part through public or private insurance schemes. Each insurance scheme represents an alternative method for pooling the risk of becoming ill and each implies a certain solidarity concept. This is illustrated clearly by looking at the two theoretical extremes of a fully private health insurance market and a completely centralised system. Although these pure forms do not occur in reality, they offer a useful starting point to understand the rationale of the idea of regulated competition.

A private health insurance market

In a private health insurance market the insured members pay premiums to the insurance funds to cover themselves against risk. Let us first look at the hypothetical situation where a homogeneous group covers itself while only some of its members will be unfortunate and will be struck by an illness. Ex ante, i.e. before it is known who will be lucky and remain healthy and who will be unlucky and become ill, the premium is paid by everybody voluntarily. Ex post, i.e. at the moment the risk occurs, the unlucky or the ill are paid out of the collected resources. Ex post there is some solidarity between the healthy and the ill individuals. However, this is a weak form of solidarity as risk-averse persons will insure them-selves out of pure self-interest.

In reality it almost never happens that risks are homogeneously spread over the population. Young persons with a favourable genetic constitution, with a high income and a healthy job have a smaller chance of becoming ill and of incurring large health expenses than old persons living in a desolated neighbourhood. In this more realistic case of hetero-geneous risks, private health insurers will be obliged to adjust their pre-miums to the individual risks of the insured, i.e. the expected level of their health care costs. Otherwise, the members with the 'good' risks would go to a competing insurer. Consequently, it may become difficult for the relatively poor and high-risk populations to find adequate insur-ance. In a private insurance market solidarity is limited to groups with homogeneous risks. Without regulation it is not possible to implement solidarity between the good and the bad risks.

However, there are also clear advantages to a competitive private health insurance market. The consumers get a menu of policies from which they can choose. If there is sufficient competition, the insurers have strong incentives to control expenditures and quality.

A public and centralised system

Let us now turn to our second theoretical benchmark, namely a public and centralised health insurance system or a single payer system. This is a compulsory health insurance system, financed through taxes or through social security contributions of employers and employees with govern-ment regulation of the health sector. The freedom of the consumers to choose an insurance policy is severely restricted. In the absence of com-petitive forces, the system may not be very responsive to consumers' preferences. Moreover, the control of expenditure operates through government regulation. It is doubtful that the government will always have the right incentives or sufficiently detailed knowledge to resist the claims of well-organised pressure groups. Very often, health care ex-penses are linked to income rather than to health care needs. This means that if the economy grows, automatically more resources become avail-able for health care. But if the economy contracts, the available resources are reduced without a reduction in needs.

The major advantage of this public and centralised system is the possibility to achieve a high degree of equity among citizens in the pro-vision of health care. The coverage of the (compulsory) insurance system can be made (almost) universal. Because competition is excluded, it can be imposed that every member pays the same premium, even if the risks are heterogeneous. It is no longer necessary for the insurance fund to charge higher premiums to its old and unhealthy members. Therefore, solidarity is no longer limited to groups with homogeneous risks. Such a strong subsidising solidarity between good and bad risks cannot be inspired by the pure self-interest of the insured members and therefore requires government intervention.

While this solidarity between good and bad risks can be interpreted as an aspect of "horizontal equity", there are also "vertical equity" aspects related to health insurance.[1] In this respect also a public system can go very far and impose what could be called "income solidarity" by linking the premium to be paid to the financial means of the insured. It is even possible to finance the whole health care system through progressive income taxes.

A regulated insurance market with risk adjustment

In a public and centralised system, equity can be imposed but incentives for controlling costs may be lacking and the freedom of choice of the consumers is severely restricted. In a private competitive system, there is freedom of choice and there are incentives to curb expenditures but there is not much room to achieve solidarity. The idea of regulated competition with risk adjustment is to look for a mixed approach which tries to combine the best features of the two extremes with an acceptable balance between efficiency and solidarity as the ultimate objective. Competition is relied upon to improve quality and efficiency; regulation is introduced for equity purposes.

Starting from a competitive system, it is important to understand first of all that a simple prohibition by government of premium differentiation will not be sufficient to achieve solidarity between good and bad risks, because it will lead to cream-skimming (or cherry-picking). If everybody pays the same premium, it becomes profitable for insurers to attract good risks and to avoid bad risks. Even if this is legally forbidden, there are all kind of tricks to avoid this legislation: selective advertising, different treatment of different insured by the staff, selective use of supplementary advantages, selective contracting with providers (van de Ven, Van Vliet, 1992). The basic purpose of the introduction of risk-adjustment schemes is precisely to make this kind of behaviour no longer profitable.

Risk-adjustment schemes can be summarised as distributing or redistributing payments to insurers to reflect more closely the expected costs of the insured. The basic principles underlying these schemes are simple. If the risk-adjustment scheme would be perfect, equally efficient insurers would charge the same premium even if the risk profile of their members is different, because the differences in the risk characteristics would be taken account of through the risk-adjustment scheme. Therefore, risk selection would not be profitable. But at the same time there remains room for competition between insurers. If there are differences in efficiency, the more efficient insurers can ask lower premiums and compete on quality. Since patients can freely choose their insurance company they will move to the insurers which offer the best balance between price and quality.

Risk-adjustment schemes can come under different variants. We will present the two most important ones.[2] In both variants there is a kind of central fund to which the insurers contribute or/and from which they receive their claims. The first system is an internal risk-adjustment scheme (figure 4.2.1) where the adjustment is done between the insurers and the central fund. Insurers with a relatively favourable risk mix of their members pay contributions to the central risk-adjustment fund. These are redistributed by the fund to the insurers with a relatively unfavourable risk structure. The insured members pay a flat rate premium directly to the insurance fund of their choice. On average, the premiums paid must be sufficient to cover the health care costs of all the insured (unless the central fund gets additional means from other sources, e.g. from government). The insurance companies are obliged to quote the same flat rate premium to all their members choosing the same insurance plan. Because this premium reflects the difference between actual costs and the risk-adjusted payments, the more efficient insurers will be able to charge a lower premium and will therefore become more attractive to the consumers. However, it does not pay to attract mainly good risks, because changes in the composition of the membership will immediately be reflected in changes in the amounts of money to be paid to or to be received from the central fund.

A second method of risk-adjustment is shown in figure 4.2.2. All concerned citizens pay a possibly income-related premium for basic insurance to the central fund. There are different possibilities here: the central fund can be financed with personal contributions, or with social security contributions from either employers or employees, or from general taxes. This central fund distributes these resources over the insurance funds by means of risk-adjusted capitation payments. A risk-adjusted capitation payment is independent of the chosen insurance fund and equals the predicted per capita costs within the risk group to which the member belongs, minus a fixed amount. This fixed amount is equal for all individuals. Individuals choose their preferred insurer and pay a flat rate premium. Because this flat rate premium in a system of risk-adjusted capitation payments covers only a part of all health costs, it will be substantially lower than in an internal risk-adjustment scheme. As before the more efficient insurers will be able to offer to the insured a more interesting menu of choice with respect to price and/or quality. But again, it does not pay to attract only good risks because this will have an immediate impact on the capitation payments received from the central fund.

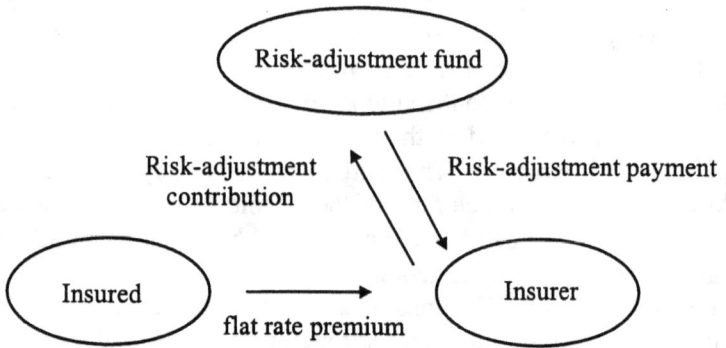

Figure 4.2.1   Internal risk adjustment

Of course, the ideal risk-adjustment schemes described here do not exist in reality. The design of a good adjustment scheme requires a lot of information on the relationship between health care costs and individual characteristics of the insured. Although perfect knowledge of this relationship is not necessary, the discrepancy between the information of the regulator (the central fund) and the information of the insurers should not be too big. The risk-adjustment formula must be as accurate as the ability of insurers to differentiate between the high and the low risks. Even this more limited objective has not been reached in actual practice - risk adjustment remains the Achilles heel of the model of regulated competition (Newhouse, 1994, van de Ven et al., 1996). It would be wrong, however, to reduce this problem to a pure technical or statistical question. We will argue that there are important ethical or political aspects involved. However, to make our discussion of these fundamental aspects somewhat more concrete, we will first describe the developments in two European countries: Belgium and Switzerland.

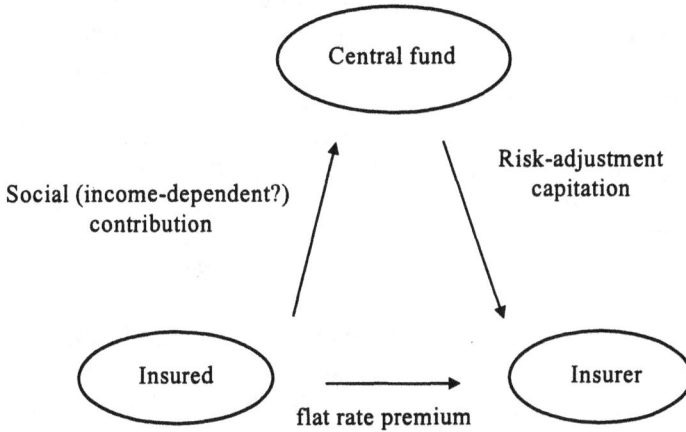

Figure 4.2.2 Capitation payments

Two examples: Belgium and Switzerland

As mentioned before, it is not at all our intention to give a detailed overview of the institutional settings and risk-adjustment mechanisms of all European countries. Instead, we concentrate on two countries which recently introduced a risk-adjustment scheme, but started from a totally different institutional setting, namely Belgium and Switzerland. These examples are chosen because they resemble more or less our theoretical benchmarks.

Belgium³

General features Belgium can basically be characterised as a public and centralised system, with a compulsory health insurance system covering the entire population. This compulsory system consists of a 'general regime', covering major as well as minor health risks for 85% of the population (employees and civil servants, retired, handicapped, widows and their dependants) and a separate 'regime for the self-employed', covering only major health risks and accounting for most of the remaining 15% of the population. The major risks mainly concern hospitalisation and special technical services. The minor risks relate to ambulatory care, medicines, dental care. The self-employed can voluntarily choose to take health care insurance for minor risks also: about 70% of the self-employed makes use of this opportunity. The two main sources of funding the compulsory system are social security contributions (proportional to income and yielding 55% of the total revenue) and state subsidies (30% of the total revenue). Individual co-payments finance the remaining 15%.

The management and administration of insurance is taken care of by a cartel of five non-government, non-profit sickness funds and one public fund.⁴ The sickness funds historically developed along political and religious lines. The national associations group a large number of local sickness funds. Membership of a fund is compulsory for employees, self-employed and retired people, but every individual can enrol in the sickness fund of her choice. Every three months, insured have the possibility to switch to another sickness fund. The compulsory insurance cover offered by the different funds and the contribution rates levied on income are identical. The sickness funds compete for new members by offering additional optional insurance for which a separate contribution is charged, by the speed of settling claims or by the quality of their services.

In Belgium, health care delivery is mainly private with both general practitioners and specialists operating independently. The patient pays by fee for service but he is partially reimbursed by his sickness fund. The fee schedule as well as the reimbursement are based on national agreements between a cartel of insurers, a cartel of representatives of the medical profession and government.

A government agency, the National Institute for Sickness and Disability Insurance (INAMI or Institut National d'Assurance Maladie et

Invalidité), is responsible for the health and disability insurance, supervises the sickness funds, takes part in the negotiation of fee schedules with the practitioners and co-ordinates health policy in general. It acts like a "central fund" and distributes the resources, collected from the employees, the employers, the self-employed and the government over the six sickness funds. There has always been much variation in the health-risks and the income levels of the members of the different sickness funds. Before the introduction of financial responsibility in the nineties, the INAMI basically pooled all the surpluses and deficits of the various sickness funds and simply reimbursed all the expenditures. This has changed since the mid-nineties.

The introduction of a risk-adjustment scheme Many observers (see e.g. Nonneman and Van Doorslaer, 1994) had the feeling that the Belgian system did not contain sufficient incentives for efficiency and cost-containment. On the contrary, since all expenditures were reimbursed and the sickness funds competed mainly on quality grounds, they could attract new members by being more lenient in their control of expenditures. Moreover, as we will argue later on, it is not at all obvious that a simple reimbursement of all expenditures necessarily leads to an equitable system.

The Royal Decree of August 12, 1994, designed to incite the insurance organisations to take more financial responsibility, was the crucial turning point. The simple full reimbursement of all health care costs to all sickness funds was replaced by a (mitigated) central fund scheme like the one described in figure 4.2.2. The Decree states that the distribution of the resources among the national associations of sickness funds should no longer depend merely on their past expenditures, but also on the (ex ante determined) risk profile of their members.

In a first step, the government sets an overall annual budget objective. This can if necessary be changed in the course of the year if there are unexpected developments. Each insurance organisation is then awarded a share of the budget in accordance with a distribution formula based on a weighted sum of two components: its actual share of real medical expenditures in the overall annual expenditures and its share in so-called "normative" expenditures, defined ex ante through a risk-adjustment formula. In 1995, 1996 and 1997, the relative weights of actual and normative expenditures were 90% and 10% respectively. The weight given to the normative component will increase over time to a maximum of 40% from the year 2000 onwards. Furthermore, the individual responsibility of the sickness funds has been limited to only 15% of their financial result in 1995, 1996 and 1997. If the sickness funds have a surplus, they may set 15% of that surplus aside in a reserve fund. If they record a deficit, they must bear 15% of that deficit themselves by drawing from their reserves or by raising their members' contributions. Here also the amount of financial responsibility will gradually increase to 25% in 2000.

Table 4.2.1 Estimation results for the active population[5]

	estimates	standard error
women	24377	8188
age 40-99	10856	4007
unemployment	33214	6426
civil servants	9919	3589
mortality	1095614	435057
disability	26843	13522
urbanisation (qualitative)	1163	226
urbanisation (density)	334	212
medical supply	1431	274
constant	508	4470
adjusted R^2	0.85	
standard deviation	217	

To develop a proper risk-adjustment strategy, it is important to determine what factors cause health care costs to vary by individual or by a group of individuals. Therefore, an econometric model has been developed to explain the level of demand in the various social groups covered by the health insurance scheme.[6] By way of illustration we give the results of the explanatory model of medical expenditure for the largest group, namely the active population of the general regime (no self-employed), in Table 4.2.1. In a first stage the construction of the risk adjusted subsidies had to be based on rather crude data at the level of the local sickness funds.[7]

We will use these aggregate data to illustrate our methodology.[8] The method used was weighted least squares, the data refer to 1995. As far as possible, the explanatory variables were expressed as a percentage of the number of beneficiaries, so that the coefficients may be immediately interpreted as monetary amounts. Medical expenditure per capita equalled 22288 Belgian Francs in 1995.

The table shows, for example, that on average a female beneficiary costs 24377 Francs more than a man, or that the medical expenditures of an unemployed person are 33214 Francs higher. The mortality rate and the disability variable are the only indications we have on morbidity. However, the coefficient of mortality is not precisely estimated and is too large. The use of aggregate data and the lack of direct information on morbidity explains the weakness of the estimates. The overall explanatory power of the regression is adequate, but there is no accurate and reliable information about the influence of all the individual factors.

Based on these estimates, one can easily "predict" expenditures for the different sickness funds on the basis of the explanatory variables in the model. It was decided, however, that medical supply should not enter the capitation payments, because the differences in medical expenditures related to differences in medical supply were deemed to be within the own responsibility of the sickness funds. We will return to the implications of this crucial choice in the following section. Risk-adjusted capitation payments were therefore calculated as:[9]

$$N_i = \sum_j \alpha_j X_{ij} - c$$

where X_{ij} are the explanatory variables for sickness fund i -note that medical supply does not enter this expression- and c is the fixed amount, referred to in the discussion of figure 4.2.2. Since the budget constraint of the central fund implies that the total budget to be distributed ω equals the sum of the subsidies given to all the insurers, this formula can be rewritten in the following equivalent form:

$$N_i = \frac{\omega}{N} + \sum_j \alpha_j \left(X_{ij} - \bar{X}_j \right)$$

where $\overline{X}_j$ is the average of X_{ij} over all sickness funds. Application of this formula is illustrated in table 2 for three sickness funds. Each row shows the effect of the different variables on the capitation payments. It turns out that although members older than 40 have higher medical expenditures, this variable has only a minor effect on the capitation payments because there is not much variation in the proportion of members older than 40 among the different sickness funds. The effects of unemployment or medical supply are much more pronounced. The results at the bottom of the table show the important financial consequences for the sickness funds of the decision not to consider medical supply as a risk factor.

Table 4.2.2 Calculation of risk-adjusted capitation payments

	coefficient α_j	variable mean $\overline{X}_j$	sickness fund A deviation from the global mean $X_{ij} - \overline{X}_j$	sickness fund A effect on the capitation payments (in BF)	sickness fund B deviation from the global mean $X_{ij} - \overline{X}_j$	sickness fund B effect on the capitation payments (in BF)	sickness fund C deviation from the global mean $X_{ij} - \overline{X}_j$	sickness fund C effect on the capitation payments (in BF)
women	24377	0.4879	0.00084	20	0.00344	84	0.00685	167
age 40-99	10856	0.3102	-0.00207	-22	0.00382	41	-0.00793	-86
unemployment	33214	0.0780	-0.01237	-411	0.02355	782	-0.00255	-85
civil servants	9919	0.0787	-0.00444	-44	-0.00868	-86	-0.00470	-47
mortality	1095614	0.0016	-0.00015	-169	0.00029	314	-0.00012	-134
disability	26843	0.0459	-0.00223	-60	0.00978	263	-0.00800	-215
urbanisation-qual.		-0.2774	-0.12055	-140	0.18258	212	-0.08253	-96
urbanisation-density	334	0.5452	-0.25452	-85	0.14818	50	0.58652	196
medical supply	1431	0.2511	-0.16842	-241	-0.01654	-24	0.55597	795
capitation payments								
all variables				-1152		1636		496
all variables without medical supply				-911		1659		-299

A provisional conclusion about efficiency and equity? In the Belgian system, insurance funds have some limited possibilities to compete, because the insured members have free choice of sickness fund and can freely move from one insurer to another. As in the central fund-scheme of figure 4.2.2, they also have to pay a small premium to the insurers, which can vary with the financial results of that insurer. However, the bulk of the financing does not come from these premiums but from the income dependent contributions to the central fund. At this moment, there is only limited premium competition. Although the financial risk of the insurers will increase in the future, it is still very small and the government bears responsibility for the majority of the health care expenditures. A more important question is to what extent the sickness funds dispose of instruments to exert a real control on the expenditures. The freedom of the sickness funds to negotiate contracts with providers is restricted. Selective contracting with providers is not allowed. Efficiency is not guaranteed by introducing financial responsibility if the financially responsible are almost powerless to influence their own financial results.

There is a real danger here, because risk selection may be easier than expenditure control. And as long as the risk-adjustment formula does not sufficiently reflect an individual's predictable future expenditures, insurance funds have substantial opportunities to cream skim. Looking into the future of the Belgian system, it seems obvious that increasing the insurers financial risk should be accompanied both by a simultaneous improvement in the risk-adjustment mechanism and by the granting of more power to the sickness funds. We will return to these more general questions after we have reviewed the Swiss case.

Switzerland[10]

General features In Switzerland also the organisation of the health care system changed rather fundamentally in the nineties (by the new Health Insurance Act - Kranken-versicherungsgesetz or KVG - of March 18, 1994 which came into force on January 1, 1996). We will first sketch the old system and then continue with the new provisions of the KVG.

Health Insurance in Switzerland is a federal responsibility supervised by the Federal Office for Social Insurance. The delivery, regulation and supervision of health care is largely the responsibility of the 26 cantons of the Swiss Federation with each canton having its own health care law.[11] Fundamental changes to the health care system require legislative reform which has to be approved by the inhabitants of a canton by direct voting.

Although before 1996 there was a voluntary health insurance scheme at the federal level, more than 99 % of the Swiss population was insured. Not only did several cantons apply regulations which made health insurance compulsory. Moreover, even where it was not compulsory, most citizens preferred voluntarily to insure. Health insurance is organised by a large but declining number of insurance or sickness funds which (before 1996) were fully responsible for the health care costs of their members. Insurance is mainly financed by the contributions of the insured. Each member of an insurance fund has to pay a per capita premium. Because premiums do not vary with income, they closely resemble those of private insurers where premiums are set on an individually risk-assessed basis and where ability to pay is not considered. The age of entry determines the premium charged by the insurance fund. This makes it very expensive for older members to move to another insurer. The lack of solidarity between the poor and the rich led to the introduction by the federal government of premium subsidies.

Patients have free choice of doctor within their canton of residence. They pay the doctors on a fee-for-service basis. The reimbursement levels for the doctors are negotiated between the cantonal associations of sickness funds and the cantonal associations of physicians. The Swiss health care system is financed by three sources, each contributing about one third of total funding. The three sources are the different levels of government (federal, cantonal and communal), the system of social insurance funds (or sickness funds) and the patients. The federal government subsidises the insurance system, whereas the cantons and communes fund the operating and investment costs of the hospital sector, as well as an increasing part of the premiums for those on low incomes. The patients make co-payments for most services such as primary care, medicines and (since 1993) hospital care.

The introduction of a risk adjustment scheme

Since the end of the eighties the health care system of Switzerland has been in a state of crisis with an increasing part of the population in favour of fundamental changes. While the Swiss system was much more regulated than our theoretical benchmark of a private insurance market, it had nevertheless many features of that latter system. It is therefore not surprising that the main problem was the gradual erosion of solidarity due to the accelerating process of risk-selection by the insurance funds or of self-selection by the insured. Because the insurance funds were allowed to differentiate premiums according to certain risk factors (age, gender,..), they were encouraged to attract young and healthy (male) members and to reject the bad risks. Having an attractive risk structure allowed some insurance funds to charge low premiums, whilst others had to increase premiums to be able to pay the health care costs of their old and sick members.

The federal authorities as well as the cantons have therefore increasingly been intervening by emergency decrees, statutory orders or changes of the law. The main tendency was the decrease of the freedom of the insurers to set premiums and tariffs, the gradual introduction of a simple system of internal risk adjustment between the insurance funds and the increase of the premium subsidies for the low income groups. As mentioned already before, the cornerstone of these developments is the new health insurance legislation of 1994, which came into force in 1996. This law introduced a compulsory basic insurance for all Swiss inhabitants with a strict definition of benefits included; an increase in the freedom of the insured to change their insurance fund, regardless of age or health status; a more explicit targeting of the subsidies with the aim to reduce the premium paid by those on low incomes; and the creation of a definitive basis for risk adjustment.

With the new measures, the government wanted explicitly to reach various goals, while keeping to the decentralised organisation of the Swiss health care system. To make the premiums for the lower income groups more acceptable, the cantons subsidise the premiums of those individuals or families whose contributions exceed a certain percentage of their income. At the same time the risk-adjustment procedure had to guarantee that competition among insurance funds was based solely on better management and higher efficiency (and not on their risk structure).

An internal risk-adjustment procedure along the lines of the scheme in figure 4.2.1 is applied in each of the 26 cantons independently. This implies that regional diversity is indirectly taken into account. Each insurance fund sets a single per capita premium for a legally well-defined health care package for each insured person in each canton. Insurers are allowed to differentiate the premiums for the regions in a canton according to the degree of urbanisation. They must offer a reduced premium for children (aged between 0 and 18 years), and they are allowed but not obliged to reduce their premium for young people in education or training (between 18 and 25 years). The insured can choose freely an insurance fund. Private for-profit insurers are included in the risk-adjustment procedure if they offer the same health care package.

The risk-adjustment procedure is based on only two risk-characteristics: age and gender. The risk-adjustment process is applicable to all sickness funds operating in a canton, and is based on actual health care costs for the basic package defined by the Swiss Health Insurance Law. The insured population of each canton is divided into 'risk-groups', based on their age and gender. Each insurance fund gives the central fund the number of insured months and total health care costs for every canton and risk-group. The total of risk-adjusted capitation claims for each insurance fund in each canton is then calculated on the basis of the differences between the effective costs per insured month for each risk group and the effective costs per insured month for a reference group, namely all men and women older than 18. Children in the 0-17 age-group are completely excluded from the risk-adjustment procedure.

A provisional conclusion about equity and efficiency? The introduction of the risk-adjustment mechanism in Switzerland was largely meant to prevent the insurance funds from risk-selecting and to increase the accessibility of the health care market. It is obvious, however, that the adjustment scheme remains extremely primitive. Age and gender are rough risk adjusters which are able to explain only a small part of the variation in individual health care costs. There still remains much room for risk selection.

The insurers can compete for members because a free choice of sickness fund is guaranteed. Compared to the Belgian case, the insurers have more and better instruments to influence expenditures. The Swiss legislation gives the insurers the freedom to introduce all kinds of managed care programs (Beck, 1998). They can have contracts with HMO's (Health Maintenance Organisations) to control costs. Here also, however, there is strong government regulation.

Risk adjustment: basic choices

Let us now return to our original questions. What can we learn from these concrete cases about the trade-off between equity (or the absence of risk selection) and efficiency? The first general lesson is obvious: it is impossible to understand the working of different systems in different countries, if one does not take into account the differences in institutional and historical circumstances in these countries. It makes a big difference whether risk-adjustment is introduced in a decentralised system for equity reasons (as in Switzerland) or in a centralised system as a corollary of the introduction of competition or at least financial responsibility (Belgium). The second lesson is closely linked to the first one but is more constructive: there is a clear relationship between the ethical and political choices made and the concrete implementation of risk adjustment. We will elaborate this second point. We will first discuss the problem of risk selection, then turn to income solidarity and finally comment on efficiency and competition.

Solidarity between good and bad risks and risk selection

We have given in the first section the usual definition of risk-adjustment schemes as mechanisms to distribute or redistribute payments to insurers so as to reflect more closely the expected costs of the insured. This definition gives the impression that the design of a capitation formula is in the first place a technical question: the larger the number of risk-adjusters and the stronger their explanatory power, the more accurate the estimation of future health care costs is likely to be. This impression is confirmed by a large part of the academic literature, which seems to accept implicitly that the better the statistical performance of the explanatory model, the better the resulting formula.[12] But if this were correct, it is difficult to explain the political decisions taken in many countries. Switzerland works with an extremely simple formula, based only on age and gender. And the Belgian case is still more striking: medical supply is deliberately taken out of the normative formula, although it clearly has explanatory power.[13] How to explain this?

Let us return to the basic rationale of the risk adjustment scheme. In a market system, the idea is to minimise the incentives for premium differentiation. In a system where the premium is regulated, the purpose of the adjustment scheme is to minimise the incentives for risk selection. Society wants to minimise these incentives because it feels that premium differentiation or risk selection respectively are ethically undesirable. But this immediately raises the basic question: is premium differentiation (or risk selection) undesirable in all circumstances? Suppose that the differences between the medical expenditures of two individuals are caused only by the fact that the first one does never consult a general practitioner but always goes immediately to a specialist (which is possible, e.g., in a country like Belgium). Should the more "expensive" individual be compensated for this behaviour? Or suppose that there is large interregional variation in medical expenditures which can clearly be related to supply-induced differences in demand. Should the insurers not get the incentives to try to curb this behaviour? Whatever the answer given to these questions, the point of the examples must be clear: "explaining" and "justifying" differences in health care costs are two different things. Defining normative expenditures is more than just a matter of statistics. It is relevant to distinguish between "is" and "ought".

The same point can also be made in another way by reasoning immediately within the context of a regression model, such as has been presented for Belgium. The estimates shown in table 4.2.1 are the best reflection possible of the way in which the different features affect observed medical expenditure. The model is far from perfect of course. The "best" possible explanatory model should forecast observed medical expenditure as effectively as possible. However, this best possible explanatory model cannot at the same time be the ideal model used for developing a normative formula: if this were true, we could more easily take observed real-life expenditures as the basis of the payment to each insurance organisation. If all real-life expenditures would be optimal from a social (or ethical) point of view, it would be rather meaningless to introduce a complicated system of ex ante capitation payments. The purpose of introducing such a system is precisely to give the insurers an incentive to act on observed expenditures.

This leads us to distinguish carefully two steps in the decision-making procedure with respect to the risk adjustment formula. The first step is to construct the best possible explanatory model. In that step normative considerations should play no role because we want to derive unbiased estimates of the effects of different variables on health care costs. The second step is the ethical or political decision to determine the characteristics for which people are to be held responsible and which therefore should not be included in the risk-adjustment scheme. That scheme should only be based on the characteristics for which society feels that individuals (and hence their insurance companies) should be compensated. Or, formulated in another way, for which one wants to avoid premium differentiation and/or risk selection. The crucial distinction between these two steps has been made carefully in the Belgian case. Medical supply has been kept in the explanatory model, because it obviously plays an important role there. It has been left out of the normative formula, however, because it was felt that the sickness funds should be motivated to do something about supply-induced variations in medical expenditures

This point of view throws a new light on the debate in many European countries about what risk-adjusters to include in the capitation formula. Rather than a technical debate, this is a debate about fundamental ethical and societal choices. Let us give some examples. Most people will agree that people are not responsible for morbidity differences linked to genetic differences.[14] If one can measure them, then they should enter the risk-adjustment scheme. The same conclusion holds for age and gender. But should we also include other factors? What about cultural differences linked to social class and income? Do we take these into account in the risk-adjustment formula or do we hold people responsible for differences in health care costs following from these cultural differences? How do we treat differences in morbidity linked to different smoking or drinking behaviour, regional variations in medical practice, subjective preferences with respect to the choice of doctor? It is clear that each of these factors will contribute to a better explanation of differences in observed health care costs. But it is equally clear that the choice whether or not to include them in the risk adjustment formula is not a statistical choice, but an ethical one. Depending on the answers given to these questions, one may end up with very different risk adjustment schemes. If society is of the opinion that people should bear responsibility for everything, a fully private health insurance market without risk adjustment is not objectionable. On the other hand, the more sensitive society is to these equity problems, the larger the set of risk-adjusters to be included in the formula.

The sensitivity to the equity problem is largely reflected in the actual schemes and in the speed with which they are introduced. Our two examples are particularly revealing in this regard. In Switzerland, starting from a decentralised scheme, only age and gender are included in a very simple risk adjustment formula. In Belgium, where the sensitivity to solidarity in health insurance apparently has much stronger historical roots, there is a complicated scheme with many risk adjusters. Let us illustrate the differences with a concrete example: the effect of urbanisation. It is well known that there are differences in health care costs between rural and urban areas. Table 4.2.1 shows some additional evidence for Belgium. Moreover, as indicated earlier, urbanisation is one of the variables taken into account in the risk adjustment formula, so that insurers are compensated for the interregional differences in health care costs, which are linked to population density and to the quality of housing. In Switzerland, where the sensitivity to the equity problem apparently is lower, urbanisation does not enter the risk adjustment scheme but insurers are allowed to differentiate the premium between more or less urbanised regions.

Two more general conclusions can be derived from this discussion. In the first place, we can now evaluate the practice of simple reimbursement of all expenditures (as in the former Belgian system) on equity grounds. Reimbursement of all expenditures means that all incentives for risk selection disappear. But this is not necessarily equitable, if one thinks that individuals should bear the responsibility for some of the factors influencing medical expenditures. In that case some risk selection (or premium differentiation) may be desirable from an ethical point of view. "Correcting" expenditures may therefore be meaningful also in a public centralised system.

Secondly, once we move into the direction of ex ante-risk adjustment, there is a danger of risk selection as long as the risk adjustment scheme is not perfect. The opportunities to cream skim will grow if one works with a simpler risk-adjustment scheme. If the available information does not allow for a rapid improvement of the capitation formula, one should think about other possibilities. One option is the introduction of mixed reimbursement schemes where the distribution of the resources is based on a weighted sum of ex ante-normative and ex post-actual expenditures.[15] As we have seen, this is the Belgian solution. Another option would be to look for a system in which the (small group of extremely) high risks of different insurers can be pooled.

Income solidarity

It can be argued that equity requires that higher income people pay larger contributions. This is definitely the opinion of a majority of Belgian citizens- but apparently this conviction is not so strong in a country like Switzerland (and still less so in the U.S.A.). The political choice about the degree of income solidarity does not interfere at all with the possible introduction of regulated competition. The central fund-scheme of figure 4.2.2 (and the Belgian experience) clearly illustrate how any degree of income solidarity can be made compatible with regulated competition on the health insurance market. One can make payments to the central fund independent of or proportional to income. The central fund can even be financed through progressive income taxes. If, by contrast, the population opts for a system with less explicit government redistribution but nevertheless wants to guarantee universal coverage, one can design a system of subsidising the premiums of the low income groups. As indicated before and demonstrated by the Swiss experience, this can be combined with the internal equalisation scheme of figure 4.2.1.

Note that when we talk about income solidarity in this context we refer to vertical equity, i.e. the possible link between the contributions paid and the income of the insured. Income may also play a role from the point of view of horizontal equity, since health care expenditures themselves (and more strongly so the health situation) are different for different income groups. The possible reasons for this correlation nicely illustrate the ethical questions raised in the previous section concerning the risk adjustment formula. On the one hand, suppose that higher income groups have larger medical expenditures because the social distance with the providers is smaller or because they can more easily afford to pay the copayments. Should income enter the risk adjustment formula in that case? On the other hand, suppose that low income groups have larger medical expenditures because their health situation is worse as a consequence of a complicated mixture of economic and cultural factors. Should income then enter the risk adjustment formula? And what in the (probably) most realistic interpretation in which the observed effect of income on expenditures results from a mixture of the two causal relationships?

Efficiency, competition and risk-adjustment

Until now we have only discussed the equity aspects of risk-adjustment schemes. But, as shown before, equity problems can be settled in an easier way by simply setting up a completely centralised system. Even in such a system, risk-adjustment may be desirable if we do not want to compensate for all characteristics leading to differences in health care costs, but as such it does not help to reach efficiency. Efficiency can only increase through the introduction of regulated markets if insurers can influence the expenditures and compete on price and quality grounds.

One can think of different instruments for these insurers. At the collective level the insurers could, on behalf of their clients, negotiate with the health care providers different possible contracts, fee schedules and quality constraints. Individual insurers could get the opportunity to go further: to collect and disseminate information on prices and quality of providers, to offer a variety of different policies, including contracts with preferred providers, to collaborate in the setting up of integrated HMO-type organisations of providers and insurers. Experience shows that these developments are inherent to or are more easily introduced into health care systems with a strong emphasis on private markets. Switzerland with its HMO-experiments again could be a European example. But even there the freedom of insurance funds to compete is curtailed by government intervention. Other European countries with a longer history of extensive government regulation and a stronger emphasis on equity have shown more reluctance to give more levers of control to the insurers. The Belgian case is typical.

It is understandable that the rhetoric of managed or regulated competition has not been very successful in convincing regulators in countries like Belgium. After all, the Belgian health care system succeeds in guaranteeing a very broad insurance coverage to almost the whole population, people are very satisfied and do not want big changes in the system (Mossialos, 1997), health care costs, although large and increasing, are not larger or more rapidly increasing than in countries where (more or less) regulated competition is prevailing- including the Big Brother example at the other side of the Atlantic. Yet if one wants to move slowly, one has to draw the consequences for the risk adjustment scheme. We have mentioned before that a deliberate choice has to be made with respect to the risk adjusters to be included in the formula and we have drawn attention to the ethical aspects of this choice. The level of control of the insurers also should play a role however. It does not make sense to decide that the effect of certain variables is within the responsibility of the insurers, while at the same time refusing to give them the instruments needed to exert this responsibility. One can therefore have doubts about the treatment of medical supply in the Belgian case. Again we reach the same conclusion as before: the development of the risk-adjustment formula is not in the first place a technical or statistical problem. It will (or must) reflect basic choices made with respect to the organisation of the health care system.

Notes

1. See Wagstaff, van Doorslaer et al. (1992) and van Doorslaer, Wagstaff et al. (1992) for an interpretation of different equity concepts in the context of health care.

2. The figures are taken from Schut (1996), who also presents a third (voucher) system, which is less relevant for our purposes.

3. Since we are advising the INAMI about the risk adjustment formula, our discussion of the Belgian situation largely reflects our own experience. This work concerning the risk adjustment formula is done jointly with a team of researchers at DULBEA (Université Libre de Bruxelles), directed by Paul Kestens.

4. The railroad employees are organised in a separate, seventh fund.

5. Definition of the variables: except for urbanisation and medical supply, all variables are expressed as a percentage of the number of beneficiaries. The variable disability gives the active population with at least one day of disability, divided by the total number of beneficiaries; mortality is the mean death rate of 4 years (1992-1995) whereas urbanisation and medical supply are two indicators based on a principal component analysis. The first urbanisation variable is based on the quality of housing, the second one on the population density and the percentage of urbanised area, medical supply on the number of general practitioners, specialists, pharmacists, dentists and physiotherapists.

6. Separate models have been estimated for the active employees and civil servants, the retired, the widowers, widows and orphans, the invalids and disabled, the members of religious communities, the active self-employed. More information about the procedure used can be found in E. Schokkaert, P. Kestens et al. (1996).

7. The magnitude of these independent regional units varies in magnitude from a minimum of about 400 members to a maximum of about 450,000 members.

8. It is obvious that individual data are absolutely necessary to derive an adequate risk adjustment formula: at the aggregate level there is not enough variation and too much multicollinearity to determine the effect of some crucial variables.

9. A more theoretical and technical analysis of this approach, based on some recent developments in the social choice literature, can be found in Schokkaert, Dhaene and Van de Voorde (1998).

10. Our discussion of the Swiss case is largely based on Schneider (1996), Beck (1997, 1998) and Beck et al. (1995). We thank Konstantin Beck for his help in explaining the Swiss situation. Of course, he is not responsible for any remaining errors.

11. Cantons can pass their own legislation, but it has to be consistent with the federal legislation.

12. Newhouse (1996) writes in his recent survey that the literature "typically uses explained variance in annual individual expenditure to judge the goodness of risk adjusters" (p. 1256).

13. In the United Kingdom also the formula for allocating NHS funds to the regional health authorities does not take into account the influence of medical supply-factors which are not a reflection of variations in legitimate need (see, e.g., Carr-Hill et al., 1994).

14. See, e.g., the empirical results in Fuchs (1997).

15. This approach is extensively discussed in the literature- see Newhouse (1996) for a list of references. Schokkaert, Dhaene and Van de Voorde (1998) show the relationship between mixed reimbursement schemes and the treatment of the disturbance term in the explanatory regression model.

References

Beck, K. (1997), Kann der Risikoausgleich unterlaufen werden? Analyse der schweizerischen Ausgleichsformel. *RPG* 3, 49-70.

Beck, K. (1998), Competition under a regime of imperfect risk adjustment: The Swiss experience. *Sozial- und Präventivmedizin* 43, 7-8.

Beck, K. et al. (1995), *La solidarité en mutation* (Cahiers d'études de la SSPS).

Carr-Hill, R.A. et al. (1994), Allocating resources to health authorities: development of method for small area analysis of use of inpatient services. *British Medical Journal* 309, 1046-1049.

Fuchs, V. (1997), Economics, values and health care reform. *American Economic Review* 86, 1-24.

Mossialos, E. (1997), Citizens' views on health care systems in the 15 member states of the European Union. *Health Economics* 6, 109-116.

Newhouse, J. (1994), Patients at risk: health reform and risk-adjustment. *Health Affairs* 13, 132-146.

Newhouse, J. (1996), Reimbursing health plans and health providers: efficiency in production versus selection. *Journal of Economic Literature* 34, 1236-1263.

Nonneman, W., van Doorslaer E. (1994), The role of the sickness funds in the Belgian health care market. *Social Science and Medicine* 39, 1483-1495.

Schneider, B. (1996), Risk structure compensation in Switzerland. in: *Risk structure compensation* (Proceedings AIM Workshop 1995).

Schokkaert, E., Dhaene, G., Van de Voorde, C. (1998), Risk adjustment and the trade-off between efficiency and risk selection, forthcoming in: *Health Economics.*

Schokkaert, E., Kestens, P. et al. (1996), Dépenses normatives des organismes assureurs dans le cadre de l'introduction de la responsabilité financière. *Cahiers Economiques de Bruxelles* No 149, 3-30.

Schut, F. (1996), Financiële responsabilisering van ziekenfondsen: motieven en methoden, *Openbare Uitgaven* 28, 164-174.

Van de Ven, W.P.M.M., Van Vliet, R. (1992), How can we prevent cream skimming in a competitive health insurance market? in: P. Zweifel, H.E.Frech III (eds.), *Health Economics Worldwide* (Kluwer).

Van de Ven, W.P.M.M. et al. (1996), Risk-adjusted capitation payments: the Achillesheel of market-oriented health care reform. in: *Risk structure compensation* (Proceedings AIM Workshop 1995).

Van de Ven, W.P.M.M. (1997), Netherlands. in: C. Ham (ed.), *Health care reform: learning from international experience* (Open University Press, Buckingham).

Van Doorslaer, E., Wagstaff, A. et al. (1992), Equity in the delivery of health care: some international comparisons. *Journal of Health Economics* 11, 389-411.

Wagstaff, A., van Doorslaer, E. et al. (1992), Equity in the finance of health care: some international comparisons. *Journal of Health Economics* 11, 361-387.

4.3 The cost of coercion: an empirical study of the willingness to pay for disability insurance

Leo J.M. Aarts and Philip R. de Jong

1. Introduction

European welfare states are facing hard times. Many consider them wasteful and unduly paternalistic. To indicate the elements ripe for change is relatively easy. But to reach political agreement on the appropriate changes, and to get sufficient social support for any proposal to curtail existing entitlements, proves difficult. The constituency of the welfare state includes not only current beneficiaries, but also older workers, persons with disabilities, and small-scale businesses owners. The incomes of these higher risk groups are protected by collective arrangements at prices that do neither reflect the full social cost of income transfers nor the extent to which they are subsidized by lower risk groups.

To promote the cost-consciousness of those covered by social insurances against wage-loss due to unemployment or disability policymakers can choose between a reduction of entitlements or an increase in actuarial fairness. Over the past two decades, reduction of entitlements was the preferred method but, more recently, policymakers have shown an appetite for premium differentiation, either as part of a statutory arrangement or by allowing private insurance companies to administer social insurances. Delivery of social insurance by a competitive market, however, is only viable if the risks covered are predictable and independently distributed within homogeneous groups. Market supply of disability insurance, therefore, is conceivable, but privatization of unemployment insurance is not.

As of 1998, the Dutch Disability Insurance (*WAO*) program uses experience rating to finance the first five years of benefit entitlement.

After those first five years benefits are funded by uniform, pay-as-you-go (PAYG), premium rates, as used to be the case for the full entitlement period. Hence, Dutch employers now have to pay both an experience rated, and a uniform premium rate to cover their statutory disability liabilities.

Introduction of differentiated premium rates in a system that used to be financed by uniform rates does not only have an efficiency effect by promoting cost-conscious behavior of the parties involved, it also affects the net utility gains/losses that covered workers get out of a compulsory insurance system. By definition, premium differentiation reinforces the equivalence between premium rates and expected damages. And, to the extent that the willingness of covered workers to pay for the statutory amount of insurance depends on the size of their disability risk, a differentiated system may well be more in accordance with the willingness to pay, and, therefore, the number of utility winners may grow.

In this paper we try to assess the utility gains or losses workers experience as a result of mandatory consumption of a fixed amount of coverage, at a fixed price, under the Dutch disability insurance program. We ignore the behavioral effects, such as moral hazard and risk taking, that insurance coverage, and the incentives engendered by its funding system, may induce. In the next section the three core concepts that determine individually varying willingnesses to pay for the statutory amount of insurance - extent of damage covered, probability of damage, and risk attitude - are derived from expected utility theory. We give a short outline of the Dutch disability insurance system in section 3, and elaborate the simple expected utility model of section 2 to incorporate the multi-period character of the disability risk. In section 5 we describe our measurement methods and data. In sections 6 and 7 we present and discuss our results. Section 8 concludes.

2. Core concepts

Disability insurance seeks to protect workers from losing their earnings (Y) as a result of disablement. If not insured, workers who are struck by an incapacitating disease or injury will fall down to a - politically defined - subsistence level (Y_s) that welfare states usually provide as a social safety net to protect the entire population from falling into destitution. Ignoring other earnings' risks, such as job loss, or a decrease in real wages, expected earnings (EY) are determined by the probability of becoming disabled (p_D):

$$EY = (1 - p_D)Y + p_D Y_s \tag{1}$$

$$= Y - ED$$

where ED, the expected damage, equals $p_D (Y - Y_s)$. Under actuarially fair pricing in a competitive market setting ED equals the premium π_{act} insurers would charge if they were to offer full coverage and ignore transaction costs: $\pi_{act} = ED = Y - EY$.

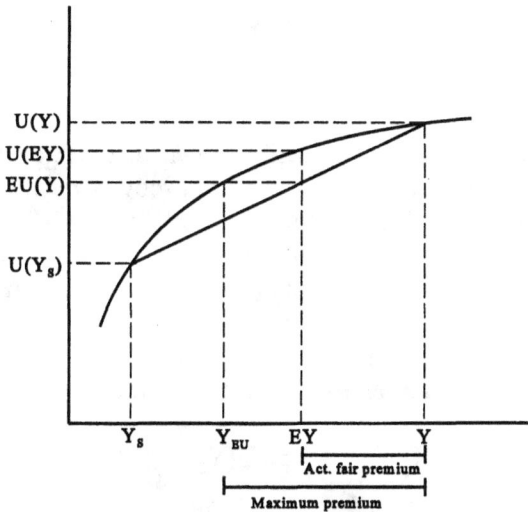

Figure 4.3.1 **Risk aversion and utility gain of insurance against wage-loss**

In figure 4.3.1 a concave utility of income function U(Y) is drawn to derive the maximum premium a worker would be willing to pay for disability insurance from expected utility theory. Without insurance the expected utility from earnings Y, given a disability risk of p_D, writes

315

$$EU(Y) \quad = (1 - p_D)U(Y) + p_D U(Y_S). \tag{2}$$

$EU(Y)$ corresponds to the level of earnings Y_{EU} which leaves a worker, characterized by earnings Y, disability risk p_D, and utility-of-income function U, indifferent between earning Y_{EU} with certainty, or earning Y subject to the probability p_D of a loss D. Y_{EU} is called the certainty equivalent amount of money (see Mas-Collel et al., 1995, p. 186 for a rigorous treatment). $\pi_{max} = Y - Y_{EU}$, then, is the maximum premium a worker (Y, p_D, U) is willing to sacrifice to buy insurance.

Barr (1993, p. 112) denotes $V = EY - Y_{EU}$ as the total value of certainty. V can also be seen as a global measure of the degree of risk-aversion of a worker (Y, p_D, U). Under a concave U(Y), which is equivalent to being risk-averse, V must be positive. Consequently, risk-averse workers are willing to buy insurance at a price that exceeds expected damages, or

$$\pi_{max} > \pi_{act}.$$

More specifically, it can be easily shown that risk-averse workers maximizing expected utility will buy full coverage if charged an actuarially fair premium (Mas-Collel et al., 1995, pp. 187-8).

Under a social insurance scheme the consumption of disability insurance is legally mandated, premium rates are set by a PAYG system, and the amount of insurance is also legally established. Usually, statutory replacement rates (or benefit-wage ratios) are less than 100 percent. Under incomplete coverage expected utility becomes

$$EU(Y|ins) = (1 - p_D)U(Y - \pi) + p_D U(Y_S - \pi + B - D); \tag{3}$$

Y|ins is earnings given an insurance policy defined by premium π and benefit B when disabled (B < D). The maximum premium a worker is willing to pay for the statutory policy, π_{max}, is now implicitly defined as the value of π that makes a worker indifferent between being insured or not, i.e.,

$$\pi_{max} = [\pi|\ EU(Y) = EU(Y|ins)]. \tag{4}$$

Likewise, the actuarial insurance premium (π_{act}) is found by setting EY|ins equal to EY. It is easy to derive that this equality gives

$$\pi_{act} = EB. \tag{5}$$

Workers will suffer a utility loss if the PAYG premium (π_{PAYG}) is larger than π_{max} as defined by (4). Conversely, they enjoy a gain if π_{PAYG} imposed by the statutory policy is smaller than π_{max}. We distinguish *absolute* winners, for whom π_{PAYG} is smaller than π_{act}, from *relative* winners for whom $\pi_{act} < \pi_{PAYG} < \pi_{max}$.

Note that our approach to coercion, and its related losses and gains, is through prices, not quantities. In this paper we derive a count of losers, and their utility loss, by comparing the individual willingnesses to pay for the statutory amount of coverage (π_{max}) with the π_{PAYG} imposed by social insurance. We do not consider the dual problem of whether covered workers would prefer a different quantity of insurance at a given price.

3. Dutch disability insurance

After a mandatory waiting period of 12 months, which is covered by sick pay, employees can apply for (*WAO*) disability insurance benefits. The risk covered by *WAO* is defined as the income loss due to the incapacity to perform commensurate employment. Until the reforms of 1993 and 1994, the concept of commensurate employment referred to one's training and work history. Under the new ruling the concept of commensurate work is broadened to encompass all generally accepted jobs that are compatible with one's residual physical and mental capabilities.

The degree of disability is determined by measuring an applicant's residual earning capacity, that is, the amount of labor income a person with disabilities would be able to earn with commensurate work, expressed as a percentage of pre-disability earnings. The degree of disability, then, is the complement of residual earning capacity. Notice that any illness or injury, regardless of its cause, entitles an insured person to a disability or sickness benefit. While other OECD countries distinguish people with disability by whether the impairment occurred on the job or elsewhere only the *consequence* of impairment is relevant under Dutch disability insurance.

WAO distinguishes seven disability categories. The minimum degree of disablement sufficient for employer based benefits is 15 percent.

Until August 1993, replacement rates only depended on the extent of disablement, and ranged from 14 percent of before-tax earnings in the 15 to 25 percent category, to 70 percent in the 80 to 100 percent (wage-loss) category. Before 1985 the maximum disability benefit was equal to 80 percent of gross earnings. As of August 1993, replacement rates also depend on age at the onset of disablement (for details, see Aarts et al, 1996, pp. 62-63). Covered wages are capped, and so are benefits. Disability benefits run out at age 65, when the national pension system takes over.

Self-employed persons with disabilities, and those handicapped from birth or during childhood, are not covered by *WAO* but by separate programs which are similar to the *WAO*. The main difference is that benefits are not related to actual earnings but to the statutory minimum wage: the maximum benefit under these programs is 70 percent of the gross minimum wage. At current exchange rates this basic benefit, which we take as the subsistence level Y_s introduced in the preceding section, amounts to about $ 900 per month.

We use the acronym *AAW* for the set of social insurances targeting people with disabilities, who are not employed or self-employed, that only award flat-rate benefits derived from the minimum wage.[1] *AAW* benefit amounts equal social minimum awards under public assistance, and are therefore part of the social safety net spanned under Dutch citizens. The main difference between *AAW* and public assistance benefits is that the first are not means tested.

The *WAO* program under which wage-related disability benefits for private sector employees can be awarded irrespective of cause was introduced in 1967. In 1970 the number of recipients of full disability benefits was 175,000. By 1980 this number had grown to about 430,000, and by 1990 to about 500,000, or 10 percent of the private sector workforce. To give an impression of the PAYG-rates that were needed to finance this runaway system: disability benefit expenditures as a percentage of GDP grew from 1.6 in 1970 to 4.1 in 1990.

After 1990 a set of measures have been taken to reduce the beneficiary volume, and to make the program more manageable in view of demographic pressures (see Aarts et al., 1996, Chapter 3). As a result, by 1996 the number of recipients of full disability benefits was back at its 1980 level of 430,000, and expenditures had decreased to 3.2 of GDP.

4. Elaboration of the simple model

The expected utility framework of section 2 assumes an instantaneous disability risk, and ignores its multi-period character. In reality disability insurance covers the risk of wage-loss during one's remaining worklife. Disability risks, therefore, do not only involve the question of whether or not damages occur, but also when, and over how many periods the loss extends until entitlements end at age 65.

The probability structure of the disability risk may be described more appropriately by positing a discrete distribution of the duration t until disability occurs. Let t_0 be the current age of a covered worker, and $t_{DI} = t_0 + t$ the age at onset of disability; then, the probability of disablement, conditional on uninterrupted labor force participation between t_0 and $t_0 + t$, can be written as

$$p_t = P[t_0 + t \leq t_{DI} < t_0 + t + 1 \mid t_{DI} \geq t_0 + t] \tag{6}$$

The unconditional probability (P_t) of becoming disabled in t periods from now writes

$$P_t = P\left[t_{DI} = t\right] = p_t \prod_{t=0}^{t-1} \left(1 - p_t\right) \tag{7}$$

Since 65 is the mandatory retirement age, we set $p_{65\text{-}t0} = 1$. By this normalization the unconditional DI-probabilities (7) can be shown to add up to one:

$$\sum_{t=t_0}^{65} P_t = 1$$

The disability conditioned earnings' risk to which a worker would be exposed if he or she would *not* be covered by the earnings related benefit program *WAO* would yield an expected stream of earnings W_t running from t_0 till $t_0 + t$ -- the beginning of the period in which disablement occurs -- or, equivalently, from 0 till t. Being not covered by *WAO*-benefits, and assuming that disablement leaves the worker no residual earning capacity, the benefit stream is defined by the flat rate *AAW* (subsistence) level. Or, using discount rate ρ to get present values of these streams,

$$EY = P_0 \sum_{t=0}^{64-t_0} \frac{AAW}{(1+\rho)^t} + \sum_{t=1}^{64-t_0} P_t \left| \sum_{T=0}^{t-1} \frac{W_T}{(1+\rho)^T} + \sum_{T=t}^{64-t_0} \frac{AAW}{(1+\rho)^T} \right| + P_{65-t_0} \sum_{T=0}^{64-t_0} \frac{W_T}{(1+\rho)^T} \qquad (8)$$

The expected utility stream corresponding to EY in (8) is defined analogously

$$EU(Y) = P_0 U(\sum_{T=0}^{64-t_0} \frac{AAW}{(1+\rho)^T}) + \sum_{t=1}^{64-t_0} P_t U(\sum_{T=0}^{t-1} \frac{W_T}{(1+\rho)^T} + \sum_{T=t}^{64-t_0} \frac{AAW}{(1+\rho)^T}) + P_{65-t_0} U(\sum_{T=0}^{64-t_0} \frac{W_T}{(1+\rho)^t}) \qquad (9)$$

Being covered by insurance against wage loss means that the flat rate AAW benefits have to be replaced in (8) and (9) by earnings related WAO benefits. Insurance also introduces a premium **rate** q which is levied on wage earnings W_t when working, and in the year of disablement. These assumptions yield

$$E(Y|Ins) = P_0 \left[\sum_{T=0}^{64-t_0} \frac{WAO_0}{(1+\rho)^T} - q W_0 \right] + \sum_{t=1}^{64-t_0} P_t \left[\sum_{T=0}^{t-1} \frac{(1-q)W_T}{(1+\rho)^T} + \sum_{T=t}^{64-t_0} \frac{WAO_t}{(1+\rho)^T} - \frac{q W_t}{(1+\rho)^t} \right]$$

$$+ P_{65-t_0} \sum_{T=0}^{64-t_0} \frac{(1-q)W_T}{(1+\rho)^T} \qquad (10)$$

and

$$EU(Y|Ins) = P_0 U(\sum_{T=0}^{64-t_0} \frac{WAO_0}{(1+\rho)^T} - q W_0) + \sum_{t=1}^{64-t_0} P_t U(\sum_{T=0}^{t-1} \frac{(1-q)W_T}{(1+\rho)^T} + \sum_{T=t}^{64-t_0} \frac{WAO_t}{(1+\rho)^T} - \frac{q W_t}{(1+\rho)})$$

$$+ P_{65-t_0} U(\sum_{T=0}^{64-t_0} \frac{(1-q)W_T}{(1+\rho)^T}) \qquad (11)$$

The definitions (8) through (11) are used to calculate both the actuarial and maximum voluntary premium rates, q_{act} and q_{max}. The actuarial rate is found by solving E(Y|ins) = EY. From eqs. (8) and (10) this yields

$$q_{act} = \frac{E[PV(WAO - AAW)]}{E[PV(W)]} \qquad (12)$$

320

where E[PV(*WAO* - *AAW*)] is the expected present value of the stream of supplemental benefits private sector employees get under *WAO* coverage upon disablement, and E[PV(W)] is the expected present value of the wage-stream before disablement. In other words, E[PV(*WAO* - *AAW*)] is the insurance liability with regard to a covered worker, and q_{act} E[PV(W)] is the premium needed to cover this liability.

Application of equation (4) to EU(Y) and EU(Y|ins) as defined in (9) and (11) gives

$$q_{max} = \left[q | EU(Y) = EU(Y|ins) \right] \tag{13}$$

for which no analytical form obtains.

The PAYG premium rate is approximated by the aggregate actuarial rate, q_{unif} imposing a uniform premium such that it covers the aggregate liability:

$$q_{unif} = \frac{\sum E[PV(WAO - AAW)]}{\sum E[PV(W)]} \tag{14}$$

where the sums are taken over the insured population. This approximation is valid if both the population at risk is demographically stable, and age-dependent disability probabilities are constant.

5. Measurement methods and data

As argued before, the critical factor determining the gains and losses induced by coercive consumption is the maximum premium rate (q_{max}) workers are willing to sacrifice to get a statutory amount of insurance at a fixed price. The obtain individually varying estimates of q_{max} empirically established measures of its determinants - covered wages (Y), disability risks (p_D), and risk preferences (U(Y)) - and estimates of their trajectories over the time interval [t_0, 65] are needed.

The dataset we use allows us to measure, directly or indirectly, each of these core elements. It is a sample of 1,268 observations of private sector employees that were extensively interviewed about their health and labor market records, their current job, earnings and household income. The employers of these sample persons were also interviewed, with respect to firm-level, financial and socio-medical, data and data regarding the sampled employee (Aarts and De Jong, 1992, chapter 4).

A drawback of the sample is that the information is somewhat stale. It was taken in 1980, which means that the mandatory social insurance policy at stake reflects the (end of the) extremely generous regime of that period, with a statutory replacement rate of 80 percent, and a very lenient attitude of the social insurance administators with regard to admissals. After 1980 both the generosity and the leniency of the system have gradually been reduced. (For a description, see Aarts et al., 1996, chapter 3.)

Measurement of W_t

Future wage trajectories which are needed to calculate the earnings streams at risk are derived from a regression of the ln of hourly wages of the sampled workers on age, education, gender, and marital status, reported in Aarts and De Jong, 1992, chapter 9, p. 262. If we write age as t the result can be summarized by

$$\ln W_t = a_0 + 3.344 \ln t - .417 \ln^2 t$$

The term a_0 contains the constant term and other, time-independent, terms of the regression.

Measurement of p_t and P_t

Previous research on this dataset was, among other things, focussed at estimating probit models to describe the process of entry onto the Dutch disability rolls. For that purpose the sample of persons who were employed when interviewed was matched with a sample of 1678 entrants to the Disability Insurance (*WAO*) scheme, also drawn in 1980. These disabled respondents, and their employers, were asked the same questions as their healthy peers. In appendix table 4.3.A1 the results of a reduced form probit using both samples are listed: the first ("healthy workers") sample are the zeros, and the *WAO* entrants are the ones. The dependent variable can be seen as the individual risk of entry into the *WAO* scheme. (The table is copied from Aarts en De Jong, 1992, p. 274.) This probit equation is used to generate direct estimates of p_0 -- the risk of disablement at the "current" age, *i.e.*, the age at sampling, and indirect estimates of p_t defined by (6) -- the conditional risk of disablement during one's remaining work life after t_0. Formally,

$$\hat{p}_{ti} = F\left[\hat{\gamma}_{oi} + \hat{\gamma}_1\left(AGE_i + t\right) + \hat{\gamma}_2\left(AGE_i + t\right)^2\right] \qquad (15)$$

with

$$\hat{\gamma}_{oi} = \hat{\gamma}_o + \hat{\gamma}'\tilde{Z}_i$$

F is the unit normal cdf, and i is the i-th sample person. Estimates of γ_0, γ, γ_1, and γ_2, are obtained from Appendix Table 4.3.A1. The ML-probit results are also used to predict individually varying DI-risk trajectories, $\hat{p}_{ti}$. The vector $\tilde{Z}_i$ contains both time-invariant and unpredictable variables. The estimates $\hat{p}_{ti}$ also yield values for the unconditional disability probabilities (P_t) defined by (7).

Specification of the utility function of income
Our dataset contains a five-level Income Evaluation Question which allows us to estimate individual utility of income functions (Van Praag and Kapteyn, 1973, Hagenaars, 1987). For the way this question runs see the paper by Bernard M.S. van Praag and Erik J.S. Plug in this volume, page 55.

If we consider the five answers -- $y_1,...,y_5$ -- to be points on the utility function of the respondent corresponding to the means of equal quantiles of the utility range [0, 1], the five answers divide this interval into five equal parts of 1/5th each. The k-th answer is associated with a utility level of

$$U(y_k) = (k - \tfrac{1}{2})/5 \qquad (k = 1,...,5) \qquad (16)$$

The five points $[y_k, U(y_k)]$, k = 1,...,5, can be used to fit for each respondent a function representing the utility function of income.

Van Praag (1968) introduced a theory of consumer behavior resulting in the proposition that the utility function of income may be approximated by a lognormal distribution function, that is:

$$U_i(y) = \Lambda(y; \mu_i, \sigma_i) = \Phi(\ln y; \mu_i, \sigma_i), \qquad (17)$$

where Λ and Φ stand for the lognormal and normal distribution functions, respectively.

323

Using (16) and (17) the information contained in the five points of the utility function can be summarized by the two parameters of the lognormal distribution function, μ, being a location parameter, and σ, a dispersion parameter:

$$U_i(y_{ki}) = \Phi[(\ln y_{ki} - \mu_i)/\sigma_i] = (k - \tfrac{1}{2})/5 \qquad (k = 1,...,5) \qquad (18)$$

Hence

$$\ln y_{ki} = \mu_i + \sigma_i u_k, \qquad (19)$$

where $u_k = \Phi^{-1}[(k - \tfrac{1}{2})/5]$ is the standard normal ordinate at $(k - \tfrac{1}{2})/5$. After adding an i.i.d. error term for all k and i to equation (19) we can estimate μ_i and σ_i for each individual by OLS.

We can now define the individual-specific utility function of income as

$$U_i(y) = \Phi[(\ln y - \mu_i)/\sigma_i].$$

The quantity $\exp(\mu)$ - the natural unit of income - is the income level evaluated by 0.5, halfway on the utility scale. As displayed in figures 4.3.2 and 4.3.3, showing examples of $U(y)$, workers are assumed to be risk-loving with respect to earnings to the right of $\exp(\mu)$, and risk-averse to the left of $\exp(\mu)$. The smaller μ, the larger the range of earnings over which a worker is risk-averse.

Having transformed the answers to the income evaluation question to yearly amounts the scale on which $U(y)$ is measured is also that of annual earnings. However, to calculate (9) and (11) expected utilities have to be taken over multi-year ranges. To expand the scale to which μ applies we define a factor M such that

$$M = \sum_{t=0}^{64-t_0} \frac{1}{(1+\rho)^t}$$

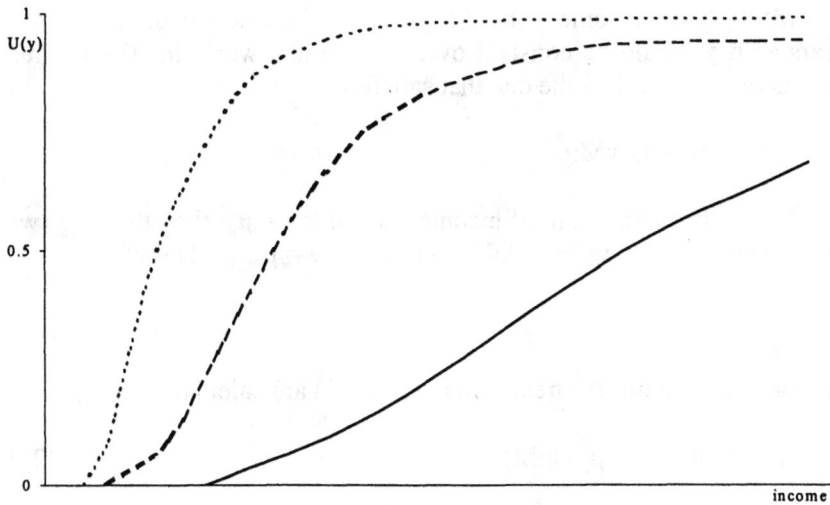

Figure 4.3.2   Examples of U(y)

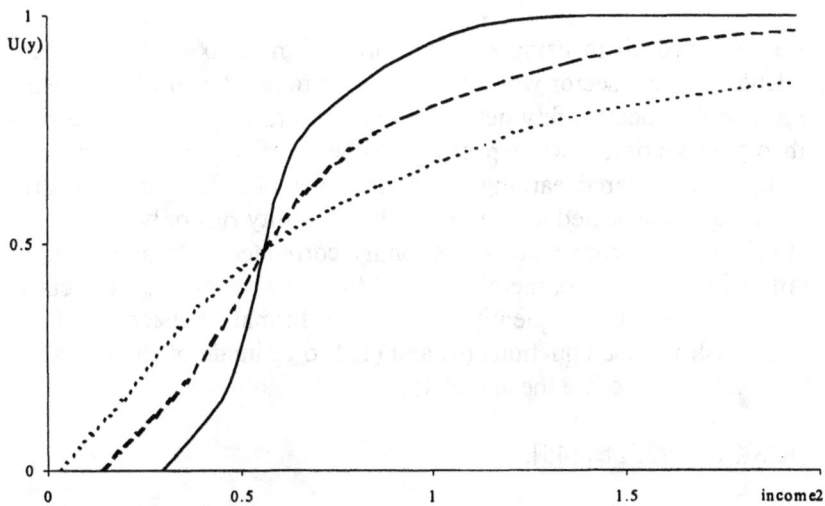

Figure 4.3.3   Examples of U(y)

325

Multiplying income y by M yields an income-stream over $64-t_0$ years as if y would be constant over the residual worklife. The desired expansion of μ, then, is the one that satisfies

$$U(y;\mu_{t0},\sigma) = U(yM;\mu_{[t0,64]},\sigma).$$

If y is the natural unit of income, so that $\ln y = \mu_{t0}$, then the $\mu_{[t0,64]}$ we are looking for follows from $\ln My = \ln M + \ln y = \mu_{[t0,64]}$. Therefore,

$$\mu_{[t0,64]} = \mu_{t0} + \ln M,$$

and the expected utility streams in (9) and (11) are calculated using

$$U_i(y) = \Phi[(\ln y - \mu_i - \ln M)/\sigma_i] \tag{20}$$

as utility function of income.

6. First results: determinants of q_{max}

As a first approach to using our measures of the maximum voluntary price Dutch private sector workers are willing to pay for disability insurance above the social safety net -- the premium rate q_{max}. From the simple theory in section 2 we expect q_{max} to be positively related with the disability risk, covered earnings, and risk aversion. The actuarial premium rate q_{act} is expected to depend on the disability risk only.

Each of these core factors is strongly correlated with age. In their operational definition we, therefore, want to neutralize any age-effects as much as possible. Consequently, to get an informative measure of the disability risk we use equations (6) and (15) to estimate of the probability of disablement before the age of 45:

$$RISK_{45} = P[25 \le t_{DI} \le 45].$$

This definition provides an age-independent estimate of the disability risk. Taking a longer age-interval -- for instance, [25, 55] -- would produce a less informative variable as the Dutch disability insurance scheme practically worked as a voluntary early retirement system for those over 45, at the time the sample was taken. Therefore, differences between those who keep working and those who end up on the disability insurance rolls fade as the upper bound of the age-interval increases. Individual variation in $RISK_{45}$ is related to job specific factors, gender and education.

An age-independent measure of covered wage is defined by the earnings stream over the complete work-life, disregarding the years before age 25:

$$PVW = \sum_{t=25}^{64} \frac{W_t}{(1+r)^t}$$

where wage-age profiles depend on education, gender, and marital status.

The attitude toward risk is measured by the Arrow-Pratt relative measure of risk-aversion, evaluated in EY as defined by (8):

$$R(EY) = -EY \frac{U''(EY)}{U'(EY)} = \frac{\ln EY - \mu_{25}}{\sigma} + 1$$

As shown in Appendix 2, the second equality follows from using the utility function (20) with $\exp(\mu_{25})$ being the natural unit of income of a respondent if he or she were 25. Through this normalization R(EY) is also age-independent.

Note that q_{max} can be written as the sum of two terms, the actuarially fair premium q_{act} and the certainty value (q_{max} - q_{act}). To see how the effect of these three explanatory variables is divided over those two parts, we regress these on q_{max}, on q_{act}, and on a global measure of risk aversion, the relative certainty value:

$$\frac{q_{max} - q_{act}}{q_{act}}$$

327

Table 4.3.1 Standardized OLS-coefficients (absolute t-values in brackets)

dependent	q_{max}		q_{act}		$(q_{max}-q_{act})/q_{max}$	
RISK$_{45}$	0.870*	-58.838	0.899*	-70.407	-0.501*	-36.166
PVW	0.247*	-17.153	0.019	-1.517	0.557*	-40.844
R(EY)	0.189*	-12.883	-0.003	-0.258	0.254*	-18.46
adjusted R^2	0.738		0.805		0.77	
#Observations	1264		1264		1264	

* significant at 5%-level

The first equation (first column in table 4.3.1), describing the relation between q_{max} and its three theoretical determinants, strongly corroborates the theory: willingness to pay for disability insurance is positively related to risk, to the loss insured, and to risk attitude. Notice that the dependent variable is a fraction of earnings covered. Therefore, the strong, positive, effect of PVW on q_{max} implies that the larger one's earnings, the higher the price one is willing to pay for insurance. This effect can be explained by the concavity of the (relevant) part of the utility function of income: as income rises equal utility losses correspond to higher monetary losses. The actuarial rate is only determined by the risk. As damages due to disablement are proportional to earnings insured, PVW is has no impact on q_{act}.

Regarding our global measure of risk aversion, $(q_{max}-q_{act})/q_{max}$, we note that the positive effect of income can be attributed to the way risk attitudes alter with earnings. Moreover, a local measure of risk-aversion, like R(EY), apparently cannot fully explain the relative value of certainty. The negative effect of risk on our global measure of risk aversion may indicate an effect of self-selectivity: the more risk-averse workers tend to look for jobs with a low risk profile. And, conversely, those facing greater risk are the less risk-averse among the work force.

7.   Further results: winners and losers

7.1 Mandatory social insurance

Two rating regimes are considered. Under the first regime all
(mandatorily) insured workers are charged a uniform contribution rate,
q_{unif}. At this rate total premium revenues equal total benefit expenditures.
Calculation of the uniform rate using equation (14) gives a premium rate
of 6.98 percent of wage income (see table 4.3.2). Under the second regime rates are uniform within groups of insured workers. When rating is
differentiated by industry, within-group uniform rates vary from 2.81
percent in the health care sector to 10.90 percent in the construction
industry (see table 4.3.3).

Table 4.3.2 Mandatory social insurance, overall uniform rates:
winners and losers (utility gains/losses (ΔU) between
brackets)

Industry (n)	q_{unif}	% absolute winners	% relative winners	% losers
agriculture (27)	6.98	41 (.11)	41 (.02)	18 (-.01)
food (63)	-	32 (.10)	35 (.02)	33 (-.03)
printing (33)	-	33 (.09)	36 (.03)	30 (-.03)
mining & chemical (76)	-	30 (.06)	39 (.02)	30 (-.03)
steel, metal & electrotechnical (182)	-	41 (.09)	39 (.02)	20 (-.02)
construction (189)	-	53 (.13)	34 (.03)	13 (-.04)
transport (81)	-	57 (.11)	31 (.02)	12 (-.01)
wholesale & retail (194)	-	30 (.09)	30 (.02)	40 (-.02)
banking, insurance (50)	-	20 (.09)	38 (.02)	42 (-.03)
other commercial (92)	-	36 (.09)	29 (.02)	35 (-.02)
health care (78)	-	12 (.07)	22 (.02)	67 (-.03)
other noncommercial (136)	-	26 (.07)	29 (.02)	45 (-.03)
Total (1268)	6.98	36 (.10)	33 (.02)	32 (-.03)
Average utility gain:	0.034			

Tables 4.3.2 and 4.3.3 show the number of workers that gain from mandatory social disability insurance, and the number of those for whom compulsory coverage implies a net utility loss. Among the winners -- workers who are charged less than they would be prepared to pay -- we distinguish between "absolute" and "relative" winners. An absolute winner is a worker who pays less than his or her actuarial rate ($q_{unif} < q_{act} < q_{max}$). Relative winners enjoy a surplus ($q_{unif} < q_{max}$) but pay more than the actuarial rate ($q_{unif} > q_{act}$). Losers are those workers that are charged social insurance contributions that exceed their maximum rate, let alone their actuarial rates ($q_{unif} > q_{max}$).

Table 4.3.3 Mandatory social insurance, sector-specific, uniform rates: winners and losers (utility gains/losses (ΔU) between brackets)

Industry (n)	q_{unif}	% absolute winners	% relative winners	% losers
agriculture (27)	7.52	37 (.12)	41 (.02)	22 (-.01)
food (63)	6.19	38 (.09)	30 (.02)	32 (-.01)
printing (33)	7.05	33 (.09)	36 (.03)	30 (-.03)
mining & chemical (76)	5.4	43 (.07)	39 (.02)	17 (-.03)
steel, metal & electrotechnical (182)	7.45	38 (.09)	38 (.02)	24 (-.02)
construction (189)	10.9	39 (.13)	28 (.03)	33 (-.03)
transport (81)	9.76	38 (.12)	33 (.03)	28 (-.02)
wholesale & retail (194)	5.84	39 (.09)	33 (.02)	28 (-.02)
banking, insurance (50)	4.78	36 (.07)	32 (.02)	32 (-.02)
other commercial (92)	6.63	38 (.09)	28 (.02)	34 (-.02)
health care (78)	2.81	36 (.05)	35 (.01)	29 (-.01)
other noncommercial (136)	6.13	34 (.07)	26 (.02)	40 (-.03)
Total (1268)	7.04	38 (.09)	32 (.02)	30 (-.02)
Average utility gain:	0.034			

Overall uniform rates Mandatory disability insurance with an overall uniform rate turns out to be gainful for over two thirds of the insured population. For 32 percent of the workers mandatory insurance implies a net utility loss (see table 4.3.2). Their average loss in utility units is calculated at -.03 (on a utility scale from 0 to 1). For the average wage earner a utility loss of this size corresponds to an income loss of approximately Dfl 1500 (or 5 percent of the average annual wage income in our 1980 sample); 36 percent of the insured population are absolute winners. Their average gain is .10 of the utility domain. For an average worker this utility gain corresponds to a wage increase of Dfl 10,000, or 33 percent. The average gain of the 33 percent relative winners is .02 utility units (corresponding to a wage increase of Dfl 1580 for the average worker). Clearly, under the Dutch social disability insurance policy that prevailed in 1980, the winners were more than able to compensate the losers.

Sector specific rates Under a regime with sector specific rates the overall number of losers is slightly smaller and the number of absolute winners increases to 38 percent of the insured population (see table 4.3.3). The size of their utility gain, however, is on average somewhat smaller. Also the average loss of the losers is one point smaller than under a overall uniform rating regime. What appears to be very different when comparing the two rating regimes, is the distribution of gains and losses over the insured population. Comparison of the two rating regimes in tables 4.3.2 and 4.3.3 proves that a regime that differentiates premiums at the level of industries produces a more even distribution of winners and losers.

For instance, under uniform rating the proportion of losers in the construction sector is only 12 percent, while that in health care is 67 percent. Under differentiated rates the proportion of losers in these two industries are 33 and 29 percent, respectively. This comparison gives an impression of the extent to which through overall uniform rating high risk industries (like construction) are subsidized by low risk industries (like health care).

7.2 Optional social insurance

From the results in tables 4.3.2 and 4.3.3 it is natural to take a further step -- let the losers opt out. Under optional insurance an adverse selection process is simulated that starts with the results in the first two tables. If the losers, who have lower risks, have less to loose, or are less risk-averse, opt out of the uniform rating system the premium rates go up.

This process of opting out continues either until convergence, or until the rate has reached a level at which everyone loses, and leaves.

The results of such iterations under overall uniform rating are presented in table 4.3.4. At convergence half of the compulsorily insured population opt out, with 72% exits in health care, and 28% in construction, as the extremes. The premium rate necessary to cover the insurance liabilities of those that stay in the system is 10.42 percent, which is 50 percent higher than under the mandatory regime. The average net utility gain (.031) is 10 percent smaller than under the mandatory regime (.034) but now nobody loses.

Table 4.3.4 Optional social insurance, overall uniform rates: winners and losers (utility gains/losses (ΔU) between brackets)

Industry (n)	q_{unif}	% absolute winners	% relative winners	% losers
agriculture (27)	10.42	33 (.10)	15 (.02)	52 (0)
food (63)	-	32 (.12)	35 (.03)	33 (0)
printing (33)	-	21 (.10)	33 (.03)	45 (0)
mining & chemical (76)	-	11 (.10)	33 (.02)	57 (0)
steel, metal & electrotechnical (182)	-	25 (.09)	35 (.03)	41 (0)
construction (189)	-	40 (.13)	32 (.02)	28 (0)
transport (81)	-	36 (.12)	32 (.03)	32 (0)
wholesale & retail (194)	-	20 (.10)	21 (.02)	60 (0)
banking, insurance (50)	-	8 (.11)	32 (.02)	60 (0)
other commercial (92)	-	22 (.11)	24 (.02)	54 (0)
health care (78)	-	6 (.08)	22 (.01)	72 (0)
other noncommercial (136)	-	15 (.07)	22 (.03)	63 (0)
Total (1268)	10.42	22 (.11)	28 (.02)	50 (0)
Average utility gain:	0.031			

When premiums are differentiated by industry an optional system would be expected to drive fewer people out than under one, overall uniform, rate. This is true for all branches reported in table 4.3.5, with three exceptions: agriculture, construction, and transport. Banning subsidies from low risk to high risk sectors means that convergence is reached only at relatively high premium rates in these high risk industries. The average rate, however, is 17 percent lower than under overall uniform rating.

Table 4.3.5 Optional social insurance, sector-specific, uniform rates: winners and losers (utility gains/losses (ΔU) between brackets)

Industry (n)	q_{unif}	% absolute winners	% relative winners	% losers
agriculture (27)	12.65	22 (.11)	19 (.04)	59 (0)
food (63)	7.93	24 (.10)	43 (.02)	33 (0)
printing (33)	8.96	27 (.10)	36 (.02)	36 (0)
mining & chemical (76)	6.15	36 (.07)	41 (.02)	24 (0)
steel, metal & electrotechnical (182)	9.03	28 (.10)	40 (.03)	32 (0)
construction (189)	n.a.	0	0	100 (0)
transport (81)	13.77	30 (.11)	27 (.02)	43 (0)
wholesale & retail (194)	9.87	20 (.10)	24 (.02)	56 (0)
banking, insurance (50)	5.99	24 (.09)	42 (.02)	34 (0)
other commercial (92)	9.81	23 (.10)	26 (.02)	50 (0)
health care (78)	4.07	23 (.06)	31 (.02)	46 (0)
other noncommercial (136)	7.72	24 (.07)	27 (.02)	49 (0)
Total (1268)	8.68	21 (.09)	26 (.03)	53 (0)
Average utility gain:	0.025			

8. Conclusions

Using empirical individual welfare functions we have tried to tackle something which is often mentioned as part of the list of potential efficiency losses of social insurance but never(?) measured - the welfare losses due to coercive consumption of social insurance. As very few datasets allow one to measure both risk and risk attitude at the individual level next to other more routinely measured characteristics we had to resort to an old data set. Therefore, the emphasis of this paper is more on method than on policy.

The outcomes show that social insurance against wage loss due to disablement financed by a uniform PAYG contribution rate is efficient in a Hicks-Kaldor sense: the welfare losses of those who lose are smaller than the gains of the winners. Charging specific rates for branches of industry does not change this aggregate picture. Thus differentiating the contribution rates, however, spreads the winners and losers more evenly within, and between sectors, by eliminating cross-subsidies among sectors.

When covered employees who lose are allowed to leave the collective system a dynamic is set in motion that converges at a point where about 50 percent of the population at risk quit. Under uniform rating workers in low-risk sectors are predicted to leave, and the collective system suffers under adverse selection, and the contribution rate converges to a level that 50 percent higher than under compulsory participation. When contribution rates are differentiated per sector the selection process works the other way: the numbers that leave the collective system are relatively high in high risk sectors, and low in low risk ones.

This paper is limited in, at least, two respects. First, we do not consider behavioral effects of going from a uniform rating system to one that uses sector specific rates. Eliminating cross-subsidies means that employers and employees in high risk sectors are more directly confronted with the cost of their risk behavior reducing a potentially substantial moral hazard component. Second, the method used in this paper should be applied to more recent data to see how risks and risk attitudes change when social insurances get less generous and lenient, and to assess the welfare consequences of such a trend.

Note

1. Until 1998, AAW (*Algemene ArbeidsongeschiktheidsWet*) was a national insurance against income loss due to disablement. For employees flat rate AAW benefit were supplemented by WAO benefits up to an amount that depended on degree of disability and earnings lost.

References

Aarts, Leo J.M., and Philip R. de Jong, *Economic Aspects of Disability Behavior*, Amsterdam-New York: North-Holland Publishing Company, 1992.

Aarts, Leo J.M., Richard V. Burkhauser, and Philip R. de Jong (eds.), *Curing the Dutch Disease*, Aldershot, U.K.: Avebury, 1996.

Barr, Nicholas, *The Economics of the Welfare State*, London: Weidenfeld and Nicholson, 1993 (2nd edition).

Hagenaars, Aldi J.M., *The Perception of Poverty*, Amsterdam-New York: North-Holland Publishing Company, 1987.

Mas-Collel, Andreu, Michael D. Whinston, and Jerry R. Green, *Microeconomic Theory*, New York-Oxford: Oxford University Press, 1995.

Pratt, J.W., "Risk Aversion in the Small and the Large", *Econometrica*, 1964 (32), pp. 122-136.

Van Praag, Bernard M.S., *Individual Welfare Functions and Consumer Behavior*, Amsterdam-New York: North-Holland Publishing Company, 1968.

Van Praag, Bernard M.S., and Arie Kapteyn, "Further Evidence on the Individual Welfare Function of Income: An Empirical Investigation in The Netherlands", *European Economic Review*, 1973 (4), pp.33-62.

Appendix 1

Table 4.3.A1   Reduced-form probit estimates for the probability of disablement

Employee-level	coefficient	(st. error)
Age	-0.0086	-0.017
Age squared (* 10^{-2})	0.0515	(0.0217)*
Female=1	0.2475	(0.0933)**
Married=1	-0.0303	-0.0839
Ndepkids	-0.0364	-0.0217
Urbanization	-0.0376	-0.0298
Education	-0.0495	-0.0269
Strenuous work record[a]	0.975	(0.1649)**
Tenure[b]	-0.2938	(0.0999)**
g(Working hours)	0.9495	(0.3565)**
Commuting time	0.0241	-0.021
Ln(other househ.inc. + 1)	0.0165	(0.0082)*
Reg. unempl. rate	-0.082	-0.1232
Previously unemployed=1	0.217	(0.0693)**
Mobility=1	0.038	-0.0602
Absence record	0.0217	(0.0046)**
Duration of complaints[a]	2.3169	(0.3238)**
Employer-level	coefficient	(st. error)
Ln(firmsize)	0.0573	(0.0149)**
Increasing employment (*10^{-2})	0.0002	-0.001
Decreasing employment (*10^{-2})	-0.0039	-0.0034
Perc. fem. employment (*10^{-2})	-0.002	-0.0012
Workers' consultation=1	-0.0783	-0.0501
Job adaptation	-0.1228	(0.0352)**
Medical guidance	-0.0549	(0.0237)*
Social guidance	-0.1584	(0.0327)**
Branch of industry		
Agriculture	-0.1171	-0.1708
Steel industry	-0.0246	-0.0914
Construction	ref.	ref.
Other industries	-0.0785	-0.0884
Wholesale and retail	-0.0632	-0.0957
Other commercial services	-0.05u8	-0.0889
Health care	-0.2884	-0.1542
Non-commercial services	-0.0126	-0.1181
Constant	-3.3511	-0.3482

-2 * Loglikelihood ratio	1393.10**	
pseudo-R^2	0.365	
#Observations	2946	

**   Significant at the 1 percent level.
*   Significant at the 5 percent level.
a   Divided by age.
b   Divided by work experience (years).

Appendix 2

$$U(y) = \int_{-\infty}^{\ln y} \frac{1}{\sigma\sqrt{2\pi}} \exp -\frac{1}{2}\left[\frac{z-\mu}{\sigma}\right]^2 dz = \int_{-\infty}^{g(y)} f(z)dz = F(g(y))$$

i) $$\frac{\partial F(g(y))}{\partial y} = f(g(y))\frac{\partial g(y)}{\partial y}$$

ii) $$\frac{\partial^2 F(g(y))}{\partial y^2} = \frac{\partial f(g(y))}{\partial y}\frac{\partial g(y)}{\partial y} + f(g(y))\frac{\partial^2 g(y)}{\partial y^2}$$

with

$$f(z) = \frac{1}{\sigma\sqrt{2\pi}} \exp -\frac{1}{2}\left[\frac{z-\mu}{\sigma}\right]^2$$

$$g(y) = \ln y$$

Hence,

$$\frac{\partial f(g(y))}{\partial y} = \frac{\partial f}{\partial z}(g(y))\frac{\partial g(y)}{\partial y} = \frac{1}{\sigma\sqrt{2\pi}} \exp -\frac{1}{2}\left[\frac{\ln y-\mu}{\sigma}\right]^2 \frac{-(\ln y-\mu)}{\sigma}\frac{1}{\sigma}\frac{1}{y}$$

$$= f(\ln y)\frac{-(\ln y-\mu)}{\sigma^2}\frac{1}{y}$$

Substitution yields

i) $\dfrac{\partial F(g(y))}{\partial y} = f(g(y))\dfrac{\partial g(y)}{\partial y} = f(\ln y)\dfrac{1}{y}$

ii) $\dfrac{\partial^2 F(g(y))}{\partial y^2} = \dfrac{\partial f}{\partial z}(g(y))\left(\dfrac{\partial(g(y))}{\partial y}\right)^2 + f(g(y))\dfrac{\partial^2 g(y)}{\partial y^2}$

$\qquad = f(\ln y)\dfrac{-(\ln y - \mu)}{\sigma^2}\dfrac{1}{y^2} + f(\ln y)\dfrac{-1}{y^2}$

$\qquad = \dfrac{-1}{y^2}f(\ln y)\left[\dfrac{\ln y - \mu}{\sigma^2} + 1\right]$

Using the results above R(y), the Arrow-Pratt measure of relative risk-aversion writes:

$R(y) = -y\dfrac{\partial^2 U(y)}{\partial y^2}\left[\dfrac{\partial U(y)}{\partial y}\right]^{-1} = -y\dfrac{\partial^2 F(g(y))}{\partial y^2}\left[\dfrac{\partial F(g(y))}{\partial y}\right]^{-1}$

$\qquad = -y\dfrac{\dfrac{-1}{y^2}f(\ln y)\left[\dfrac{\ln y - \mu}{\sigma^2} + 1\right]}{\dfrac{1}{y}f(\ln y)}$

$\qquad = \dfrac{\ln y - \mu}{\sigma^2} + 1$

338

4.4 Some issues in aged care expenditure in Australia

Ching Y. Choi

Introduction

There are concerns, in many countries, that health and aged care expenditure is growing at a high and unsustainable rate. In Australia (where there is a universal health care system and a well-developed aged care system both funded largely from government taxation) there are concerns that the rapid growth in the 1980s and the early 1990s in government funded aged care expenditure is not sustainable. There are reports to government that project or assume very high rates of growth in health expenditure because of the ageing of the population. These reports called for an immediate curtailment of health and aged care costs (Economic Planning and Advisory Council 1994 and National Commission of Audit 1996). The assumptions behind these projections have been variously questioned. (Gibson and Goss, 1998).

This paper looks at the level and pattern of aged care expenditure by government. It describes the main areas of expenditure in aged care, and argues that the controls put in place in each of these areas to contain costs have resulted in a manageable increase in government aged care expenditure.

Major areas of aged care expenditure

Older persons in Australia have access to mainstream social security and health care systems and the specialised aged care system. The main expenditure areas funded by government are:

- the government age pension (including veteran's pension),
- hospitals,
- medical services (including general practitioners and specialists as well as pathology and imaging/screening services),
- pharmaceutical services,
- residential aged care services (nursing homes and hostels), and
- non-residential services (home and community care).

Age pension ($16,000 million, 5 year real growth 20%)

The age pension, funded out of Commonwealth government taxation, is subject to a means test on income and assets. Generally the family home is exempt. In the 1970s, those aged 70 and over were exempt from the means test, but this exemption was removed in the mid-1980s. The age pension is also subject to tax. The qualifying age was 65 years and over for males, and age 61 and over for females in 1996-97. In 2013, the qualifying age for women will be increased to 65, the same as that for men.

With the ageing of the population, age pension outlays have increased rapidly since 1975-76. In 1991-92, legislation was passed to make it compulsory for employers to contribute to employee superannuation. The rate of contribution was set at 4% of the employees' salary in 1992-93. At present (1997-98) it is 6%, and will rise gradually to 9% in 2002-2003.

Table 4.4.1 Superannuation coverage by age group (1996)

Age	% of employees with superannuation cover
15-19	51
20-24	86
25-34	90
35-44	91
45-54	92
55-59	89
60+	73

Source: Australian Bureau of Statistics, Yearbook 1997.

This legislation has the effect of rapidly increasing the number of employees having superannuation coverage, from 52% in 1990 to 80% in 1992 and 86% in 1996. The coverage by age group as at 1996 is shown in table 4.4.1.

The relatively lower coverage in the age group 15-19 years is affected by many in casual jobs that do not attract compulsory superannuation contributions. The figure for those aged 60 years and over is not useful as it is affected by the large proportion of people in this group who are no longer employed.

The high coverage of those in the prime working ages would indicate that they should be able to finance some or most of their income needs when they reach retirement, as intended by government. With compulsory superannuation and means testing of the age pension in place, the very rapid rise in government expenditure on the age pension may be reduced in future in spite of the continuing ageing of the population. The success of any means testing of the aged pension and compulsory superannuation scheme to reduce reliance on government would, of course, depend on how financial arrangements of retirees might affect their eligibility for government funded pensions.

Hospitals ($3790 million, 5 year real growth 13%)

Public hospitals in Australia are administered by State and Territory governments with part funding from the Commonwealth. While in the 1980s, States have provided more funds to hospitals than the Commonwealth, this has reversed since the early 1990s. In recent years, Commonwealth funding has exceeded State funding by a small margin. Treatment in public hospitals as a public patient is free of charge to Australian residents under the Australian Medicare scheme. (Medicare is a universal and very popular scheme funded by tax. It provides a rebate for visits to doctors, other medical services such as pathology and imaging services, and provides free public hospital services.) There is no choice of doctor when treated in a public hospital as a public patient, and there are waiting lists in public hospitals for elective surgery. Patients can choose to be treated as private patients in public hospitals with their own choice of doctor. In these cases, a charge is made.

There is a continuing debate on the containment of hospital expenditure and the services they provide. The Commonwealth government

341

attempts to limit its contribution to the States under the Commonwealth/State Medicare Agreement. State governments recently introduced case-mix funding in order to plan their funding of hospitals and to ensure that they obtained increased output per dollar spent.

Private hospitals handle about 31% of all hospital patients. These hospitals are not covered by the Medicare scheme, and patients are insured in a health fund or make independent out-of-pocket payments. Hospital insurance is offered by private funds to cover hospital treatment in either private or public hospitals. Premiums are high and benefits paid do not always cover 100% of costs. There is also little incentive for the young and healthy to join the funds. The population coverage of private hospital insurance has been dropping since Medicare was introduced in 1984.

Hospital utilisation is higher for older people than for younger people, both in terms of 'separations' per 1,000 population and the average length of stay (AIHW 1997, p25). Expenditure in hospitals is high for those aged 75 and over (and also for females at child bearing ages). In 1993-94, those aged 65 and over consumed about 34.7% of hospital expenditure (Mathers et al. 1998 p 36). This figure was 34.6% in 1989-90 (Goss et al, 1994) showing little change since the late 1980s. These figures compared with around 12 percent for the population as a whole.

Older patients in hospitals cost more because they are admitted more often and because they stay longer than younger patients. While older patients do stay longer in hospitals, an early study showed that only a very small proportion of older hospital patients are very long stay patients (more than 34 days) - between 0.8% to 1.3% in 1988-89. Most of these patients were discharged to the community, and only a very small proportion was transferred to a nursing home. In terms of bed days used, these older long stayers who were transferred to a nursing home used 7% of all bed days (Renwick, Gillett and Liu, 1992). With the length of hospital stay being reduced rapidly in recent years and the increased provision of aged care in the community (see later section), it is unlikely that this has become more serious.

A recent study of the case-mix funding for elderly patients in several Victoria hospitals has shown that elderly patients do not cost more although they do stay longer in hospitals (Duckett and Jackson, 1998).

342

Medical services ($1559 million, 5 year real growth 36 %)

Medical services include expenditure on consultations with general practitioners and specialists as well as pathology tests and screening and diagnostic imaging services. It also includes medical services provided to patients in private hospitals. Medical service providers receive rebates from Medicare. A schedule of fees has been established and benefits for services provided by private practitioners relate to that schedule. Doctors are not obliged to adhere to the schedule fees, but if they charge above the schedule fee, the patients must pay any additional amount. This 'gap' is not insurable.

Government pays a benefit of 85% of schedule fee. Many doctors choose to only charge 85% of the schedule fee, so the patient does not have to pay. Any charges above the schedule fee are paid by the patient. This is to encourage patients to see doctors who charge the schedule fee and directly bill the government. The schedule fee is adjusted regularly, and there is debate on whether the schedule fee is adequate. The setting of the schedule fees is the main mechanism of control over medical services expenditure.

Medicare covers all permanent residents in Australia. There is no restriction on the choice of doctor and the number of times a person sees a doctor. The lack of a 'cap' on medical service usage is often considered as a weakness in the Australian Medicare system in terms of expenditure control.

The level of use of medical services is higher among older people compared with younger ones. It is estimated that, in 1993-94, 24% of medical services were used by people aged 65 and over who comprised about 12 per cent of the population. This compared with about 20% in 1989-90.

Pharmaceutical services (780 million, 5 year real growth 85%)

The Pharmaceutical Scheme (PBS), funded out of the taxation system, subsidises the cost of a wide range of drugs. Patients are grouped under two categories. Concessional beneficiaries, generally people of lower income and receiving various forms of government benefits, pay a set contribution for each item of drugs, currently around $3.20, irrespective of the cost of the items. This contribution is indexed each year. General

343

beneficiaries, ie all others, pay a higher contribution for each item. Their contribution is also indexed and is at present up to a maximum of $20 for each item. If the cost is less than $20, the patient pays the total cost. The pharmacist claims the difference between the contribution and the basic price of the item from the government.

The PBS also includes a safety net that sets separate upper boundaries for concessional and general beneficiaries, beyond which all costs for drugs for the rest of the year are met by government.

The items that attract benefits, the basic price and the benefit level are reviewed regularly. These reviews are the main mechanism for the control of government pharmaceutical expenditure, as there is no 'cap' on the number of items and repeats used by patients. Recently, government has encouraged the use of generic drugs rather than brand name drugs in an attempt to reduce costs and would only refund the cost to the value of the generic drugs if they were available.

As would be expected, usage of pharmaceutical items is higher among older people compared with younger ones. It is estimated that, in 1993-94, 31% of pharmaceutical services were used by people aged 65 and over who comprised about 12 per cent of the population. In 1989-90, this proportion was about 35%.

Residential care (nursing homes and hostels) ($2366 million, 5 year real growth 16%)

Nursing homes and hostels are a central part of the Australian system of long-term aged care. Until early 1998, nursing homes and hostels were funded differently and they have catered for people with different levels of dependency - nursing homes for very frail older people while hostels for those with a lower level of dependency. Funding subsidies were higher for nursing homes than hostels. Both nursing homes and hostels charged daily fees, but hostels also charged new residents who are capable of paying an accommodation bond that provided funds for refurbishment and new buildings. Nursing homes were not allowed to charge an accommodation bond and did not have the same potential to build up a pool of funds for large scale refurbishment.

Government provided means-tested recurrent subsidies to residents (which include an amount, often considered insufficient, for up-keep of the premises). Government also provided capital grants for building hostels and not-for-profit nursing homes. Available capital grants for hostels were instrumental in encouraging the building of more hostels.

Residents who were government age pensioners were required to pay 87.5% of their pension as fees to nursing homes and hostels. Residents of hostels who had income above the government pension were charged an additional fee. However, for nursing homes, those who can afford to pay were not charged an additional fee until March 1998.

In the 1970s, there was a very rapid increase in the number of nursing homes and beds because government responded to the lengthening of nursing home waiting lists and provided subsidies for both capital and recurrent purposes. There was also a large movement of dementia patients out of State psychiatric hospitals into nursing homes and this movement was made possible because of the expanding (and Commonwealth funded) nursing home sector (AIHW 1993, p 204).

In 1985, government commissioned a review of nursing homes and hostels, and initiated a process of reform. The key components of the reform were a progressive reduction of nursing home beds, a substantial increase in hostel places, increases in the range and level of non-residential services, and the development and extension of assessment procedures to increase the appropriateness of service use.

The Review proposed to maintain the existing national ratio of 100 residential care places per 1,000 persons aged 70 years and over. However, it recommended substantial change to the balance between nursing home beds and hostel places. This was to be achieved by reducing the ratio for nursing home beds from 67 (in 1985) to 40 and to increase the ratio for hostel places from 32 in 1985 to 60 by the year 2011. The intention was to counter some inappropriate admissions to nursing homes and to expand hostel and home and community care. The desire of older people to remain at home was also recognised and the expansion of home and community care was an important policy change to respond to this desire. Home care services of a more intensive nature (called Community Aged Care Packages) were introduced since the reform, and the target of 60 hostel places was revised to 50 hostel places and 10 community aged care packages by the year 2011.

The reduction of approved nursing home beds since the 1980s has meant that there has not been a great deal of new investment in nursing homes in the last 15 years. This is particularly the case with for-profit nursing homes that did not attract separate capital fund. In recent years, the amount of capital grant funding provided by government has not been sufficient for replacement and up-grade (Gregory 1994, p10). Many of the existing nursing homes are now old, needing refurbishment and not ideal, with some 40% of residents living in rooms of 4 or more people. The industry generally does not generate enough funds through fees to refurbish run down nursing homes. There is increasing pressure on nursing home operators to raise additional money for this purpose.

Population ageing and the reduction of nursing home beds meant that the dependency levels of residents in both nursing homes and hostels have risen, and there is an increasing need for highly dependent hostel residents to move to nursing homes. However, while hostels have vacancies, nursing homes are mostly full and have long waiting lists. The scarcity of nursing home beds is particularly a problem for couples with different levels of dependency who could not be accommodated in a single establishment. This means that a couple may need to be separated if one partner is offered and accepts a nursing home bed.

In late 1997, government made further major changes to the residential aged care system. The separate funding of nursing homes and hostels was simplified by bringing these two sectors together under the Aged Care Structural Reform Package. It took into consideration the increasing dependency level of both nursing home and hostel residents, and the consequential need for residents to move from hostels to nursing homes.

This reform introduced new income testing arrangements for fees, means tested annual accommodation payments, and a new accreditation and standards system.

Fees

A basic fee of $21.10 a day was set from March 1988 for pensioners. For non-pensioners and part-pensioners, the basic rate is $26.40, and depending on their income, the maximum fee payable by them is $63.30 a day (all rates are indexed). The fee paid by residents is not affected by their level of dependency. Level of dependency affects the amount of subsidy government gives to the aged care facilities.

Accommodation payments

Accommodation payments are levied by the operators of aged care facilities to enable the up-keep and improvement of the building qualities and standards. Two types of accommodation payments are levied and they are regulated by government.

The first is a one-off accommodation bond levied by the facilities on residents entering hostel level care. Most of the bond is refunded when the resident leaves the facility. While the bond is not capped, accommodation payments are not allowed to be so high as to leave the residents with less than $22,500. This arrangement is a modification of the accommodation bond that had operated for hostels in the past.

The second is the accommodation charge for residents entering nursing home level care. This charge is means-tested and residents who cannot afford the charge are not asked to pay. Before the 1997 changes, nursing homes could not charge an accommodation charge or bond. The 1997 changes were designed to align nursing home level residents with hostel level residents. Initially, government intended to allow facilities to levy a bond similar to that paid by hostel level residents. But this was objected to vocally by the public and was dropped in favour of an annual charge that is not allowed to exceed $4,380 a year. The annual charge is paid for a period of up to five years. However, aged care facilities are allowed to provide places or beds with higher levels of accommodation, food and other services. Places or beds with such extra services attract accommodation bonds.

The administration of the policy on accommodation bonds and charges is complex. Income and asset testing for new entrants and the treatment of hostel bonds on transfer from hostels to nursing home level care are complex. Options for delayed payments are also available so that charges (with interest) can be deducted from the estate of a former resident. Government has a Financial Information Service to assist people who may have difficulties in understanding the income test and payment requirements and options.

While the policy change is designed to bring the nursing home and the hostel sectors together, it will take some time before this can be achieved, as the physical structure of hostels and nursing homes will need to be changed to make them suitable for both types of residents. Aged care facility operators may also find the accommodation charge to be too small, compared with the bond, to bring in enough funds for immediate major upgrade of their facilities.

Aged care facilities are now subject to accreditation by the new Aged Care Standards Agency. Any facility that is not accredited by January 2001 will no longer receive government funding.

Funding of aged care residential facilities

Recurrent funding of nursing homes and hostels is based on the level of dependency of the resident. The 1997 change to combine nursing homes and hostels has given rise to a new dependency and funding classification scheme for residents in the combined facility. The Resident Classification Scale has 8 categories, with categories 1 to 4 representing high care levels and 5 to 8 representing lower care level. The amount of subsidy is dependent on the level of dependency of the resident. Initial evaluation of the new scale for the combined facility has shown that the amount of subsidies has increased (Australian Catholic Health Care Association, Newsletter, April 1998).

Capital funding of the new facility is now available from the pool of funds collected as accommodation bonds and accommodation charges.

Australian nursing homes cater also for younger disabled persons. It is estimated that about 5% of nursing home expenditure in 1993-94 were consumed by younger persons under the age of 65.

Non-residential care (Home and Community Care) ($651 million, 5 year real growth 46%)

Australia has a large and varied non-residential aged care system, the core of which is the Home and Community Care (HACC) system. HACC is jointly funded by the Commonwealth and the States. HACC was implemented in 1984-85 by pulling together a variety of home based services and has been greatly expanded since. Real growth in government expenditure in the first 5 years of operation (from 1985-86 to 1991-92) was 104%, and it has since grown further by 26% to reach $651 million in 1995-96. Although HACC services are not fully means tested, clients who can afford to pay are asked by services providers to pay for HACC services. There are plans in most States to move towards a more uniform charging policy for those who can afford. This is in line with most Australian welfare and social security programs and benefits.

The range of services available under HACC includes home help, personal care, food services, community respite, day care centres, transport, home maintenance, and home and community nursing. More recently the Community Aged Care Packages (CACP) were expended. Expenditure on CACP was $33 million in 1995-96 and is expected to grow further in the coming years. Respite care programs are increasingly established, both in residential facilities or community centre settings and/or at home, to give carers breaks from their caring responsibilities, to enable them to care for their older relatives or friends for longer.

The policy towards encouraging and funding more home and community based care rather than residential care is driven not only by the higher costs of residential care in general. The policy recognises the desire of many older people to remain in their home and community for as long as possible. As a result the burden of carers are becoming heavier. The government recognises this, and in April 1998 announced a large increase in funds to expand the Community Aged Care Packages, to support carers and to provide more respite care.

Home and Community Care caters for both the young and the old. It is estimated that about 75% of HACC expenditure was consumed by people aged 65 and over.

Aged Care Assessment Teams are established throughout the country to provide screening of older people who may need HACC assistance or who may need to be admitted to a residential facility. These teams work mainly from community and public hospitals and are staffed by health professionals. Admission to residential facilities requires an assessment by an Aged Care Assessment Team and the Teams also refer people to HACC services.

The cost of aged care

The complex systems of health and aged care in Australia described above indicate that government expenditure on health and aged care is large and increasing. This is particularly true when the population has grown older in the last twenty years. This is shown in table 4.4.2.

Table 4.4.2 Australian population aged 65 and over (1976 - 1996)

June Actual	Percent of population aged 65+	Population 80+ as a % of 65+
1976	8.9%	17.4 %
1981	9.7%	17.6 %
1986	10.5 %	18.7 %
1991	11.3 %	19.7 %
1996	12.0 %	22.0 %

In 1975-76, 9% of the Australian population was aged 65 and over. Of them, 17 percent was aged 80 and over. These proportions increased to 10.5% and 18.7% respectively in June 1986 and to 12.0% and 22.0% in June 1996.

The ageing of the population in the last twenty years have seen an increase in both health and aged care expenditure, but not in an unmanageable way. Both health expenditure in general and aged care expenditure grew at a rate higher than the growth of the GDP. But there has been sufficient growth in GDP that the proportion of GDP and all government outlay that go to health have not increased greatly, and the proportion that go to aged care have remained rather stable.

Health expenditure

Health expenditure in Australia has grown at an average rate of 3.9% a year in the last 10 years (constant prices), slightly above the growth of the GDP. For the past 6 years, health expenditure has remained at about 8.5%, having risen from around 7.5% in the early 1980s. This places Australia in the middle range of OECD countries, with the USA at around 14%, France at 10% and Sweden, New Zealand and the UK at around 7%. Health spending is affected by the age structure of the population, and Australia's population is relatively young compared with many European countries but is similar to those of the USA, New Zealand and Canada.

About 68% of health expenditure is funded by governments (46% Commonwealth and 23% States), and 32% by the non-government sector (health insurance premiums and out of pocket payments). The government component has remained relatively stable; it was slightly over 70 % in the early 1980s.

The above health expenditure figures are for the population as a whole. Government expenditure on persons aged 65 and over (including both health and community services) are estimated below.

Aged care expenditure

As a % of GDP, government outlay for aged care has remained relatively stable; it was 5% in the mid 1970s, increasing to 5.3% in the 1980s and remaining at around the 5% level until now. In the last 10 years in real terms (1985-86 to 1995-96) Australian GDP has grown 36%, while aged care expenditure has grown 31%.

Table 4.4.3 Constant price expenditure on aged care (1996 - 1996)

	1975-1976	1980-1981	1985-1986	1990-1991	1995-1996
	$ millions (1989-90$)				
Age Pension	8557	10281	11192	11611	13936
Hospitals	2055	2389	2775	2960	3345
Medical services	551	344	855	1009	1376
Pharmaceutical	298	215	285	371	688
Nursing homes	732	979	1562	1787	1909
Hostels	31	39	78	182	368
Non-residential**	43	86	240	393	575
Total	**12268**	**14332**	**16987**	**18313**	**22197**
As % of GDP	5.2%	5.3%	5.3%	5.0%	5.1%
As % of government outlay	14.6%	14.6%	12.6%	12.7%	13.3%
As % of health, social security & welfare outlay	43.5%	44.4%	38.9%	35.9%	32.9%

Includes veteran pensions
** HACC, CACP, DNCB, and ACAT.
Source: Australian Bureau of Statistics, Year Book, various years, and Australian Institute of Health and Welfare, unpublished data.
Notes: Estimated for persons aged 65+ using the following factors: hospitals (.347), medical services (.2404), and pharmaceutical (.3098), in Mathers et al 1998. p 36, and nursing homes (.95).

As a proportion of all government expenditure (and in particular as a proportion of expenditure on health, welfare and social security), expenditure on aged care actually declined quite markedly since the 1970s. This has certainly been caused by the large increases since the mid-1980s in government expenditure on the unemployed and on the family (for example, single parent payments and childcare assistance).

Table 4.4.3 sets out the constant price expenditure on each area of aged care.

Conclusion

This paper has described in very broad terms the Australian aged care system and how expenditures on aged care are or are not subject to controls. The data show that in the past twenty years, the population has aged a great deal exerting pressure on aged care services. In this period, changes have been made to various aspects of the aged care system. These changes are designed to maintain care at an affordable level and also to introduce some control over costs.

There are continuing debates on the impact of ageing on aged care expenditure and the sustainability of the current level and expected increases in health and aged care expenditure. Many in Australia argue that the Australian health and aged care systems have coped well the ageing of the population so far and that the present trend in expenditure in Australia could accommodate an older population such as those in Europe (Gibson and Goss 1998, Goss et al. 1994; Howe 1997).

The data presented in this paper show that the improvements in aged care services in the last twenty years have been made possible by the growth of the economy as measured by the GDP. Economic growth allowed more funds to be made available for government services, and some of these additional funds have been allocated to aged care services.

The calls on government funds have come not only from aged care, they have come from other sectors. It appears that other areas of social concern such as unemployment, family services such as childcare and family payment, have received a level of government funding at least equal to aged care for the improvement of their services.

References

Australian Bureau of Statistics, Year Book Australia, Canberra, AGPS, various years.

The Australian Catholic Health Care Association. (1998) Outcomes of the Review of Resident Classification Scale.

Australian Institute of Health and Welfare (AIHW) (1997). Australian hospital statistics 1995-96. AIHW cat. No. HSE 3. Canberra : AIHW (Health Services Series No. 10).

Australian Institute of Health and Welfare (AIHW) various years, Health Expenditure. Canberra: AIHW (Health Expenditure Bulletin Series)

Australian Institute of Health and Welfare (AIHW) (1996) Australia's Health, 1996, Canberra

Australian Institute of Health and Welfare (AIHW) (1997) Australia's Welfare: Services and Assistance, 1997, Canberra

Duckett, S.J., and Jackson, T.J., (forthcoming) Do the elderly cost more? Casemix funding for the elderly patients in acute inpatient settings, in Nursing Older People: Issues and Innovations, Nay R (ed.) Malcolm and Petty Publishers.

Economic Planning and Advisory Council (1994), Australia's Ageing Society, EPAC Background Paper No. 37, January 1994, AGPS, Canberra.

Gibson, D., and Goss, J., The coming crisis of Australian aged care: fact or fiction?, Unpublished paper, AIHW, 1998.

Goss, J., et al. (1994) Economic perspective on the health impact of the ageing of the Australian population in the 21st century, paper presented to the 7th National Conference of the Australian population Association, Canberra, 1994.

Gregory, R.G., (1994) Review of the structure of nursing home funding arrangements, Stage 2. 1994, Department of Human Services and Health, Canberra.

Howe, A., (1997) care costs of an aging population: the case of Australia, Reviews in clinical gerontology, 1997 7; pp. 359-365.

Mathers, C., Penm, R., Carter, R., Stevenson, C., (forthcoming) Health system costs of diseases and injury in Australia 1993-94, Canberra, AIHW.

National Commission of Audit. (1996) Report to the Commonwealth Government, June 1996, AGPS, Canberra.

Renwick, M., Gillett, S., and Liu, Z., (1992) Long Stay older patients in acute hospitals: are they bed blockers? Australian Health Review, Vol. 15, No. 3, 1992, pp. 284-298.

List of contributors

Leo J.M. Aarts
E.M. Meyers Institute for Research on Law,
Faculty of Law,
Leiden University, The Netherlands.
Aarts & De Jong Consultancy and Research,
The Hague, The Netherlands.

Helen Barnes
Lecturer of Social Policy,
University of North London, U.K.
Former Senior Research Fellow,
Social Policy Research Unit,
University of York, U.K.

Andrew Bershadker
Associate Professor of Econommics,
Department of the Treasury and
Department of Economics,
University of Wisconsin, Madison, Wisc., U.S.A.

Jonathan R. Bradshaw
Professor of Social Policy,
Department of Social Policy and Social Work,
University of York, U.K.

Ching Y. Choi

Head Welfare Division,
Australian institute of Health and Welfare (AIHW),
Canberra, Australia.

Stefan Felder
Professor of Health Economics,
Otto von Guericke University,
Magdeburg, Germany.

Katja Forssén
Assistant Lecturer,
Department of Social Policy,
University of Turku, Finland.

Colin Gillion
Director Social Security Department,
International Labour Office,
Geneva, Switzerland.

Mia Harkovita
Researcher,
Department of Social Policy,
University of Turku, Finland.

Robert H. Haveman
Director of LaFollette Institute of Public Affairs,
Professor of Economics,
University of Wisconsin, Madison, Wisc., U.S.A.

Estelle James
Lead Economist,
Policy Research Department,
The World Bank,
Washington, D.C., U.S.A.

Philip R. de Jong
Professor of Economics of Social Security,
Erasmus University, Rotterdam, The Netherlands.
Aarts & De Jong Consultancy and Research,
The Hague, The Netherlands.

Nadine Lefaucheur
National Centre for Social Research (CNRS),
Paris, France.

Erik J.S. Plug
Associate Professor,
Faculty of Economics and Econometrics,
University of Amsterdam, The Netherlands.

Bernard M.S. van Praag
Director, Foundation for Econometric Research (SEO),
Professor of Economics,
Faculty of Economics and Econometrics,
University of Amsterdam, The Netherlands.

Lee Rainwater
Professor of Sociology,
Department of Social Sciences,
Harvard University,
Cambridge, Mass., U.S.A.

Martin Rein
Professor of Social Studies and Planning,
Department of Urban Studies and Planning,
Massachusetts Institute of Technology,
Cambridge, Mass., U.S.A.

Stein Ringen
Professor of Sociology,
University of Oxford, U.K.

Erik Schokkaert
Professor of Health Economics,
Centre for Economic Studies,
Catholic University of Leuven, Belgium.

David Vanness
Graduate Student,
Department of Economics,
University of Wisconsin, Madison, Wisc., U.S.A.

Carine Van de Voorde
Senior Researcher,
Centre for Economic Studies,
Catholic University of Leuven, Belgium.

Barbara L. Wolfe
Director, Institute for Research on Poverty,
Professor of Economics and Preventive Medicine,
University of Wisconsin, Madison, Wisc, U.S.A.